Hi Lo to
HOLLYWOOD

Books by Max Evans

Bluefeather Fellini
Bluefeather Fellini in the Sacred Realm
Bobby Jack Smith, You Dirty Coward
Broken Bones and Broken Hearts
Faraway Blue
The Great Wedding
The Hi Lo Country
Hi Lo to Hollywood
Long John Dunn of Taos
The Mountain of Gold
My Pardner
One-Eyed Sky
The Rounders
Rounders 3—A Trilogy
Sam Peckinpah—Master of Violence
The Shadow of Thunder
Southwest Wind
Spinning Sun, Grinning Moon
Super Bull and other Escapades
This Chosen Place
The White Shadow
Xavier's Folly and Other Stories

Hi Lo to HOLLYWOOD
A Max Evans Reader

Max Evans

Texas Tech University Press

This book was set in Berkeley Oldstyle ITC, Copperplate Gothic BT, and Snell BT. The paper used in this book meets the minimum requirements of ANSI/NISO Z39.48-1992 (R1997). ∞

Design by Melissa Bartz

Endleaf map © 1998 courtesy James R. Gober

Printed in the United States of America

Library of Congress Cataloging-in-Publication Data
Evans, Max.
    Hi Lo to Hollywood : a Max Evans reader / Max Evans.
      p. cm.
    ISBN 0-89672-404-2 (alk. paper)
    1. Western stories. 2. Western stories—Authorship. I. Title.
    PS3555.V23A6 1998
    813'.54—dc21   98-35709
                                      CIP

98 99 00 01 02 03 04 05 06 / 9 8 7 6 5 4 3 2 1

Texas Tech University Press
Box 41037
Lubbock, Texas 79409-1037 USA

800-832-4042

ttup@ttu.edu

Http://www.ttup.ttu.edu

Contents

5. Magazine Articles

Foreword

It might appear odd for the director of one university press to be writing a foreword to a volume published by another university press. And so it is.

I left the New York publishing world in 1976 to move west to Oklahoma. I think it fair to say that at that time my knowledge of the West was pretty limited. I knew that it had innumerable great streams and rivers that fit well on the end of my flyrod. I *thought* it was filled with colorful characters, some wearing braids, feathers and fringed buckskins sweeping the plains astride saddle-less horses, others wearing oversized hats and uncomfortable boots, riding atop well-appointed horses, carrying six-guns with which they blazed away at anything that hindered their progress. The stream topography I knew from some first-hand experience. The rest I had gotten from those unimpeachable sources, pulp westerns, television, and Hollywood. It did not take long working with the University of Oklahoma Press's Indian and western history lists to convince me that just about everything I thought I knew about either American Indians or the West was wrong.

In 1980 I moved to Albuquerque to be director of the University of New Mexico Press. The press had considered reprinting a book by Max Evans called *Long John Dunn of Taos*, but, sometime before I arrived, had decided against the reprint. For months the press staff had attempted to return the book, sending it several times to the wrong Max Evans, who dutifully returned it each time with increasingly unfriendly notes. The last, waiting on my desk when I arrived, just read in very large, bold handwriting: "I am not THAT Max Evans, and I didn't write this damned book!"

Being too new to the job to know what a press director was really supposed to do with his time, I decided to find the real Max Evans. A trip to the university library produced an armload of books by Max, most of them relatively short volumes that I figured even I could read without tiring my lips too much. Little did I suspect what a pleasure and what an education on the twentieth- century West awaited me. After a couple of weeks of almost continuous reading, I knew I had to meet the author who could convey so much about the land, the animals, and the people who struggle, triumph, fail, live and die in the real Southwest. Max Evans conveyed more with fewer words than any prose writer I had ever read. Three of the short novels are included in this volume: *Xavier's Folly, One-Eyed Sky*, and *My Pardner*. Each is a masterpiece of storytelling. *One-Eyed Sky* is an exceptionally fine piece whose protagonists are an old cow and a coyote doing their best to provide for and protect their offspring. The late John Sinor, a highly regarded syndicated columnist, once wrote that Max knew more about how animals act, and think, than any other writer he had ever read.

From another southwestern writer whose office was close to mine, I got Max's telephone number and arranged the first of countless legendary lunches. I will not go into detail about those lunches, except to say that they usually took a full turn around the clock; and, among our most notable accomplishments, we bagged a mountain lion without ever leaving the comfort and safety of Baca's Bar and Grille. The UNM Press went on to reprint several of Max's short fiction works, including the three just mentioned, and one collection of nonfiction pieces, *Super Bull and Other Stories*, the title story of which rounds out this volume. It is a fine piece on one of New Mexico's great ranchers, Jimmy Bason, and his attempts to corral and control an animal that is just a little better adapted to the land than he.

Since I left Albuquerque, an act which by itself could account for ninety percent of Max's increased productivity over the past ten to twelve years, we have worked together on four books: two original novels, *Bluefeather Fellini*, and *Bluefeather Fellini in the Sacred Realm*; one original nonfiction book, *This Chosen Place: Finding Shangri-La on the 4-UR*, a history of one of Colorado's most famous ranches, as well as a biography of its current owner, Charles Leavell; and a special edition of *Rounders 3* illustrated by Grem Lee, a well-known cowboy artist who is also from one of New Mexico's most historical ranching families. Max's personal introduction to that volume is included here, and I highly recommend it to anyone interested in the source of the writer's inspiration.

A mountain of well-deserved acclaim has been accorded Max and his writing by far more qualified critics and writers than I. His deep understanding of and love for the Southwest and its peoples, and his ability to convey that understanding with humor and compassion, is unmatched. This volume, covering several genres and most of Max's writing career, aptly demonstrates the breadth and depth of that understanding, humor and compassion. Read. Enjoy. And I think you, like me, will hope that there is a lot more to come from Max's pen.

Luther Wilson, Director
University Press of Colorado
Boulder, Colorado

A Dedication of High Respect

To
Martin Scorsese and L. Q. Jones

My deepest thanks to long time friend and great character actor, L.Q. Jones, for having the good sense to mention Sam Peckinpah's name when he told Mr. Scorsese about *The Hi Lo Country*.

Highest possible regards to one of the world's great film makers, and savers, Martin Scorsese, for reading the book and understanding why Peckinpah had spent a quarter of a century trying to get it made into a film, and as an added bonus—hiring one of the most intense and dedicated men I know, Stephen Frears, to direct it.

To
Charles H. Leavell and Oliver (Grem) Lee IV

Two men of the toughest emotional strength in existence, partnered with great wives, Shirley Leavell and Debra Lee. Both men have forged ahead despite tremendous physical handicaps.

Charles Leavell conquered the international business world and fulfilled his greatest dream by creating a conservation-recreation paradise on his 4UR guest ranch near Creede, Colorado. My book *This Chosen Place* tells of Charles' life and his wondrous paradise. Grem Lee, despite spells of temporary blindness and hospitalizations, has become a first-rate wildlife–ranch life artist. He gave me the authentically perfect illustrations for *Rounders 3* that I had so long hoped for.

To

Mattie Field
and family

Lifetime friends of my family, with whom we share a mutual respect for art and the great prairies from Bronco to Ruidoso.

To
Walon Green

A talented producer-writer-director of the film world. Among his many credits are: *The Wild Bunch, Hill Street Blues, LA Law, ER,* and now *The Hi Lo Country.* My hat's off to him for breaking the back of the *Hi Lo* script when so many others had failed.

To
Rudd Simmons

Producer on *The Hi Lo Country* and my new-old friend, who held the shooting together through first scouting over two thousand miles of locations in a terrible drought and later in freezing snow, alternating with wheel-bogging mud.

To
Dale Walker

A world-class Jack London scholar, editor, and a first rate writer of countless non-fiction stories and books and the greatest supporter of writers *out of the West* I can remember. Besides—and even rarer—he is a damn good guy.

Muchas gracias, amigos.

Introduction

I'm amazed. I never thought I would see a lifetime collection of my own favorite stories. These selections include short novels, forewords and introductions to other writers' books, essays, magazine and newspaper articles, and short stories. Four of the latter were the first serious writing I ever attempted. They are: "A Man Who Never Missed," "Sky Of Gold," "Blizzard" and "The Wooden Cave." I included these early stories (which were written in a total of four consecutive days—one day each—back in 1950) because I liked the *idea* of each one, even though I was incapable of doing a first-rate story in such a short time. A story without an idea is nothing but an exercise. "Sky Of Gold" inspired me to make over thirty years of notes and observations that resulted in the greatest two novels of my life, *Bluefeather Fellini* and *Bluefeather Fellini in the Sacred Realm*. "The Wooden Cave" and "The Call," like several of my other short stories, were magic realism long before the term was invented.

One of the great failings of the human creature is *the forgetting of beginnings*. We become so brainwashed in the imagery of the instant that we lose track of the beginnings of our work, our loves, our pains, our first experiences. These beginnings make us what we are now—what we will become. It is important for me that these four *starter* stories are included alongside some of my later, more mature, work for I, too, have the same failing of forgetting the genesis. And I hope that some young, truly dedicated, beginning writer will see here that no true idea is ever wasted.

It is apropos that Texas Tech University Press is publishing this work since I was born at Ropesville (Ropes) just twenty miles south of this noted campus.

Perhaps not too surprising, some of my own personal favorite stories could probably be ranked as my best. Odds and emotions suggest that *One-Eyed Sky* is my best short novel, and the

"The Call" word for word, is my best short (under 1,500 words), short story. I also think that the long essays on director Sam Peckinpah and John Milton, are as good as I have done in that field. The short essay "Song Of The West" is my favorite in that length. The introduction to the book *Spirit Ascendant* (Red Crane Books) on the life and art of the great santero and symbolist, Patricino Barela, of Taos was written with all the emotion I have.

Before I go on, let us stop and settle something in our minds of the randomness of literary endurance. More than likely it will be after the year 2050 before any true indications of which writers' work survived from the preceding century. A quick rundown of the history of literature since Shakespeare will prove the great surprises in store for readers yet to be born. By 2050 most of the famous, rich, best-selling authors of today will have been buried and forgotten along with their billions of words. The same number of academic and critical pets of the present will have blown away in the smoke and fog of uncertainty. Not all, for sure, but most. History is surprising, heartless, and certain, in the fragility of lasting reputations.

I remember back in the 1950s reading Somerset Maugham and thinking he was a master stylist and a great observer of the human condition. He was required reading in a majority of schools—I haven't heard his name mentioned in twenty years.

In the 1960s, I discovered Joyce Cary. I believed then and I believe now, that *The Horse's Mouth, Mr. Johnson,* and *Charley Is My Darling,*—each totally original and different from the other—are three of the greatest and best balanced tragicomedies ever written. However, no single one of these is as great as the proven survivor of tragicomedy, Cervantes *Don Quixote.* It is difficult today to find a Cary book, even in rare book stores. It is even more difficult to find anyone who knows of him.

More recent writing in the tragicomedy vein, near the center of the Southwest, William Eastlake must be mentioned. His Cuba, New Mexico, Indian trilogy that included *The Bronc People* was quite popular in his chosen land up until the eighties. Like Cary, about a generation before him, Eastlake is being unjustifiably ignored by most of the critics and the public. I have enormous respect for individual works by many southwestern writers including Frank Waters, John Nichols, Denise Chavez, Ed Abbey, Tom Lea, Harvey Ferguson, and Conrad Richter, but none have surpassed the most ineluctable tragedies of human life, kept in balance by a natural humor, as Eastlake did in his Cuba trio.

I have loved and enjoyed the words of Katherine Anne Porter, ("Pale Horse, Pale Rider," "Noon Wine") but she also seems to have been relegated to diminishing attention mostly in her native state of Texas. Among others, the works of Colette have long enlisted my deep admiration. Right now she will at least enter into the early part of the next century intact. I believe Porter to be her equal. One slowing vanishing, the other holding on. How can a person possibly make reason out of this? I have proven nothing here except to declare a few of my personal puzzles and choices. Only the unseeing filter of time, and possible chance, will reveal the rapidly shrinking number of survivors. Since we are all temporary to one degree or another we should be humble and at the same time thankful for whatever tracks—no matter how few— we make in the vanishing desert of words.

I am astounded that some of my own works have been in print for forty years and realize they may all have vanished before I do. Knowing this however, makes what you have between these covers more precious than platinum or even a green-grass rain. I do not write just about white people, Indians, Hispanics, or any other group except in the proportions they exist in the region I know best—the Hi Lo Country—and in my personal life. This is not to be politically correct or incorrect, but simply to be true to what existed and portray as authentically as possible all the people of this vast land.

The short novel *My Pardner* was inspired by actual happenings when I was ten years old. That is the year learned psychologists assure us is the final digit in the shaping of one's total life. Perhaps they are right. That two month odyssey gave me survival instincts still in effect today. I made myself older in the book than I actually was so it would be more believable.

One of my favorite short novels *Candles in the Bottom of the Pool* was left out because it is presently in two anthologies: *Spinning Sun, Grinning Moon* (Red Crane Books), and *Western Hall of Fame Anthology* (Berkley/Jove). There are no cowboys or cowgirls in this contemporary story of the mystical Southwest. It has been anthologized eight or nine times, and I have always been very fond of this work.

You might wonder why this tome is titled as it is. When you read the section entitled "Introductions and Forewords" about two other books, *Rounders 3* and *The Hi Lo Country* I believe you will understand. To continue *The Hi Lo Country* saga, it is now a major motion picture with Martin Scorsese (*Raging Bull,*

Goodfellas, Casino) as the executive producer who made the project possible and hired Stephen Frears (*Dangerous Liaisons, My Beautiful Launderette, The Grifters*) as the director, with a screenplay by Walon Green (*The Wild Bunch, The Hellstrom Chronicles*). It stars Woody Harrellson, Billy Crudup, Patricia Arquette, and Penelope Cruz and includes a wonderful supporting cast of Sam Elliott, playing against type, Willy Nelson, Katy Jurado, James Gammon, Cole Hauser, Jacob Vargas, and Enrique Castillo. At this writing the twenty-five minutes of cut film we have seen is powerful and feels real. Two of the principals who have seen the near final cut have called it an exceptionally fine film. You can judge for yourself as it will be released December, 1998. I will stick my neck out and predict that Billy Crudup will become a *lasting* household name.

In some of the enclosed stories you may find the Sam Peckinpah–*Hi Lo* connection repeated for a total of about two minutes of reading time. Please forgive me because I felt it only fair that the stories appear in full as they were written at the time.

It is both a jolting and highly pleasant surprise to realize through these works how many physical and emotional wars one can survive in a long, busy, plunging life. Early on in my thirties, many academics supported my work, but as my writing remained eclectic a lot of them quit me. Among those who stayed hooked without reservations were the Dean of Southwestern writers, C. L. (Doc) Sonnichsenn and John Milton of the noted *South Dakota Review*. The wheres and whyfores of all this can be gleened from this book.

At first this lessening lack of attention puzzled me. Then I realized in this age of endless sequels, copycat killings, and fad-after-fad followers, to a degree that would embarrass lemmings, it is now against the law to be original in any line of endeavor, much less writing. Even if I wanted to, it is too late for me to do a damn thing about it. I have literally thousands of different stories and hundreds of paintings in my head that can only be put down if some scientific genius invents a "forever pill" for this dimension. In lieu of that, I am just going to keep right on scribbling as long as they manufacture ink and I can hold a pen. I hereby make a little medicine prayer that you enjoy at least a few of these stories. Since they are my favorites I surely did. With a good nights sleep, I may start one of those beginnings again tomorrow.

Max Evans
Albuquerque, New Mexico

1
Short Novels

Xavier's Folly

1

The creature moved across the hill, struggling through the thick black grass with determination. Xavier Del Campo opened his eyes a little more and watched the bug straining through the jungle of hair on his heavy arm. The sun formed tiny prisms of light here and there. He imagined they were shining on a vast stage and he could see Tamara, the great Russian ballet star, pirouetting under their golden glow. He could hear the music, especially the strings, and then she finished. The applause shook rocks loose in the earth. She was beckoning him to come and share her glory on the stage. Imagine!

Xavier lifted his head from his arms and slowly sat up, rubbing the heavy curled hair on his head. He stared off at the blue hump of the Rocky Mountains rising like prehistoric monsters out of the earth. His eyes looked above them into the sky. He liked to look at a cloudless sky since he discovered that it was full of holes. He was entranced by the firmament. The holes pulsated with greens, pinks and purples. He felt sorry for people who just saw the sky as a blue curtain. They were missing so much. All they had to do was really look. That's all.

His wife was one of those who missed. Shortly after they were married he was pursuing his hobby of 'sky staring' when she stepped out of the house to hang out the wash. She asked, as she walked past him, "An eagle?" When he didn't answer, she asked, "A hawk?"

"Look at the sky," he said, "it's full of pretty holes."

She cast a suspicious eye upon him. Seeing he was serious, she snorted. "It's your brain that's full of holes."

Their relationship had deteriorated after that. His great Mexican eyes dropped back down to the sage-covered foothills of the mountains. He could see their little house and sheds there. Lonely. Aloof. He tried not to think of her but it was no use. Tonight he had to tell her of his great plan. A feeling of dread caressed his short, muscled body. He stood up and looked at the ditch in front of him. Manuel usually dug the ditches while Xavier tended to the fitting of pipes. He didn't mind digging, but it took up valuable time. As a plumber, Xavier was an artist. All metal fit perfectly and was sealed the same. He was immensely proud that his pipes never leaked. Never. Now, however, he must dig. Yesterday he paid Manuel so it was reasonable to figure that today he was drunk. Xavier might have joined him but he had to save money. It would take a lot of cash to fulfill his plan. He already had thirty-seven hundred dollars hidden in a bucket behind the outdoor privy.

He lifted the pick from the loose dirt and stepped into the ditch to dig. The steel point pierced the earth and bit away chunks as he swung up and down in powerful rhythms. The spring air was not hot, but sweat soon darkened the underarms of his shirt. When had he promised his clients to have the plumbing installed? They came every day from town to check on his progress. They were anxious to move into their new adobe. It was expensive living in a hotel, they informed him.

Xavier swung faster and harder at these thoughts. Today, though, they failed to come and he dug straight till dark, almost finishing the ditch. He dug it over three feet deep so the harsh winters could never freeze the pipes. All his customers complained at his seeming slowness, but later they commented on the perfection of his skill and recommended him to others. He was never without work.

When he could no longer see clearly what he was doing he dropped the pick, got in his faded old red truck and headed home. It had to be tonight. Yes, he had to tell her now. He took a short cut around the town of Taos, chugging into the foothills towards the light in the window that glowed deceivingly warm. A coyote loped across the winding road in front of him, glancing sideways, and vanished in the sage and darkness.

The two old cur dogs moved off the porch and barked a half-hearted welcome. As he got out of the truck the dogs smelled his legs and waved their tails so slightly it was only a suggestion. He thought that somehow they had adopted a certain attitude of their mistress.

3

As he opened the door he wondered why he didn't detect that contentment that men were supposed to feel on the return to the hearth. Where was the surging pride in a hard day's work to share with his lady?

She and her two daughters were just finishing the evening meal. One girl was fourteen, the other sixteen—Suzanne and Suzette. They had the same gray eyes of their mother, watery, dull and somehow appearing a bit out of focus. They moved these orbs slightly upward in greeting. Both had buck teeth and when they smiled their lips pulled back and a wad of flesh wrinkled up over the gums. It had come to Xavier on occasion that their mouths reminded him of a mule's behind when he strained to pull a deep plow through dry earth. He had long been curious as to what their real father looked like. But he would never know for the man had died years before, from the bellyache. Xavier would soon understand more about his demise.

Marion looked up, saying between chews of spaghetti, "You're late. We went ahead and ate."

"Aw, that's all right. I'm not very hungry anyway." He washed his face and hands in a tin pan of cold water and sat down. The girls got up and went to their room. He watched them go, shaking their rounded tails far more than the dogs. He reached for the bowl and took the little bit of spaghetti left. As he buttered a cold biscuit, she poured him a cup of warm black coffee. He ate. She sat.

He knew exactly what she'd say when she did speak.

"When are you gonna finish the Bently job?"

"Next week if Manuel gets over his cold."

"Cold? He's too full of wine to catch anything. You said you'd put in our plumbing when the Bently job is done."

He took a long drink of coffee and tried very hard to see out through the old adobe wall. In fact, he tried to *be* outside. It didn't work.

"You been sayin' you was gonna put in our plumbin' after every job for a year now. It's gettin' embarrassin' to explain to folks. The girls are ashamed to bring company home. How can they explain to their friends that they have to go outside to the toilet? Some plumber you are."

Xavier never knew why he said it. The statement was against his nature and made his important announcement much more difficult,

"It's cleaner to crap outside."

4

He knew he'd stepped over the bounds with her. When she was mad she pulled at her stringy, mouse-colored hair and squinted her eyes. She was pulling and squinting right now.

"You tryin' to get funny with me or sumpthin'?"

"Marion, I got something important to tell you."

"You tryin' to get funny, huh?"

"Marion, I . . ."

She got up from the table and started gathering the dirty dishes. She took his coffee before he was half through and made a lot of noises doing all this.

"You smell."

"Smell what?" he asked.

"You. You, that's what. You smell like a boar hog. If you'd put a bath in at least you could take a shower before settin' down at the table with us."

"I'll take a tub bath tonight," he placated, "but first I want to tell . . ."

"Imagine havin' to bathe in that old tin washtub. A plumber's wife. Jist imagine," she said.

"Now, Marion, I promise. I'll even promise on a Bible." He walked over and got the book out of a dresser drawer to show faith. "Now see here, I got my hand on this Bible."

She stopped washing dishes and glared at him. "Well?" she said, waiting, almost believing him now.

"All right now. I promise on the word of the Lord that as soon as I put on my ballet presentation I'll put in the plumbing. "

"Your what?" she shrieked.

"The great Tamara. I'm going to bring her to Taos. I'm going to present her."

Marion just stood and squinted till she couldn't even see her eyes, only a tiny thin line where they had been. She was almost pulling her stringy mouse-colored hair out by the shallow roots. What poor Xavier didn't know was that Marion had married him to get her plumbing installed. She had always intended to kick him out just as soon as that was accomplished.

Finally she said in a deadly flat tone, "I always knew you was crazy. I knew it from the first time you was tryin' to find holes in the sky. Ballet? Ballet? My God! I ought to have you locked up!"

"But . . . but ballet is beautiful."

"My God! There ain't anybody in Taos that even knows how to spell the word. Beautiful my wild ass."

5

Xavier rubbed at his curly hair and twisted around on his feet still holding the Bible as if God himself might just materialize from the pages and smight him dead. His stomach hurt. How was he going to make her understand?

"Just because folks don't know is no reason that they can't learn to like beautiful things."

She hurled the dish towel across the room and sat down on the battered-up divan. "Beautiful. Beautiful, he says. All I ever want in the world to make it beautiful is a bathroom and now you tell me that I have to wait while you bring a bunch of idiots here to dance around on their toes. I'm tellin' you, you even bring it up and the people of Taos'll laugh you plumb into Texas. My God! Toe dancing! People never was meant to dance on their toes. They might as well try swingin' from their tails like monkeys."

She got up and went in to talk to her daughters. He could hear sounds from the room, but he couldn't make out the words. For this he was thankful. He got himself a cup of cold coffee and sat down trying to think.

She came out slamming the door with a victorious air about her sagging breasts. She stopped in the middle of the floor, her feet spread apart like a boxer's, and said, "You know what we're gonna do?"

He looked up at her, knowing that whatever they were going to do would not be to his benefit.

"We're going into town first thing in the mornin' and we're gonna draw ever dime out of the bank." She smiled now like a coyote with a rabbit by the hind-quarters. "And we're gonna hire Ben Gonzales to put in our plumbin'. There won't be no cockeyed ballet, no nothin'." She paused, relishing the sad look on Xavier's face, and then threw the coup de grace at him. "Now won't the folks of Taos get one hell of a laugh outa the fact your competitor is puttin' in *our* plumbin'? Huh?"

Things didn't get any better that night. Xavier had his choice of sleeping on the divan, which had springs that punched one's body, or sleeping out back in a shed with the goats. He wrapped up in an old rag rug and said to the goats,

"Don't worry, it's just for tonight."

Marion lay in bed and exulted over her move. Not only would she make a laughing stock out of Xavier but she'd run him off as soon as the plumbing was installed. She had recently learned that the useless looking sagebrush land her first husband had left her could be turned into a housing development. At least that

6

marriage had paid off. The land ran all the way into the timber on the mountains. The realtors told her she would make a fortune, but it would take time. In the meanwhile she'd get her bathroom and then run Xavier off before he could share the benefits from any real estate profits. Marion was a lady who made plans.

Out back with the goats, Xavier thought of himself as a coward. He just couldn't muster up the guts to tell her there was only four dollars and thirteen cents in the bank. But with all his immediate troubles, and the fact he'd been demoted to the animal shelter for the night, he dreamed big dreams.

Xavier's mother and father drowned in a flash flood when he was ten years old. He was sent to live with an uncle and aunt in Los Angeles. His uncle was a plumber and Xavier was apprenticed. He learned how to cut and thread pipe; how to measure and fit; how to melt the lead and permanently seal the joints. He learned fast. The first two years he went to public school, but then he had to quit because he became too valuable to his uncle to be wasted on reading and writing.

They lived upstairs in a very crowded section of old houses. At night, after helping his aunt do the supper dishes, he'd sit out on the walk-up porch, look at the city and conjure up visions of all the things the millions of people were doing at that moment.

Across an alley was an empty-looking old building. One night a light beamed from the big window and there for the first time he saw ballet. A lady had opened a dance academy.

At first, Xavier thought their actions very strange and foolish, but each night he was drawn back to watch. Gradually he began to feel the grace and dignity, and finally he had the courage to slip down to the window for a closer look. He was entranced.

There was one long-haired girl who looked to be of his own blood—Mexican. She seemed to float when she leaped. He kept hoping that she would truly learn to fly with a hawk. Each time she danced, his muscles twitched in his short frame with her and for her. He fell in love with her; he fell in love with the dance. A thirst was upon him. Oh, he didn't deceive himself that *he* would ever dance. Not with his build. He would simply look like a fat rubber ball bouncing about. No, he participated with his soul.

Finally a night came when all the parents arrived to see the results of their money and their children's dedication. Xavier had saved pennies for weeks so he could attend. His uncle laughed but his aunt smiled, somehow knowing.

When the lights came on and the long-haired girl was spotlighted, he thought he'd faint it was so lovely. As she danced in the dark with the light following, it became a glorious, sensuous thing to Xavier. He felt that he himself was the light and that he completely enveloped her while she moved with the grace of a Maltese cat.

He waited outside that night as the people left chattering with their children and friends. When she came out (he never remembered her name) he touched her on the arm and said,

"You . . . you are beautiful."

She stunned him with a smile that radiated right straight through his heart. Then he ran.

2

Xavier was grown now. He was a master plumber. He had returned to his own beloved Southwest and started a business in Taos. Then one day a movie called RED SHOES came to town. It was an old and timeless film. Never, not even in Los Angeles, had he seen anything so hypnotic. The dark, flame-lit red hair of Moira Shearer floated with her like thousands of tiny writhing snakes. Her white face and body were from other planes; they were from heaven. When she had thrown herself from a window in front of the train, he'd died with her! And when the camera had shown the red satin shoes and the pink tights with the blood coming through, he'd died a thousand times more. But even so . . . What a film! What a lady! What a dance! Finally he knew what the word "magic" really meant. It meant ballet.

Later he saw a photographic study of Tamara in a national magazine. He looked at it until the pages were worn and shredded. He knew now what he must do. He knew what he was born for—his whole purpose. He would die to accomplish it. He would bring the great Tamara here to Taos and present her. He could see it now: XAVIER PRESENTS.

He had already started saving his money for this dream when he met Marion. She had seemed so sweet when she invited him up for supper. He'd even been treated with a smattering of kindness from her daughters. The food had seemed all right, too, for her flattery had numbed his tastebuds. And in the dark that night she had felt good.

As always, though, the light finally comes. The woman was as obsessed with indoor plumbing as he was with ballet. He could not afford to do the work on her home. That would take time and money away from his presentation. If only he could have told her sooner, but until tonight he always got a knot in his throat and could never say the words. Now he had a knot in his stomach as well.

The goats kept him awake most of the night trying to eat the rag rug right off his body, and so when the first rooster crowed, Xavier, stiff and sore, arose. He had dug in the earth all the day before and bedded on it all night.

It took the sun awhile to climb the other side of the mountains. They seemed flat and black against the rising oranges and yellows, but once the mighty globe shoved its brilliant sabers of light between the peaks, the mountains took form and suddenly the valleys were violet and the hogbacks golden and green.

The chickens scratched around and started visiting. A bird talked somewhere out in the sagebrush. A trailer-truck groaned over a rise on the highway below. A thin blue haze hung over Taos from early morning piñon fires. The two curs moved over against the adobe wall where its reflection would give them a double warmth.

Xavier took his morning relief behind the privy, staring at the spot where the money was buried. He had an urge to dig it up but knew that Marion and the daughters would be awake. He was hungry. He headed for his truck, not looking at the house. He walked in an arc to the conveyance as if a pressure exuding from the house had pushed him off a true course.

The old motor choked and spit. Xavier pumped the gas pedal with some hint of desperation, glancing at the house, expecting Marion to crash right through the thick walls and devour him. Finally, the motor, gas and sparks all coordinated and Xavier raced the truck backwards, bumping up on top of a huge clump of sage. He then gunned it in a circle, hit the road hurtling back and forth across it, settled down and rolled on to town.

He had breakfast at a truck stop and went to work. Manuel was there. He was hanging on the pick where it appeared to be stuck in the bottom of the ditch. He had swung at the earth with admirable intent, but the earth had jumped up, meeting his move halfway and jarring his whole body, as sometimes happens when one steps from a curb that is not supposed to be there. For the moment, he was taking no chances on any kind of movement.

Manuel was about three times as long and not a great deal bigger around than the pick. He had spent so many years digging that the instrument was simply an extension of his arms. No matter what his physical discomfort, the visual aspects suggested a very long-armed man leaning comfortably on the world. Xavier's closer inspection of Manuel's face, however, gave the truth away. Sweat was protruding all over his forehead, and his Adam's apple chugged up and down in his throat, necessitating as many swallows to keep the wine down as it had taken to get it there in the first place.

Xavier asked a silly and unnecessary question, as most people seem to do at moments like this, "How you feeling?"

Manuel allowed the question to reverberate through his head a moment until it had time to settle down. "I feel *lack* I been *shoot* at and *mees, sheet* at and *heet.* "

Xavier felt he needed no further description of his associate's condition and he entered the house and went to work. In spite of the various forms of turmoil within him he worked harder, faster, and more efficiently than ever. When the Bentlys arrived that afternoon and posed their perpetual question, he could honestly tell them they could move in three days from the present one.

By late afternoon Xavier was so delighted with the fine day's work that he decided to help Manuel in his recovery. They stopped in at the Chico Bar for medicinal purposes only. As the wine was repeatedly served there was a distinct change in Manuel. There was no doubt that he now felt as good or maybe even better than he had the night before. Not only did he do a Mexican hat dance without a hat, but by midnight he was singing "Guadalajara" and envisioning himself as the Caruso for the entire Spanish world. How the rest of the patrons saw him remains private with them, for all had learned long ago that Manuel's skinny muscles were like those of an eagle. You don't mess around close up with eagles.

Occasionally, certainly not on purpose, Xavier's thoughts drifted to Marion's home on the hill. He knew she'd be waiting for him. However, these thoughts were fleeting indeed for Chico's place exuded warmth, companionship and safety.

By one o'clock he knew that Manuel was in as good condition as it was possible to attain in that length of time, and so he pondered on his own pleasures and there by the music box he conjured up the great Tamara. My, what a talent! She could even dance to "Guadalajara." She whirled and turned and leaped and flew, and smiled at him, then vanished behind the multi-colored music-maker.

The two o'clock closing time came. This did not deter Manuel. He took several bottles of wine and his boss home with him. They sat on the porch out of courtesy to Manuel's wife and seven children. Xavier insisted they must not enter and disturb their sleep. He had not considered that they would probably wake up the entire neighborhood.

They talked of many truths, and spilled a few lies. Xavier told Manuel about the ballet. But Manuel thought it was some kind of Indian corn dance and said many toasts to his Indian brothers.

". . . and to you, Xavier, my boss, one man who helps makes piss on this earth. Marries gringo womans, and dance with Indians.

Manuel went to sleep on the porch. Xavier took a bottle of wine, crawled sleepily into his truck, and headed home. He drove up just as the sun knocked the shadows out of the sky. He'd been gone exactly twenty-four hours. He was no longer afraid. He knew what he must do and that was it. He'd tell Marion and make her understand. Xavier took another drink of wine just to be sure he wouldn't forget.

The new sun had slightly blinded him, and it was a moment before his eyes adjusted to the room. It didn't matter that much for the voice was everywhere. It ricocheted from wall to wall, spun in circles, and danced up and down. It whizzed around in his head, kicking his stomach from the inside. A Neanderthal instinct caused him to move around so that the table was between himself and the strongest point of emission. It was fortunate that Marion had no training in baseball, for Xavier would already be dead. Things, heavy things, were zapping through the room along with the voice. It's possible that her aim became faulty because of her movement around the table to get nearer her target. Xavier himself moved to get farther away from the catapult. Fortunately, she was just no good on moving objects.

"Where is the money? The money? You . . . you . . ."

She stopped, sputtering, desperately trying to find words that would express her deepest feelings and a weapon that would kill.

Xavier had never been able to say the right things to his wife. In their moments of forced communication such as now he was a total flop. As she hesitated in her fury he stuck the bottle of very cheap wine out in front of him and politely suggested,

"Would you like a little nip?"

Before she could answer he took a large swallow, watching her around the edge of the bottle. This was no time to get careless.

Marion found words again, "Son-of-a-bitch! Son-of-a-bitch! Son-of-a-bitch!"

The daughters were bravely yelling encouragement to their mother while at the same time wisely staying behind a bolted door.

Xavier, like most honest people, was a poor liar. It comes from a lack of practice. He ventured, "I . . . I lost the money gambling."

"Liar! Liar! You lying bastard!"

He realized that she'd caught on. He had no time to dwell upon it, though, for she now expressed many of those deep feelings she'd been searching for. "I'll have you jailed. I'll sue for the money. I'll sue, you hear?"

Xavier said, "Now, honey . . . " How he came up with that sweet word he could not comprehend.

She went on: "All my life I've had to go outside to the toilet, in blizzards and blazin' sun! It ain't right! You . . . you worthless little pig! You think fixin' a place up is paintin' the toilet door blue! That's all you've done since we've been married! You didn't even bother to fix the cracks. The wind freezes my ass off in the winter and melts it off in the summer.

Xavier now realized that it was either indoor plumbing or Tamara. No compromise was to be reached. His decision took no struggle at all. He set the bottle down on the table, toward her side. She glared at it, breathing so hard that her drooping breasts actually pushed out momentarily. Her eyes were squinted so that Xavier doubted if she'd ever be able to get them fully open again. There was no use concerning himself about the anger or the disarray of her hair.

She said with meaning, "You son-of-a-bitch. "

As always, Xavier spoke the improper words to her even thought he did so with restraint and a certain touch of politeness, "I wish you'd quit calling me by your family name."

That certainly did it. She went right over the table, grabbing the wine bottle on the way. Xavier turned and ran for the door. But now the odds were finally fulfilled. She hurled the bottle and it went straight to its mark, thudding against the back of Xavier's skull just as he was trying to escape through the screen door. He was propelled out and off the porch, face down, in the dirt. The cur dogs were both barking and nipping at him as he stumbled to his feet. The world tipped and rocked, trying to flatten him against its bosom. He could hear the screams behind him and feel the breath of the dogs on his legs. He stayed upright. It wasn't easy either. He managed to fumble his way into the truck and release the brake just as Marion reached out to claw his eyes. But the truck was moving, and as he jerked the door shut it knocked her down. He gave the motor a turn and the saints were kind—it started. He rolled swiftly down the hill and didn't even glance in the rear view mirror.

3

It took nine stitches to sew his head up and the knot throbbed a week, but he and Manuel worked and worked and worked.

Xavier went to see the attorney, Mr. Granger. He smiled at the little plumber, and said, "Yes, I was in show business for awhile. It's possible that I could use some of my old connections to find Tamara for you." He made it seem like a very difficult task before he was through. The truth was, Xavier had barely left the office when Granger called a performers' guild in New York and acquired the address of Tamara's agent.

The agent said there was a possibility that in late summer Tamara might have time for a night in Taos. It would all be up to the cash offered, availability of proper music, etc., etc. Granger let Xavier wait three weeks before telling him about the ten minutes of calls.

In the meanwhile Xavier rented a very small room in an alley, barely big enough for a cot and all his tools. He ate all his meals right from the cans and had no luxuries. He now worked at night when the houses were new and empty, and by sleeping little and worrying much was accumulating more money all the time. The cache behind Marion's house still had to be recovered, but he simply couldn't bring himself to invade her domain as yet. The new scar on his head still itched.

Marion had told around town that he had attacked her in a drunken rage and she'd fought for her life. She had the law arrest him, but it was only a formality. They quickly observed that she didn't have a scratch on her and Xavier had a nine-stitch hole in his head.

Granger finally received word from Tamara and she could stop over, enroute from Chicago to Los Angeles, the twenty-first day of August, for one night. The cost, Granger said, would be thirty-five hundred and expenses. Actually it was twenty-five, but Granger had to live like anyone else.

He explained to Xavier that at the Met and other large theatres Tamara worked with a sixty-piece orchestra, and he was having some difficulty convincing them that even though they could only deliver thirty pieces it would be very satisfactory. For a moment this shocked the ecstasy out of Xavier's body, but Granger told him not to worry because he had to make a business trip to Denver soon and he would take care of all the arrangements.

"Strings," exulted Xavier. "Get lots of strings."

Now the word was around town about Xavier's madness and he was greeted with, "How's the impresario today?" "Give my regards to Broadway," and such like.

He rented a small lot in the desert on the opposite side of town from Marion. About thirty yards back from the highway, he started building his stage. Local jokesters called it the 'poor man's Met.' At first the verbal cuts had hurt but now he just worked, and dreamed. He tied on to the power line and when he wasn't plumbing at night he sawed, measured, and gradually nailed his stage together. It would be an outdoor stage with the whole vast southwest as a background. He built a railing for the orchestra. He did Tamara's stage with fine wood, solid and smooth. He put up poles on the corners and in the middle, and strung small ropes crisscrossed over it. On these he hung scores of tiny colored flags.

When the last piece of red cloth was draped, he walked excitedly out into the desert, not looking back till he was on a promontory a good half mile distant. Then he turned; the beauty almost overwhelmed him. It was like a carnival, so gay and joyous. It was alive and breathing. It was his . . . his and Tamara's. The local populace drove by and laughed; strangers stared in wonder at the apparition, but Xavier loved it.

Then Granger called him in for a meeting. It was decided that the cost of attendance would be a flat five dollars. It was now time to have the show cards printed. Xavier had already worked out the design and color. When he took his idea to the newspaper for printing he never dreamed they would do a story on him.

In a few days he got the eighteen by twenty-four inch cards. They were grand—red and yellow with black letters and a photo of Tamara. His name was right next to hers. They read:

XAVIER PRESENTS
The
GREAT TAMARA
Ballerina Supreme

They gave the date, hour and price of admission, as well as the location (as if everyone in the whole of Taos County wasn't aware of that). He proudly drove around town putting the cards in every saloon, gas station, and shop. He even put them up in the court house and the county jail. This activity turned almost every individual in town into a comic. Oh, the wise remarks that exist in doubting souls.

Xavier went about building the benches and stringing the lights. He had to import an electrician from the Little Theatre in Albuquerque to install the moving spots. These were covered with pink gel to soften the glow. He kept the man two extra nights just to be sure they were of a proper quality for his Tamara. Yes, she was *his* right now, and forever, no matter what. The electrician would return, for a price, the night of the big DO.

Then the local paper came out with these large letters on the front page: LOCAL PLUMBER TO BE IMPRESARIO???? and the story followed. In spite of the question marks, the local comments of ridicule slowly subsided. They gave glances of fear now, barely smiling. Hadn't the paper actually said the ballerina was coming? What if he really pulled it off? From some of those who had teased the most he now got an occasional, hesitant pat on the back. They were having third and fourth doubts. Everyone fears a winning except other winners.

Marion had received an advance on the land development and had Ben Gonzales up at the house putting in her plumbing. She was so excited about this that she only had time to curse Xavier about one hour out of three. She got a lot of extra work out of Ben by flattering him and stating that he was lucky. Xavier would be broken and shamed out of the county and he'd have the plumbing business all to himself At this thought she started working on Ben in other ways as she had once done to the little ballet producer. The lady was determined to have her own personal plumber.

Manuel didn't really know what was going on, but with a sense of destiny, he dug deeper, faster and longer, than any man in the history of Taos. It was a busy time for plumbers.

15

4

As mid-August came the town of Taos filled up with tourists. Each day hundreds passed through on their way to Colorado, but many stayed. The motels were ninety percent full and the plaza was overflowing with visitors, in varying percentages, from all the states. The Chamber of Commerce and one drug store handled Xavier's tickets. To everyone's amazement except Xavier's, they were sold out by the sixteenth. There were requests for standing room. Many had agreed to bring their own seats and sit in the desert itself.

On the morning of the twentieth, Xavier handed over the needed funds to Granger. The attorney, knowing Xavier's fine earning record, had given checks for the orchestra, etc. Xavier had taken care of all construction, printing, and the like.

Granger raised pencil from paper and said, "Now, that takes care of everything but Tamara and the hotel bill."

Xavier was thanking Granger, "Mr. Granger, I don't know how to . . . "

"Now, now, Xavier. It's all in my duties. Nothing to it. just glad I could be of help. We're proud of you here in Taos." He took on his courtroom voice now, rubbed his prosperous stomach, and continued, "Very proud indeed." And then as an afterthought, "It looks like you're going to have a financial success on your hands as well." And he smiled at Xavier like Santa Claus' great grandfather.

Xavier had several hundred dollars left but he could avoid it no longer, he had to go to Marion's and get his buried money. In the adventure, the glow of creating a classic presentation, he'd kept delaying his duty on the hillside until he'd hidden it so far within himself it had actually been forgotten. Well, the dark of night was well suited for digging up money buried ten steps behind the wooden outhouse with a painted door. Even the wise old coyote knew things like this. Xavier had always believed in following nature whenever possible.

Now he would go out and make his last inspection, because tomorrow he would be too busy. The day was warm, the blue grey foothills rolled up merging with the base of the mountains. An aura hung over it all . . . an unseen mist that caused the rays of the sun to break into infinitesimal sundrops exploding in the air with billions of tiny sparkles. The soft sound of a dove cooing caressed the bright air. The bobcat and the coyote rested in the first jumble of rocks, digesting food from last night's hunt, waiting for the moon again. The gophers and the rats were in their dens hiding from the sun. Some of them would not escape the night hunters. Some would. Bugs and lizards crawled under small rocks. The snakes waited in the shade of the sage and cactus and watched their movements. Higher up in the aspen and pine, deer fed, becoming lazy and fat. But at the first explosion of the fall hunter's gun, they would quiver, run and hide, trying to survive. Some wouldn't. But all the movement Xavier could see in this expanse was a hawk circling and the slight stirring of the flags as they made love to a fluctuating breeze. Behind the mountains the clouds rose, shoving up like sails being raised on giant sky ships. Their heaviness turned their bottoms dark with shadow.

The mood of the day, of the time in Xavier's existence, had caught him up in a reverie of dreams, of glory. Then the first heavy drop of rain hit his shoulder. He looked up. Two more splashed against his face. Then it came down hard, fast, clean and pure. The curtain of moisture moved on over his kingdom and down the hills to the west wetting a path perhaps two thirds of a mile wide.

The freshness of everything was almost more than Xavier could take. What luck! The dust would be perfectly settled for the crowd tomorrow night.

Xavier checked out the ticket sales and the hotel reservations. He called on Granger again to be sure about the orchestra. All was in order. His universe was complete, or would be, after a little trip to the *casa* in the foothills.

At dusk he bought a box of dog biscuits. Then he went to his crowded room and fed himself a can of Vienna sausage, some crackers and an apple. He lay down on the cot to wait. The alarm was set for two o'clock. That would get him at Marion's about three when she would be sleeping the soundest. The girls didn't concern him. They were too lazy to wake up. Sleep avoided Xavier that night. There was too much to think about on the morrow, not counting the risk of facing Marion tonight. He rubbed the scar on his head. The alarm rang, and he quivered all over from shock at the sound.

The moon was almost full. It shoved the blue lights out over the sage and made Xavier wish for total darkness. He thought that the earth's second biggest spotlight was not needed this night. He pulled from the highway, turning off his lights before he did, drove up a little draw and hid the truck. He put on his jacket and emptied the dog biscuits in one large pocket.

He used the country road for awhile, trying to walk softly. He felt that every step was surely jarring the foundations of the house and rattling dishes in the cupboard. He envisioned Marion sitting cocking the hammers on a brand new shotgun. If she hadn't hated the outdoor privy so, he was sure she'd be waiting there to blow him in half, cursing the undone plumbing while he kicked his last.

Sure enough, when he was within a couple of hundred yards of the house the two dogs ran around barking like never before. Xavier knew they sensed his fear. He jumped off the road behind some sagebrush and held his breath. Xavier *tried* not to *be*—to exist—but he *was*. He was right here cowering while the money resided up there in an unfeeling bucket not caring whether he recovered it or not.

Inside, Marion pushed at Ben Gonzales' sleeping back until he awoke. "There's somethin' out there, Ben."

Now Mr. Gonzales had labored day and night getting her plumbing all in order and had finally finished the task that very evening. He was tired. "Ish jiss a coyote," he mumbled, and went back to sleep.

Xavier moved up to meet the dogs and whatever other demons lurked there for him. He knew now what courage it took for a foot soldier to attack hidden machine guns and cannon. As he neared the dogs, or vice versa, he tried whistling to them with friendship. He really didn't know if he was making a sound or not. Dogs are supposed to feel vibrations beyond the capability of the human ear, and he was not about to exude enough air for Marion's ears.

Now the dogs faced him and they had a combination of irritated barks and disgusted snarls for their former half master. He pitched some biscuits in front of them, whispering love songs as hard as he could.

"Oh, you beautiful dogs. You kind-hearted dogs. You wise and thoughtful dogs. You hungry dogs. Dogs are my friends. Hello, my friends."

It worked somewhat. They did grab up the biscuits greedily. And then stood back with bristles up, growling softly to see what kind of trick or treat was next. Xavier was busy. He made a wide circle to come in behind the outhouse, all the time dropping

18

biscuits to the growling dogs and trying to watch the door to Marion's house. He listened hard, too.

The dogs had decided to adopt the ancient attitude of let's wait and see. They had a growl bottled up just at the end of their tongues ready for instant action if the biscuits were stopped permanently. The jacket pocket was only half full now. Xavier would have to work fast.

And then he saw! The outhouse was gone and all the ground around had been graded smooth! There was Gonzales' work truck. No doubt Gonzales also occupied his late unlamented bed. To save his life, his soul, his presentation, he could not divine the spot where the small structure of relief had stood.

Christ! If he'd just had enough sense to bring along his electronic pipe locator there would be no problem. In a small hysterical moment he thought about borrowing his fellow worker's. It was probably in the back of the truck. However, the truck's proximity to the doorway of Marion's house forbade that.

The dogs were circling now, feeling his anxiety and letting little portions of growls escape. Any moment they might go the whole route. He pitched them two more biscuits, buying time. He thought. Not an easy thing to do either. Watching the door and the dogs he spotted a stick in a pile of wood that had once been the privy. If he remembered correctly the contents of that little building had been somewhat above the level of the earth. That would mean it would be mixed with the soil that covered it.

He made a wild guess as to its location and an even wilder decision. He must become a dog. He threw the rest of the biscuits out around him and dropped down on his hands and knees, punching at the earth, looking for a soft spot, and sniffing back and forth from side to side like a thoroughbred trailhound. At this unusual action the dogs even forgot the biscuits. They growled and let out two rather confused barks.

Marion was not going to accept the coyote theory. This time she kneed Gonzales in the kidneys and forced him up. He stumbled around trying to find the bedroom door.

Suddenly Xavier plunged the stick into soft soil and he got the scent all right. There was no doubt at all. Now he moved back and forth trying to define the edges of the covered hole, sniffing, dropping his head right to the ground to better pin down the outer edges correctly.

Gonzales finally found the door and sort of wobbled through the kitchen and looked out. He tried to rub the sleep from his eyes and then he saw through the blur that there were three dogs in the dimming moonlight. He disgustedly made his way back to the bed and said, "Jish another dog."

Xavier drew the line in the soil and stood up putting his heels on it and took ten steps straight toward a prominent sagebrush. He knelt and scooped the few inches of dirt from his beloved bucket, pulled it out, stood up, looked at the house, then at the dogs. They were doing their growling trick louder now for they realized they had a real thief in their back yard.

Xavier started his circle away from the house, again whispering loving words to the dogs as he went. His steps got faster as they got louder. Then he broke into a run. Now dogs have a great attraction to anything that runs from them, whether it be rabbits, cats, cars or plumbers. They pursued. Loudly. They nipped and circled, making all kinds of exciting noise. Xavier was fending them off fairly well with the bucket. Since he was going downhill and also nearing his means of escape, his speed increased. So did that of the dogs.

Marion sat straight up in bed and suddenly reached over and hit Gonzales on the side of his snoring head. He never did know how he got the sore spot nor why he'd awakened so suddenly.

Xavier made his truck, opened the door, and as he jumped in one of the dogs latched on to his coat tail and the other to his leg. But nothing could stop him now. He kicked them loose and the truck responded to his desire by starting right off and he drove like hell for town as the greatest day of his life announced itself beyond the mountains in the perpetual sky.

5

Granger had volunteered to take his private plane and pick up Tamara and her three associates at the Albuquerque airport. The orchestra was coming in on a chartered bus from Denver. The stage was as ready as it would ever be. Manuel was given the day off and all work stopped. Xavier went to J. C. Penney's and bought a new suit, tie, shirt, socks and even underwear. None of it quite fit, but then creative people are sometimes shoddy in their dress.

The local newspaper carried a half page on the activities and said that representatives of two major TV networks would cover the show out of Albuquerque. Everywhere Xavier went he found

.riends. New friends, old friends, and friends of friends. He just wandered around accepting the attention with smiles and thanks but his mind was on the night. Tonight, yes tonight, he would actually cast his eyes on the moving, living, lovely flesh of Tamara. Had any man in all time ever been so blessed? He said a quiet prayer of thanks. He was so happy and full of wonder that he failed to notice a twenty-mile long column of white clouds peeking constantly higher over the Rocky Mountains.

He checked at the Chamber and the drug store. All tickets were sold. They had even sold out of standing room. The town was full of people and a crowd was gathering in front of the Taos Inn. Everyone wanted a glimpse, a touch, a part of the great Tamara.

He worked his way through the crowd to the lobby where he was welcomed by the mayor, the chief of police, the hotel manager, newspaper and T. V. reporters. He was frightened. He was numb. He was in agonized ecstasy. The clicking cameras, flashing lights, and pointed questions, whirled around Xavier in a blurred vortex.

Then he heard the noise and all the flesh moved to the door. He just stood in the lobby and waited. He could not push to see her. It had been too long. It was a long wait of only a minute. His hands perspired and he rubbed them over and over against his coat. He didn't want his right hand wet when he finally touched hers. His feet had melted to the floor. He felt if he took a step part of the hotel rug would pull up and go along with him.

Then he saw Granger smiling, gregariously efficient, leading . . . leading . . . yes, it was Tamara. The lovely Tamara! He saw her dark eyes floating ghostlike through space up to him and he took her hand in both of his and kissed it. That's all he remembered until someone handed him a cup of tea in her suite.

Her wardrobe mistress was busy unpacking. The ballet master and manager was on the phone long distance already planning the next show in another city. One helper held two elegant Afghan hounds on a joined leash and constantly answered the door. With haughty politeness he refused to allow anyone to enter. Granger and the mayor were the only local people present.

Tamara was giving orders on clothing and food for after the show like a true and crowned queen. Xavier was amazed that she was only five feet one and ninety pounds. In her photos she looked six feet tall. In fact, she appeared that now.

21

Suddenly she turned full on Xavier, asking, "Mr. Del Campo, could we order you drinks, food, anything? I do neither until after the performance."

He shook his head no, and choked that he would wait too. Then he took a swallow of the tea he had forgotten all about. He couldn't believe he was actually talking with her. They were saying words to each other across the room. They had shared eyes while doing so. She was far more beautiful and graceful than could be imagined. Every move was a poem . . . no, a symphony! Xavier dared not even blink his eyes for fear he'd miss a priceless gesture.

The low distant growl of thunder came to him subconsciously but he ignored its existence. Granger walked and looked out the window towards the mountains. He didn't comment, but gave Xavier a quick glance.

The next hour was a fog to Xavier. He did remember later that she'd commented on the beauty of the land around and how refreshing to perform out of a big city in such clean air.

Outside, and above, the clouds humped over the mountains and spread across the foothills and the valleys. They were dark and solemn like dynamite just before the spark touches. They boiled now and moved together, and the lightning burst out of them, crescendoing sound across the land and shaking the windows of the hotel.

Then there was a pause. A stillness. Tamara, busying herself with her wardrobe, glanced at the window and then at Xavier. Xavier stared into the bottom of his teacup. He was afraid to feel—to know. Then it came, great gushes of water splashing against the panes with its brother wind, running off the walls and joining the little rivulets on the ground. The thunder and lightning became the same sound now, the same entity. So did the beating of Xavier's heart. No one talked for awhile, then Granger and the mayor said they'd call the airport for a weather report and left.

Tamara made light chatter and smiled at Xavier many times. He just sat smiling, with his face. A small smile to be sure, but there, just the same. The storm seemed to talk louder and pound harder.

Suddenly Tamara sent her entourage away. She brought him another cup of tea, and as she bent over he saw the ocean of her eyes. The waves splashed against and over his whole being.

She was at the phone talking. He did not hear. Then the waiter was there, and they sat across a table from each other. There was food he didn't taste, champagne he didn't savor, and talk he didn't hear. But he felt. Had any man *ever felt* all the things he had in the last few seconds, minutes, hours, eternities?

She left him and went to her bedroom, motioning him to wait. Then she came into the room in the dress of the dying swan. She danced. The entire orchestra was down in the bar drinking, but Xavier heard them playing, playing, playing. She floated and flew. Xavier swore to Manuel later that there were whole minutes when she didn't even touch the floor. And then she died. Just for him. Fluttering the life from flesh that had become that of the most graceful of all the world's creatures—the white swan. The bird lay there dead but the lady slowly rose and bowed to him. He clapped so hard his head jarred, and just as his dreams had predicted she came to him, taking his hands, saying,

"Thank you, Señor Del Campo, thank you from the bottom of my soul."

She led him to the door and whispered that it was late. Then she bent slightly and kissed him on the mouth, holding his head in her hands with infinite tenderness. Her eyes spread around him and went with him into the hall, keeping him warm and glowing. It was midnight. He could not go out the front and see anyone. He could not share this moment. It was his alone. He moved to the end of the hall and stepped out onto a fire escape. He walked down it into the wetness of the same alley he lived on. The rain was over. The eaves still dripped a little. The clouds were spreading apart, making holes for the light of the moon. One beam hit a puddle in front of him. He splashed into the blue mirror.

6

It was never known if anyone drove along the highway at sunup the next morning, but if so, they would have seen the open air stage where the little colored flags hung limp, wet and heavy. A closer examination would have shown a short chunky man standing there looking at his muddy feet. He took two timid steps forward, raised one leg and whirled almost all the way around on the wet wood. And then he smiled.

One-Eyed Sky

1

The cow lifted her muzzle from the muddy water of the tank. She must go now. Her time was at hand. She could feel the pressure of the unborn between her bony hips. With the springless clicking tread of an old, old cow she moved out towards the rolling hills to find a secluded spot for the delivery.

It was late July and the sun seared in at her about an hour high. The moistureless dust turned golden under her tired hoofs as the sun poured soundless beams at each minute particle of the disturbed earth. The calf was late—very late. But this being her eighth and last she was fortunate to have conceived and given birth at all.

The past fall the cowhands had missed her hiding place in the deep brush of the mesas. If found she would have been shipped as a canner, sold at bottom prices and ground into hamburger or Vienna sausage. Not one of the men would have believed she could make the strenuous winter and still produce another good whiteface calf. She had paid the ranch well, this old cow . . . seven calves to her credit. Six of them survived to make the fall market fat and profitable. The coyotes took her first one. But she had learned from that.

She turned from the cowtrail and made her way up a little draw. Instinct guided her now as the pressure mounted in her rear body. It was a good place she found with the grass still thick on the draw and some little oak brush for shade the next sweltering day. The hills mounted gradually on three sides and she would have a down-grade walk the next morning to the water hole. She had not taken her fill of water, feeling the urgency move in her.

24

She found her spot and the pain came and the solid lump dropped from her. It had not taken long. She got up, licked the calf clean and its eyes came open to see the world just as the sun sank. It would be long hours now before the calf would know other than the night.

It was a fine calf, well boned and strong, good markings. In just a little while she had it on its feet. The strokes of her tongue waved the thick red hair all over. With outspread legs it wobbled a step and fell. She licked some more. Again the calf rose and this time faltered its way to the bag swelled tight with milk.

The initial crisis was over, but as the old cow nudged the calf to a soft spot to bed it down, her head came up and she scented the air. Something was there. As the calf nestled down with its head turned back against its shoulder, the old cow turned, smelling, straining her eyes into the darkness. There was a danger there. Her calf was not yet safe. Nature intended her to eat the afterbirth, but now there would be no chance. She stood deeply tired, turning, watching, waiting.

2

The coyote howled and others answered in some far-distant canyon. It was a still night. The air was desert dry. It made hunting difficult. It takes moisture to carry and hold a scent. Her four pups took up the cry, hungry and anxious to prey into the night.

She, too, was old and this, her fourth litter, suffered because of it. She was not able to hunt as wide or as well as in past years. The ribs pushed through the patched hair on all the pups. They moved about, now and then catching the smell of a cold rabbit trail. Two of the pups spotted prairie mice and leaped upon them as they would a fat fowl, swallowing the rodents in one gulp. It helped, but still they all felt the leanness and the growling of their bellies.

The old coyote turned over a cow chip and let one of the pups eat the black bugs underneath. They could survive this way, but their whole bodies ached for meat.

They moved up to the water hole as all living creatures of the vast area did. The old one had circled carefully, hoping to surprise a rabbit drinking. But there was none. They had already worked the water hole many times before with some success, but now its banks were barren. They took the stale water into themselves to temporarily alter the emptiness.

The old one smelled the tracks of the cow, hesitating, sniffing again. Then she raised her head to taste the air with her nostrils. The pups all stood motionless, heads up, waiting. There was a dim scent there. Not quite clear. The distance was too far, but there was a chance for meat. A small one indeed, but in these hard times the mother could not afford to pass any opportunity. With head dropping now and then to delineate the trail of the old cow, the old coyote moved swiftly, silently followed by four hungry pups copying her every move.

3

Eight miles to the north a cowboy sixty years old, maybe seventy—he had long ago forgotten—scraped the tin dishes, washed them briefly, and crawled in his bunk against the line camp wall. He was stiff and he grunted as he pulled the blanket over his thin eroded body. The night was silent and he thought.

Outside a horse stood in the corral. A saddle hung in a small shed. In the saddle scabbard was a .30-30 for killing varmints. If he had a good day and found no sign of strays in the mighty expanse of the south pasture he could ride on into headquarters the day after next to company of his own kind. It really didn't matter to him so much except the food would be better and the bed a little softer. That was about all he looked forward to now. Tomorrow he, too, would check the water hole for signs. He slept.

4

She couldn't see them, but they were there. Their movement was felt and the scent was definite now. She moved about nervously, her stringy muscles taut and every fiber of her being at full strain. When they had come for her firstborn she had fought them well, killing one with a horn in its belly and crippling two more. But finally they had won. The calf—weak as all first calves are—had bled its life into the sand of the gully. She had held the pack off for hours until she knew the calf was dead and then the call from the blood of those to come had led her away to safety. It had been right. All her other calves, and the one resting beside her now, had been strong, healthy.

The scars showed still where they had tried to tear the ligaments from her hocks in that first battle long ago, she had been

26

sore and crippled for weeks. A cowboy had lifted his gun to relieve her misery. But another had intervened. They roped her and threw her to the ground. They spread oil on her wounds and she recovered.

She whirled about, nostrils opening wide from the wind of her lungs. Her horns automatically lowered, but she could see nothing. She was very thirsty and her tongue hung from the side of her mouth. She should have taken on more water, but the enemy would have caught her during the birth and that would have been the end. She would have to be alert now, for her muscles had stiffened with age and the drive and speed she had in her first battle were almost gone. Then too, in the past, many parts of nature, of man and animal enemy had attacked her.

In her fourth summer, during a cloudburst when the rains came splashing earthward like a lake turned upside down, a sudden bolt of lightning had split the sky, ripping into a tree and bouncing into her body. She had gone down with one horn split and scorched. Three other cows fell dead near her. For days she carried her head slung to one side and forgot to eat. But she lived.

Later she had gotten pinkeye and the men had poured salt into her eye to burn out the disease.

And she had become angry once while moving with a herd in the fall roundup. She had been tired of these mounted creatures forever crowding her. She kept cutting back to the shelter of the oak brush and finally she turned back for good, raking the shoulder of the mighty horse. The mounted man cursed and grabbed his rope. She tore downhill, heading for the brush, her third calf close at her side. She heard the pounding of the hooves and the whirr of the rope. Deliberately she turned and crashed through a barbed wire fence, ripping a bone-deep cut across her brisket. In that moment the man roped her calf and dismounted to tie its feet. She heard the bawling, whirled, charged at the man. She caught him with her horn just above the knee as he tried to dodge. She whirled to make another pass and drive the horns home. Then another man rode at her and the evil, inescapable snake of a rope sailed from his arm and encircled her neck. Three times he turned off, jerking her up high and then down hard into the earth, tearing her breath from her body until she stood addled and half blind. Then they stretched her out again and turned her loose. She had learned her lesson hard. During the stiff winters and wet spells she limped where the shoulder muscles had been torn apart.

But the worst winter of all was when the snow fell two feet deep and crusted over, isolating the herd miles from the ranch house. During the dry summer they had walked twice as far as usual to find the short shriveled grass. She and the others had gone into the winter weak and their bellies dragged in the drifts. When they tried to walk on top of the white desert the crust broke and they went down struggling, breathing snow and cold into their lungs, sapping their small strength. The icy crust cut their feet and they left red streaks in the whiteness. And the wind came driving through their long hair, coating their eyes and nostrils with ice. They'd wandered blindly, piling into deep drifts, perishing.

Finally the wagons—pulled by those same horses she had hated so much—broke through the snow. They tailed her up and braced her and got some hay into her mouth. Once more she survived.

The old cow had a past and it showed in her ragged, bony, tired, bent, scarred body. And it showed in her ever-weakening neck as the head dropped a fraction lower each time she shook her defiance at the night and the unseen enemy.

The moon came now and caressed the land with pale blueness. It was like a single, headless, phosphorescent eye staring at the earth seeing all, acknowledging nothing. The moon made shadows and into these she stared and it would seem to move and then she would ready herself for the attack. But it didn't come. Why did they wait?

The night was long and the moon seemed to hang for a week, then the sun moved up to the edge of the world chasing the moon away.

Her tongue was pushed out further now and her eyes were glazed, but she stood and turned and kept her guard. She saw the old, mangy coyote directly down the draw facing her, sitting up on its haunches panting, grinning, waiting. It took her awhile to see the pups. They were spotted about the hills, surrounding her. But these did not worry her. They would not move until the old one did. Nevertheless she cast her dimming eyes at them, letting them know she knew—letting them know she was ready.

The calf stirred and raised its head and found the glorious world. First it must feed. She moved swiftly to it, watching the old coyote as she did so. The new one struggled up, finding its way to the teat. The cow saw the muscles tense all over the old coyote. Its head tilted forward as did its pointed ears. Then it

28

moved from side to side, inching closer at each turn. The pups got to their feet, ready for the signal. But it didn't come. The old coyote retreated. It was a war of nerves. And because the coyote fights and dies in silence, when the time arrived there would be no signal visible to the cow, only to the pups.

Now the calf wanted to explore. It wanted to know into what it had been born. Already the color and the form of plant and rock and sky were things of wonder. There was so much to see and so little time for it. Again the mother bedded down her calf— a heifer it was—and soon the warm air and full stomach comforted it.

By midmorning the coyote had faked ten charges. And ten times the cow had braced to take the old one first and receive and bear the rear and flanking attacks until she could turn and give contest. She knew from the past they would all hit her at once, diving, feinting, tearing from all sides. But if she could keep the calf from being mortally wounded until she disposed of the old one they had a chance. But with each rise in temperature, with each drying, burning moment of the sun without water, her chances lessened.

By noon the heat was almost blinding her. She felt the trembling and faltering in her legs. All the old wounds were making themselves known now and her tongue hung down, parched and beginning to swell. Her breathing came hard and heavy. The nostrils caked from the powdered dirt of her restlessness and her eyes filled around the edges and watered incessantly. But the coyote waited. And so did the old cow. Life had always been a matter of waiting—waiting for the calf each year, waiting for the greenness of spring, waiting for the wind to die and the cold to quit and the snow to melt. But, win or lose, she would never see another spring. They would find her this fall and ship her away to the slaughterhouse. And if they didn't, the winter, the inexorable winter winds, would drive through her old bones and finish her. But now she had a chore, a life-and-death chore for sure. She would do her natural best.

In the middle of the afternoon she imagined she could smell the water, so near and yet so far away. She bawled out of her nearly closed throat and the tongue was black, and down the other side of her mouth thick cottonlike strings of saliva hung and evaporated in the interminable heat. Her legs had gradually spread apart and she wove from side to side, taking all her strength now just to stand. And right in the pathway to the water sat the laughing coyote beginning to move back and forth again, closer. Closer. As the sun moved lower and lower, so the coyote came nearer, lying down, looking straight at her.

The coyote lay very still, nothing moving but the pink tongue. Yellow eyes watching, glowing like suns. Ten minutes. Twenty minutes. The coyote came from the ground without warning, straight in and fast. The cow knew the others were coming too. She braced herself.

5

The mother coyote followed the trail into scent range of the old cow. Her nostrils told her of the new one. Cautiously she moved up now, almost like a cat. The young tried mightily to do as well. It was no use. The quick, intense movement of the cow revealed her knowledge of their presence. They would have to wait. Methodically she went about spotting her young. She ringed the old cow in, giving soundless directions to her pups to stay put.

The scent of birth, the calf, the old cow brought taste glands into action. The natural impulse was to attack as their stomachs drew narrow and craving. But the coyote could tell from the alertness of the old cow that an early assault would be sure death to some. The hours would be long but the cow would weaken. Much of the moisture had been drained from her body in the birth. The sun would be their ally. They could have the early luxurious feast of the tender veal, and the lean meat of the old cow would last for days—even with the vultures and the magpies to contend with. She could fatten and strengthen the pups and make them ready for mating as her mother had done her. Yes, her mother had been a good teacher and she had learned well. She had been taught to hunt under rotten logs, cow chips and anthills for insects in case of hard times. The field mouse had often saved her from starvation. The lowly grasshopper had filled her belly many times and given her strength to catch larger, tastier game. She learned to steal into a hen yard, make a quick dash, throttling the fowl and escaping before the rancher could get his guns. All of these things she had taught or was teaching her own. But now must come the ultimate lesson—how to down and kill an animal weighing as much as fifteen of their own kind. Besides, they were desperate in their near-starvation.

The old coyote took the main chance in locating herself in the path of the water hole. This was the weak point and she must handle it with care, cunning and courage. She could not fail, for they too would weaken in the long vigil.

She carried a .30-30 slug in her belly from the past. She only felt it on cold or hungry nights. Her tail was shortened and ugly at the end. Her ear was split and torn. A scar ran across her back. One foot was minus two toes.

The ear and tail wounds had come about at the same time. She had learned a hard lesson from this action. She was almost grown then and hunted with the rest of the litter. They had stopped behind a clump of bear-grass, watching the pickup truck circle slowly. They had seen these things before, but no danger had threatened. Suddenly the thing stopped. From its back dropped six large, running hounds. Two teams.

The coyotes moved out too late. Instinct split them in three directions. But the hounds had their speed, and in less than a quarter of a mile each team had downed one of the brood. She alone escaped. On a little rise she whirled watching the hounds bear down on her brother and sister, crushing the life away with their awful fanged jaws. She sailed down from the hill and at full speed crashed into the nearest team, knocking them loose and giving her brother a chance to rise. But it didn't work. Two of the hounds flung the wounded one against the earth again. The third gave chase. She strained away in terror, knowing she could not compete with its size and strength. The hound reached for her throat but missed her and ripped the ear apart instead. They both rolled in a choking spurt of dust. As she rose, the hound clamped her tail. She broke free leaving a humiliating part of herself in his jaws. The chase was more uphill now, and she learned that hounds slowed on that sort of run and never again was she caught on the level or going downhill. She escaped. Alive. Wiser. Alone.

She learned to respect the metallic wheeled things for another reason. She had watched one from a safe distance, as far as hounds were concerned, and suddenly a black something stuck from it and then something struck her in the belly, knocking her over and down. It had been close. She bled badly inside and by the time the bleeding clotted she was very weak from hunger. All that saved her was the finding of a wounded antelope dragging itself into the tall grass of the prairie to die. But now she could smell a gun from a considerable distance. They would not hurt her again in this manner.

31

Her first sister had eaten poison and died before her eyes. They would not slay her in this vile way, either.

The scar on her back had come from one of those men who whirl the rope and ride horses. She was looking in a sheep pasture for a lamb to carry to her first litter of pups. She was so intent on her job she did not see the cowboy coming through the gate some half mile distant. But as he neared she felt him even before she cast her glance back over her shoulder. He came on full speed on a fast quarterhorse, whirling the rope. She did not know what it was, but she felt its danger as she did that of a gun. He was upon her and she heard the whirr of the rope mingled with the ground-jarring thump of hooves. She hit the manywired sheep fence without slacking speed. She went through, tearing her back on the vicious barbs. Her neck was sore and twisted for many days. But she lived to hunt again.

The worst of all were the steel jaws the men put in the earth. Once, when she had been hungry, the scent of hog cracklings, and also the urine of one of her own, came to her. Bait. This gave her the confidence to inspect even though the faint scent of man was intermingled. The jaws had grabbed her as she vainly leaped away. She struck the end of the chain where it ran up out of the ground and tightened between the trap and the heavy rock that anchored it. She fought wildly and in great pain for a while, gnawing at her foot until exhaustion stilled her violent action.

She studied the rusty, hard, impersonal steel. It had her. But if she was to die she would do it on the mesa—her home. Foot by painful foot, yard by wrenching yard, she dragged the rock. The man had intended her to hang the trap in some brush flexible enough to keep from tearing the foot loose. It hung, all right, hundreds of times, but never for long.

It took her two days to get to the edge of the mesa. The foot was swollen almost to the knee joint now and her yellow eyes were red from suffering. Then the stone hung between a crack in the rocks. She fell off the other side and rolled down the rough boulders. The trap and a part of her foot remained in the rocks.

She lived again, less able than before.

Under the recent rising of the staring moon the coyote studied the old cow. It was obvious she was weakening. Soon she would lie down and then . . . but the old cow stood and at the break of day she suckled her young, looking straight at the coyote and shaking her head in answer to the coyote's slavering jaws.

The coyote moved in now, taunting, teasing, draining another ounce of strength from the old cow.

The sun came soon, hot and red, striking the old cow in the side of her head. The pups squatted and waited with hunger pounding at their every nerve.

By midday the old coyote could feel the muscles trembling and jerking with weakness in her forelegs and the stomach walls seemed glued together, devouring themselves. She now badly needed water and food. At times the earth diffused into the molten rays of the sun and it looked as if the cow had dissolved. At other moments she bunched her muscles imagining the cow attacking. She sat with her tongue out and an eternal laughing expression in all her face except the eyes. They seared through the sun's rays, hungrily, with a quiet desperation and sureness.

The old cow's head was dropping now. She was slipping fast. But still she stood and every time the coyote moved in her snake-track advance the cow raised her head a little and tossed the pointed swords.

There was no backing out now. No changing of plans. The old mother coyote and her brood would soon be so weakened they would surely fall prey to one of their many worldly enemies. Survival now meant the death of the old cow.

The coyote drew in its dry tongue and dropped it again into the dry air and waited. The sun moved on and the old cow's legs spread a little more. The coyote could see her weaving and straining to stay upright. The tender, living veal of the calf lay folded up beside her.

Now the time was present. She sent her message of alertness to her pups. They stood ready, watching, muscles bunched, hearts pounding above the strain of hunger, thirst and heat. She moved forward and lay down to deceive the old cow. Motionless she waited and waited more. All of her being cried to lunge forward, but still she waited. She had decided on the cow's muzzle. She would dart in between the horns, locking her fangs in their breathing softness, and hang on until the aid of her pups downed the old cow. Then? It would be over shortly. A bit torn here and there and the loss of blood would finish her. Then the feast.

The burning eyes of the old coyote and the old cow were fixed on each other now. They both knew what they must do. The old coyote sent the unseen, unmoving signal to her pups and she came from the ground at the same instant, aiming straight and swift between the horns of the old cow.

6

The man arose from the bunk as stiffly as he had crawled into it. It was not quite daybreak. He clothed himself and pulled hard to get his boots on. He built a fire in the squatty iron stove and put the coffeepot on. Then he washed his face and hands in cold water. He placed a skillet on the stove by the coffeepot. Methodically he sliced thick chunks of bacon from the hog side. He took the last of the sourdough batter, tore small balls from it, placing them in a dutch oven on the stove. This done he rolled a smoke, coughing after the first puff. Soon he had a large tin cup of scalding coffee. Another cigarette, another cup. Then he ate. He wiped up the syrup on his plate with his bread. He washed the utensils and put them back on the shelf. He, or someone else, would be here another time. He went out to the corral.

If he was lucky this day and found no strays he could head for the main ranch house tomorrow morning, or if the moon was good he might ride on in tonight. He had two horses here. One ran in a small horse trap adjoining the corrals. The other he had kept up for the ride today.

He brushed his horse's back with his hand and under his belly where the cinches would fit to be sure nothing was lodged in the hair that would cut or stick. He bridled and saddled, put on his chaps and spurs and led the horse up a few steps before mounting. He rode him around the corral several times to limber him up. Then he dismounted, opened the gate, got back on, and rode south just as the sun was melting the night.

It was eight miles in a beeline to the water hole. If there were a stray in the huge pasture it would be nearby. He would probably have a twelve-mile ride, what with checking out the sign in the draw and gullies.

The sun was up now, hot for so early in the morning. It was the kind of day that made all living creatures seek shade. Well, he had always wanted a little place with lots of shade trees and water. Especially water. It wouldn't matter how big it was if there was just plenty of water. He would never forget the drought that had sent his family to the final sheriff's sale and moved them from their ranch into a tent on the edge of the little western town to take other folks' laundry, charity, handouts. His pa had already loaned him out to local ranchers. So, he just took a steady job with one of them. At first he worked only for his board and blanket. He gardened, he milked, he shoveled manure out of barns. He patched roofs. He rebuilt corrals. He chopped a whole year's supply of firewood. He ran rabbits in holes and twisted them out with the split end of a barbwire.

And then the drought was over and the grass and cattle came back to the land. He was promoted to horse wrangler which only meant one more chore. He was up before anyone in the morning riding into the horse pasture, bringing in the day's mounts for the cowboys. But things finally got better. His boss saw him top out a waspy bronc and he was allowed to ride with the men. He got five dollars a month and felt proud. Mighty proud. He learned the ways of the range and the handling of cattle and horses. And at the age of seventeen he could draw down twenty dollars a month with room and board. By the time he had worked on ten or twelve different outfits and reached the age of twenty-five he could demand and get thirty dollars a month. Things weren't all bad.

Then a fellow cowboy with a talent for talk convinced him they were in the wrong business.

"Now look here, Snake" (that was his name at the time from being bitten by a rattlesnake), "we're makin' thirty dollars a month, right?"

"Yeah. "

"Well, how much you figure a broke-out saddle horse would bring?"

"Oh, round thirty, forty dollars."

"There you are. Now, if a man could ride out say eight or ten a month?"

"I'll have to get a pencil. Besides where you goin' to get that many horses and how much you got to give for them?"

"That's just the deal. Up north in the rough country there's hundreds of wild horses. Now, I had some experience at catching them boogers when I was a kid. We're crazier than hell stayin' around here when we can get rich on our own.

So, he took all he had, two hundred and ten dollars, two head of saddle horses, one saddle, four used ropes and moved north with the talkin' cowboy. The money went fast. It was used to buy packmules and supplies.

They pitched camp and started riding the hills and canyons for sign. The horses were there, all right. But a man could ride all day and never actually see anything but tracks. They were wilder than deer by a whole lot. So the two cowboys set to work building brush corral traps in the narrow part of some canyons on the trail to the watering places. Then they built a round pole corral near camp to break the horses out. It took some wild reckless riding to pen these animals but pen some of them they did. Then they found the horses fought like bobcats and it took some doing just to get a rope on one and snub him up. It was impossible to drive them, so they tied a twisted rawhide garter on one leg. The circulation was cut off and the leg became numb and useless. It wasn't so hard to handle them then.

That was only the beginning of their troubles. When they castrated the studs, half of them died. Most of the rest lost their spirit and became dead-headed and listless.

After a good try they drifted out of the rough country ahead of the winter snow. They had two half-broken mares. But it beat walking because without them that's exactly what they would be doing. Well, they went back—at thirty a month—to the cowpunching job they had left. He started saving again. Finally a rancher offered him a foreman's job at thirty-five a month and he could run as many head of his own cattle as he could acquire.

After a few months, when he had some cash to go on, he made his move. He began trading with the Mexicans. A few dollars down, a worn-out saddle, an old rifle and so on were his barter goods. In three years he had built his herd up to sixty head of cows, twelve steers and two bulls. They were a mixed lot and they were his, but the land they ranged on was not. He still couldn't figure why his boss had been so generous. Another thing he couldn't figure out was why the owner and two of his hands did so much riding without him. He didn't ask questions because it looked like a man would be a fool to tinker with good times. They were mighty scarce.

His boss sent him to a roundup over west at a neighboring ranch. His job was to check out any of their strays and deliver them back to the home range. It was a big outfit and the roundup went on for several days. The last of the work was done right at headquarters. The cowboys ate at the cookhouse. There was a pretty little brown-headed girl doing the cooking. Fine tasty chuck it was. She was the owner's daughter, Nelda.

Well, he kept eyeballing her and she kept glancing back. He was pretty good-looking at that time . . . in a rough, healed-over way. The aging and scars of the tough life hadn't taken hold yet. On the last day before he started home with his gather he asked her for a date, and he damn near fainted when she accepted.

He borrowed a buggy and picked her up late Saturday afternoon. They went to a dance at the schoolhouse. She was all decked out in a long, flimsy, turquoise dress that hugged her up close around the waist and bosom. Her hair just sparkled like her brown eyes and that was like a fall sun striking new frost on a golden aspen leaf. He was so scared and so cockeyed proud that he danced every set with her, even though he had a heck of a time fending off the other cowboys.

About four o'clock in the morning a little before daybreak when the music was slow, he walked outside and leaned her up against the building. While the coyotes howled out in the prairie he pulled her up hard and said: "I . . . I love you. I sure do."

Although she didn't say anything she let him know how she felt with her arms and her eyes. Sweet.

They went steady then. His luck just kept running. He got into a poker game with a bunch of mining and timber men and won six thousand dollars. That was more money than he had seen all his life put together. He couldn't wait to get over and tell Nelda.

They rode together in the hills and he loved her and she loved him. He told her about the money and how it was not only burning a hole in his pocket but was burning right smack through his leg.

"Snake," she said, "you've got a good start on a herd and the Larking place is for sale. We wouldn't owe more than eighteen thousand."

Eighteen thousand dollars! It scared him. It was beyond him. He would never make it. He just couldn't take on a woman like her, the daughter of a big rancher, owing that kind of money.

Well, he got drunk in town and didn't show up for work. The boss fired him and told him to come and get his cows, at the same time he said there would be no hurry about it. Somehow it didn't make sense.

Snake stayed in town that fall and on into the winter trying to make up his mind what to do. In the meantime the money was going steadily out for whiskey and gambling.

The winter came and a blizzard hit. Most of his cattle walked off into deep drifts of snow and froze to death. By the time he sobered up it was spring and he was broke.

Then the law came and took him. His ex-boss was right there shaking his head and saying he couldn't believe it, after all he had done for him. They railroaded him and now he knew that he had been a blind and a cover-up for the rancher's thievery. He got a year and a day. After three dreary months inside the prison wall he planned to kill the man who sent him there, but then they put him out on the prison farm and he reasoned it wasn't worth it.

He didn't return to the home country for a long time after his release. Nelda married someone else and he kind of regretted he had been so undecided.

He tried a lot of things after that, plunging hard to come back—prospecting, timber leasing, nothing worked out. He was trying to keep from going back to punching cows. He took a job as a dude wrangler in Yellowstone Park. His natural friendliness, his knowledge of horses and everything attracted a lot of business. He had several chances to marry rich widows and cowboy-smitten girls. But he never could decide when the time came. He had heard that all was not roses and sweet violets with the rich dames. A man had to go around with his hand out all the time.

At last, though, he chose to take on this woman from St. Louis. She had come right out and told him she would buy and pay for a ranch, stock it in his name and put some money in the bank in the same manner.

Then he got drunk in Pony, Montana, on bootleg whiskey. It poisoned him and he was laid up out of his head for sixty days. The doctors almost gave up on him. By the time he came to and acquired strength enough to walk and talk, the widow had disappeared. The wrangler who had taken his job ran off to Mexico with her. If only a man could ever make up his mind at the right time he would have this world singing *his* songs he figured.

He kept trying and bumming around into one thing and another. He damned near starved. The years were beginning to show. Finally he returned to his old country and the only thing he really knew—punching cows. The wages were one hundred and twenty-five dollars a month and board. That was tops, as high as he could go in his profession. It was a job that took guts, natural skill, and understanding of the earth and its animals, both wild and domestic, though the present wages wouldn't buy as much as twenty dollars had in his youth. But there he was now riding the draws around the water hole looking for sign and finding none.

It was midafternoon and hot. If he turned back now he could make it in a little after dark, saddle a fresh horse and go on into headquarters. It was three days till payday. He could take his check, go into town, buy a new pair of jeans, a new rope, maybe a new hat. If he was careful he might have enough left over to get a little drunk and maybe even play a little poker. He really needed a pair of new boots but anything worth working in cost between forty and fifty dollars so he would just have to wait till next payday—or the next.

He decided to go on and check the water hole just in case he had missed something. It would cost him another night in the line camp but, after all, what was one more night alone to him? He saw the usual sign of wildlife and was surprised to find the day-old tracks of a cow. One lonely cow. She must have strayed in here to calve, he thought. He could tell by the way her hooves splayed out and by the withered cracks around the edges that she was an old cow.

As he followed her tracks up the trail he noticed that a coyote and four pups had been ahead of him. Probably went right on, he thought, and then an uneasiness came over him. Man, it was hot. He pulled his hat back and wiped the sweat from his forehead and out of his narrow sunwashed eyes. The cow had turned off across a small ridge and he saw the tracks of the coyotes do the same. Pretty soon he felt the horse bunch under him. The head came up and the ears pitched forward. He thought he heard a sound, a cow bawling maybe, but he wasn't sure. He got down and tied the horse to a bush.

He removed the .30-30 from the scabbard and started easing forward. He was slow in his movement because of the stiffness from the long day in the saddle and many years of breaks and bruises. Then he was on his belly crawling forward feeling an excitement that he couldn't define. It was more than the hunter's blood surging now.

He raised up carefully from the side of a yucca plant. He saw the old cow first and then, slowly, one at a time, he located the coyotes. They hadn't seen or heard him yet because of the dryness and lack of wind.

He eased the rifle and sighted down it at the old mother coyote as she moved forward. Just as he started to pull the trigger she lay down right out in front of the old cow. For some reason strange to him he held his fire.

7

In the little hollow where the man, the coyotes, the cow and her calf lay there was concentrated the most life for miles in every direction. Five miles to the north and west in the cedar- and piñon-covered hills twenty-six buzzards circled and lighted

39

on the remains of a cow downed two days before by a mountain lion that lay now in the coolness of the rocks with a full belly; to the east another pack of coyotes was desperately stalking a herd of swift antelope with no luck at all.

A hawk circled curiously above the draw with the man and the animals, smelling meat. The land itself was covered sparsely with buffalo and grama grass and, everywhere, the yucca plants bayonetted the sky. Now and then in meandering, meaningless lines, the land was cut by wind and water erosion forming a rolling, twisted terrain that on the face of a man would have portrayed deep torment.

The man felt the trigger of the rifle with his finger. The hammer was thumbed back. His cheek lay hot and sweating along the stock. The sights were centered on the thin rib cage of the coyote lying so very still. He could tell by the torn, powdered earth around the old cow, standing, swaying so weakly with far-drooped head, that she had held them at bay a long number of hours now.

His eyes raised again and counted the pups. One shot would do it. He must have killed two or three hundred of these animals, these varmints, these predators. He was a good shot. He would not miss. His eyes were in the second sight that comes briefly to older men. He could see almost as good as he could at twenty-one. His stomach was hollow. And he thought vaguely that it had been many hours since he had eaten or drunk. It came to him then that the creatures before him had been much longer without repast.

A sudden admiration came over him for the old, hungry, thirsty coyote and the old, hungry, thirsty cow eying each other in the golden blazing, dying sun. His duty, his real job, was to kill the old coyote and as many of her young as possible and drive the old cow to water, carrying the calf across the swells of his saddle for her. In a day or two she would have her strength back, then he could drive her on to the main herd. That was his job. But he didn't move and all of his long life came to him now as he studied what he saw before him.

The old coyote knew what she must do and she was doing it with every particle of cunning, courage and instinct in her emaciated body. Her pups must be fed and she must, too, if she was to survive and finish their training.

And the old cow had long ago reconciled herself to her fate. She would stand and fight—win or die.

The indecision was not theirs. This trait was his and had always been so.

Time became a vacuum in the floating dust. The bawling of the old cow, just a whisper now, came to him. The coyote lay like dry wood. The pups watched her, their bodies slowly evaporating in the ceaseless sun. It was everything.

His lungs ached from the shallow breathing, but still he could not move the finger that fraction of an inch that would end it. Time. Timeless time.

Then the old coyote attacked as if hurled from the earth. The pups charged down. The man fired but the bullet struck into the shoulder of one of the pups instead. The momentum carried it forward and down and over. It kicked its life away. He raised the gun and fired again. The hindquarters of another pup dropped. He levered another shell and shot it though the head.

As the old coyote came in, lips peeled back, fangs sharp and anxious, the old cow pulled a tiny ounce of strength from her heart—a little reserve she had saved for her young. She shuffled forward to meet the terrible threat.

The sound of the shot had caused the old coyote to veer just a fraction at the last thrust, and it was just enough. The lightning-splintered horn of the old cow drove between the lean ribs and she made one upward swing of her head. The horn tore into the lungs and burst the arteries of the chest apart. The coyote hung there. The cow could not raise her head again. She fell forward crushing at the earth. When she pulled her head and horns away the coyote blinked her yellow, dying eyes just once. It was over.

The other two pups ran out through the brush. They were on their own now.

The calf got to its feet and sucked a little milk from the mother's flabby bag. The man went back to his horse wondering why he had shot the pups instead of the old one. For a moment he had known. But now the knowledge was gone.

In a little while as the sun buried itself in the great ocean of space behind the earth the old cow, her calf at her side, stumbled downhill to water.

The Mare

It was the most fantastic story Forest Ranger Joe Healy had ever heard. "It just can't be," he said in stunned disbelief. "Don't you realize if she's over thirty years old, that would make her almost a hundred and twenty in human terms?"

"Yeah, something like that," Randy Lindsey answered. "She does truly exist. I first spotted her tracks about three years ago, and I felt just like you until I finally saw her for real a couple of months back. Yeah, she's up there alright."

Randy was a young cowboy who worked for Jimmy Bason's F Cross Ranch. Bason leased out most of the grassland on his hundred thousand acres, so he needed only his son, Brent, and one extra cowboy to help take care of his small herd. Jimmy was lucky . . . Randy was a "throw back" of the Old West. He liked living by himself in a line-shack, and preferred to work with horses instead of a pickup truck. He wanted to carry on the old-time traditions.

The two men were sitting at a table in the one-bar, two-church town of Hillsboro in southwestern New Mexico. The bar also had the only restaurant available for thirty miles.

Ranger Healy knew that Randy would never lie to him about a thing like this, but he found it almost impossible to believe that a horse could have survived, totally alone, for all those years. He leaned forward across the plate of red chile burritos and the bottle of beer, saying softly, "Does anyone else know about this?"

The young cowboy said, "Only Jimmy Bason . . . and he don't want anybody to know. He says the do-gooders and the do-badders will both try to capitalize on her." He paused. "In fact, he'll probably fire me if he finds out I slipped up and told someone."

Joe laughed softly, "You don't have to worry, Randy, I won't tell anybody except my daughter. She's crazy nuts about animals, you know. That's why she's definitely decided to become a vet.

42

And, by dogies, she'll never have another chance to see anything like this. That mare has to be some kind of miracle. My God, even gentle horses, that are pampered and cared for, don't live that long. I'd say this is about the rarest dang thing I ever heard of. It's like being first in line at the Second Coming. Yeah," Healy said as if to himself, "Pauline's got to see this horse."

Randy reluctantly agreed to describe the area the mare currently habituated. He was unaware that their conversation was being overheard by a vacationing young reporter for an El Paso, Texas, newspaper, who was sitting at the next table with his wife and two children. The young man hurriedly grabbed a pen and pad from his pocket and, with noticeable excitement, started scribbling.

Joe Healy drove the pickup, pulling a trailer containing two good saddle horses, as near as the rough terrain would allow, to the designated wilderness area. He and his fifteen-year-old daughter, Pauline, quickly set up camp. They had enough supplies to last over a month if that's what it took to find the wild mare. They had come prepared and totally dedicated.

They rode the piñon-and-cedar-covered foothills. Then made their way up to the edge of the tall pines on the mountain. They roamed for five days looking at the ground, hoping to find a sign of the horse. Even in their anticipation of the latter, they still enjoyed the markings of the other wild creatures. They actually saw twenty or thirty deer, ten elk, a coyote, many kinds of birds, and even glimpsed a black bear disappearing into a patch of heavy timber.

On the sixth day they found her hoofprints. The tracks were at least a week old, but to the Healys, they were as new as first frost. The excitement of discovery surged through all the tissues, nerves and thoughts of their bodies, but nevertheless, on the seventh day they rested themselves and their horses.

Pauline said, "Daddy, if she's never had a colt, she's still a filly no matter what her age, right?"

"Now don't get technical on me, Pauline. As old as she is, we're gonna call her a mare."

Pauline pushed her long, blond hair back from her face, and said in a soft voice filled with wonder, "She's really out there. We've found her unshod hoofprints. Poor thing . . . all alone. Just

43

think of all the bad weather, and the predators, and the loneliness she has endured, and now she's so old. Wonder how she's done it?" Her blue eyes widened in astonishment at the frightening images.

Joe Healy searched for a special answer for this question, but he could only come up with "It does seem impossible. She must be blessed. That's the answer, Pauline. She's blessed."

Father and daughter rode out of camp at dawn the next day. The two had spent a restless night, but now they were keyed up and tuned in to the whole world. It was midafternoon when they found some more recent tracks—these were only a couple of days old. Joe recalled Randy saying, "I was ridin' old Birdie, when I cut my first sign of her. I just knew she had to be the last of the wild ones. I never had a feelin' like it before. It was sorta like I'd just invented the first saddle." Healy was having some of the same feelings now. A sense of the primordial permeated his being. He couldn't have been more in awe if he'd just come face-to-face with a living dinosaur or the Loch Ness monster.

Pauline almost cried aloud, but instead, she let the tears rivulet silently down her cheeks. To her it was a sacred moment and she looked up to the heavens. In the distance, she saw several buzzards circling. She lifted her wide, blue eyes above the birds to a patch of sky and then on above that she saw something that caused her to cry out, "Daddy, look! Look way up there!"

He looked in the direction of her pointing, but his vision missed what she had so briefly seen. His eyes moved, by nature and training, back down to the tracks they had been following. Pauline reined her horse in line. Now her eyes were focused on a movement nearing a huge cumulus cloud. She stared in wonder.

The mare was born in the spring of the year the Space Age dawned. In October 1957 the Russians fired Sputnik I into the heavens. It circled the globe at altitudes ranging from 141 to 588 miles above Moscow and Washington, D.C. It traveled at 14,700 miles per hour. The people of the Soviet Union rejoiced and justifiably felt enormous pride. The Americans were embarrassed and scared. There was an outcry for more defense spending and the whole educational system of the free world altered. The emphasis was placed on science. Literature, all the arts and old-time basic schooling were greatly neglected. The Space Age and the mare had been born.

Far below on the solid rocks of the Black Range, the colt frolicked, nursed and grew stronger daily. She did not know, or care, about this monumental change in the world. From the beginning, she was more agile and faster than the other colts in one of the dozen or so scattered bands of wild horses. Her chestnut coat glistened in the sun and her large, dark eyes were full of adventure and mischief.

Her first winter was an easy one with little snow. The horses fared well in the rolling hills between the private ranches and the national forest area, but the springtime came dry and the grass was short.

The ranchers moved their cattle into the wild horses' domain under individual leases with the government. There was competition for the shriveling grass between the wildlife, the mustangs and the domestic cattle. The ranchers and Forest Service joined forces to get rid of the wild horses.

They built log-pole traps around waterholes in an attempt to capture them alive. They tried roping the young, the old or the lame. This effort only delivered ten head of the wily bunch, and in the process they crippled three cowboys, one ranger and twenty-two of their tame horses.

The ranchers and Forest Service executives argued over other means to dispose of this threat to the welfare of their cattle and consequently their families. During one of their meetings, word came of a forest fire in the area. It had been started by lightning from a small, shower cloud. The flames caused the dry trees and vegetation to snap and pop like infantry machine gulls.

One small band of horses was trapped and perished. All living things ran together now, to escape the inferno. Deer, elk and cattle raced alongside coyotes, bears and cougars. Rabbits dashed in and out of the flames until some caught fire and fell in kicking, smoking bundles. Everything attempted to escape in a terrible panic. Most small things like lizards, ants, grasshoppers, spiders, tree worms, squirrels, skunks, and nestlings were cooked as black as the forest floor.

The colt raced beside her mother as the dominant stallion of the band circled, squealing commands, kicking, biting and trying to drive his harem and offspring to safety. The prevailing southwest wind joined in the chaos and whipped the flames in circles and drove it forward with destructive speed. The smoke could be seen one hundred aircraft miles away in El Paso, Texas. Fire fighters tried to organize, but their efforts were futile against the raging force.

Then the winds suddenly quit as if on command from the gods and the fire died out at the banks of the North Percha Creek. It had decimated the five-mile width from the upper Animas drainage to the creek. The existing forage would be much sparser now.

The ranchers moved their cattle back to the home ranches with great effort and much loss of weight. The decision was made—the wild horses had to be destroyed. They organized and came with camping gear, horses and rifles. They rode for weeks driving their prey into the burned areas where they killed them.

Joe Healy's father, John, who was a ranger at the time, led the onslaught. He instructed the Rangers and cowboys to try to "bark" the wild horses. That is, shoot them through the top edge of the neck knocking them unconscious so they could be saved for live capture. It didn't work. The fire, followed by the cracking of rifles, the squeals and groans of dying animals, created a madness of desperation. The stallions lost control of their bands and ran about as erratically as their broods. Over a hundred and thirty horses were slaughtered.

The area became, and looked, like a battlefield. What with the dead horses scattered about through the massive burned area and the buzzards gathering from miles around to join the coyotes, bobcats, bears, lions and other meat-eating predators to feast on the carcasses.

The Rangers and ranchers agreed there were none left to scatter the seed. They were wrong by *one*.

The yearling colt had been barked from a long distance and when she regained consciousness, she raced blindly across the scorched earth through the stench of the rotting bodies and kept on going up and up until the greenness of undefiled timber surrounded her. The sweat had turned to a lather over her entire body and her lungs bellowed in and out in painful gasps.

She kept going until she was deep into the high forest and her legs began to tremble and caused her to fall over and over. Then she stopped. She could move no more. She was sore and weak for several days before she found a spring and enough feed from brush and the scant grass to live. She was totally confused about where she was or what had happened to her world.

Then the late-summer rains came and the earth was soaked, cleansed, revitalized, and so was the colt. The soreness and the gauntness disappeared. She was alone in several hundred thousand acres of wilderness. But she lived.

The rains had made good feeding for the grazers, and the remains of the horses and the other burned animals gave plentiful food to the predators. This one winter, when she needed help so much, the fanged animals had no need of her flesh.

The spring grass and vegetation came again. She was feeding and nourishing her muscles and bones, and rapidly growing into a fine two-year-old equine specimen. She looked better than she felt. The flashes of fire still raced behind her eyes, and over and over she heard the death screams of her mother. Sometimes she would hold her head high, with nostrils straining wide, thinking she smelled the smoke from the scorched forest floor and the rotting flesh of her family and ancestors. After these flashbacks of horror, she would tremble and run about, trying to escape the imagined destruction. Finally, she'd calm and return to her normal watering, feeding and exercising. The fearful images slowly grew dimmer as she grew older.

She was walking to her secret waterhole when the warning chatter of a tassel-eared squirrel become louder and more urgent. It was October the first, 1961. Roger Maris, who played baseball for the New York Yankees, had just hit his sixty-first home run of the season, breaking Babe Ruth's old record. Just as the standing ovation of the crowd drew him out of the dugout for the second tip of his cap, a heavy force hit the filly on the back.

The lion had leapt from a limb above her and dug his foreclaws deep into her neck. His rear claws were locked into her hips. With powerful, open jaws and long, meat-ripping fangs, he reached for the place where the neck bones join the skull. The instant she felt the force of the lion's weight, and the sharp pain of its claws, she bolted straight into a heavy growth of young trees. Before the lion could close his jaws on the death spot, a limb smashed into his forehead and dragged him off her back. In so doing, the claws raked through her hide and into raw flesh plowing permanent lines and eventual scars on both sides of her neck. The claw cuts were painful for a while, with the swelling and draining, but they healed. From then on, her mind was alerted to the warning sounds from other possible victims of predators.

The five-mile-wide and ten-mile-long burnt area had come back lush green. The grass and brush had fought the timber seedlings for space and won. The small surviving trees were scattered widely apart. All the new growth made, for a few years at least, lush summer grazing. For a long time she spent as much of her life here as possible. The trees were so far apart that she could watch for the death drop from above and avoid the tearing claws of the lion. The deer felt as she did, and grazed right along side her. In the fall and early winter she and the other foraging creatures would move high up, out of the healed area, and feast on the oak brush and mountain mahogany pine, putting on fat to hold them through the sometimes hard winters.

She wasn't so lonely anymore. She had the company of wild turkeys, band-tailed pigeons, quail, squirrels and chipmunks, blue jays and mountain grouse, hawks and eagles. Some of the creatures lived at all altitudes, changing locations with the seasons and the food growth, while others were found at only certain heights in special terrain. There were many creatures here she would have to study in order to live out her allotted span of years.

Fortunately, she had found a secluded spring soon after the earlier holocaust. The timber and rocks, while completely encircling it, sat well back from the waterhole. On this special terrain she could drink peacefully, knowing that she wouldn't suffer a sudden attack. She maintained a constant alertness as far as her knowledge at this point allowed.

In late September, she went to the spring and found it frozen over. This was a new surprise . . . another type of warning she must learn to heed. There was much more danger on this mountain than the long-toothed predators, and after this winter she would always remember that early ice and falling leaves, along with higher, more frigid winds, meant heavy storms soon. She didn't have that knowledge frozen into her genes at the time the great snow came.

The dark clouds moved in formation, low, caressing, over the peaks, like Alexander's legions. And underneath them the wind fought with the trees, thrashing them about in agony and sending the flying things coasting up and away on its mad currents. But below, where the wind was less, many of the four-footed animals failed to move out in time.

The snow stuck for a moment on the millions of branches and limbs before being shaken loose by the wind over and over, thousands and thousands of times. The white, frozen crystals were swept and piled into massive drifts higher than the mare's head. She was all right for a few days, pawing the snow down to the little clumps of bunch-grass and oak brush.

She rapidly consumed all edible food in the small radius she was able to control. Soon she had to struggle harder, pawing into the deeper drifts. Her exertions caused rapid weight loss. Her lungs had to pump more warm air which formed ice crystals around her nostrils and eyes restricting her breathing and vision. She was in a white, frozen world and was quickly turning into an immobile ice sculpture.

She could only paw feebly now, and began to lose interest in making any effort at all. She was dozing. Her weakened neck allowed her head to drop down almost to knee level. She felt warm, dry, and totally without concern for food or anything else. Soon one foreleg slid out to the side. She was teetering with her whole body about to fall over, but she felt as if she was running in the summer warmth again with the gray male colt. They were jumping about, dodging and chasing each other with their short tails in the air, and heads up like the Royal British mounts. They were full, free and safe. It was a glorious moment.

Suddenly then, she was certain that she smelled the smoke, envisioned the fire, and heard the squeals and screams again for the first time in months. The fear became so real she began actually running from it. Then she whirled and ran back towards it, craving its imagined warmth. After bursting through drift after drift, she began to feel the cold again, but kept plunging through the forest down, down, always down. Eternity returned. She now fought to reach lower ground as years before she had struggled for the high.

Her lungs pained terribly as she sucked in more and more frozen air, just as she had once breathed the hot ashes and fire-scorched winds. As before, there came a point where her afflicted lungs could not supply enough fuel to keep her body moving. She stood quivering, and made loud gasping sounds as she tried to take in the warmer air of the foothills.

When she could finally see again, she discovered that the drifts were much smaller here. There would be no problem pawing through to the grass and even some of the bushes could be reached with hardly any effort at all. She survived until spring once again. Never, not once, would she be trapped in the high country by the felonious storms.

By spring, she had gained back almost all her weight and strength when she spotted two black-bear cubs climbing over and around a dead log, chasing and cuffing one another about in the purest of fun. One fell, hanging on just a moment before tumbling the short distance to the ground. The mare, feeling good after the grinding winter, eased forward in a friendly gesture to the cub. They had barely touched noses when the little bear whirled and scampered away, and the mare heard the loud "whoof." The sound was followed by a blasting slap to her side and neck. The mama bear had been plunging downhill at such speed that her swipe at the mare was slightly off. The blow to the horse's neck and ribs had not been the solid finishing strike the bear had intended. Even so, it knocked the mare stumbling to the side. Her neck and rib cage were numbed where the mighty paw of the five-hundred-pound beast had struck.

As the bear whirled back to finish the mare off with her teeth and foreclaws, she received an unpleasant surprise. The mare's adrenaline had flushed up ancient resources of genes. An old experience imparted the knowledge to her brain that her numbed body could not outrun the bear. She whirled and started kicking back towards her attacker. The bear stuck her lower jaw right into one of the mare's hooves when it was at its apex of power. The bones cracked like a bull elk stepping on a tiny dry stick. The other hoof caught her on the left eye, chipping the skull around the socket in several places and knocking the bear's remaining vision askew. In a few weeks the coyotes got the cubs and the buzzards discovered the starved body of the mother bear.

The mare's left shoulder had torn tendons that caused her much pain as she traversed the uneven ground trying to feed. Another wide scar undulated with the muscles beneath the skin from the blow of the bear. Since she hadn't fully recovered from the decimation of the winter, it would be late summer before the scar healed and the soreness left her.

By early October, she was well and sufficient winter fat was already on her bones. With this recuperation also came a feeling of longing. Something was missing—something that was a part of her—something that she had every right to be sharing. The vacancy left an aching in her heart, her womb, and her animal soul.

She thought she saw a blur of her own kind, her own blood, in the bushes and trees, but no matter how hard she looked and searched, the images she ached to define would not come clear. This ineluctable feeling pervaded her all during, and past, the twenty-second of October, 1962, when the Cuban missile crisis began. President John F. Kennedy ordered the blockading of Cuba and revealed the discovery of Soviet missile bases on Cuban soil through air reconnaissance photos. The President went on television and gave media interviews in the Oval Office. The two leaders of the superpowers exchanged many accusations and threats. The hearts of the world stood still in dread.

For six days, the mighty powers threatened and blustered. US bombers, loaded with atomic bombs, flew patterns up to the edge of Soviet territory by the hour. The warships were about to pair off for battle. The Russians, vastly outnumbered in the nuclear bomb category at the time, held out six days before they gave in. Never before had the world been so close to destruction in just a few minutes of madness. It has been debated ever since whether Kennedy saved the world by calling the Russians' bluff or gave it away by not taking Cuba while it was in his grasp.

During the six days of worldwide tension, the mare grazed contentedly and enjoyed the cool nights and warm days of autumn in peace. The forest has many eyes and ears, watching, listening, always aware, and now she knew how to use them to her advantage. These animals would voice the movements of danger to her instantly. She only had to listen and act to be safe.

As the other world started breathing again, but as yet looking over their collective shoulders, the mare spent a mild winter with plenty of forage. When spring came, some tiny bit of fat was still left under her long winter hair. She would soon be slick and shiny.

After many years of gaining knowledge through painful experiences and her natural force of observation, she finally chose her favorite spot for repose. About halfway down, between the jagged peaks of the high mountains and the lower meadows, there was a mesa with Mimbres Indian ruins on top. From here she could walk around the edges of the pueblito and observe the far-spreading wilderness in every direction, just as the Indian occupants once had.

Here in her part of southern New Mexico, hundreds of these ruins existed. Some archaeologists dated them back a thousand years, but the exact time period is as much in dispute as how an entire nation of mostly peaceful Indians vanished completely. They did leave behind them, their rock houses, burial grounds, stone and bone tools, arrowheads, and traces of jewelry. However, there were very few implements of actual war. Their main gifts to history were their wonderfully constructed, and uniquely designed black on white pottery.

Here in the ancient ruins, the mare felt a comfort and peace greater than in any other spot in her domain. When the hidden blood-longings and blurred visions came to her, she headed to this spot to share it with the ghosts of its former inhabitants like retreating to a Benedictine monastery. She heard drums and chants and sometimes saw incomplete images in the air, but she didn't know what they were—only that she was comforted.

After the time of the Mimbres and before the time of the satellites, there had been many battles in this part of her range. Geronimo, Chief Victorio, and Old Nana had made this area their last hideout from pursuing cavalry. Only half a mile below her, an isolated squad of buffalo soldiers from the 9th Cavalry had encountered a small band of Apaches. It became a running battle. A black sergeant named Moses Williams, realizing two of his wounded Buffalo soldiers were surrounded, charged back, catching the Apaches by surprise and saving the soldiers' lives. Sergeant Williams was awarded the Congressional Medal of Honor.

In 1963, President John F. Kennedy was assassinated by Lee Harvey Oswald in Dallas, Texas. It shocked a nation and a lot of the world into near paralysis. People will never forget where they were when they heard the news. The mare knew none of this, nor would she have cared, for hers was and had truly been another world. Much more would pass in both dimensions.

The mare was honored in the year of '67 by the weather. The forage was plentiful from the summer rains and the snow of the high country had melted early. She prospered . . . but in the cities of America the flower children came to full bloom, shouting peace and free love, while the rock music cascaded its battering, and often deafening, beat across the land and cheap dope altered minds and history forever. In the Haight-Ashbury district of the lovely city of San Francisco, the children lay about the streets with minds bent and bodies so inert they could barely follow up on the prevalent misguided theory of love being free. They had presumably started out innocent and wound up tasting the refuse of the gutters, seeing visions of such complexity that for many there was nothing left but the accidental and sometimes purposeful ultimate quest—suicide.

That same fateful year ended in near tragedy for the aging mare, even more innocently than it had for the children of the streets. She wanted companionship . . . a direct communication of some kind. During one of those periods of deep loneliness, she was craving something like the image she saw reflected in the water as she drank from her favorite spring. That's when she followed and, in a friendly gesture, stuck her muzzle down to a porcupine. The animal with thirty thousand barbs swung its short tail and imbedded fourteen of them into the left side of the mare's nostrils and face.

In a couple of days one passage was swelled completely shut and the other barely open so that she gasped for breath even while standing still. She started losing weight and strength immediately. The swelling and pain grew so great that she would rub her face against trees, rocks, bushes, the earth itself and sling her head in circles trying to dislodge the darts.

Now the coyotes witnessed this and stalked her. They were far too smart to risk her deadly hooves, if she had been well. Due to their small size, they could only down big game when it was ill or injured. By her erratic actions, the coyotes knew she was both. So they patiently circled and watched, for days. Even with all her pain, the mare watched them too. She turned her rear to them, ready to strike out hard with her hind feet.

Slowly, some of the quills worked their way out, while only a few burst open the swelled spots at her rubbing. She was forced to graze solely on bush leaves. It was slow and painful. She was weakening fast.

Finally one coyote leapt at her nostrils. While she was busy with the first, the other tried to hamstring her. The coyote did manage to get hold of her muzzle just long enough to puncture it. This helped the poison ooze out, and the swelling started down. She kicked the other one in the side and sent it rolling down an embankment with three broken ribs. The wise coyotes left her alone and chose to dine, that day, on game already dead.

She could eat better now and gradually the barbs either worked all the way out or a protective gristle formed around them. She became strong again. It seemed that no matter how long she lived and how much knowledge she acquired, there was still wisdom to be gained that could come only from pain. Just the same, she knew, and had survived, most of the deadly dangers of the wilderness at least once. She had paid a highly inflated price to gain a few years of relative tranquillity.

The last year of the sixties was a good one for her. Most of her scars and injuries were healed. She spotted a bobcat on a rare daylight foray. It crouched in the grass stalking a quail. That same day Armstrong and Aldrin would complete one of mankind's most sought-after dreams. They landed a space ship on the moon. Scores of millions of people worldwide were tied with invisible ropes, to their television sets. The bobcat didn't know any more about this than the mare. It was hungry and the solution to that problem hid motionless in the grass some ten feet ahead.

The cat's ears twitched ever so slightly, trying to catch any sound or movement from the intended victim. The soft, furry belly was actually touching the ground at its lowest point. Its short tail switched once as the cat leaped forward. The quail raised up, took three strides and winged into flight. About four feet off the ground the bobcat's claws hooked into the bird's belly. As they fell back to earth, she locked her jaws on the last flutterings, and crouched, holding it tightly as she looked about for any competition. As soon as the bird was dead, the cat took off towards its den in some rocks out of the mare's sight.

That same day, as the mare wandered, browsing in the brush, a golden eagle dropped from the sky into an opening, hooked its powerful talons into a fat rabbit and flew up to some bluffs to dine. The forest gave sudden voice with squirrels and birds chattering, then became cautiously silent again. This was all so natural in her life that the mare took only a cursory glance at the necessary killing. This golden eagle had landed, and so had the one on the moon. One in an action as old as animal history and the other as new as birth. New worlds had surrounded the old forever.

A mother elk tried to graze while her bull calf lunched greedily at her bag with switching tail. Three forest moths played in and out of a sunbeam like happy, little angels. The mare, witnessing all of this, would have fed in contentment except the yearning for something more of her own self struck her several times a month now.

She might have felt better about one human endeavor presently occurring if she had known about it. A lady known as Wild Horse Annie from Nevada, had raised so much hell, enlisted so many supporters, and grabbed so much attention from the media, that a federal law was passed protecting wild horses. Of course, it came far too late for the old mare's immediate ancestors. As her life moved in its eternal cycle of daily survival, the world around her was accelerating with a momentum that seemed to gain in speed like a great boulder rolling down a mighty mountain towards a tiny village.

In 1972, the Arabs put an embargo on oil, and while millions of Americans waited in line for hours at gas stations frustrated and unable to move, the mare browsed on luscious foliage and enjoyed an unhurried, uncluttered existence.

Oil prices escalated, and some poor nations became rich and many rich countries poorer. Wealth shifted about like the hearts of young lovers. The Watergate scandal dethroned a president and his men, changing the political attitudes and history of the free world for decades yet to come.

During these outside occurrences, the old mare had, on several occasions, seen a flash of gray in the timber and brush to the east of her Mimbres ruins lookout. She knew somehow that this was a replica of herself. She felt a kinship here at the ruins, and she had the same feeling for the glimpses of gray. She now took excursions trying to get a solid sight or smell of her illusory relation. But none came—no matter how long she wandered about on swiftly tiring legs, or stared with her dimming eyes, or sniffed with her knotted, scarred muzzle. The only place she could conjure up the flashing vision was from the same spot on the east side of the Mimbres ruins. There only. But she kept on searching, season following season. She would return to the magic spot and wait, sometimes hours, sometimes days, until forced to move away for food and water. But the gray thing began to appear more often. She felt warm and elated at each sighting, even if it was blurred and filmy.

Things had been working in her favor for several years now. A chief forester named Aldo Leopold had written an enormously influential essay entitled "The Land Epic." It led to the creation of a huge official wilderness area named after the forester. The mighty Black Range was to the west of the free area. Gerald Lyda's Ladder Ranch, one of the largest and most famous in the Southwest, touched it on many sides. The Cross Triangle joined to the north and Jimmy Bason's to the east. The old mare lived, protected, right in the middle of it all.

Now that no private vehicles could ever enter her area, she sometimes watched the backpackers walking into the Animas Creek area to camp and relish nature. She would watch them through the bushes, standing as motionless as an oft-hunted buck deer. As long as they didn't carry cracking rifles, as did those who hunted yearly in the lower country, they were nothing but a pleasant curiosity to her. Many elk had migrated across the Black Range from the Gila Wilderness to hers. She enjoyed their presence and bugling calls, but it did little to allay the growing sense of an impending personal event.

Friday, September 18, 1987, the two-hundredth anniversary of the Constitution of the United States, the mare spent looking out the canyon from the ruins, hoping her gray companion would show. It was an anxious day for others as well.

The Polish Pope John Paul II arrived in San Francisco toward the end of what would probably be his last junket to the United States, amidst about two thousand picketing AIDS victims and sympathizers. The Pope kept calm.

Headlines around the nation said that the United States and the Soviets had reached an accord on diminishing the number of missiles in the world. When the mare had been born into the Space Age, America had far superior numbers of arms, but now on this day, the Soviets were ahead. Not many people on either side really believed the negotiations were being held for the good of all mankind.

As patriotic parades were held all across the land on this great day, the old mare went on, patiently looking. Then she saw it. Now the gray mist had taken on a little more solidity and form. Her heart beat faster. The figure didn't disappear this time but stayed just inside the bushes as she strained harder than ever before to see and realize what part of her it was.

The year of the celebration of the Constitution passed with many wars in effect. In Lebanon, Afghanistan, all over Africa. The Iranians and the Iraqis went on butchering one another and the ships of the world filled up the Persian Gulf supposedly to protect oil tankers for the Western world market. While the old mare looked for her compatriot there were, in fact, over forty blasting, slashing, mind-numbing wars being fought, and oddly mostly ignored by the preponderance of the world's population.

The calendar moved on into the presidential election year, with the candidates made up of preachers and lawyers. The old mare's body was as ravaged as the polluted and war-torn earth. The scars on her neck, ribs and shoulders from the attacks of the lion and the bear looked like little, erratically plowed firms. Her back was swayed, her eyes were dull and clouded over. Her once long, flowing mane and tail had been matted and stuck together with burrs and stickers of all kinds for years. The natural indentations above her eyes were sunken, creating round shadows. Her ribs looked like wagon bows sticking through thin, worn, chestnut-colored cloth. The old gunshot wound in her neck hardly mattered in comparison with all the rest. Her tattered ear bent over like one on a generations-old toy rabbit. She had spent her extended life searching for *peace*, hurting nothing except those who sought to destroy her breath and blood.

Unbeknownst to her, children of the cities, farms, and ranches ran around playing astronauts and aliens from outer space instead of cowboys and Indians as they had at the time of her birth, and most of their lives as well as those of their parents were hourly directed by computer buttons and little images on various screens. Her natural methods of survival had mostly remained the same through her decades here in the Aldo Leopold Wilderness. These ancient rhythms went back to the forest fire, to the conquistadors, to Spain and Egypt, and throughout history. Since the beginning of man, her ancestors were hunted for meat or used as beasts of burden, as creatures to make war with, and at times for racing, hunting, and even many forms of pure pleasure.

Her genes cried and tugged at her being, taking her back sixty million years to the Eocene epoch, or time of the Dawn Horse, when she would have been the size of a small fox terrier. Now as she strained ever harder to make the gray object clearer, she heard the Indian ruins and the accompanying chants become louder. The fuzzed objects were suddenly delineated. Some of the Mimbres Indians were dancing in a circle of spectators. Their brown legs and feet moved faster and faster as the drum's volume increased. Her heart beat in synchronization with them as she looked across the canyon and back to the Mimbres.

She was extremely excited, but a mellowness absorbed her at the same time. The drummer's hands, at their ultimate speed, pounded the hide drums and the moccasined feet thumped the earth with all the skill and power left in them. Intense vibrations filled the air and permeated everything. The sound and movement stopped at its peak—and for just a moment so did the universe, in total quiet and stillness.

Then four elders squatted in a rectangle. Each one took a turn standing and making a gesture with both hands in supplication to all four winds. A medicine man and a medicine woman stood before the mare now, and in contrast to the former solemnity of the ceremonies, radiated smiles of love and compassion towards her.

The medicine man reached into a doeskin pouch and gathered a handful of seeds from all the vegetation of the land. He leaped high in the air and hurled the seeds out over the mare. The seeds turned into uncountable bluebirds. They flew up, up and dissolved the thin mists of clouds across the sky, and moved ever higher, growing into numbers so great they became a solid mass of blue. The birds moved past the sun and the bright land of the sky was reborn.

Just as the medicine man landed back on earth, the medicine woman leapt upwards in a floating jump. She, too, reached into her doeskin bag for seeds, also throwing them above the mare as her compatriot had done. These turned into multitudes of white doves fluttering skyward forming a great flat-bottomed, castle-domed cumulus cloud. She drifted back to earth standing next to the man. Both lifted their arms above their heads and yelled with all the force of their throats and lungs. Their cries were a mixture of all living things of the mountains—the lions and the insects, the bears and the bobcats, the hawks and the hares. All.

The mighty crescendo of sound moved up and became a symphony of drums and hand-carved flutes, spreading so wide it finally softened to a simple, sweet sigh. Instantly the Mimbres Indians vanished from her vision as they had so many centuries before from the earth.

And now, across the eons right to the present, she saw the grayness move out of the brush and become circular movement. It was a great, shining, gray stallion who pranced with arched neck and high-tossed tail, back and forth directly across the canyon at about her level. Her scars were no longer felt, nor the stiff limbs, nor any of the lumps of the years. She was possessed with an inner feeling of permanent warmth and peace. Her eyes became so sharp she could see the nostrils of the stallion flare as he turned his head to nicker and squeal to her. She heard it as clearly as the bells of Notre Dame, and knew all its meaning as she always had and always would. She saw the stallion racing across the canyon, through space, towards her, mane and tail streaming. Then he sailed up and up above the grass the brush and the trees. She whirled agilely about, leaping down the rough terrain and then ascending sharply, racing in a soothing, golden vacuum straight towards her mate, at last.

At the very moment Pauline Healy had yelled for her father to look in the sky above the descending buzzards, an El Paso reporter, a photographer and three cowboys, who were expert ropers and trackers, were moving their pickups and gear towards the Healy's camp. If the Ranger and his daughter had been listening into the quietness, they would have heard the truck engines straining uphill.

From another direction came the chawp, chawp, chawp of the helicopter as it passed over Jimmy Bason's Ranch loaded with people from the Associated Press. The Healys didn't hear the sounds below because the discovery that lay before them blocked out all else.

The Ranger felt his horse's muscles tense beneath him and saw three coyotes scatter away from a chestnut carcass.

He said with an infinite loss in his voice and a painful expulsion of breath, "Ohhhh . . . nooo. We're too late! The coyotes and buzzards have already beat us to her."

Pauline's wide, wondering eyes were locked on a movement in the sky. She did not hear her father, or see the signs and activity on the ground. Three tiny clouds, each one bigger than the other, raced across the blueness to the cumulus cloud and right up on top of it. There the girl saw a stallion, a mare, and a colt playing together in the upper mists and lights of the massive formation of white moisture. They were silhouetted proudly against the sky. Forever. Anyone could see them who knew how to look.

With an imponderable smile on her suddenly beatific face, the girl said softer than the whisper of a saint, "There will never be another her. Never."

Old Bum

"Hey, Mark, guess what I've got in here," Tom Creswell said, clicking his store-bought teeth and licking his lips as he pointed to the trunk of his old Plymouth. His watery, light blue eyes were almost gleaming.

I figured by all this facial action that he surely must have a forty-pound sack of diamonds in there. It turned out to be almost that rare and priceless to us "great-white" hunters—even if I was three-sixteenths Indian.

Tom C. was a sixty-odd-year-old rock mason, and we were partners in the rock building business; and we were friends in fun, drinking and coyote hunting. He was a "hound-dog man" from all the way back to the first hunting genes.

He opened the trunk and out jumped this black and tan coon-dog, and looked all around the wide-open grasslands of northern New Mexico. That was back in the early fall of 1947, when Tom introduced me to this creature that would alter my entire life.

"What do you think about this old hobo? I reckon he's just what we need for our hunting," Tom C. said with a certain pride.

"Why it's a flop-eared trail hound," I said, surprised. "What in the hell are we going to do with him? He couldn't catch a coyote in a month of hard running."

"Coons, Mark. We'll use him on coons. We can double our hunting and trapping income in no time atall."

I believed him. That's the way it is with mentors. You have to believe everything they say even if it's wrong. Of course, mentors are so seldom wrong you are supposed to just let it whiz right on by. Code of the West, you know?

"Where did you get him?" I asked.

"Found him about a quarter of a mile out of Grenville, walking smack down the middle of the Denver/Fort Worth railroad.

He looked like he was on the trail of a fast freight. I just whistled and he came to me."

There is a lot of good hunting in the rolling hills of northeastern New Mexico, and Tom and I hunted with dogs all the time. We hunted for the hides and the bounty. We had never used anything except long-legged, long-jawed running dogs—greyhounds, stags and Russian wolfhounds. So, this trail-hound was something new.

Before I get carried away about this wondrously unpredictable creature, I think it's fair to tell why the ranchers commissioned Tom Creswell and me to hunt coyotes for them.

I have on occasion helped ranchers pull calves from birthing heifers to save the lives of both the first-time mother and the new calf. It can be an agonizing struggle taking hours to inch the calf out of a heifer with bare hands or a pulley. The suffering is often great for all concerned. Sometimes it fails and one or both is lost. After one of those successful deliveries, a rancher will usually ride back the next day to check on the animals that feed, clothe and give life to his tough world and family. He expects to see a mother-licked-clean, big-eyed calf, bucking and playing around with his little contemporaries; or, sucking white liquid growth from its mother's swelled bag; or, having done that, sleeping off its contented fullness in the green grass of spring. However, if this rancher sees buzzards circling before he gets there and then just finds small bits of his protégé scattered about the land from a coyote's fangs, and sees and hears the heifer walking and bawling, looking for her firstborn, her untapped milk painfully filling her udder until it drips out wasted onto the earth, the rancher gets real mad. He has lost part of the family's survival here, and he has lost something he gave his heart and hands to bring to the world.

Once I was sitting, waiting for Tom C. to deliver a load of rocks to a windmill site for building a tank on Jim Ed Love's JL Ranch, when his son Clyde drove up in a pickup checking on things. We were visiting about the lack of rain, the price of cattle, the best bar in Raton and the best hooker in Juarez, when we heard a calf bawl over a hill to the north.

"Something's getting after that calf," Clyde said. "Come on."

So I jumped into the pickup with him and he gunned it over to a gate. I leapt out, opened it, and he slowed just barely enough for me to get back in. Then we ran smack up against a sheer-drop arroyo. We bailed out and scurried to the top of a rise and saw a sight to make a rancher sick.

Two grown coyotes had hold of an early calf. One held onto the tail that was already chewed down to a nub, while the other had it by the muzzle. They were methodically circling. The calf would drop soon, and then they would tear it into shreds and feast.

We both yelled as we ran downhill. The coyotes turned loose and ran up on a hill where they stopped to watch us. They always know if you have a gun or not. I could tell by their boldness they had a den of pups nearby. The little white-faced—now all red—calf had its tail torn off to the spine. Its eyes were bitten blind and its muzzle hung in shreds of bloody meat. The poor little thing sensed we were not the enemy. Seeking some kind of comfort, it kept rubbing up against our legs, smearing us with blood. It was beyond help. Clyde grabbed up a ten-inch sandstone rock and hit it between the eyes as hard as he could strike. It went to its knees, then rolled over, jerked a couple of times and died. We both understood that was all that could be done.

We numbly wiped the blood from our Levi's the best we could with wads of bunch grass, then slowly, silently, walked back to the pickup. I looked up on the hill. I couldn't see the coyotes now, but I knew they could see us. In a little while they would come back, satiate themselves, taking a stomach full back to their den to regurgitate for their pups' sustenance—just as natural to them as moonlight. It was just as natural for the rancher to try to kill the coyotes to protect his own family. That is what the ranchers hired Tom C. and me to do for them. A terrible impasse.

I had to explain this distasteful truth so the monumentality of what happened later to make me quit hunting forever can be somewhat better understood.

Anyway, this new dog, this stranger in a lonely land of lonely people, would somehow become the cause of my soul-tearing turnaround. We called him Old Bum, instead of Hobo, but we sure never dreamed that he would live up to his name the way he did and turn into a real out-and-out mooch. We soon found out he had all the vices of his two-legged brothers: heavy drinking, staying up all night at poker games, chasing the opposite sex, and finally even becoming addicted to hillbilly music. And with all this going for him, it turned out that he was also a downright snob. However, in the beginning he was a hunter tried-and-true, even though he was somewhat strange about his methods.

Back when this all happened—in the late forties—my eyesight was perfect, but the totality of my vision was sometimes cloudy. It's hard enough to get a young man to change his mind about a way of life he loves, but to have it altered in one day—with a single mysterious action that lasted less than a couple of minutes—is miraculous.

Now as I look back forty-five—or is it fifty?—years, I marvel at how that old flop-eared hound indirectly led me to such a dazzling enlightenment. And he wasn't even there at the time. Maybe that was part of it.

It was right after I returned from fighting with the combat infantry in Europe, and all that ground-tearing, sky-piercing madness that went on there, that I finally joined up with Tom Creswell. Since he was about thirty-five years older than me, he became my rock-mason mentor. Before the war I had learned the finer points of hunting and trapping from him, and now I was honored for him to teach me how to select, size, smear cement and lay rocks, so that they could form a water tank, a good horse shed, a milk house or a fence.

I was able to keep my wife Ortha, and four-year old daughter Connie, well-fed and clothed and living in a house that sat on a hundred and ten acres just on the edge of Hi Lo. We had a milk cow and laying hens that were fat and producing. It was good to be young.

The cattle ranchers around Hi Lo had been making a lot of money for the first time in quite a spell because of the demand for beef during World War II. The price of cattle just kept going up. Even in those boom times, only a very few had running water in the house or indoor plumbing. Some had electricity supplied by wind motors, but mostly they used kerosene or carbide lamps. The only TV in the whole Hi Lo Country, that I knew of, was in a bar in Raton about thirty miles to the west. Some people had battery radios for their only worldly communication. In 1947, ranchers still kept milk cows, laying and eating hens, and butchered their own pork. This not only made economic sense but people were still fearful because of the drought and the Great Depression of the thirties which was still fresh in their minds. Even so, these extra chores made it especially hard on the ranch women who were always overburdened anyway.

In spite of the somewhat primitive living conditions, they were busy expanding and improving their land holdings, which meant the big lizard swallowing the little lizard just like always. Tom C. and I prospered by specializing in building rock stocktanks for them, and since the coyote population was increasing at the same time the calf losses were, it wasn't too hard to convince the ranchers over this vast lonely spread of land to contract us to hunt coyotes at ten dollars a pair of ears.

So, there we were, "settin' purty." We were getting paid for laying rocks way out in the boonies and drawing down ten dollars a kill for the predators we pursued anyway just for the thrill of it. Oh yeah, I almost forgot. On top of the rancher's bonus, we got between five and fifteen dollars for each coyote hide. These extras made it possible for us to support our hunting habit without taking too much out of our construction income.

Coyote hunting was a pretty expensive sport. We had to feed the running hounds, buy traps and gasoline, replace busted tires, steel springs, burned out pistons on our pickups, and also, there were those drinks we had to buy in the bar while bragging about what great dogs we owned and what cunning, courageous hunters we were. We didn't really need drinks to tell these heart-rapping, mind-jouncing tales, but it made everybody more interested in listening. The stories were so wonderful and wild that we had to tone the truth down most of the time. Of course, everybody thought we were stretching things a little—like most other sportsmen have to do. Not us, though. You could bet your sister's drawers on that. This will be better understood after witnessing a few of the incidents that happened after Old Bum came into our lives. To be fair, he entered lots of lives.

Ortha had always been fairly patient with me and Tom C. talking about our adventures until Old Bum came along and we got to making her listen to the endless adventures about him. I really had not noticed it as closely as I should—ain't that a failing in most men? But she had taken to going off in another room and reading *Ready Romance Magazine* when we started up our natural hunting conversation. It wasn't long until she included *Romantic Interludes*, *Always Love*, and *Hearts the Same* on her subscription list of literary pursuits. Since we didn't have any TV and the batteries on the radio were dead half the time, I read some myself. I liked Jack London and James M. Cain the best.

Now, looking back on it, I swear it seems impossible that I didn't see the train coming while I was sitting on the crossing. I reckon I misled myself by the fact she still kept the house, yard, my daughter Connie and herself neat and clean, the garden watered, the meals cooked, and took care of the cow and chickens. At that time she was getting only one or two headaches a week at bedtime, but when those increased to three and four, any idiot should have caught on that aspirins were going to be useless.

Ortha was a hard working, loving woman built as well as a quarter horse mare. She had green eyes that could have been worn as emeralds on a queen's necklace, lips as lucious as strawberries, and teeth so even and white that brushing seemed like a waste of time, and a voice that rolled out soft words to make warblers and jazz musicians bow down in homage; and I didn't appreciate her as much as I did my hounds. I was a master fool and then some, but I didn't get the illumination until the sun had already set.

I told Tom C., "Blessings be, ole partner, I do believe she almost smiled at breakfast this morning."

He just looked at me blankly, his mind on our upcoming hunt: "Sounds promising."

How does the song go? "So far, far away and forever ago." Something like that, I do believe. As I sit here in a comfortable lawn chair looking over the barns and the big house in the middle of four green, landscaped acres that belong to my daughter, Connie, and her husband, Jack Oldham, I can see as clearly as nightlightning back to those days before I quit hunting so suddenly, forever.

Yeah, Ortha did leave me, and she took my precious little Connie with her to stay with her folks in Texas until we could get divorced and she could start a new life. No use going on much more about that, except to say that Ortha married a realtor from Fort Worth. Connie grew up beautiful as all the fresh colors sprouting from the earth after a spring rain, and as smart and graceful as a circus pony. Ortha turned back to her naturally decent self and let Connie spend a month or so with me every summer way out here in the Hi Lo Country. Before I could say "General Patton" or "Holy hallelujah hell" Connie was in her second year in college at University of Texas in El Paso. She wrote and said she would be out in a week to stay a week.

At the time, I was building—Tom C. had finally retired because of arthritis and one short leg—a stock tank for Jack Oldham, a young rancher over south of Raton. I took Connie with me one day. Jack came by to check out the project. I'll never know how it happened, but Connie wound up married to him four months later. Jack was director in a Raton bank, owned some interest in a producing coal mine, and kept this great house just on the edge of the northeast city limits. We got along like coffee and doughnuts.

Since I was so handy with rocks, and not too shabby with wood and nails either, my son-in-law kept me working on the ranch for years. When I started to stumble over little tiny pebbles and lean permanently to the northeast, he let me have the guest house in town, and all I had to do was keep the four acres slicked up some and look after the twin boys, Fred and Ted, whenever Jack and Connie wanted to go off to Acapulco, Las Vegas, Nevada, or Hillsboro, New Mexico, for a little of the so-called "rest and regeneration."

Like I said, this very day I was sitting in one of those outdoor chairs Connie kept all over the yard, letting the early summer sun loosen my old muscles so they didn't bend my bones. I felt good. All the family, and a couple of the twins' high school friends, was all out at the ranch, riding and roping to beat seven hundred, I reckoned.

Anyway, I kept dozing some and everytime I woke up a little my mind's eyes went traveling into the past about thirty miles east to the lonely village of Hi Lo. For some reason I kept seeing all that malpai, sandstone, wind-ripped country and everywhere I looked I seemed to see Old Bum who was the critter that led up to my neck-snapping, nerve-cracking turnaround. Like the song goes, "Long away and far, far ago," or something like that.

Anyway . . . we were mighty restless waiting for nightfall so we could get Old Bum out in the field. Tom C. chose the Cimarron River country below Folsom for our first venture. Cottonwood trees lined the banks of the creek, and enough perch and other small crustaceans inhabited it to entice the coons. When the coon hunts, that's when we hunted him.

We bailed out of a pickup truck carrying a twenty-two rifle, a powerful flashlight, two running hounds and Old Bum. The moon was just beginning to climb over the hill, casting black, night shadows all about. The crickets and a billion other insects sang their eternal songs.

"What's that?" I asked quietly after hearing a noise.

"Deer, I think," Tom whispered. "They come down at night to graze in the rancher's alfalfa patches along the river."

I listened to the whomping noise they made as they ran back towards the hills, and then I said, "Well, that's one thing in Old Bum's favor. He doesn't run deer."

"Yeah. Now, let's hope he doesn't take after a porcupine and get his head loaded up with quills."

We shut up then and began to hunt. Old Bum was moving ahead in erratic circles, his nose to the ground and his tail sticking straight up in the air. He acted like a real "cooner." The running dogs just walked along taking a sniff of the air now and then, mostly watching the new, short-legged member of the pack, insultingly, as if they wondered what a snail was doing trying to run with the racers.

Then we heard him bawl. Just once, that's all. The running hounds took off with their long legs eating the ground. I snapped on the flashlight. Tom and I tore through the brush, falling now and then but following the course of the river just the same. Then we heard the hog-like squeal of the coon.

"Here, Tom!" I yelled, flashing the light on the frenzied battle.

It was a huge boar coon. The running dogs had never been on a coon hunt before. They were having trouble deciding on the proper method of attack. The coon was up and down, rolling over and over, slashing with his razor-sharp teeth at the hounds. Finally, Brownie, half stag, half grey, and the heavier of the two, got the throat. Then Pug, the Russian wolfhound, moved in to the brisket, crushing down with powerful jaws. The coon was finished. And where do you suppose Old Bum had taken hold? The tail, that's where, and almost halfheartedly at that. I reckon he figured this end didn't have any teeth.

We caught two more coons that night. Old Bum would work out ahead and jump one. The running dogs would listen for his single squawk, then they would move out fast and down the coon before he had a chance to climb a tree. It was a new and exciting hunting combination—the trail-hound to track, the running dogs to catch and kill. As far as Old Bum was concerned, that was just the way it was from the first coon on. He refused to get in close enough to be bitten by the wildly fighting coons. He acted a little stuck-up about it, as if he figured the smelling part of the job was the most important. He wouldn't lower himself to the actual bloody business of fighting.

Overnight, the big dogs had developed a reserved admiration for one whose special talents they couldn't match. The combination improved as the dogs learned to get into the neck quicker by throwing the coon on his back. Old Bum would voice his single bawl. That was like a trigger to the other hounds.

All that fall we hunted up and down the Cimarron with Old Bum, taking about forty coons. We hunted at Weatherly Lake and caught eighteen nice ones. Just three coons made their escape to the scattered cottonwoods that entire season. The eighteen skins brought only about three dollars and fifty cents each, but that was better than a bee in the ear. Hey! Whiskey was thirty-five cents a drink, the jukebox was a nickel a song—six for a quarter—and a loaf of bread cost the same as a shot of the brown whiskey. Two coon hides would finance a small meal, a small drunk, and a big hangover. Those were the good old days and nights—or so it seemed for a while.

Naturally, we began to brag a little about our coon hunting prowess. Then in the natural process of things, we got to wondering how Old Bum would do on a coyote hunt. I wish we had never thought of that.

We turned the hounds out about a mile and a half from Cow Mountain. It was good rolling country. The coyote had about a hundred yard start. The running dogs leaped out of the back of the pickup. They sailed smoothly across the grasslands after the coyote, who was now racing madly. If a person had never run coyotes, there is no way to explain how your entire body and probably your boots, hat and underwear are flooded with adrenalin to the point of feeling as if you were swimming in it. Your heart knocks ribs apart and causes lungs to swell like helium balloons. We once ran right through a rock wall, actually speeding up before the pile of rubble settled behind us. Crazed. Nuts. A person is instantly hurled back in to the time before the wheel was invented and fire was something that only flashed down from the sky in a storm or boiled up from volcanos. Ancient emotions. Raw. Facts.

Well, anyway, Old Bum hit the ground on his short legs, rolled over about three times in a cloud of dust, then got up and headed in the wrong direction. He had been knocked silly from the fall, causing his inner-head compass to spin erratically.

We could see the running dogs pull up closer and closer on their coyote in long, graceful, ground-eating strides. Then one hound was alongside the coyote. He reached over, took hold of the coyote's neck and down they went! The other dogs piled on. But where was Old Bum? Well, he had accidentally jumped the running mate to the other coyote and was running as fast as his legs would carry him in pursuit. The coyote just loped along, easily outdistancing him. Teasing.

We drove on to where the other running hounds were scattering the coyote's insides across the prairie. We pulled the dogs off and loaded them into the pickup. Then we started looking for Old Bum.

Way off to the west, we could see two tiny clouds of dust heading into the hills. Old Bum didn't show up again for twenty-four hours, and when he did he was chewed all over, his ears ripped, and his nose was covered with cuts. It looked like the coyote had led him into an ambush, where several of the varmints had given him a real working over. We felt mighty lucky to have him back alive. He seemed to appreciate breathing, however painfully, himself. We never took Old Bum coyote hunting again. It wasn't the thing to do. I don't think he wanted to go anyway.

We did use him that winter to trail animals that had escaped with our steel traps. He proved invaluable on the trap line, paying for his upkeep many times above and beyond.

I didn't know then, as I've already explained, what was slowly separating me from my family. I started spending quite a number of evenings up on the main street of Hi Lo—which consisted of four blocks split by Highway 87. There was just too much going on up town, and I didn't want to miss any of it. Well, this move, as it turned out later, didn't do me much good, but what it did for Old Bum was something to sit down with my head in my hands and ponder about.

The first step in his changeover from a damned good coon dog to a hard-drinking hound—if not a downright drunkard—came about one Saturday afternoon in the Wild Cat Bar where the sidewalk curb was smack up against the aforementioned highway.

Hi Lo is a little cowtown—population of about one hundred and fifty—on a long piece of pavement from way down somewhere in Texas into, and across, northern New Mexico. To the south of town is Sierra Grande Mountain. Some claim it to be the largest lone mountain in the world. It is forty-five miles around the base and about nine thousand feet high. It takes a full day to hunt around its edges. To the north, east, and west is rolling gramma-covered rangeland broken now and then by a steep, jagged, malpai-studded canyon—the Carrummpah. There were two grocery stores, Chick Johnson's small hotel, two cafes, an all-night service station and two bars. The bars are the busiest places in town. The ranchers, cowboys and odd-job boys—like me and

Tom C.—all hang out there when they come to town. They do a little drinking—sometimes a lot of drinking—and catch up on the gossip, find out who won the latest street fights and other such sporting activities.

The bars are directly across the street from each other; the Wild Cat to the south, the Double Duty to the north. It was very convenient for all concerned. If a fight started in front of one, the customers of both places had what you might call ringside seats. If a feller was a little wobbly on his feet and wished to change company, he could just aim himself right straight across the highway and he would be pretty sure to hit a bull's-eye as far as bars are concerned. There wasn't enough traffic in those days to worry about the odds of getting run over.

The wind blows in Hi Lo at least two thirds of the time. It comes howling around the Sierra Grande Mountain in a grass-bending fury. I think the reason so many fist fights break out is because the people are all on edge from bucking this infernal wind. In fact, after all these decades I've had to think about it, I know that's the main reason.

That Saturday, I left Old Bum in the pickup and walked into the Wild Cat to do a little visiting. It just happened that a friendly pitch game was going on in a booth, and several wind-bent, sun-cured cowboys were standing at the bar giving Lollypop, the bartender, a lot of business. It was a cold day, but the Wild Cat was warm, and the only wind blowing inside was some cowboy bragging about what a bronc rider and calf roper he was. And then, I just couldn't help myself, I began to brag a little about Old Bum.

As the talk got mellower, somebody suggested that it was a dirty, stinking shame to leave such a remarkable dog out in the pickup where he might catch cold or get snake bit or something. We invited Old Bum inside. He stopped just past the door and looked the place over like General Montgomery surveying a battlefield. For a minute we were afraid he wasn't going to like the place. All of a sudden he trotted over to the bar, wagged his tail just a tad and stared right straight up at the bartender. That was too much. The thirst pains showed up so strong on Old Bum's face that we kindhearted cowboys, railroaders and rock masons just broke down and bought Old Bum a double shot.

The bartender set it on the floor in front of him. He looked at it. He looked at me. Then he ran his tongue out and took a lick. Something happened right then and there to Old Bum. Sort of a quiver came over him, and after the booze he went. In his hurry, he turned the glass over, and about half of it poured out on the floor. But it didn't evaporate or get stale, or go to waste or anything like that. He licked it right up, almost taking up what was left of the design from the linoleum-covered floor.

A lot of cheers went up. Over and over the glasses were set up for the greatest of all coon dogs; this aristocratic reveler; this friend of man and his vices, as well; this cool cucumber of a canine; this . . . aww hell, there were no words to describe him that first night of his debauchery. As the song says, "Away so far, so long ago."

The pitch players couldn't hear their bids, so they got up and joined the party. After a while somebody punched the jukebox full of nickels, and Old Bum sort of waltzed over and cocked his head to one side. Whenever a hillbilly tune came on, Old Bum would throw that proud, flop-eared head up and join the singing. We all agreed that he sounded better than some of the records. When anything played other than hillbilly, the head came down, the tail stopped wagging, and a sad, sour expression came over his face.

After a time Old Bum wobbled over to the door and scratched to get out. I figured maybe he was sick or something, but it turned out that he, unlike most of us, knew when he had had enough and wanted to get some sleep. This animal seemed to have had experiences we would, or could, only guess at. I helped him into the front of the pickup, not wanting him to suffer from the wind.

About four hours later, I decided it was time to go home. Every time I tried to open the pickup door to get in, Old Bum would snarl and leap at me. It came to me then that he understood himself a lot better than we did. This wasn't the first time for him. Far from it. He probably knew he got mean when he reached a certain stage and wanted to bed down before he got unfriendly and hurt somebody.

I waited down at the all-night station until about daylight. I stumbled back up to my pickup feeling worn out and sleepy. Old Bum didn't make a move. He was lying there passed out, snorting and jerking once in a while as he dreamed his private dreams of the past. And what a past he must have enjoyed. I was certain of it.

I crawled in real slow and careful, and then drove the half mile home just as the sun came up. Since I lived right in the edge of town at that time, I don't know why I didn't just walk on home and turn the pickup over to that dog. But, of course, that would be letting him take advantage of me. Just because Old Bum pulled this one big drunk was no sign he was going straight to hell as fast as he did, but it was a slight indication. Just like it was with my own family, I didn't move soon enough with Old Bum to prevent the sure deterioration. Anyway, I carried his sleeping body into the house with me.

We both woke up lying side by side on the living room floor. For just a minute I felt like running outside with Old Bum and keep going till we fell off in a deep, dark, secret canyon. It was too late. Ortha was already making extra loud, banging noises cooking breakfast. She saw us both struggling to survive, and she didn't say "Good Morning." In fact, she didn't speak at all.

My little Connie made an effort to be her true, sweet self, but soon leapt away from the breakfast table, running outside for an early playtime, shouting, "That dog stinks." I didn't know which one of us she really meant.

When I saw Ortha wash the butcher knife for the seventh time, I got out of there and headed for town. I suppose, for a spell anyway, me and Old Bum sort of got lost in the wicked wilderness. It's hard, all these years later, to realize how thoughtless I could be with the exuberance of youth driving me on and on.

I quit working rocks with my mentor. The reason being, I decided to become a painter—not a house painter, but the other kind who paints pictures. Tom C. never said much about it, but I could tell he was deeply hurt by the foolish actions of his protégé. I still hunted with him though. He had to give me credit there.

Levi Gomez, a part-Spanish, part-Apache, part-French, part . . . I don't know what . . . artist friend, was showing me some "bultos" (standing figures of saints) he had carved from cedar. He told me that some people knocked down as much as twenty bucks apiece for such like. I was somewhat amazed at this. A few days later I read in the *Saturday Evening Post* about a cowboy artist called Charlie Russell receiving thousands of dollars for just one painting. This seemed like a good idea to me. Why shouldn't a rock mason/coyote/coon hunter have just as good a chance at getting rich and famous as a dumb-ass cowboy? I know it sounds stupid now, but during those old times at Hi Lo I believed almost everything was possible.

So Levi and I discussed things over a quart of good brown whiskey and decided we would set up a studio and get rich. We sure did the first, but we missed the last by a country music mile.

Next door to the Double Duty bar (that's the one across the street) was an ugly old building held together by a bunch of brown rusted tin. We rented one end of this for fifteen dollars a month.

I bought a lot of paint in little metal tubes, some brushes made out of camel hair, a sketch pad and a few canvas boards, and started painting horses and cowboys. You talk about going crazy. For a while it was hard to tell which was the horse and which was the cowboy. Whenever I finished a picture I would tack it up on the wall at a fancy price. I had gone that silly. No one else in that country did any serious painting. We soon found out that the citizens of Hi Lo didn't have much interest in art of any kind, so we went it all alone.

We got an idea then that we might attract a little tourist trade if we had a sign. So Levi painted us a fancy one and we nailed it up on the front of the building. We called our place "Ye Olde Masters Art Gallery." Nobody ever stopped by. It took a while for us to catch on to the dearth of cultural interest along Highway 87 at that time.

Our only company was Old Bum. He hung around the gallery with us most of the time. Well, no wonder. We fed him there; it was out of the wind; and it was really handy to both bars. It was also a great place for him to sober up and recover from his hangovers. At these times he didn't tolerate any talk or bother. More than one person in town was snapped at for trying to pet him when he was under the influence. He was a pretty severe art critic, too. Every time I asked him how he liked one of my paintings, he'd scratch on the door wanting out.

In small country towns, cats and dogs roam free. There are no restrictions on a pet's freedom except whatever the owner wants to impose. So, it didn't surprise me one day when I drove into town to do some painting, to see about nine dogs all in a fighting pile. I caught glimpses of what I knew were parts of Old Bum. I jumped out of the pickup and tried to knock them off of him with a long-handled shovel I always carried in the back. When they all left, there lay Old Bum bloody and chewed all over. His tongue was hanging out, and it looked like it had already turned blue. I was sure he was dead.

I laid him in the back of the pickup and started to drive the short distance downtown to tell Levi the bad news. I glanced into the rear view mirror to check for traffic before I pulled onto the highway, and durned if I didn't see Old Bum get up and jump out. He ran across the pavement in pursuit of the same little black and white female that had started all the trouble. How Old Bum succeeded in this love affair, against such great and resentful odds, no one could guess, but there was no denying the five little flop-eared, half-breeds born a few months later.

One afternoon I was standing out in front of our "unvisited" gallery, leaning against a telephone pole just soaking up some sun. Old Bum was squatted on his hunkers beside me trying to recover from a little overindulgence of the night before. I studied the condition of our old friend. He was a mess. His eyes were red and watery from his heavy drinking, and there were scars over his whole body. His ears were in little threads and knots out at the ends where they had been bitten so much. But he was tough, and a real mixture of contradiction. A lot of big dogs chewed him up, but none of them ever made him run. He was too high-classed to pitch in and fight an over-matched coon, but when it came to privileges with the female, he would fight any dog in town right to the death.

As much as he admired the women folks of his own kind, he couldn't stand the human breed of female at all. He was strictly a man's dog. I imagine that came about somewhere in his past when a strong, wise woman must have told him to straighten up and do right, or he was going to be shunned. Ortha was telling me the same thing in her own way, but like I said, I'd gone over—way over—the dark crack in the earth and couldn't see any daylight.

Old Bum had been around town long enough now to have a regular circuit worked out for himself. He stayed at the gallery until we began to run out of money and could't feed him what he liked. After that, he just dropped by to give the critic's cold eye to our art work, or whenever he was too drunk to make it to his more distant hangouts. Everyone on his appointed route was a bachelor.

Pal England—one of the more sporting lads in town—lived with his retired, widowed, old father. Pal had a short leg from parachuting into a bad landing after his bomber was shot down over the Third Reich, and had spent a spell in one of their P.O.W. camps, so the government gave him a small pension for his short leg and long memories.

Pal said, "By all odds, I should be recognized as the town drunk since Vince Moore's unintentional retirement, but Old Bum has more experience, so, I'm giving him the title for now."

Vince Moore had held the undisputed title a long time before Pal. He was a part-time bootlegger who had moved his large family into town after being *nudged* out of his single section of land. He proudly claimed the title of official town drunk. He once told me, "I've been drunk for forty years because I'm afraid of falling dead with a hangover." His worrying all that time was wasted. As he was hurrying to his outhouse one of those Hi Lo wind gusts blew the roof off and knocked him as dead as last year's Christmas tree. If any creature had a chance to match these great accomplishments of the past, it was Old Bum.

Knowel Denny, a foreman on the railroad, lived across the tracks about three hundred yards from Pal. They were close friends, and Old Bum liked them both. They made quiet talk and always had something good cooking on the stove, like venison stew, or biscuits and gravy, and other tasty handouts that appealed to his taster.

Another place the old hound visited was down to the east about a quarter of a mile at Rube Fields'. Rube was an old-time well driller and widower. Rube's specialty was chile and beans. Old Bum kept pretty well-fed by making his circuit.

Besides the food stations, he checked on the bars three times a day. The first inspection was around ten in the morning to see if any holdover party from the night before was still going on; then again about three in the afternoon when the pitch and poker games were on the way; and, of course, around nine or ten at night when the more serious drinking was beginning. He would stand up close to the bar and look sad, and somebody was bound to take pity and give him a refreshment.

Old Bum's obvious enjoyment of country music (his favorite singer was Eddy Arnold) would cause somebody else to buy him a drink, so he could relax and more fully enjoy this place of country culture. A couple of drinks and he was well on his way to becoming part of the musical entertainment.

He had a knack for hearing, smelling, or in some way sensing a really jam-up, bottle-throwing, fist-fighting party. Whiskey, female dogs, and fist-fights were the things that exicited him most. When a fight would break out, Old Bum would jump around, all alert, not missing a punch. But he never took sides.

The only time I remembered him showing any pity on a loser was when I made a feeble effort to save him from the fun and drinking that was making the both of us wobble and shake like a gravel separator. I told this big cowboy, that worked for the JL

Ranch, that I didn't want him or anyone else giving any more drinks to my hunting dog.

He turned away from the bar, looking at me as if I was that sneaky bronc that kicked him in the belly last week, and said quietly, "He's just a dawg."

Talk about foolish, I replied, "No, he ain't just a dawg. He is a first class coon hound, and you're going to ruin his smeller."

The cowboy grabbed my collar and the seat of my Levi's and hustled me outside faster than thought. That's as fast as it gets.

He said, just as he hit me in the nose, "You got it wrong, partner, It's your smeller, I'm gonna ruin."

He did. It always turned to the southwest after that. I went face down in the gutter of the sidewalk with his two hundred and more pounds on top of me flailing away from my kidneys to my ears with fists as hard as horseshoes. While the old boy had me down where the sidewalk joins the highway, trying to push my face into the gravel, I kept turning my head to the side to avoid permanent implants. Every time I turned, Old Bum would lick me with a long, wet tongue right across my eyes.

I gasped, "Why don't you get the s.o.b. on top of me by the throat, if you love me so much."

After a while, Levi came and picked me up and led me over to Ye Ole Master's Gallery and helped me wash the road tar and gravel from my face. He picked up one of the cedar bultos—Saint George, slayer of dragons, I think—and said he was going over to beat that cowboy's head into pudding with it. I said, "Naw, Levi, let it go. Killing a cowboy with a saint is not going to be good for our artistic image." He reluctantly saw the wisdom, and all soon became calm.

As time passed, Old Bum's personality changed along with his appearance. He was becoming jaded, stuck-up and more than half cranky. During this period, somebody shot Old Bum in the shoulder with a twenty-two rifle. An amateur horse doctor said to leave it alone and it would heal around the bullet. Which it did, but it gave him a kind of stiff-legged limp in his left front leg. It made him appear to walk in an even more stuck-up manner. By this time he had also acquired a big rip over one eye leaving a scar that added to his aristocratic appearance, looking more like a monocle than anything else. He also became very possessive about his territorial rights, as well. Not only did the sidewalks belong to him, but so did four blocks of Highway 87. Sometimes when he was crossing from one bar to the other, he would stop right in the middle of the highway and just stand there with his head up looking mighty important through his drink-blurred eyes. Many times we would hear tires screeching against the asphalt and know someone was trying to miss killing the current town drunk. He would not move, nor bat an eye, with a ten-ton truck bearing down on him at top speed. It was the greatest wonder in the world that Old Bum didn't get a lot of sober people killed.

Finally to my great relief, after I had made about a thousand sly hints, people began to worry about him and sort of by mutual consent we decided to cut him off the bottle for a while and try to straighten him out. Trying to be an inspiration to him, I quit drinking myself. Tom C. was thrilled when I said I was ready for another hunt now.

Old Bum had been sober for over a week when we decided it would do him good to take him coon hunting and get him interested again in what he was born and bred to do. We didn't have any trouble finding him, but we were about three hours too late. Some tourist had stopped for a drink on his way up to Colorado, and Old Bum had slipped in, looking kind of lost and pitiful. Before long he had beggared himself a load-on.

Tom C. had spent his long life hunting and handling hound dogs, but this presented a brand new problem.

I said, "We might throw him in the river. It could sober him up."

"It might work at that," Tom C. agreed.

Old Bum loaded into the back of the pickup with the other dogs without any trouble. He was at this happy stage now, but if we had waited another hour to rescue him from the saloon and demon drink, it would have been too bad. The big running dogs gave Old Bum some strange looks, wondering what in the world had happened to their faithful, helpful hunting partner.

When we unloaded, down on the Cimarron, it was dark and cloudy. My flashlight beam knocked a bright round hole in the night. We eased up beside Old Bum and pushed him off into the river with a big, wet splash. He crawled up out of there shaking the water from his hide and struck out for the brush without giving us a glance.

Suddenly we heard him bawl. And bawl again, then again. He had never bawled over once before. Tom C. and I looked at each other. The running dogs were already racing after Old Bum ready for the easy kill.

"What in the world do you think he's got treed?" I asked.

"Well, I sure don't know, but it's bound to be something different. I ain't never heard him bawl twice before."

"Yeah," I said. "I guess he finally had the 'one too many' drinks we all talk about but never believe."

We headed out as fast as we could. The other dogs—always silent hunters before—were barking and growling in sounds of dismay and puzzlement. All of a sudden the light beam found them. A bull! Old Bum had treed a big, white-faced bull. The bull lowered his head and charged Old Bum at full speed. The dog sort of stumbled out of the way, still making that loud bawling noise. The bull whirled, pawed the ground, snorted and charged again. He didn't miss Old Bum three inches. The other hounds had become so excited they had forgotten their training and were running in circles around the uneven contest like amateur cheerleaders when the baton is dropped.

"A hell of a big coon!" Tom C. yelled.

"Yeah," I answered. "We've got to do something quick, Tom, or that bull's going to kill Old Bum."

The bull charged. We scattered and ran for the pickup. I tried to lead him away from the much slower Tom C. I was successful. He hooked me under one leg with a horn and tossed me like a wet dishrag up on the hood of the pickup. While at the apex of this unwanted fight, I threw the flashlight at a clump of bunch grass. The bull took in after the light until he decided he was in the wrong pasture. We were saved. I rolled over on the ground, my breath knocked loose, wondering if I was dead. I knew I was alive when I heard the bull tearing up brush heading for the hills.

Then Tom C. shined the lifesaving flashlight in my face and asked, "You all right?"

I sat up. I moved. I felt of my legs and all. I couldn't feel any rips in my skin and everything seemed to be in its rightful place. Before I could determine an answer, Old Bum was in my lap licking my face like it was smeared with wild honey. You can say, or think, whatever you want about this animal that had created all the fun and excitement, but he and that slobbering tongue of his always came to the aid of the down and out.

I stumbled to my feet saying, "I'm the luckiest man alive."

"I reckon we all are," Tom C. said with profound truth.

We just breathed in the moonlight a while, not talking. There was a little numbness in my leg where the horn had hooked under and it was beginning to swell a little. I was thanking God and all his kinfolks that that was the extent of the damage. I could have been standing there with my entrails or my privates in my hands. It was at least an hour before we gathered the dogs up and headed for town.

On the drive back home that night, my mentor told me something special. He lifted the wrinkled little tan hat from his head and ran a large, perpetually chapped hand through his thin gray hair, as he tried to push his false teeth solid with his tongue so he could speak clearly, he said, "You know something, Mark? To be conceived is dangerous to life, but being born is even more so."

Later—after my semi-retirement in Raton—I would remember what he said, because now all these medical scientists were telling us that just about everything, including ice cream, eggs, beef and even dreaming, would kill us. The old man's wisdom became even more special by the day. Like I said before, that's what mentors are for, but I didn't understand all he meant back then.

The next day when the boys asked how we did on our hunt last night, we said, "Not much good. Too dark." Old Bum didn't show the least sign of shame.

A few weeks later, Levi and I were working at the gallery while my sore body loosened up. Old Bum had not had a drink since the night of the coon hunt. His eyes looked a lot better. All evening, though, we noticed how restless he was. Ever so often he would get up and walk to the door. He didn't scratch to get out, so we didn't pay much attention. Then he started whining.

Levi said, "I believe he needs to hunt a post."

I let him out. I didn't know we would never see him again and it would be decades before I would know all that happened.

Tom C. and I had finished putting some new rigging on the pickup with two compartments in the bed. We had rope pulleys attached to sliding gates on the bottom half of the backend. Each pulley was clamped by opposite windows on the truck cab. When we spotted a coyote, we could jerk the back gate open with the rope and let out one team of dogs at a time. This way we would always have a fresh team ready. We figured we could double our production of coyote ears for the ranchers' bounty. We could hardly wait to try it out. For some unexplained reason, I was determined to take Old Bum along. Tom C. thought I was crazy. Just the same I had the urge for his company; but we couldn't find him anywhere and nobody in town would admit to having seen him. Later, of course, the story would leak out. It always does in these little one and two bar towns.

It was one of those days that the poets talk about happening just once in a lifetime. Everything changed forever that day for me. Everything.

I felt a little vacancy for Old Bum as we drove by Weatherly Dam on out to Pete Jones' outfit for our first testing of the fancy-rigged coyote truck. Pete's ranch rolled downhill north to Carrummpah Canyon and creek. We drove on down about a half mile this side of the canyon's rim, knowing from many years of past hunts that most flushed coyotes would head straight towards their protective wildness.

The dogs moved about restlessly in the back, knowing we were hunting, but not yet used to the new setup. In spite of my prior emptiness, because of the missing flop-eared hound, my heart was jump-starting as I stared across the yucca-dotted grassland. I was gripping the steering wheel so hard my hands were almost numb. I could smell coyotes. I couldn't see them yet, but the scent-notifiers in my brain already were stirring little squirts of adrenalin all through my body.

The wind was whipping the gramma grass in golden rhythms. The electricity that generates somewhere in the brain and the heart was sparking fiery impulses through the flesh of my entire being. Old Tom C. was leaning stiffly forward with both of his huge knobby hands gripping the dashboard with desperate force. They looked as strong and hard as the thousands of rocks they had shaped into beauty and usefulness. His eternally weakening, blue-grey eyes seemed to project tiny rays of light ahead trying to call back the sight of his younger days. I nearly always spotted our prey first, but when the ancient hunter's blood started pulsing and pumping, Tom C. never quit trying. In these few moments out of eternity, it seemed that we were separated from the usual progression of earth, moon, sun and stars. It was as if our limited chunk of this hard wind-agitated land had been removed to another time and galaxy for our own special events of life and death to occur.

I spotted the mother coyote's ears. They were shaped wider, different from the sword-like blades of the large yucca clump she watched us through. I drove on silently, trying to keep all the tearing turmoil in my body from exuding out so the dogs would not pick up the silent message and start raising hell too soon.

Tom C. had already felt it, but our blood communication was so perfect the only sign he showed was the rising of his chest trying to keep his lungs in place. That's the way it is with long time hunting partners.

The coyote had four pups, three-quarter-grown, lying low in the tall grass, but I spotted their outlines because their bodies created a motionless little void in the ocean of wind-dancing stems. She was sure we were going to drive on by and miss her, I knew. We were very close to that point you can never return to or from. That immeasurable portion of space where everything will happen.

I kept my foot easing up and down delicately on the accelerator, trying to keep the mother coyote from noticing any untoward movement. I wanted to get exactly between her and the canyon, hoping we could catch her and maybe one of the pups before she could head for the canyon's safety.

Just a few more yards now. The world was a blur of red. There was no breath. The wind had no air for that moment. Then it all exploded at the same precise instant.

I hit the brakes. The mother coyote knew we had spotted them. She whirled, racing east, followed by her scattering pups who looked back at us in a quick hesitation as they tried to follow their mother's lead and at the same time satisfy their curiosity of our movement. It was a fatal half-second of hesitation. Tom C. jerked the cage rope and one team of the hounds leapt upon the ground. I jerked the other rope and now two teams were stretching full out. Their long legs were just graceful, ground-swallowing blurs.

Our timing had been exact as a dagger tip. The first team downed a pup—one by the neck, the other at the brisket. The wind had whipped the battle-dust away by the time Old Pug and Brownie had caught the mother. Just as hundreds of times before, Brownie raced right up parallel, reaching his mighty jaws out clamping down on the neck of the coyote. They rolled completely over twice before Brownie would stand up still crushing the neck. Before the coyote had a chance to rise, Pug was there to secure the prone position and demise of the coyote by crushing the ribs right into the heart and lungs.

Tom C. and I were so caught up in this moment of intense action and sudden death, and the unspoken success of our first hunt with double teams, that we forgot all about the pickup.

I raced afoot across the rolling world towards the kill, driven on by things so old, so deeply rooted, that I would have dived off a

81

twenty-foot bluff without hesitation to be there at the moment of the ultimate. The kill!

Tom C. stumbled along behind, his old heart unable to supply enough air to fuel his movements any faster. Then it happened. My eyes, trained so long to seek out the tiniest form and movement, flashed uncontrollably to the three pups racing for safety over the crest of a hill perhaps an eighth of a mile distant. Two of them disappeared, and thereby lived as their many millions of years of genes instructed them. But one stopped. The universe stopped. Then, as always, it exploded again. The pup, without any hesitation charged back down the hill, gathering speed in its descent, heading straight for the trio of Pug, Brownie and its dying mother. It charged with all the speed of its body, with all its ancient fury, into the two hounds whose combined weight and bulk was at least eight times that of the pup. His momentum knocked both dogs loose from the mother. It bounced over the dogs in a complete flip, rolling over several times, stumbling up stunned.

The hounds were also momentarily numbed. The pup's action had no place in their world of directed instincts. For an unmeasured space of time they hesitated. Then all their million of years of trained genes took control and they downed the addled pup and killed it almost instantly.

All this had happened before our eyes in just under two minutes. But somehow in that tiny space of clock time, a millennium had whizzed by.

I was still standing motionless except for the wind pushing me. The act of the coyote pup was beyond any scientific knowledge in existence. I knew I had witnessed a true sacrificial event against all human knowing. I was numbed and humbled beyond speech.

Old Tom C. finally stumbled up beside me, gasping. He, too, had extended his heart's strength as far as it could be crowded without its own final explosion. He hesitantly reached one of his great old hands out to my shoulder for support. It was trembling so that it shook my body, and myself, back to awareness of this present world. His painful breathing body struggled to keep him upright one more time, through one more hunt. Finally, he was composed enough to stand without using my body as a brace.

Then he said, quietly, "I never saw anything like that in my whole life. Have you, Mark?"

"No," I answered, and the single word was taken away by the wind.

We loaded our dogs and the three dead coyotes—when there should have been, by all the laws, only two. I drove back to town. Neither one of us talked for a spell. We just stared straight and far down the road. I knew I could never hunt coyotes again. Not ever. I didn't.

That same fateful day, Ortha had left for Texas with my sweet little Connie, but I've already told about that. My wife didn't leave me for chasing women. She left me for running coyotes.

As I sit now in this comfortable lawnchair thinking back, re-living those days decades ago, I realized how lucky I was to wind up here comfortable and being able to help my loved ones now and then. It had been luck when Tom C. had introduced me to Old Bum. It had been luck when I found out a couple of years back where, and how, that flop-eared wonder had disappeared from Hi Lo. Well, I'm using that world luck a lot, but I know it plays a big part in everybody's life one way or another, but then maybe it isn't just luck. Maybe it's more. I don't know for sure, but I have a feeling it is.

Anyway, back to how I finally got a tracer on Old Bum's disappearance. My son-in-law is sure enough enterprising in a lot of different ways. As a good example, he was the first one around here to make his cowboys use two-way radios as they rode in pickups or horseback across his hundred and eighty thousand acres of land. The working cowboys checked into headquarters with the ranch manager every scheduled hour of each working day. It wouldn't be long before they would be riding with two-way videos and a little compact camcorder as well. Then the ranch manager could just set there on his butt watching wall-sized pictures of the ranch and all its operations, giving orders while he had his ice tea or hot chocolate—according to the time of year.

The open range cowboy was gone before 1900, then the barb-wire cowboy gave way to the pickup cowboy, and now they were going to be forced to move over for the electronic, hi-tech cowboy. Oh, dear Jesus, help us all. So much for the individual-ism that used to mark the American cowboy.

When the government agency poisoned the coyotes, and trapped all the mountain lions, the deer became so thick they were dying of starvation; so, my go-getter of a son-in-law just set up a hunting outfit. Every fall, Jack and the entire family, and half of the cowboys, guided, fed and entertained, charging hunters from Oklahoma and Texas lots of money for each deer bagged. The smart son-of-a-gun was profiting from everything being forced out of balance. It would no doubt teeter and tilt again before long, but right now he was doing a hell of a balancing job with all the misunderstanding going on between the ranchers, the world-savers and most of the Washington D.C. ding-a-longs. One thing for sure, when the newest tehnological medium comes on the market, my son-in-law will be there the next day to haul it to the ranch. If politics has become the newest religion, appealing as far left as atheism, and as far right as the most rabid fundamentalist, then television is its Pope. Jack knew how the media used these infinitely advancing sciences for ever growing power. He would always make their knowledge his own.

Mind you, I'm not trying to shovel any of my personal notions off on anybody else. However, revealing the so-called "progressive attitude" of my son-in-law shows what a vast change has occurred in the world—and, in me—between the time I first met Old Bum and the four-odd decades later when I finally learned what happened to him.

A while back—before Jack got everything organized to perfection on the hunt, two-way radios and all—everyone used to gather here at the Raton house before going on down to the ranch. So now, as much as I enjoy keeping the stock tanks and house all in top shape, about all I contribute to the actual hunts are a few hound dog stories.

I don't hold it against anyone who hunts the right way, don't you know. It's just that I personally never can, nor ever will, hunt again, after that single portentous day when I knew for sure Old Bum was gone, my wife and child were gone, and I had witnessed that coyote pup sacrifice his life over there east of Hi Lo.

It was only two, or maybe three, years back that I was visiting with some of the excited men as they checked guns, bedrolls and all that stuff before the big event on the oak-brushed mesas and in the canyons of the ranch. I was telling this hunter, Jim from Oklahoma, about some of our adventures with Old Bum when he interrupted with a look on his face like he had just shook hands with God and been assured he had a first-class reservation to heaven waiting with his name on it.

"That dog wasn't a black and tan was he?" Jim asked.

"Yeah. Yeah he was," I said.

"That dog wasn't the one whose floppy ears looked like they'd been run through a CIA shredder, was he?" Jim asked and inched forward on his chair.

"That's his ears, all right," I agreed, getting pretty interested in the questions.

"That dog didn't limp from a bullet wound in his left front shoulder when he got tired, did he?"

Now that long-unused hunter's adrenaline and consequent electricity was stirring up in my body. "He did that exactly and for sure." I almost yelled.

Leaning forward with his eyes stretched open, Jim whispered, "And he only bawled once when he treed a coon, didn't he?"

"That's him. That's Old Bum!" I yelled this time loud enough to make the ears spin on a stone statue.

"Old Bum, huh? Well, we called him Old Traveler," Jim said.

"Same thing," I said.

Then we both began to babble, trying to talk at the same time like folks do on those TV talk shows, or when they've been drinking too much. Just the same, I found out Jim's grandfather, and some friends, had stopped in Hi Lo for a beer, and they wound up buying Old Bum from Rube Fields, the well driller. That old scoundrel.

It seems that somehow a party got going, and Rube had started feeling so good he thought everything in the world belonged to him, including Old Bum. After listening to Rube brag, for a total of two hours, about what a hunter the dog was, these guys from Oklahoma just bought him—for an undisclosed price—to shut him up. It didn't matter if it was fifty dollars or fifty million, they still got the bargain of their lives, when I think about what's truly valuable on this circle of fire, air, water, and rock called earth.

With his still-keen ears, Old Bum had heard this party in the making. Then someone invited him into the Wild Cat. They all broke down and let him join the party, but he fooled everybody—just like he always had. He would not take a single drink no matter how he was enticed. As impossible as it seems—even now—Old Bum had quit cold turkey when he found out that stuff made him pick fights with thousand-pound bulls.

Jim's grandfather had hauled Old Bum back to Laverne, Oklahoma, near the west edge of the panhandle, and gave him to Jim for an early Christmas present; then took them on a coon hunt.

"Traveler didn't stay home a lot," Jim continued, "but he always came back. Seemed like he knew when a man was getting a bad case of hunter's itch." The young man was smiling all the time he talked now. So was I. "I was afraid something would happen to him," Jim continued, "and tried to keep him penned up, but that didn't work at all. He wouldn't take a lick of water or a bite of food until I turned him out of the dog pen. I mean to tell you he would have starved himself plumb to death before he would give up his freedom. I just gave in and let him go his own way. Sometimes when he'd come home he'd be full of new scars from fighting and chasing the gals."

"Wonder how old he was when he died?" I asked.

"Oh, I don't know Mr. McClure, but we had him seven years. My dad said he was durn sure over a hundred years old in human time. You know, I rode the school bus to and from school, because in those days we lived four miles from Laverne on a farm. Whenever Old Traveler was home, he'd wait for me halfway across the front yard. That's as far as he would come to meet me. He'd wag his tail about one and a half times and give me a glancing lick on the leg. You had to know him to understand that this was as joyful a greeting as he was gonna give anyone."

"Yeah, I remember."

"Then one day he wasn't there. It was nothing unusual, but somehow I knew in my gut he was gone for good. I looked everywhere for him, but found nothing. I guess he just traveled on." Jim paused, and became quieter. Then he added, "One thing for sure though, I'll forget a lot of people before I do that old dog."

"Yeah, son, I savvy that clear as morning dew." I didn't want to talk about Old Bum the traveler any more right then myself.

Now I sit here enjoying recollecting.

Tom C. went back to his childhood home in Missouri to die and was buried by the side of his young wife. I still miss him very much. Knowel Denny, Pal England, Rube Fields and a lot of other sporting boys and girls are up on Graveyard Hill north of town.

I remember Levi Gomez telling me one day, "You know what, Mark? Original thinking and doing are deadly. I'm leaving this burg." He moved west over the Rocky Mountains to Taos and became a truly distinguished "Santero." His saints carved from cedar wood were blessed by the Pope and his work was collected by rich and famous people from far away places. He's gone, too.

And me, old Mark McClure? Well, I really wasn't much of an artist anyway, so right after Levi left Hi Lo, I quit painting, and started back laying rocks and doing odd job carpenter work. I kept seeing these people's houses all over whose poor walls were covered with bad paintings forced on them as gifts from friends. Seems suddenly half of America started doing these westerns and scenery paintings—as the locals called them. This world needed a lot of fixing, but one more bad painter sure wasn't going to help it.

I don't know hardly anyone at Hi Lo any more. One of the two saloons is gone and the other will surely follow. Now it would be impossible to get up a poker game in a month of Saturday nights. When Old Bum left, he took part of a spirited era with him. Hell, that wise old dog saw it coming and allowed himself to be sold so he could ride, instead of walk, out of a country soon to turn more boring with each hour. In these little towns, on far scattered ranches, people were now getting their secondhand thrills from the perversely soul-diminishing, possessive little box called TV; and being told every single second—on one channel or another—how to vote, how to love, how to die, how to everything.

There ain't even any more hillbilly music. It's called country, country western, rock-a-billy, country rock, country this and rock that. One thing though, there are still hundreds of thousands of acres of grasslands out there broken by lonely malpai and sandstone mesas. Maybe it's even lonelier between the far spread ranch houses than it was in my time.

There are more raccoons, antelopes and deer out there now, and, in spite of all the programs of poison, airplane hunters, and all that stuff, the coyotes are still howling when they damn well feel like it, and the Hi Lo wind blows their messages across a deaf world.

Boy howdy, and gobblin geese, this late spring sun feels good to my old ex-hunter's bones. It is also a grand and comforting feeling to know that dogs and coyotes are equally as important as kings, queens or cockroaches. Of course, it's probably not, but the sun seems like it is shining just special for me today. I keep looking down the graveled driveway for Old Bum to come limping in from some kind of chase bringing along his great zeal for life as the most precious of gifts. I don't worry about him because if he doesn't show up today, he will tomorrow, or in a day or so after that, for sure. Like the song says, "Long ago and far away..."

My Pardner

1

After twenty-odd years, the image of Boggs is just as clear as the day he came walking towards me with his head leading his body a few inches. His skinny legs were bowed like a bronc rider's, but he wore the bib overalls of a farmer and a dirty old brown hat that flopped all over. Both boots were run over in the same direction, so he leaned a little to the left all the time. His nose was big and flat, and his mouth so wide it turned the corners of his face.

As he moved closer, I could see that there was only one crystal in his thin-rimmed glasses. A funny thing though—he had one eye gone and the crystal was on that side, leaving a single blue eye beaming from the empty gold rim.

He swung the heavy canvas bag from his back to the ground and stuck out a hand saying, "Reckon you're my pardner Dan. Well, it's shore good to meet you. I'm Boggs."

"Howdy, Boggs," I said.

"Why hell's fire, boy, you're purty near a grown man. Your pa didn't tell me that. How old are you, boy?"

"Twelve goin' on thirteen."

"Hell's fire, I was punchin' cows with the top hands when I was your age. By the time I was fifteen I was out in Arizona mining gold."

Suddenly I felt real small. Course I didn't weigh but ninety some-odd pounds. But I'd felt pretty big a while ago when Papa had handed me the map and the three dollars and said, "It's up to you, son. I'm dependin' on you and Boggs gettin' those horses to Guyman, Oklahoma, by ten o'clock July nineteenth." He had gone on to explain that we'd be out on the trail nearly sixty days because every other day he wanted the horses to rest and feed so's they'd get in looking good and ready for the big sale. That was the key thing to remember: balance the moving and the stopping so the horses would pick up weight.

I looked over at the corral and counted five mules and sixteen starved, ragged-looking horses of every color. Well, Papa had more confidence than I did, but I couldn't help swelling up a little when he shook hands and said, "I ain't worried a peck." But then Papa had lots of guts. Here we were on the edge of Starvation, Texas, living in a shack that was held up by hope, on land that the drought had singled out to make an example of. Half farm, half grassland, and only half enough of either one.

At heart Papa was more of a trader than a land man. He'd traded for a hotel once in Starvation, but when the drought came a few years back, everybody left Starvation except the pensioners, the postmaster, and a few others too broke to go. Then he traded the hotel for a herd of goats, and the goats for some dried-up milk cows, and the cows for a truck, and the truck for a car. Somehow or other I liked the old Ford better than the hotel. Anyway, in between he kept something to eat on the table and Ma made it taste good.

Well, lately Papa had done some more figgering. The drought of the thirties had broken and people were putting a lot more virgin land into wheat and cotton. They'd need lots of horses to plow with. Most folks still hadn't gotten used to the idea it could be done cheaper and better with a tractor. The way Papa looked at it was this: by July 19th all the wheat farmers would have their wheat in and by then the grass would be made for the stock to finish fattening on. People would feel like buying horses for the next plowing. That is if it rained in early July. The spring rains had already been good. So, Papa had started trading for livestock, and finally come up with this ugly bunch. He and Uncle Jock would head up north about a week before we were due and get the sale handbills out and so on. Uncle Jock was an auctioneer, so it wouldn't take much money to pull it off. If everything worked right, we might be able to pay the mortgage, buy some seed, and put in a crop of our own the next spring.

Boggs said, "Let's git goin', boy."

My horse was already saddled and I'd thrown the rotten old pack on the gentlest of the mules. I had two blankets, a jacket, a stakerope and a sack of dried apricots tied on it. That was all. Papa had said we could find *plenty* to eat along the way. He hadn't explained exactly how.

Boggs hung his canvas bag on the pack and fished out an old bridle. Then it dawned on me he didn't have a saddle.

I said, "Ain't you got a saddle?"

He grunted, caught a bay out of the bunch, grabbed his mane and swung up bareback. We turned them out and started across the mesquite-, shinnery-, and grass-covered pastures to Oklahoma.

Boggs rode out front and led the string. They weren't hard to lead, because they were in such poor shape, but riding the drag was something else. They just wanted to stop and eat all the time. I was riding back and forth every minute yelling them on. All the same I felt great again—sorta like a man must feel on his first ocean voyage.

Along about noon I could feel my belly complaining. We rode up to a windmill and watered the horses. After my horse had finished I got down and took a drink. Then I reached in the pack and got a double handful of apricots, and handed some to Boggs. He spit out his chew of tobacco, wiped his mouth, and threw in the whole batch and went to chewing.

When he finished, he said, "Boy, get up on that horse. I want to show you something." It took me kind of by surprise but I crawled up. "Now look here," he said. "Look at your knees. See how they kind of bend when you put 'em in the stirrups. Now look here," he said, walking off. "See them pore old bowed legs of mine? Why you could run a grizzly through there without him even knowin' it. Now ain't that a disgrace?" he said.

"I don't see as it is," I said, having always felt bowed legs to be some sort of badge of honor.

"Well, by jingos!" he said. "You don't see, boy? You don't see? Do you realize that I'm a highly educated man—havin' traveled far and wide and knowin' all about the isns and ain'ts of the world? Young feller, I'll have you know that at one time I was made a bona fide preacher. Yessir, a man of the Lord dwellin' in his own house, spreadin' the true and shinin' light. But what happened?" And he jumped around in his runover boots waving his long arms in the air. "What happened?" he shouted, putting that sky-blue eye on me. "Here's what happened," he said as he squatted down and pulled off his boots and overalls and waded out into the dirt tank. "Look," he said, "look at them legs. By jingos and hell's fire, boy, how would you like to be baptized by a preacher with a pair of legs like that?"

I burst out laughing, even though I was half scared I'd made him mad.

"There you are," he shouted, running out of the water. "That's another thing that happened . . . peals, barrels, tubs full of laughter burstin' across the land. You see, Dan"—he suddenly lowered his voice and it was like dragging satin over satin—"a young boy like you with his bones still growin' and shapin' should never ride a saddle. Otherwise your legs will get bent like mine. A long trip like this will doom the young sapling. Let me have that saddle, son, and save you this terrible disgrace. Grow up straight and tall like Abe Lincoln. And besides"—he leaned at me with his hand in the air signaling for silence—"besides, when our duty is done I'll buy you the fanciest present this side of the pearly gate."

Well that was fancy enough for me. I just crawled down, unfastened the cinches and handed him my saddle. He threw it on his bay horse, then went over to the pack and took out a half-gallon crock jug.

"Cider," he said, tossing it over his arm and taking a long pull. "Ain't good for young'uns," he said, corking the jug. "Cures the earache. Always got an earache." He rubbed one ear and put the jug back inside the bag. Then he took out a long plug of tobacco and really bit him off a chew. "Let's git goin'," he said, and we struck out.

About five hours later the horses quit. There wasn't any way to keep them all moving at once. Well, I had an inkling why. My belly was just plain gone. It had lost confidence in ever being fed again and had just shriveled up to nothing.

Boggs rode back and said, "We'll pitch camp right over there." He pointed to a dry lake bed with a heavy growth of mesquite most of the way around its edges. Off to the northeast I could see a clump of trees sitting like a motionless prairie ship in a green grass sea. I knew there was a ranch house there with beans and bacon and good black coffee, but it would be late the next day before we'd, make it. Tonight we'd dine on apricots. Dried.

We unsaddled the horses. I took my rope and staked out one for a night horse. I wasn't worried about the others running off. They were too hungry. Besides, they would be easy to hem up in a fence corner about a quarter of a mile off.

I spread my blanket out and Boggs reached in his canvas bag. He had another pull of ear medicine. He fished around in the bag and came up with a coffeepot and a little dutch oven. Then he said, "Gather some wood, boy. I'll be back in a minute." He struck out in that rocking-chair walk of his, leaning to the west.

I started picking up dead mesquite limbs, watching every now and then to see what Boggs was doing. I could see him twisting some loose wire on the corner post. I didn't know what he was up to, but if a rancher caught him we'd sure be in trouble.

He came back carrying a six-foot strand of barbwire and said, "Come on, let's git goin'."

I followed. We walked out through the mesquite. All of a sudden he yelled, "After him! After him!"

I saw a cottontail rabbit shoot out between us. I took after him feeling like a damn fool. The fastest man on earth can't catch a rabbit. Well, that cottontail wasn't taking any chances on it. He ran and jumped in a hole. I stopped, breathing hard, but Boggs just ran on past me, right to the rabbit hole. He squatted down, took one end of the wire and spread the strands about two thirds of an inch apart. Then he bent about ten inches of the other end out at forty-five degrees. He put the forked end into the hole and started twisting the wire. To my surprise the wire went right on down, and even passed the spot where the hole turned back. Then I could see him feeling his way. His eye was bugged out in concentration. His face was red and sweating. Then he gave another couple of twists and said, "Got 'em, boy. Now the secret is, *not* to bring 'em up too fast or you'll pull the hide out and they're gone. If you bring 'em up too slow then they'll get a toehold and the same same thing will happen."

He backed up now and I could see the rabbit.

"Grab 'im!"

I did.

"By jingos, he's a fat one. A regular feast," he said, and he wasn't joking.

We built a nice fire and Boggs scraped the fat off the rabbit hide, then we cooked him in his own juice. I'm telling you that rabbit woke my stomach up and really put it back to work. We finished it off with a cup or two of black coffee and half a dozen apricots. The world was all of a sudden a mighty fine place.

I leaned back on my elbow and watched the flat rim of the prairie turn to bright orange. High above, some lace clouds got so red for a minute I thought they would just drop down and burn a man up. Then the cool violets and purples moved in and took over. Bullbats came and dived in the sky in great swift arcs, scooping the flying insects into their throats. The crickets hummed like a Fordson tractor, and away off the coyotes started their singing and talking howl.

Then Boggs said, "Boy, you ever been to Arizona?"

"No."

"Course you ain't. But you will. That's a great country, boy. That desert and all that gold just waitin' to be dug." He went on a little while and I looked at the sky full of stars and my eyes got heavy just trying to see past the first bunch. Then his voice came again, "I'll tell you all about Arizona one of these nights, boy, but right now my ass is too tired."

I could hear the horses grazing nearby, snorting now and then, slowly in contentment. The fire was a small red glow teasing the night goodbye. I slept.

2

"Let's git goin', boy."

I sat up in my blankets.

"Here." He handed me a cup of hot coffee, and kicked dirt over the fire.

It was just breaking day. I swallered the scalding stuff and tried to stand up. This took some doing. I was sore and stiff in every joint, but that wasn't what bothered the most; it was my hind end. The rawboned back of the saddle horse had rubbed my rump like grating cheese. I had to walk with my legs spread apart. It was not a good condition for horseback riding.

The sun got hotter. My setter got rawer. Every little bit I'd slide off and walk, but the insides of my legs were galled so bad I couldn't keep up with the slowest of our horse herd. There was nothing to do but get on and go.

By eleven o'clock I was hurting so bad, and the sun was so hot, I got somewhat ill-tempered. I was cussing Boggs, not altogether under my breath. "You old liar and conniver. You old nutwut. You old . . ." It eased my pain.

By two that afternoon we pulled up to the trees. There was a water tank about fifty yards long and a windmill pumping at each end. But the ranch house had long been unoccupied. It looked like now it was occasionally used as a temporary camp for cowboys. It was a disappointment. While not thinking about my sore bottom, and when not cussing Boggs, I thought about the beans and bacon, hot gravy and biscuits we'd have had at the rancher's table. I just got down and lay in the shade and listened to my belly growl.

After the horses watered we turned them all loose in a little horse trap where the grass was coming good.

"Reckon there's any rabbits around here?" I asked Boggs, chewing on an apricot.

"Might be," he said, looking in the tank.

"There ain't no rabbits taking a swim in that tank," I said.

"You're right, boy, but I'm tellin' you there's some catfish in there."

"Catfish?" I said, bolting up out of the shade.

"Yessirree Bob."

Then I settled back down. "Well, we ain't got no way to catch 'em. Guess we better get to lookin' for a rabbit."

"Now look here, boy, you're givin' in too easy. We're goin' to have an ample amount of rabbit before this trip is over anyway, so let's try doing a little thinkin'. It's all right to go through life just plain feelin', that's fine, but when your old gut is cryin' 'hungry' to your soul, it's time to think. You hear? Think!"

Well, we walked around the yard. If you could call his bow-legged and my wide-spraddled motions walking. We went into the ranch house: nothing but an empty table, cupboard and four chairs. Out in a shed, we found some tools, old and rusty, a can of axle grease, and a stack of empty feed sacks tied in a bundle.

Boggs said, "Look here, the great gods above done smiled down on us poor sinners. By jingos, boy, we're in for a treat." He gathered up the sacks and out we went.

After untying and splitting the sacks, he spread them out on the ground and began sewing them together in one big sheet. Then he tied some rocks along the bottom, put sticks on each end for handles and we had us a dandy good seine.

Boggs went back in the shed for a minute. "Here, boy," he said, handing me a can of axle grease.

"What's that for?"

"Rub it on your hind end."

I just stood there holding it in my hand.

"Well, go on," he said, "we ain't got much time."

I rubbed it on. It was sticky and left me a little embarrassed when I walked, but it did ease the pain.

"Pick you out a couple of them sacks to ride on tomorrow."

I did.

"Now, come on, boy. We're wastin' time."

Boggs told me to go to the deep end and start throwing rocks into the tank and yelling. He said this would booger the fish into the shallow water so we'd have a chance at them.

About middle ways down, we shucked our clothes and waded in. I sure was glad I had applied the axle grease in the right place. That water would have really finished chapping me. I pretty nearly choked to keep from laughing at Boggs' bowlegs until he got them under water. The seine was spread and he told me to keep the bottom just a little ahead of the top so the fish couldn't get underneath.

"Now, boy, move in steady to the corner and when I yell, come out with the bottom first and hold tight. Then give a big heave out on the bank."

We moved along.

"Haawwww!"

Up we heaved. Sure enough there were seven or eight nice cats, three perch and a goldfish. I didn't heave quite enough and two of mine fell back, but the next trip through we got another good catch and Boggs said, "Hell, that's all we can eat, so let's go swimming." He put the fish in a wet gunnysack and we took a cooling swim.

When we crawled out the sun felt good for a change. Just when I thought I was going to faint from hunger and the extra exercise, Boggs said, "Boy, get out there and get a bunch of mesquite wood."

I went after it. When I got back with the first load he had dug a hole about a foot deep and a yard long. He built a fire in this hole and I kept packing wood for it. After the fish were cleaned and wrapped in some pieces of brown paper sacks we'd found in the shed, he mixed up a batch of mud and rolled them in it. When all the wood had burned down to glowing coals, be buried the fish in them.

We waited and we waited.

"Don't you think they're done, Boggs?" I asked feeling the saliva run into my mouth.

"Not yet."

"Lord, I'm starving. Looks like to me those coals have done gone out."

"Not yet."

Finally, he took one out and broke it over a rock. The baked mud fell away and there it was, the juicy white meat of the catfish. Everything was soon gone but a pile of bones cleaned as slick as crochet needles.

All the next day we let the horses rest, water and eat. We did the same. Then on the move again. The wide green tablecloth of a prairie soon turned to shinnery bushes and sand where the sun was meaner and the earth drier. We ate rabbits and apricots until the apricots were gone, and that left just rabbit.

Then we could see the little clumps of trees increasing in the distance, and we knew we were finally on the edge of the farm country.

We checked our map. If we were lucky, we could make it to a Mr. Street's farm before night. He was supposed to be a friend of Papa's. Papa said Mr. Street was a pure farmer and wouldn't have any pasture grass for our horses, but he would have plenty of cane bundles to give us. It was here I was to buy two hundred pounds of oats out of the three dollars and start graining our herd.

As I followed the old white horse into Mr. Street's road I finally figured out why he was behind the others all the time—one ankle was twisted just enough to make him slower. He was a stayer though. I was getting to feel friendly toward him and wouldn't have liked any of the other horses back with me.

I went up to the front of Street's house, leaving Boggs out in the road with the horses where they grazed along the bar ditch. It was a neat, white house with a paling fence around it, and a few elm trees scattered about the place. I could see a big barn, several corrals and feed stacks. Down below the house was a shack for the Negro hired hands. Mr. Street was rich. I could sure tell that.

I tied my horse at the yard gate, went up to the door and knocked. It didn't feel as if anyone was home. I couldn't hear a sound. Then I knocked again and waited. Just as I raised my hand, the door opened.

"What'd you want?"

I looked up and up and sideways and all around. That door was full of woman. I felt like I was standing at the bottom of a mountain.

"Well, what'd you want?"

"Is Mr. Street in?"

"What'd you want?"

"My papa . . ."

"Your papa? What about your papa. Come on, boy, speak your piece."

"Well, uh, my papa is a friend of Mr. Street's."

"Who is your papa?"

"Ellis Thorpe."

"You know any Ellis Thorpe, Nate?" she said back over her shoulder.

"Yeah, used to," he said. "Ain't seen him in years."

I never saw such a woman—little bitty ankles with massive muscular legs above to hold up the rolls and rolls of blubber that ran right up under her ears and spread over her cheekbones so it made her eyes look little and mean. Sure enough they were.

"Well, what do you want?" she asked again.

"Papa said you might put us up and feed our horses for a day."

She went in and talked to Nate in low tones. Then she filled the door again.

"Nate says times have been hard what with overcoming the drought and all, but he says you can bunk down at the shack with the help and you can have all the bundles you want at a nickel apiece."

"I, uh . . .

She started to shut the door.

"Just a minute," I said, and pulled out the three dollars. "I guess we'll take two bundles apiece for the horses. How much'll that be?"

"How many head you got?"

"Sixteen horses and five mules."

"Forty-two bundles at five cents." She counted on her little short fingers "Two dollars and ten . . . er . . . twenty cents."

I handed her the three and she brought me eighty cents change. She slammed the door.

I felt sick. There went the grain money. I'd already started letting Papa down.

We took the horses to the corrals and started pitching them the bundles. Then Nate came out and counted them. He was a little man with a quick, jerking motion to everything he did. When he was satisfied we hadn't cheated him he said, "Tell your pa hello for me," and walked off.

Over on the other side of the corral stood four big, fat Percheron work horses. They made ours look like runts, and I began to wonder if Papa had a good idea or not.

It was almost night when we walked down to the workers' shack. Three little Negro kids grinned at us from the steps. Boggs spoke to them and a man came to the open door.

"Howdy. What can I do for ya?" he asked.

"Well, Mr. Street said we could bunk with you tonight."

"Sho, sho, come in," he said. "I'm Jake."

He introduced us to his wife, Telly. She was almost as big as Mrs. Street, but somehow in a different way. There was something warm about the place.

Boggs sent me to get our blankets and his cider jug off the pack saddle. Telly sat out three cups and they all had a drink.

"Sho fine," said Jake.

"Better'n fine, Telly said.

"Best cider in Texas," said Boggs, winking at them, and they all busted out laughing,

Then Telly fixed us a big stack of hot cakes, and set a pitcher of black, homemade molasses on the table. I smeared a big dip of churn butter between about six of them and let the molasses melt all over. I forked three strips of sowbelly onto my plate and really took me on a bait of home cooking. Then two tin cups of steaming coffee finished it off.

A while after the eating was over the three grownups went back to that cider jug.

Every little bit Boggs would say to Jake, "Ain't you got a bad earache, Jake?"

"Sho nuff, Mr. Boggs, I do. I ain't never knowed a ear to hurt like this'n."

Telly said, "Well, you ain't sufferin' a-tall. Both my ears done about to fall off."

The only earache I'd ever had hurt like seventy-five. I never could figger out how these people were getting such a kick out of pain. I spread my blankets on the floor and lay down to get away from all this grown-up foolishness.

It was soon dawn again, and it was Boggs again.

"Let's git goin', boy. Leave the eighty cents on the table for Jake."

I was too sleepy to argue.

We moved the horses out fast. Then I said, "Boggs, where's the pack mule? We forgot the pack mule."

"Shhhh," he said. "Shut up and come on."

In a little while, maybe three quarters of a mile from Street's, I saw the pack mule tied to a fence. On each side of the pack saddle hung a hundredpound sack of oats.

"Where'd you get 'em?" I asked bristling up.

"From Street."

"That's stealin'!"

"No, it ain't, son. I've done him a real favor."

"How's that?" I said smartly.

"Why, boy, you ain't thinkin' again. This way him and your pa will remain friends."

I studied on it all day, but I was a full-grown man before I figured it out.

"Well, anyway that's too much for that mule to carry," I said.

"That shows how little you've been around the world, boy. That mule is plumb *underloaded*. When I was mining out in Arizona we packed four hundred pounds of ore out of the mountains. *Mountains*, you hear. This mule is at least a hundred pounds underloaded."

"Oh," I said, and we moved out with me staring that old white horse square in the rump.

3

Afer a while we stopped at a little grassy spot along the road and poured out some oats. Those old horses were really surprised.

"You know something, boy?" Boggs said, filtering a handful of dirt. "This here's sand land. Watermelon land. They come on early in this soil. Fact, just about this time of June."

He raised his head kind of sniffing the air as if he could smell them. Then he got up and ambled off through a corn patch that was up just past knee-high. I sat and watched the horses eat the oats thinking what a damn fool Boggs was for figuring he could just walk off across a strange country and come up with a watermelon. I'd stolen watermelons myself, and I knew better than that.

The ponies finished their oats and started picking around at the grass and weeds in the lane. I began to get uneasy. Maybe somebody had picked Boggs up for trespassing. Then I heard singing. I listened hard. It was coming through the corn. I heard loud and clear, "When the saints . . . Oh, when the saints go marching off. Oh, when the saints . . ." closer and closer till I could see the long stringy figure of Boggs, and the watermelon he had under each arm.

"Had a little trouble finding two ripe ones. Most of 'em's still green."

I didn't say a word.

He took out his long-bladed barlow and stuck her in a melon. It went *riiiiiip* as it split wide apart like a morning rose opening up. I knew it was a ripe one. He cut the heart out with his knife and handed it to me. I took it in both hands and buried my head plumb to my nose in it. Good. Wet. Sweet. Whooooee.

I ate every bit of that watermelon except the seeds and rind and my belly stuck out like I'd swallered a football. Boggs didn't waste much of his either. It was a mighty fine lunch.

When we stood up to mount our horses, I said, "Boggs, sure enough how'd you know them watermelons was over there?"

"Look right there in them weeds under the fence."

All I could see was a bunch of flies buzzing around. I walked over. Sure enough there was a half-ripe watermelon that somebody had busted open the day before.

"I just figgered nobody could carry one any further than that without seein' if it was ripe. Knew they had to be close by."

"Oh."

We got our horses and rode. We soon came to the main highway to Brownfield, Texas. According to Papa's map we'd be riding along this bar ditch for a long spell now. It was late afternoon and that watermelon belly had disappeared and the usual holler place was making itself known.

We looked around and finally found an old fallen-down homestead out in a cotton patch. It was vacant, and there was a lot of weeds and stuff growing around the barns and old corrals for the horses to feed on. But we still had to water them. The windmill was cut off and if we turned it on in the daylight somebody might see it and maybe have us arrested for trespassing. We had to wait for dark.

Boggs said, "Let's see if we can find a rabbit."

We'd already lowered the rabbit population of west Texas a whole lot but I was willing to thin it out some more. We rode along the fencerows, all around the old place, but there wasn't a cock-eyed rabbit to be found. About half a mile from the homestead we looked out over a weedcovered fence. There was a farmhouse with chickens, milk cows, chickens, some white ducks in a little pond, chickens and dogs.

"By jingos, boy, how'd you like to have some roasted chicken tonight?"

"Sure would, Boggs, but we ain't got any money."

"Money? Why only a sinner against mankind would pay money for a chicken."

"What do you mean?" I asked, feeling fingers made out of icicles grabbing my little skinny heart.

"I mean we'll procure them chickens. Now you know the lady of that house is overworked. She's probably got six kids to look after besides her old man. All them ducks to feed, and the churnin' to do after milkin' those cows. Now it's just too much to ask of her to take care of that many chickens and gather that many eggs, ain't it?"

I started to say it was stealing, but my belly set up those growling noises again and I felt my legs trembling from hunger weakness.

"What about the dogs?" I asked.

"No bother a-tall. I'll take care of the dogs while you steal the chickens."

"Me?"

"You."

"Now listen. . ."

"Now you listen close and I'm going to tell you how to get the job done. Why hell's fire, boy, you're just the right size for such an operation."

I wondered how in the world it could make any difference to a chicken whether I weighed ninety pounds or two hundred.

"Now about them dogs. I'm goin' to go off to the right of the house and howl like a coyote. The dogs will come out barkin' and raisin' cain at me. It'll throw everybody's attention in my direction. Get it?"

I swallered.

"Now the minute you hear me holler and the dogs start barkin' get to that henhouse. Here's the secret of chicken stealin': first, a chicken sleeps pretty sound. About the only thing that will wake 'em is one of their own taking on. *That* you have to avoid. Be as quiet as you can gettin' into the henhouse. When you're used to the dark so you can see a chicken, grab her right by the throat and clamp down hard so's she can't make any noise. Then just stick her head under her wing. A chicken's so dumb it won't make a sound. Now as soon as this is done carry her outside and do 'er round and around in the air," he said, and made a circular motion with his arms held out. "Like this. She'll be so dizzy, it'll take 'er ten minutes to stand up again and that much longer to get her head out from under her wing. You can steal a whole hen-housefull in twenty minutes."

"Do we want 'em all?"

"Hell's fire no, boy. Just one apiece."

Darkness came and the lights went on in the farmhouse. Every once in a while the dogs would bark. I think they heard us.

Boggs said, "Let's git goin'."

He circled off to the right of the house and I eased along to the left behind the henhouse. When the dogs started barking, I stopped. They quit for a minute and I heard that coyote Boggs hollering his head off. I dashed up to the henhouse with my breath coming in quick gasps and cold prickles just breaking out all over. I was scared but at the same time thrilled. I slipped around to the door and fumbled for the latch. The noise pierced the night like a runaway wagon. It was too late to back out now. Besides, I was too durned hungry.

I heard the chickens stir and talk a little as I went in. I stood still just a minute. My heart thumped louder than the chickens. I could make out a dark mass over on the roost. I moved as quietly as I could with my hands outstretched. The dogs were really raising the dickens over on the other side of the house. I wondered if maybe they had Boggs down chewing on him.

Then my hand touched a chicken neck. I squeezed tight and holding her with one hand I stuck her head under her wing with the other. Outside I went. Whirl that chicken I did. I plunked her down and she just sat there like Boggs had said. This gave me confidence. In a half a minute I had another one outside on the ground all dizzy and still. Then I relatched the door. That Boggs had started me thinking tonight. I grabbed up a chicken under each arm, and sailed out of there.

Boggs got back about twenty minutes after I did.

"What took you so long?" I asked, feeling kind of important.

This seemed to rock him back for a minute, then he said, "A funny thing, boy. Just as I raised my head to let out that coyote yell, a sure-enough live one beat me to it. I just hung around a few extra minutes to see what'd happen."

The cooking took place.

The eating took place.

The sleeping with a full belly took place.

And I dreamed.

4

We went through Brownfield before sunup, right into the heart of cotton country. It stood up straight and green everywhere. In a few more weeks the hard, round boles would form. Then in the fall they would burst open into the white white of ripe cotton. The fields would fill with bent-over pickers dragging long canvas bags behind them and their hands snaking cotton from the vine to the sack. Wagons by the hundreds would pull it to the gins, and the gins would hum day and night for a brief spell, cleaning and baling the cotton for shipping and sale all over the world. Now, it was still, and hot, and green.

The people in the autos traveling parallel to us all waved. I guessed it had been a long time since they had seen a remuda of horses on the move. All the horses, except the old gray, were beginning to pick up flesh. just the same, I couldn't help worrying some. In the first place, if that thieving Boggs got us in jail, our time schedule would be thrown off, and one half day late would be just the same as a month. I couldn't figger Boggs out. One minute he'd be preaching and the next he was stealing. Sometimes his speech was like a school professor's, and then like an uneducated dunce. On the other hand, I would have starved nearly to death without his help. We were hungry most of the time anyway. Besides worrying about letting Papa down, all I could think about was getting enough in my belly to last a whole day.

We moved on through Meadow, Texas, and then out to the edge of Ropesville. We had a two-day hold up here if we wanted it. There was a patch of heavy grass by the road where a sink hole had held back some extra moisture from the spring rains. We decided to take a chance on the horses grazing alone on the road while we did a little exploring. This was risky because if someone took a notion to impound our horses, we were done. It'd cost five dollars a head to get them out. That would be impossible to raise in time to make the sale, but Boggs had said, "Our luck's holdin', son. You can't beat luck—even with thinkin'. The odds are that no one'll think but what the owner is keepin' his eye right on 'em. You got to be willin' to take chances. The way to survive this world is knowin' when to duck. That time generally comes when a man has made a mistake while takin' a chance. Now you take my whole durn family. Ma, for instance. She died having me cause she didn't reckon she needed a doctor. Now my brother got killed robbin' a bank. He walked in when two plainclothesmen were making a deposit. He should have watched *everybody* instead of just the guard. That sister of mine jumped in the Rio Grande to save a drowning boy. The boy caught hold of a limb and swam out—she sank. Pa didn't do so bad. I don't reckon you can hold it against a man for gettin' choked on a piece of bear meat. By jingos, boy, you can't hold that against a man, especially since he killed that bear with his own hands swingin' an axe."

"No," I said, "you cain't."

"You're right, boy."

We cut across a pasture looking for a place to hide the horses for a couple of days. The nearest house was about a half mile away, and we had to get out of its sight.

"Looky there!"

"What?" I said.

"A rat's den!"

It was a whopper—three feet high and six or eight feet in width and length—made up of broken mesquite limbs, thorns, bear-grass leaves and cowchips, with numerous holes woven in and out.

"Rats!" he screamed into the air, throwing his long arms up as if seeking the help of the Almighty. "Rats! Rats! Rats! Oh gracious and powerful Lord give me the strength to wage battle against these vilest of creatures. Pass on to me a small portion of your power so that I may stand strong and brave through the conflict about to come upon us. Lend me some of your skill and eternal magic while I slay the carnal beasts. Guide and protect this innocent young man as he follows forth the bugle's glorious call."

I was getting boogered and looked all around to see what might be fixing to tear us in pieces when he jumped from his horse and handed me the reins.

"Here, boy, this is your duty. Hold the mounts that we may yet escape to wage war another day."

He raced to the large pile of trash and put a match to it. A lazy rope of smoke rose, then burst into flames. Boggs had secured a long, heavy mesquite limb and he had it drawn back in a violent gesture.

"Ah, you four-legged offspring of the devil, I have turned your own fire and brimstone against you. Seek ye now the world of the righteous."

Well, they started seeking it. Rats were fleeing the burning nest in every direction. Boggs was screaming and striking with fury. Dead rats soon covered the ground.

"There, pestilence!" he shouted as he bashed one to a pulp. "Die, evil creature of the deep. Return to your ancestor's wicked bones. Bring the black death into the world will you? Destroyer of man, his food, of his life. Die, rats, die!"

When he could find nothing else to strike at he turned to me breathing heavily, still waving the stick.

"Rats have killed more people than all the wars combined. Did you know that, boy?"

I shook my head "no," trying to quiet the nervous horses.

"Well, they have. They are man's one mortal enemy. They live off man's labor, off his love for other things. They can't survive without man. It's a battle to the great and final death. People shouldn't fight people, they should fight rats. Here, give me my horse."

He dropped his stick on the dying fire and mounted.

"We better get out of here," I said. "That smoke will draw some attention."

"Just the opposite, if it's gone unnoticed till now we'll be safe in pasturing our horses here. Let's git goin'."

I was in such shape after the last few minutes of action that I just rode obediently along and helped gather our horses. It was almost night and that same old weakness of all day without food was upon me. It never seemed to bother Boggs, or at least it didn't show. He rammed a plug of tobacco in his mouth and chewed on it awhile. He seemed to be studying hard.

Turning to me all of a sudden, he spoke. "Boy, I'm takin' you out for a steak dinner."

"We ain't got any money."

"That's right, boy."

"Well?"

"Don't ask so many questions. Would you like a steak dinner? It's too late to catch a rabbit."

"Yeees," I said meekly.

Ropesville, Texas, had two tin cotton gins standing huge and sightless like blind elephants. The cotton lint from the ginning last fall still hung in dirty brown wads from the phone and light wires and in the weeds and grass around the town. It was a small place, maybe a thousand or twelve hundred people in and around the town. But it was a big town to me this night.

We tied our horses in a vacant lot off the main street. I was scared plumb silly. I had no idea how Boggs was going to get us a steak dinner without stealing it. And I just couldn't figger any way to steal it without a gun.

We marched right around to the first restaurant we came to, stepped in and got us a table.

A woman came over smiling like she meant it and said, "Good evening."

"Evenin', ma'am," said Boggs.

"A menu?"

"It's not necessary. My pardner and I desire one of your finest chicken-fried steaks."

There wasn't any use ordering any other kind of steak in the backwoods of west Texas in those days. They all served the one kind.

"Would you kindly put a little dab of mayonnaise on our salad? And pie? What kind of pie you want, boy?"

"Apple?"

"Apple for me, too, ma'am."

"Coffee?"

"Coffee for me and orange soda pop for the young un.

"All right." And she went away writing.

In a little bit there was a whole table load of stuff. I stuck my fork in the steak and sawed my knife back and forth. I put a great big bite into my mouth. Whoooeee! Was it ever good. Before I hardly got it swallowed I took a big bite of the mashed potatoes on the plate and another of salad. Then when I got my mouth so full I could hardly chew I'd wash it down with a big pull of orange pop. Great goin'! For a minute I quit worrying about how we'd pay for it.

The time came to face up to it. Boggs was finished and so was I. The lady came over and asked if there'd be anything else.

Boggs said, "Another soda pop, coffee and the check please."

Well, I drank on that soda and watched Boggs. I'd been scared plenty on this trip already, but he was really headed for the deep end now. Every once in a while he'd grab out in the air like he was crazy. Then I saw him put his hand over his coffee cup like he was dropping sugar in it. But the sugar was in a bowl.

All of a sudden he straightened up and said seriously, "Lady. Lady, come here."

The lady walked over smiling. Boggs pointed silently into his coffee cup. She looked. The smile crept off her face.

"I . . . I . . . I'll get you another cup."

"Lady," Boggs said under his breath, "I don't want any more coffee—that ecstasy has been denied me now and probably forever. One of the true pleasures of life will now raise only a ghastly memory to my mind at every thought. I feel I should bring suit against this cafe." Boggs rose now and so did his voice.

The other customers had stopped eating and the woman ran to a man behind the counter. He looked up, listened and walked over to our table.

"Please, please," he said. "Just quiet down and leave. I'll take care of the check."

Boggs stood a minute with his gleaming blue eye on the man. "Very well," he said standing there with his head thrown back, "but you haven't heard the last of this yet. Boy, let's git goin'."

As I walked around the table I leaned over just a minute and looked in the coffee cup. There were two big, fat flies in there and only one had drowned.

5

Boggs woke me up praying. I'd slept late for once; it was nearly noon. All we had to do this day was feed and water ourselves. It didn't sound like much but it could turn into quite a chore. Anyway I heard this voice taking on. I raised up in the blankets and tried to rub my eyes open.

"Lord, now listen to me close. We're goin' to be in the land of plows and man-planted things for over eighty miles now. It's goin' to get harder and harder to live off the land. We made a promise, me and Dan, to deliver these fine horses on time and in good shape. We got to keep that promise one way or the other, Lord. All I ask of you is to help me think. And listen, Lord, if I mess up, which being one of those so-called human bein's I'm liable to do, I want you to know I ain't blamin' it on you. Amen, Lord." Then looking over his shoulder at me he said, "Mornin', boy. It's a great day. Care for a cup of coffee?"

"Uh-huh." I looked at it to see if there were any flies in it.

Then he said, "When you finish, let's go to town."

I swallered. We went.

We were riding along the highway when he spotted a big piece of cardboard leaning against the fence. He got down and cut out a couple of eight-inch squares. Then with a stubby pencil he wrote on one: I'M DEAF AND DUMB. This one he hung around my neck. On the other he wrote: I'M BLIND. This one was his. I didn't need any explanations this time to figure out what we were fixing to pull.

He took off his glasses and put on a pair of dark ones he had in his canvas bag. He put his floppy old hat in the bib of his overalls, pulled his yellow hair down over his forehead, and rubbed some dust on his right eyelid. When he closed it, it looked sunken like his blind one.

We tied our horses in the same alley, and started down the street carrying a large tomato can he got from the bar ditch.

"Now, boy, if anybody tries to talk to you just shake your head and make Indian sign language."

"I don't know any Indian sign language."

"They ain't nobody goin' to know the difference. Here, boy, hold my hand. Cain't you see I'm blind?"

I took his hand and walked into the lobby of the town's only hotel. I held the tomato can out in front. An old lady put down the newspaper she was reading, reached in her purse and dropped fifteen cents in the can. She rubbed me on the head saying, "What a pity."

I blinked my eyes real hard for her.

The man at the desk gave me a dime and on our way out a man and his wife stopped and watched us. The man fetched a nickel out of his pocket but his wife glared and gouged him in the ribs with her elbow. He came up with fifty cents this time.

The drugstore was next. We left there with nearly two dollars. Boggs dragged his feet along, not only looking blind, but acting like it. The grocery store was good for eighty-five cents. Then a garage for forty. A little girl with a nickel in her hand kept following us around from place to place, running out in front once in a while to stare at us. All of a sudden she ran up and dropped the nickel in the can and gave me a kiss. If my knees had been trembling before they were going in circles now. Boy, I sure wished I had time to get to know a girl who would give up a bar of candy and a kiss for a dumb boy and a stranger at that.

We made it on down to a red brick building at the end of the street. There was a bank and a dry-goods store. The bank was closed but the dry-goods was worth ninety-five cents. By the time we'd covered the entire north side of the street we had fourteen dollars and sixty-three cents. We went into the alley to count it.

"By jingos, we're rich," I said. "I ain't *never* seen so much money."

Boggs smiled clean around his face. "I used to make this much in a day when I was panning gold in Arizona."

"How come you left?"

"The gold was gone."

"*All* gone?"

"Hell's fire, no, boy, not all of it, just all of it in this one spot. I'm goin' back some day. Besides, I decided to try to find my gold already coined in the form of buried treasure. So I left Arizona and went treasure huntin' up at Taos, New Mexico. You ever been up there, boy? Course you ain't. I keep forgettin' you ain't been out of west Texas. Well, Taos is one of them adobe towns full of Mexicans, Indians, gringos and nutty artists. A feller had sold me this treasure map and told me to look up a *bruja*. You know what that is? Course you don't. Well, it's sort of fortune-teller and witch combined."

He gave that tomato can full of money a good rattle and went on, "Well, I found her. Yessir, by jingos, I found her all right, and she said the map was true and the treasure was buried there, but a lady had built a house over it. So we went to this lady and she said she could tell by the map her bedroom was right smack over the treasure, and if we'd split we could tear up the floor and dig it up. Well, I tore up the floor. The *bruja* said, 'Dig there,' and I dug. I had dirt piled all over the place. Pretty soon the *bruja* said, 'The devils are at work and they have caused us to dig in the wrong place.' Well, sir, she grabbed a poker hanging by the fireplace and rammed it about three inches into the dry hard ground and said, 'There! There it is!' Hell's fire, I stood right there and pulled on that poker, trying to get it out of the way so I could dig. And the harder I pulled, the deeper in the ground it went. When it went out of sight I naturally couldn't hold on any longer. Now I ain't the kind of feller to scare easy, but I broke into a run and I ain't been back to that insane town since. Ain't hunted much treasure either."

"What about the floor?" I asked.

"I never did write to find out."

He would have gone on for two hours telling me yarns, but I suddenly remembered how hungry I was so I said, "Let's go over to the cafe' and buy us a big dinner. I'm starvin'."

"Now there you go, not thinkin' again. We just can't go in there like this. If they catch us faking this blind act, to jail we go.

Come here," he said, and ducked my head under a water faucet and washed me off. Then he pulled out a dirty comb and slicked my hair back. "Take off your shirt and turn it wrong side out. Now," he said, "you can go over to the store and get us some grub. Hell's fire, you look just like the mayor's son. Don't hardly know you myself."

He handed me a list and I walked over to the store. I got cheese and crackers, a loaf of bread and four cans of sardines for tonight. Then I got us another big bag of those dried apricots and a slab of cured bacon. We could take these along with us and they wouldn't spoil. Besides, we had lots of money left. I went all the way and bought Boggs two new plugs of tobacco and me a Hershey bar.

We rode out to our camp that night with Boggs singing "When the Saints Go Marching Off," just chewing and spitting between notes.

6

The next day we just loafed around and watched the horses graze. It was the first time we'd been sure of eating for over one day at a time.

Boggs said, "Boy, you ain't wrote a line to your mother since we've been gone."

"She don't expect me to."

"That's right, boy, she don't. But that ain't keepin' her from hopin'. Now is it?"

"I reckon not," I said, getting scared again.

Boggs tore a piece of brown sack up and handed it to me along with a stub of pencil.

"I ain't never wrote a letter home," I said.

"Might as well start now," he said. "It ain't much work and it'll do your ma a lot of good. It'll even make you feel better. You can drop it in the mail when we ride through Ropesville."

Well I was out of arguments with this man Boggs, so I wrote my first letter home.

Dear Ma,

I'm sending this letter just to you cause I expect Pa is gone off somewhere on a deal. He generally is. How is old Blue and her pups? I sure hope we can keep the brindle one. He's going to make a real keen rabbit dog. I can tell because the roof of his mouth is black. That there is a sure sign.

Did the old red hen hatch her chicks yet? I hope she saves all of them so we'll have fried chicken this August.

Me and Boggs are making it just fine. Ever time he talks it's about something different. He kind of puzzles me.

Is the cow giving lots of milk? I bet her calf is fat. Are you going to try and can everything in the garden like you did last year? Don't work too hard on the garden or the canning either.

This man Boggs is a funny feller. Sometimes I think he's the smartest man in the world and sometimes I think he's the dumbest. Are you getting any sewing done? Don't worry about patching my overalls for school. I just plain know we're going to get into Oklahoma with all these horses and make us rich. The horses are looking better.

Love,
Your son Dan

There was no question now, the horses were putting on good solid meat. I could tell by looking and I could tell by my sore hind end.

Ropesville had been good to us. We fed regular—regular for us, and the horses had done the same. Besides, we had some money in Boggs' pocket and some sowbelly and pork and beans in that pack. Things looked better all the time. That's what I was thinking about five miles out of Ropesville when I noticed the old gray horse throw his head back and stop. The horse in front of him had also stopped and was holding up one foot.

"Boggs," I yelled, "come here. Something's wrong with this bay horse."

Boggs reined back and we both dismounted. He picked up the forefoot and examined it. I could see it was a bad cut.

"He stepped on a piece of glass, looks like to me," Boggs said.

I walked back a few steps and sure enough there was a broken bottle.

"What do we do?" I asked, fearing what he'd tell me.

"There ain't a thing to do, boy. With the best of care this horse is going to be lame for a month or more. The frog is cut deep. We'll just have to leave him. I'll go up here to this farm and see what we can work out."

111

He was gone maybe ten minutes before he returned with a man. They both looked at the foot again.

Boggs said, "He's yours if you'll doctor him."

"I'll give it a try," the man said, looking worried.

"Now listen," Boggs said, "soon as you ease him up to the barn throw some diluted kerosene on it. It might burn him a little but it'll take a lot of soreness out quick. Then make a poultice out of wagon grease and churn butter. The grease will keep the flies from getting to it and the butter will take out the fever."

"I'll give it a try," the man said again.

I wanted to say that my hind end could still use some of that butter, but I felt too bad about the horse. Now we were falling short on delivering the goods and we had a long way to go yet.

"Let's git goin', boy."

I rode along now feeling blue and upset. After a while I thought I might as well try to cheer myself up so I started trying to guess what the fanciest present this side of the pearly gates would be. Maybe Boggs would get me a new hat. Or even better, a new pair of boots. I'd never bad a new pair of boots—just old brogan shoes. It was a disgrace. Why, I'd be thirteen my next birthday. And that birthday was tomorrow according to the calendar in the Ropesville café.

All of a sudden Boggs rode back. "Look there, boy, there's Lubbock."

"I was there once," I said, blowing up a mite. But I was really too little to remember. The tall buildings stuck up out of the plains so's you could see them for miles around. "Man that must be a big town."

"Naw, it ain't nothin', boy. You should see Denver, or San Francisco or Mexico City."

" You been all them places?"

"Hell's fire, yes, and a lot more besides."

I still wasn't going to give up on Lubbock. "How many people you reckon lives there?"

"Oh, maybe twenty-five thousand."

I whistled.

"See that building? The tallest one?"

"Yeah."

"Well, that's a hotel. I still got a suitcase in there. One time I was driftin' through here and went broke as a pullet bone. I figgered and figgered how to get out of that hotel without paying."

"You was thinkin'," I volunteered.

"By jingos, you're right, I sure was. Well I took a shirt and put all my other clothes, all my shaving equipment and some crooked dice I happened to have with me, in this shirt. Then I tied it up in a bundle so's it would look like a bundle of dirty laundry. As I stepped out into the hall, one end of that shirt came open and dice and razors and all sorts of stuff fell right out on the floor. A porter and two maids just stood there and stared while I gathered it all up and tied it back tight. That was where they let the hotel down. Before they could get to a service elevator to squeal on me, I was already down three flights of stairs and asking the desk man where the nearest laundry was. Well now, once ole Boggs got outside I was gone. That little Ford car just purred me right out of town."

"Ain't that cheatin', Boggs?"

"Why, Lord, no. What's the matter with you, boy? That's what you call tradin'. I left them a sure-enough good, empty two-dollar suitcase for a week's rent and feed."

The closer we got to Lubbock the more my eyes bugged. It sure was a whopper. We skirted around the west side of town next to the Texas Tech campus. Boggs pulled up.

"Here's a nice little pasture to hole up in. I've got to get on into town and do a little shoppin'. You'll have to stay here with the horses, boy. Part of my shoppin' you wouldn't understand anyway.

Well, just as we were unloading the pack mule, we heard a truck coming. There were two men in it and one of them said, "What the hell you think you're doin' turnin' a whole herd of horses in my pasture? I'm a notion to impound 'em."

Well, my little skinny heart was tearing my ribs out. That was all we needed to fail Papa completely.

"Why, my good sir," said Boggs, "let it be my pleasure to inform you kind gentlemen that we have merely paused a fleeting moment in our travels to relieve for an instant the burden of this fine pack mule. I am a preacher of the gospel. Myself and my young apprentice are heading north—our eventual destiny to be deepest Alaska. There we intend to bring about a revival of the Eskimos that will shake the northern world. Our horses we shall trade for reindeer upon our arrival. There are some things a reindeer can do that are beyond the capabilities of the American horse. Suffice it to say that with another moment's kind indulgence we shall wend our way over the great horizon to far distant shores."

One of the men just stared puzzled, the other one said, "Well, I don't know about that."

"And what, my beloved fellow inhabitant of this celestial globe, can I inform you of?"

"Jist git out, that's all, jist git out." They drove away mumbling under their breaths.

"Well, we shall skirt on around town, my boy. There's a canyon full of grass to the north of town. Yellow House Canyon by name. We shall perhaps find a better sanctuary there."

I was wishing he would shut up that silly talk and quit practicing on me. Hell's fire, I was ole Dan.

It took us another hour to skirt town and sure enough there was a nice little canyon with lots of grass. We pulled up and pitched camp.

Boggs said, "Now get a good rest. There's plenty of grub for a change. I'll see you afterwhile." He rode off on a black, leading the pack mule. I had me a nice meal. Worried awhile about losing the horse and finally fell to sleep.

It was getting somewhere close to ten o'clock the next morning when I heard a heck of a yell. I looked up and there came Boggs down the other side of the canyon. He kept yelling and singing. And that mule was having a hard time keeping up with him. There was stuff hanging all over the pack.

"Happy Birthday, Dear Dan'l, Happy Birthday to You." He was really singing it out and swaying in the saddle till I was certain he'd fall off. He jumped off his horse and shook me by the hand so hard I thought he was going to unsocket my arm. He lifted the jug from the pack and said, "Here's to you, Dan'l, and a happy birthday it's goin' to be. I got no more earaches, Dan'l. Whooooopppeee! Happy birthday to you!" He ran over to the pack and grabbed a secondhand No. 3 washtub. "Gather the wood, boy."

I knew better than to do anything else. But since the mesquite was thin here I had a devil of a time keeping him supplied.

He dumped a ten-pound sack of flour in the tub. A five-pound sack of sugar followed. Then he threw in a can of baking powder, and I don't know what else. He wouldn't let me stay to watch. Said it was going to be a surprise. I watched for a minute from off a ways. He ran down to a little muddy spring with a rusty bucket and got some water. Then he stirred it all up with a mesquite limb.

Well, when I got back with my next load of wood, the fire was blazing under this tub, and he said, "Here's your surprise, boy.

It's a chocolate cake. Now what boy on this earth ever had a chocolate birthday cake like that?"

I had to admit that I doubted if there had ever been such an event take place before. Well, I kept carrying the wood. And he threw it on the fire and stirred. After a while the cake started rising. He kept shushing me to walk quiet.

"Hawww, boy, watch your step, you'll make this cake drop."

Well, I figger that nine hundred buffaloes could have stampeded right past and that cake would not have dropped. In fact it rose up in the air about eighteen inches above the rim of that tub and just ran out in all directions. Boggs had taken his earache medicine and bedded down.

For a while I thought I needed his help when it looked as if the cake would fill the canyon, but when it finally cooled and I took a bite I was real glad he was asleep. I choked for thirty minutes. After I got finished choking, I hauled most of it off and fed it to the magpies. I didn't want to hurt his feelings. I should have had some consideration though for the magpies, but in those days I was just a growing boy.

7

We worked our way north of Lubbock through country spotted with cotton fields, sorghum—thick and heavy leafed—and here and there the brown stubble rectangle of an oat patch already cut and stored. On past Plainview we got into some grassland again, and that's where something happened.

We were moving out of a small draw through some cutbanks when the old gray horse pulled out of line reaching for a special clump of grass. I reined over to the edge of the sharply sloping cutbank and yelled "Haaarr" at him. Just as I did, my horse bolted to the side and I went down hard against the ground. I was sort of off balance laying on the slope of the cutbank. I reached up to get hold of a thick clump of grass to raise myself, when I heard the rattle. The snake lay coiled on a level patch. That's what had boogered my horse.

We looked each other right in the eye. I strained my left arm where I held the grass clump. The snake struck out right at my head, but he was short an inch or two. Now, I *was* in a fix. I could tell the grass roots would give way if I put any more weight on them. If they did, I'd slide right on top the snake.

His little black eyes looked at me over his darting tongue, and suddenly they seemed as big as light bulbs. And that forked tongue popping in and out was nothing to make me happier. I could feel the sweat all over, and a ringing in my head. For a minute I nearly fainted. Then for some reason I thought of Papa and how he was depending on me. If I panicked and got snake-bit the whole thing would be blown up. Everybody's hopes would be done in. But I didn't know what to do. If Boggs just knew, but of course, he couldn't. He couldn't see me. I'd just have to hold on as long as I could, and maybe the snake would go away. It wasn't advancing, but it wasn't backing up either. It just lay there coiled, its head in striking position, shaking those rattlers a hundred miles a minute. I kept feeling like I was sliding right into those fangs. I couldn't move, but just the same I pressured my belly into the dirt hoping to hold.

Then I heard the voice coming, easy and sure. "Don't move, Dan boy. Boy, you hear me, don't you? Well, keep still now. Just a little longer, boy."

I didn't even twitch an eyeball. I saw him crawl into my range of vision. He had a stick held out in front of him and he was kind of humming the same note over and over and twisting the end of the stick in a slow circle. Closer, closer, hum, hum. The stick circled near the snake's arched neck. Nothing but the tongue and the rattlers moved now. Then the head shot out and Boggs scooped the snake onto the end of the stick and hurled him way down to the bottom of the draw.

I was paralyzed another moment. Then I leaped up screaming, "Kill him! Kill him, Boggs!"

Boggs sat down beside me, and said, "Now, just calm down, boy. You're fine and the snake's fine."

"Ain't you goin' to kill him?"

"Lord a Mercy, no, I ain't goin' to kill him. Why, that poor old snake's in the same war we are."

"War?"

"Sure enough, boy, he's fightin' those pack rats harder'n we are."

I forgot all about the loss of the horse, and when I found out that Amarillo was a bigger town than Lubbock I even forgot about the rattlesnake for a while.

I did wish I could go uptown and see all the sights, but Boggs said that would come for me soon enough; besides, we had to stay on the march and take care of our horses now.

8

Between the towns of Amarillo and Dumas, Texas, runs the Canadian River. We drove our horses along the highway until we spotted the long, narrow cement bridge crossing it.

Boggs threw up his hand and stopped the horses. He rode back to talk to me.

"I don't believe we better try to take the horses across the bridge. We're goin' to block too much traffic. And besides we've got to have a permit, as well as the highway patrol to watch both ends. It's too late to get either now. We only have one choice, boy; that's bend the horses back to a gate and ride east down the river till we find a crossing."

This we proceeded to do.

I could see the storm sweeping toward us from the west and north. It must have been over a hundred miles in width. We had to cross the Canadian before it hit. This river is nothing to play with. It is full of quicksand and bogholes, and when it rains heavily to the west a front of water drops down out of New Mexico and west Texas with great force and speed.

Most of the time, though, the Canadian is a quiet river. Many places in its bed are as wide as the Mississippi, but during dry spells only a few small, red, muddy streams trickle through its bottom. Cottonwoods break the treeless plain along its banks, and cattle come to water from it for hundreds of miles up and down. Wild turkey, quail, coyotes, antelopes and many other kinds of wild game love the Canadian. But to man it is always treacherous.

For ten or twelve miles on each side are the sand hills—thousands upon thousands of tiny, rough, ever-changing hills of sand—spotted with sage, shinnery, mesquite and yucca. The yucca was green now, and the pods were soon to open their beautiful, milk-white blooms.

We rode hard, pushing the horses through and around over the sand. The old gray could only be moved so fast. So that I was constantly having to yell and crowd the poor thing. But he did his best for me.

There was no sun as the huge cloud blanket moved on towards us and shadowed the land. The lightning was cracking so fast now that the thunder was a continuous roar, never letting up but varying its sound like rolling waves. Even without the sun it was hot—sure enough hot. The horses were lathered white. And my almost healed-over hind end was sweated to the back of my mount. The Canadian looked fifty miles wide to me but was actually only about three-eighths where Boggs finally chose to cross.

I crowded the old gray down into the clay and sand of the bottom. There were tracks where a cowboy had crossed here. The forefront of the storm clouds was moving up over us now. I kept glancing up the river, fearing that wall of water I knew had to be moving upon us from the west. The wind was intense and the horses' manes and tails blew out almost parallel with the ground. We struck a few shallow bogholes where our mounts went through to the hard clay underneath.

Way up the river bottom I could see the rain reaching out into the banks and I knew a head of water was racing right along with the storm. I saw a small tornado drop down out of the sky for the ground and then return like a hand reaching out of a shawl to pick up something. Several writhing snakes of cloud broke loose in torment. I could hear the roar of the rain above the thunder now and its chorus—the river.

I almost panicked and left the old gray horse. More than anything I wanted to get out of the river bottom and up to the banks above the cottonwoods. Even if there was a tornado there. And there *was* one just beyond. I could see the inverted funnel ripping at the earth. Black. Mad.

Now we were on a huge sandbar that carried all the way to the bank. There was no turning back. There was no detour. Underneath the slight crust of its top was quicksand. Deep and deadly. The sand shook and quivered like Jello. The bank was nearer now.

The old gray stumbled and the extra force against the ground broke the crust. He went in up to his belly. I rode up beside him and pulled at his mane. My horse was sweated and excited and almost jumped out from under me. For a moment I thought the quicksand would get him. The more I pulled, the more the old gray fought, the deeper he sank. I was crying and begging the old horse now. And it wasn't just because it meant another loss to Papa, but it was a loss to me. He was my friend, this old horse.

And then I heard Boggs. He was riding back across the bar. "Git, boy! Look!"

I saw the terrible churning wall of dirty, red water racing at us. He slapped me hard up the side of my head and said, "Ride!"

I rode on by the old gray and I saw his nostrils almost tearing his face. His eyes rolled back as he sunk to his withers. In his eyes there was an acceptance along with the terror.

We rode up on the bank as the rain hit us harder and the edge of the tornado squalled on by. I got one glimpse of the old gray straining to throw his head above the river's blood, and then he was gone.

It rained for two hours and then the sun came out. We were very cold and very wet. It didn't even bother me. The river would be up all night. We gathered our horses and moved on across the sand hills. I didn't look back.

9

I had a numb feeling as we rode along. We were getting into the last stages of our drive, and we were two horses short. It was just plain awful to let Papa down. I was sick thinking about it.

We reached the edge of Dumas, Texas, on a Sunday. We knew that was the day, for the churches were filled with singing and shouting. I watched Boggs up ahead. I could almost see him quiver, he wanted to get in there and go to preaching so bad. He raised his hand and stopped the horses. They milled about and started grazing on somebody's lawn.

He rode back to me. "Boy," he said, "it's takin' all my will power to stay out of that church. I'd like to go in and talk that Reverend into ten minutes with Boggs. There's a lot of sinners in there and they think they're saved, but ten minutes later I'd have 'em lined up and headin' for a baptizin'."

It sounded like he wanted me to say "Go ahead." So I said, "I'll watch the horses, Boggs, if you want to go in."

"That's a magnanimous gesture, boy, but I reckon we've got to do somethin' about replenishin' this herd of horses. We just cain't let your papa down. And besides, your ma is staying back there worrying herself sick about the mortgages and all that. Now the way I got it figgered is this: these little west Texas towns all have baseball teams. Today is bound to be Sunday. There'll be a ball game around here somewhere."

Well, he was right. We found the baseball grounds out on the edge of town in a big opening. We turned our horses loose on the grass and rode over where a man was dragging the field down with a tractor and scraper.

119

"Yes, sir, there's going to be a ball game," he said, taking a chew of the tobacco Boggs offered him. "Spearman, Texas, will be here in just a little while. They've got a good team but we've got a better one."

"Is that so?" Boggs said. "What kind of pitchers you got?"

"One good 'un, and one bad 'un."

"Sounds about right."

I was sure puzzled about Boggs' interest in baseball, but since we were going to graze the horses awhile we might as well have a little fun watching a baseball game.

The crowd began to gather early. They came by truck, car, wagon and horseback. The teams began to warm up their pitchers and everybody was getting excited. Seems like this was an old rivalry.

I followed Boggs around till he found the manager of the Spearman team. This man also chewed tobacco, but when Boggs offered him a chew he reared back and looked out over his monstrous cornfed belly and said, "That ain't my brand."

Boggs said, "How much would it be worth to you to win this game?"

"Well in money, not much. I only got five dollars bet on it. But in personal satisfaction, my friend, it would be a strain for a millionaire to pay off."

I could tell the way he talked they were going to get along.

"Did you ever hear of Booger Boggs who played for the East Texas League?" Boggs asked.

"Sure. Everybody's heard of Booger Boggs. Why?"

"That's me."

"Ahhhh," and he started laughing and laughing. "You're jist a farmhand. Maybe a bronc rider, by the looks of them legs."

Boggs was quiet for once. He let the manager finish out his laugh then he said, "Can you catch a ball?"

Sure. I *am* the Spearman catcher."

"Well, go get your mitt and get me a glove and ball, my dear associate."

While the unbelieving fat man went after the equipment, Boggs started warming up his arm, swinging it around and around.

"Now, son," he said to me, and I knew he was really going to get serious because of the "son" bit, "this old arm ain't in much shape and it'll never be any good after today, but I just want you to know I'm going to give 'er all I got."

"You goin' to pitch?"

"You just wait and see."

He threw a few soft ones at the manager and then he let one fly that purty nearly tore the catcher's arm off. I knew he was going to get his chance. He went around and started a few conversations.

"You folks from Dumas don't know when you're beat. I'm goin' to sack you boys out today." As usual when they looked at Boggs everybody just laughed and laughed. That's what he wanted them to do.

One of the sporting boys said, "If you're goin' to pitch I'd like to lay a little money on the line. Now, if you ain't just a blowhard, why don't you put your money where your mouth is?"

"Well now, I ain't got no money, my dear compatriots, but I've got something better," and he swept a long arm at our horses grazing off a ways. "I'll bet any four of that fine bunch against any two of yours."

One man got so carried away he said, "I'll bet my good wagon and team with the grain and laying mash that's in it and a box of groceries to boot."

That was the only bet Boggs called. They shook hands and had plenty of witnesses.

The game started. I watched Boggs fan three Dumas men in a row. Then Spearman got a man on base. The next two up for our side struck out and the Dumas catcher threw our man out trying to steal second. Then Boggs fanned another and two grounded out to shortstop. And right on into the sixth inning scoreless. Then I could tell Boggs' arm was weakening. A Dumas batter swatted a long, high fly that should have been an easy out in left field. The fielder just plain dropped it. The man scored standing up.

Well, Boggs took off his glasses, pulled out his shirttail, and went to cleaning that lens. He took his time about it. Everybody was wondering what difference it could make if he cleaned a glass that fit over a blind eye. So did I.

The Dumas fans were naturally rawhiding him quite a bit and the Spearman team was getting uneasy. I watched him closely. He was up to something. I knew that no matter what Boggs was, I'd never see another anywhere like him. Come to think of it, that's a whole bunch to say about any man. He was at *least* three different men and maybe a dozen.

When he got through cleaning his glasses he slowly put them back on. Then he took off his hat and his glove and held the ball high in the air. And he shouted so that everybody quieted down.

"Lord, up there in the great universe, heed my call. Lord, I'm goin' to ask you to put some devil on this ball. Just let me use him a little. I want a devil curve and a devil drop and a devil fast ball, and I'll guarantee you that the end of the game will belong to you, Lord. What I want is victory. Now I know you heard me, Your Honor, Lord. So it's up to me. And if I don't win this game bring a bolt of lightning down upon my unworthy head and bum me to a cinder. Amen and thanks."

I looked up in the cloudless sky and thought that even the Lord would have to strain to get lightning out of that blue sky.

He pulled his hat back on tight, picked up the glove and ball, squinted out that glassless rim, took a big spit of tobacco, and let fly. No matter what happened to this game it was quite a sight to see him pitch. Those runover high-heeled boots, bib overalls, and that old floppy bat sure were different to say just a little.

That ball whistled in there so solid and fast the batter fell down hitting at it. Boggs didn't waste any time now, just wound up once and let fly. The ball broke in a curve and the batter nearly broke his neck fishing for it. The next one was a drop—breaking sharp and clean. The umpire yelled, "Strike!" and thumbed him out. A great roar went up from the Spearman rooters.

After that is was a walk-in. Boggs had shot his wad on those three pitches. He was faking his way now. The spirit of the home team was broken. The Spearman players started a seventh inning rally and the way they batted I could have been pitching for them and they would have won.

The game wound up nine to one and we had us a team of horses, one of which was a mare with a colt by her side, a wagon, a lot of feed, plus a big box of groceries.

Boggs was carrying his arm at his side. It was obvious he'd never pitch again, not even for fun.

10

When we headed out of Dumas the next day I was sure a happy kid. As soon as Boggs was up ahead where he couldn't see I just plain let loose and bawled. After that I felt fine.

Now our only problem, if we were lucky, was the time. We were a half day behind. At the same time we couldn't push the horses too hard or it would gaunt them and the buyers wouldn't pay enough. I drove our wagon with my saddle horse tied behind. We'd taken the pack off the mule and so we all moved out pretty good.

Wheat country sprung up all around now. The plowed fields contrasted to the rich green of the sorghum. There was a zillion miles of sky all around. The farms and ranches looked peaceful and prosperous, but every little bit I could see where the drought still showed its fangs—fences buried beneath drifting sand, fields barren and cut to clay beds. But this new idea of contour plowing, so the land wouldn't wash, was sure enough helping. I didn't like to remember the dust that came and choked and killed and desecrated the land like the earth had suddenly turned to brown sugar. I liked to think about the green growing things. But I was young and I know I'd never have appreciated the wet years without the dry ones.

Night and day became almost the same. We didn't sleep or stop much and when we pulled into Stratford, Texas, in the upper Panhandle, we were dead tired. We camped about four or five miles from town. It was so thinly populated we could see only one farmhouse close by.

We ate, turned the horses loose to graze, all except the one we left tied to the wagon eating grain, and went to sleep.

As usual Boggs was up before the sun. "Go drive the horses over close while I fix breakfast. That way we'll save a few minutes."

I saddled up and rode out through the mesquite. I was surprised the horses weren't nearby because the grass was good everywhere and they like to stay fairly close to the grain. I tracked them a ways and blamed if they hadn't walked right up to this farmhouse. There they all were in a corral. I felt a hurt come in my belly. A hurt of fear. Those horses durn sure hadn't penned themselves, and we were on somebody's private land. I didn't have long to wait, before I found out whose.

He sat on a big plow horse holding a shotgun, and spoke in a mean voice, "Thought you'd be around directly. Well now, boy, where's your pa?"

"At Guymon, Oklahoma."

"Guymon, huh? Well now, ain't that interestin'. What's he doin' off up there?"

"Waitin' for me," I said, swallering and feeling the tears start to burn. I choked them back.

"Who's helpin' you with these?" He motioned the shotgun at the horses. He was a short man but broad and big bellied. He wore a tiny hat that just barely sat on top of his head and his mouth hung loose around his fat face. I couldn't see his eyes, just holes in the fat where they were.

"I reckon you know you were trespassin'?"

"Yes, sir."

"Well, cain't you read?"

"Yes, sir."

"Well, then how come you didn't heed my 'posted' sign?"

"Didn't see it."

"Well"—he started nearly every sentence with well—"I'll tell you one thing, young man, you'll look the next time you come around my place. You got any money?"

"No, sir."

"Well, now ain't that too bad. I'm just going to have to ride into town, get the marshal, and we'll have to have a sale to justify the damage to my land. Five dollars a head, that's the law. If you cain't pay, I take the horses."

"But we ain't got anything else, no way to live . . ."

He interrupted, "Well, you should've been thinkin' about that when you rode on my place and started destroying my grass."

"Please."

"Too late for that, sonny."

I had to stall for time. I said, "Look, mister, I know you're goin' to take my horses, but first, before we go, could I have a drink of water?"

"Ain't no harm in that," he said. "But hurry it up. I ain't got all day."

I went over to the horse trough and drank just as long as I could. I thought I saw something moving out near our camp.

"Hurry it up, sonny. Get on your horse and let's go."

I walked up to my horse and picked his hind foot up. I glanced under his belly and I could see Boggs snaking along from one yucca clump to another, and it sure looked like he was *eating* yucca blooms. The damn fool was going to get himself shot sneaking up this way. My horse heard him and pitched his ears in that direction.

"Here, sonny, what you doin'? That horse ain't lame. Now get up on there before I give you a load of this here buckshot."

I got up on my horse just as Boggs raised up and broke into a wild, arm-waving, screaming run right for us. The froth was streaming out both sides of his mouth. His one eye gleam'ed right at us just like a wild man's.

That horse under that man with the shotgun just snorted and jumped right straight up in the air. When his hoofs hit the ground, there wasn't anybody on his back. That feller came down hard and the shotgun blew both barrels. The horses and mules broke out of the corral and ran back towards our camp snorting and blowing to beat seventy-five.

I finally got my horse calmed down and when I did I saw Boggs sitting on top of the feller who once had a shotgun. He reached over and tapped him up beside the head with a rock. The man slept. Boggs got some rope from the barn and tied him up.

"Go round up the horses," he said, as he stuffed the man's mouth full of shirttail.

I soon had them cornered, and tempting them with a little oats in a bucket, I made them follow me over to the wagon. By then Boggs was back. We caught our team, hooked them up and got to hell out of the country as fast as we could.

We rode on now through the day and into the night, and then again. We let the horses have twelve hours on grass and a big bait of grain just before we crossed the state line into the Oklahoma Panhandle. The last lap now.

This strip had once belonged to Texas until around 1850, when they sold it to the United States as part of the territory including New Mexico, Colorado, Wyoming and Kansas. It had been known as the "strip" and "no man's land" until 1890 when the strip was made a part of the Oklahoma Territory.

It was part of the great plains we'd just come across. These vast regions shot northward all the way through the Dakotas, Montana and into Canada. My hind end felt like we had covered our part of it.

Late in the afternoon of the next day we spotted Guymon. We unrolled the map out of the oilcloth wrapper and studied it.

"The sale is tomorrow at noon," Boggs said. "That means we need these horses in there at ten o'clock like your pappy said. The buyers like to look before the biddin' starts."

"We're late," I said, feeling cold and weak.

"No, sir, we turn up here about a mile and then it's nine more northeast from there. If we ride way in the night we can make it."

"But the horses'll be gaunted down."

"No, we'll feed them a good bait of grain and give them till eight in the morning to graze. If we find grass where we stop we'll be all right."

"If we don't?"

125

"Like I said, son, there's risks in everything. That's where the fun comes in life."

"Let's git goin'," I said.

We pushed the horses on. They didn't like it and kept trying to graze in the bar ditches of the country lanes. We made them move. I left it up to Boggs to lead, hoping hard he was going in the right direction. For a long time we could see the orange light of the farmhouses sprinkled off across the prairie and once in a while a car light moved in the night. Then all the lights were gone except those of the stars and a half moon. It was enough. I nearly went to sleep several times, but I'd wake up just before falling off the wagon. It seemed like we'd ridden a hundred years to me. My body was still working but my mind had long ago gone numb.

Then there was Boggs. "Take a nap, son. There's plenty of grass for the horses right along the road. I'll stay up and watch 'em."

I crawled in the wagon bed fully intending to sleep an hour or so and then relieve Boggs. It didn't work like that. The sun was up and warm when he woke me.

"Get up, boy, and let's have another look at the map."

I raised up fumbling sleepily for it.

"Here it is!" he cried. "Here it is! Look, two dry lake beds, then take the first turn to the left for one mile. Look—" He pointed up ahead and there were two dry lake beds. A tingling came over me. Boggs handed me a cup of coffee and said, "Just a minute and I'll fix you some bacon."

"Don't want any."

"Let's git goin', Dan boy," he said, grinning all over.

It took us a while to get hooked up and on the move. The colt bounced saucily beside the wagon. The horses were full and although they weren't fat, they had lots of good solid meat on them. They were strong, tough, and so was I. I was burned brown as a Comanche warrior and my hind end had turned to iron.

Papa saw us coming and headed down to meet us in his old Ford. He jumped out and said, "Howdy, fellers. Why look at Dan. Boy, you've growed a whole nickel's worth. Have any trouble, Boggs?"

"No, sir, not a bit."

I didn't tell Papa any different. Besides he had such faith in us he didn't count the horses. If he had he'd have found there was one extra.

The sale went over big for us. Uncle Jock really got his best chant going. When it was all over Papa had cleared over twenty dollars a head on the horses and nearly thirty on the mules. Ma could rest easy and go ahead and plan her garden for the next spring. Papa gave me three whole dollars to spend just any way I pleased.

Soon as we got home I went over to Starvation to drink a few orange soda pops and get my present from Boggs. He didn't show up the first day and he didn't show up for a whole week. I was getting a trifle worried but figured maybe he'd had to go plumb up to Lubbock to find me the new pair of boots. I'd made up my mind that's what he'd give me for using my saddle.

Well, on the eighth day I ran into him coming out of Johnson's Grocery, and said, "Hi, Boggs."

"Well, howdy yourself, Dan. How've you been?"

"Fine," I said. "Did you get me the present you promised?"

"Just a minute, boy," he said, and walked back in the store. He came out with a nickel pecan bar. I took it. He said again, "Just a minute, boy," and went back in the store.

I figured he must be getting my present wrapped up pretty for me, so I hunkered down on the porch and started eating my candy bar. It sure was thoughtful of Boggs to feed me this candy while I was waiting. I'd eaten about half of it before I noticed the funny taste. I took a close look. That candy bar was full of worms. Live ones.

I got up and went in the store. I walked on towards the back figuring Boggs was behind the meat counter. Then I saw this table that said: ALL CANDY ON THIS TABLE PRICED ONE CENT. There were lots of those wormy pecan bars among them.

He wasn't at the meat counter and I asked, "Mr. Johnson, do you know where Boggs went?"

He said, "No, I don't. He walked out the back door."

Well it finally glimmered in my little brain what had happened. I got mad. Real mad. I got me a board and I went all over town looking. I was going to knock his head clean off if I found him. It got dark. I waited at the back of the pool hall looking through a window for him. I waited till it closed. I waited till the whole town closed. I was in such a rage I nearly died.

I never found Boggs. In fact, I never saw him again. I don't know where he came from and I don't knew where he drifted to. But by jingos I sort of miss him. After all he *was* my pardner.

2
Essays

Sam Peckinpah: A Very Personal Remembrance

It's a hard thing to do, this remembering—but forgetting is impossible after twenty-five years of hell raising, dreaming, creating, fighting for things and against things, loving and dying, with Sam Peckinpah. Once he touched your life, even briefly, he became unforgettable; and so are many of his films.

When a magazine editor asked me if I'd like to do a story on Sam, I seriously hesitated. I knew that all the major news sources of the world would be out with stories and opinions on the recently deceased movie director. What would be left to say? We agreed that I should try it the only way possible—from a very personal, almost private, point of view.

It all started when Sam read my New Mexico novel *The Hi Lo Country* in publisher's galleys. He called my agent and said, without abbreviating, "I want to meet the s.o.b. who wrote that book."

The agent called me in Taos, all excited that this hot young director was interested in my novel. He was already adding up his percentage while we talked on the phone. Now, I had spent most of 1960 in Hollywood on assorted movie deals pertaining to my novel *The Rounders*. Hearing the promises of stars, directors, producers, agents, and Sunset Boulevard con men had created within me a great yearning for a return to Neanderthal times.

I hadn't yet seen Sam's *Ride the High Country*, so the trip was just another bothersome gamble to me when we met at a Polynesian restaurant on Ventura Boulevard. We had lunch, drinks, talk, and a bunch of fun. The friendship that began there lasted twenty-five years. We saw a lot of things through the same prism. He had a deep feeling and understanding for my novel and for the land and people of New Mexico. I was amazed and pleased.

The parties, the dreaming, and the labor had begun. Our agents were working out details for Sam to option *The Hi Lo*

Country. In the meantime, I went to a studio screening and saw that he'd already stolen part of it. It was a TV movie directed by Peckinpah called *The Losers*, starring Lee Marvin, Keenan Wynn, and Rosemary Clooney, a comedy about two cowboys who come to town in a battered pickup and get into trouble while trying to have fun. I didn't mind that the theme was almost identical to my book *The Rounders;* I was kinda proud, in fact. But in the last reel, I recognized an entire chapter lifted from *The Hi Lo Country*, down to almost exact dialogue. I was slightly disenchanted with Señor Peckinpah.

I eagerly anticipated our dinner meeting that night on Sunset. He beat me there. I walked up to the table and said, "Hey, you . . . I just saw *The Losers*, and you didn't even bother to change the dialogue."

He gave me that slow, impossible-to-understand, dark-eyed look he'd later become famous for, and said quietly, "Of course. It just shows you what good taste I have. What are you drinking?"

Well, just what could I say to that? Besides, it was a really fine film (eventually it ran five times in prime time).

He did option the book in a few days at a fair price, and from his own pocket. He bought it several more times through the years. We horse-traded it back and forth until there was such confusion we had to hire a gang of lawyers to straighten everything out. It's mine now, and I'm sure going to miss our trading. One thing about Sam, he never played cheap. When he optioned a book or just asked you to dinner, he laid down his own money even if he had to borrow it.

Sam was hired by MGM to direct *The Cincinnati Kid*, with Steve McQueen, Edward G. Robinson, Karl Malden, and Ann Margret. It was a brief but happy time, because our book was scheduled to follow. Then the crap started, and it would never end.

The shooting went well for four days. Then Sam insisted that a nude scene was needed in the story line. MGM refused, but Sam cajoled a crew and a star, and sneaked into the studio at night, and filmed it anyway. He was fired over a scene that would rate only a PG today. (Ann Margret was filmed nude *under* a fur coat). We both died a little bit together right there. MGM canceled out the deal with Sam on *Hi Lo* as well as *Kid*.

The big trouble for Sam was just around the corner of the barn. He was shooting *Major Dundee* in Mexico. It starred Charlton Heston and a group of Peckinpah's repertory actors. Total conflict of viewpoint developed about the script, the shooting—the whole concept of the picture. Even though the powerful Heston came to Sam's defense and offered to give up his entire salary if the director could remain in control of the editing, it was still taken away from him and cut up like mountain man jerky.

Sam called from Mexico and invited us, my wife, Pat, and our twin daughters, Charlotte and Sheryl, to spend the summer at his Malibu place, called "the birdhouse," saying he would join us as soon as the Mexican disaster was complete. I was working on a new book, so we just loaded up the typewriter and took off.

These were great times. We became acquainted with Sam's family . . . his sister, Fern Lea, brother-in-law, Walter Peter, and their three small daughters, Stephanie, Suzanne and Michelle. Sam was recently divorced from Marie, mother of his four children—three daughters Sharon, Kristin and Melissa and one-year-old son, Matthew. All our children, and those of visiting friends, were in the seven and younger age bracket. Fortunately they were all simpatico. Sam loved them—all of them. No matter what else is ever written or said I will always remember Sam's love and vast generosity to his children and his friends.

I was now involved in many Hollywood projects, and commuting from Taos, New Mexico, became very complicated, so we decided to move to Studio City for at least a school year. Sam had moved to a house on Broadbeach. The weekends at Sam's picked up where they left off. We all went to Sam's—he, after all, was the one with the ocean—where the joy of youth, of creativity and a machete-edged lust for life were centered.

Regulars who dropped by these gatherings included Lee Marvin (who once magnificently played, in the kitchen, a scenario of two fighting roosters by himself and made it believable), Robert Culp, Warren Oates, Vera Miles, Jim Hutton, the master composer Jerry Fielding and his wife, Camille, stuntmen, crew men and women, and Chalo Gonzales with his relatives from Mexico. It was a circus by the sea gone happily mad.

Many, many things worth telling happened at these pleasurable events, but there's only one little antic I want to detail. Matthew, Sam's son, had just learned to walk, and he also learned to remove any encumbering clothing almost as soon as it was put on him. I guess the sand was more comfortable to him when it wasn't trapped inside his training pants. He would play happily around the cooking area. I was standing watching Sam baste the meat with beer, when I felt a sudden dampness on my leg. I looked down to find Matthew calmly peeing on my pantleg. Sam noticed, too, and said just as calmly, "He's putting his mark on you. It's a sure sign he loves you." I guess it was, because every once in awhile he irrigated Sam, too. Matt is six feet tall now, and has been in the Marines, like his father was.

Sam then married the fine Mexican actress Begonia Palacias. They would divorce and remarry, then divorce again and remain close friends. She was with him when he died.

Along with all this fun, there would be days and weeks of dedicated hard work, along with the dealing that everyone in the picture business goes through every week of their lives. About this time I sold Sam a thirty-minute contemporary comedy script called *The Horse Traders*. He loved it. He had it sold to CBS. I was ecstatic. I would be able to write three or four books from the proceeds. Sam found out that the CBS man was in my agency and that they were taking 10 percent off the top. It's unfair, but was standard procedure then and to a degree is now. We were really needing money, but Sam killed the deal in a thirty second phone call.

Sam then decided he would try to get another book of mine called *My Pardner* made. He said if I could get it to Henry Fonda and he liked it, we could get it produced. I told him Hank had already read and loved it. We set a meeting for the three of us at a restaurant on Santa Monica Boulevard.

Hank and I arrived first and waited for Sam at the bar. Both Sam and I had great respect for Henry Fonda, but Fonda had never met Sam. Sam finally arrived, and let me tell you that I was feeling good. Here I had two friends who were among the world's best at their occupations. We all had respect for the project. How could we miss? Sam didn't kick over the table or throw glasses at anyone and shout expletives as he'd done on several occasions at and with me. No, he was a perfect gentleman, discussing the project in the softest, most delicate terms with Henry all during the delicious luncheon. Hank grunted and smiled, nodding his head as if in agreement. I, too, tried to be a gentleman, only ordering one unnecessary drink and staring at the terrible paintings on the wall as if they were Van Goghs while humming silently to myself and feeling sure these two worthy companions were securing our future forever. Sam smiled. Hank smiled. I smiled. The entire world was full of golden joy.

The luxurious glow was maintained all the way until after the parking attendant had delivered Sam's car to him. He shook hands with us, smiling again with what seemed to me great and deserved satisfaction, mumbling something about getting together and making the picture. As we watched his car move away, Hank put his hand on my shoulder and said, "Max, I never heard one damned word that man said."

My whole body dropped down in my Luchesse boots and spilled out on the concrete. I knew I'd never be able to get them together again, and I never did. You see, Sam had developed this habit of talking so low the listener had to strain, I mean *strain*, to hear at all much less analyze what he did decipher. The director had developed this trait gradually over the years in dealing with the higher echelons of Hollywood. It was a protective trait. A tape recorder couldn't decipher his part of the conversation and the opposition could never pin him down to an exact statement. A clever and advantageous ruse for sure, but he'd used it so long it had become natural and he would sometimes confuse and put off people like Henry Fonda that he really cared for. A lot of interviewers were fooled by this, thinking he was shy and withdrawn, until those times when the whispers would instantly, shockingly turn into the roar of the tiger. Then you could visualize the birds and beasts of the jungle taking wild, erratic, and usually fearful flight. He was—ask some masters—a consummate actor himself. So, out of a strong survival instinct, he became a complex and deadly opponent, even those times when he deliberately appeared weak.

After the fiasco of *Major Dundee* and *The Cincinnati Kid* debacle, Sam was effectively blackballed as a director. No one would touch him. For three years he had to survive by working on other writers' lousy scripts, sometimes under assumed names or without credit.

For a short while he had a writer's office at MGM. I met him there one Thursday afternoon. We were looking forward to a long weekend at Malibu with a few good friends. We made one of those fateful decisions that seem to come so naturally to writers and other fools: "Hey, let's have two for the road." "Yeah, sounds keen to me."

One young executive who looked about like Rock Hudson in his prime, accompanied by two lackeys, entered the open door to Sam's office. As I recall, they came in peace with an offering of friendship. At least on the surface, I knew these brave power brokers were some other kind of symbol to Sam when he *didn't* offer them a drink but *did* raise his glass to me in a toast to them. He spoke softly, graciously, of the many wondrous attributes of the leader of the trio. How he would without doubt someday be the head of this great studio and oversee majestic productions that would reek of much gold and have the qualities of a Tolstoy. I barely caught his last few words: "Max, let's castrate these cats." I jerked the desk drawer open, yellin' "We'll use the bedeezers on 'em." (That instrument, used by cowboys on bulls, has handles that force two clamps together, supposedly relieving the male in question of his virility without any blood or pain.) Of course, every studio desk should be required by law to contain one of these humanitarian tools. This drawer didn't!

The trio was running over one another, all hitting the door to the long hallway at once.

Sam shouted, "A knife! A knife will have to do. Here's a good sharp one!" As we all thundered down the hall, as they say in the old-time westerns, Sam screamed, "Bulldog the one on the right!"

I yelled back, "No! No! I'll flank the fat one on the left." Just as in the movies they just barely got the office door shut and locked as we hit it. We could hear them shuffling furniture inside. They were safe. So were we, I thought, if we could get out before security got us. We did; and I'm sure glad we didn't catch them. The rest of this story would certainly have been different.

The executive very shortly quit the studio business and married a world-famous actress of stage, screen, and television. I hope in some way that Sam and I contributed to the executive's long and successful marriage.

We had a lot of ridiculous laughs that weekend, but on Monday morning Sam Peckinpah found that the lock had been changed on his office door. His brass nameplate had also vanished.

Sam had taken it upon himself to financially support a couple of dozen people, but at this time (1965) he didn't have enough money. It was a long, dry struggle for him and, I would suppose, underneath a degrading one. He kept on fighting the world of film and having fun in between regardless.

Finally producer Dan Melnick gave him a break. He fought to let Sam direct Katherine Anne Porter's "Noon Wine." Sam cast Jason Robards, who wasn't any darling of the chosen few at that time either. They made a classic out of a classic. The public loved it, and the critics raved. Sacrificial Sam was back in town. Even so, it took a lot of effort for producer Phil Feldman and studio head Ken Hyman to get Peckinpah on *The Wild Bunch*. It also took a lot of guts. They had heard hundreds of stories about his difficult, explosive personality. They persevered anyway, and the movie worked magically. After the mighty struggle for its production a few scars were healed. Sam was a contradictory hero again, but this time around he became a worldwide celebrity.

He was even more contradictory to his few surviving friends. Sure he'd once tried to drown me and I'd broken his leg for it. He'd thrown a glass full of whiskey at me simply for speaking to a professional hooker friend of his while he had left the room momentarily. Even so, he once sent his secretary all the way from CBS in Burbank with cash when he heard I was broke. I was staying at actor Morgan Woodward's house in the Hollywood Hills when the hundred dollars arrived without my asking. You can forgive a person for many foibles when he makes gestures like that.

Sam admitted his plentiful sins and didn't apologize for them. I, too, have many sins. We were simply friends. No apologies needed.

We were bound together by *The Hi Lo Country*, both the book and the land, and we worked together on it for years, no matter which of us owned it at the time. There were several producers hired and a few scripts written on it. Sam did one from my treatment for Marvin Schwartz at 20th Century Fox. He always thought it was his best work and tried many times to buy the rights back from Marvin.

Sam made several, mostly anonymous, trips to New Mexico picking up atmosphere for his script and optimistically looking for locations. On one trip I introduced him from Clayton, New Mexico, to Taos, then to Silver City, as a pharmacist from Fresno. He got a huge kick out of it. He loved to play games.

Sam spent more money, love, labor, and time on *Hi Lo* than any other property, and yet he only got about twelve minutes of it on the screen in *The Losers*. I'm glad now he stole it. He told me several times while we roamed the state and he was becoming part of the land, "I'll make it if it's the last thing I ever do." I'm honored and humbled at his great failure.

When Peckinpah started *The Ballad of Cable Hogue*, he showed me the script and asked me to do a little acting job and possibly add a few rewrite suggestions. I was to ride shotgun to Slim Pickens on a stagecoach. I accepted. I'd long had an idea of doing a book about "behind the scenes" action on a Peckinpah picture. This was my chance—and I did the book.

The firing and hiring on *Major Dundee* had made minor history, and Sam's stripping all the clothes off one of the producers and leaving him standing nude in the Mexico City airport had only added to the titillation. On *The Wild Bunch* the situation had only increased. After *The Wild Bunch*, Sam now intended to make a picture, as he later described *Cable Hogue*, "about a man who found water where it wasn't, about love . . . it's also about God."

The gentle and lovely *The Ballad of Cable Hogue* was to bomb at the box office, but it would break all records for firing and hiring. The headquarters at the hotel in Echo Bay, Nevada, fifty-three miles out in the desert, created part of the problem. There was no town, no shopping center, no Seven-Eleven . . . just the hotel surrounded by a million miles of desert, rabbits, wild burros, rattlesnakes, and coyotes.

Sam intended to bring in a film of high quality on, or below, budget. The rain and the isolated location changed all that. After the first two days of shooting it rained for the next fifteen straight. That's right. Fifteen consecutive days of flooding in a sand-blasted desert, and we had no interiors to speak of. The entire cast and crew were jammed together in one place day and night. It created a madness in all concerned. Some took to drink and gambling, others wanted to fight and fornicate.

Most of the filming was in the Valley of Fire, fifteen miles from the hotel. One cold, breezy day when we were all standing freezing, waiting for the sun to peek between the clouds so we could finish a shot, Slim Pickens announced, "I sure wish I owned this here Valley of Fire." He paused and waited for the stunned reaction—which he got—then continued, "I'd sell the sucker and buy me a place in Oregon."

Another time when we were all walking down to the set, Slim stopped and said in his most country talk for all to hear, "If a bunch of hippies was to stumble on this scroungy cast and crew they'd turn around and run themselves to death across the desert."

It helped Sam; it helped us all. Sam loved Slim. Hardly anyone in the world knows, or would believe, that they were both mystics. The old cowboy actor had pneumonia twice on the picture, resulting in the loss of part of his lung. Sam treated him with complete concern, calling doctors himself, and assigning me the job of staying with Slim all the time he wasn't sleeping.

The tensions grew, the budget went way over, the shooting was, thanks to nature itself, spasmodic. Out of a crew of 80, Sam fired 36 and 14 quit.

The picture, though, was one of Sam's finest . . . a tender, tough look at a man and a woman and their blossoming love in a harsh, unforgiving setting. The authorities didn't believe in Sam or the picture, but now critics are beginning to admit it's a classic. Few have seen his great original cut of that film, or the originals of several of his other pictures. I wish they could.

After several divorces and strangled love affairs, Sam moved to a mobile home (he called it a trailer house) at Paradise Cove, Malibu. It was an unusual trailer. Many parties, deals, and other activities occurred here. A parade of actors, screen writers, journalists, musicians, cowboys, and bums from around the world made pilgrimages to this little building. It was full of his treasured books, paintings—even a couple of original Picassos.

I stayed there many times. One occasion I would like to forget, but can't, concerned Sam's health. He was dying, but absolutely refused medical help, or any other. He couldn't eat. His body shrank and his mind clouded. (He was supposed to be preparing to shoot *Bring Me the Head of Alfredo Garcia.*) Katy Haber, his extremely talented executive secretary, and I were having to lead and half carry him to the bathroom. Day after day he lay in bed throwing up, refusing whatever food Katy served him. He was living on vodka and little red, hard-kicking pills, either one enough to wipe out the average man in his condition. He became so weak, we had to totally carry him. Having spent many months as a combat infantryman in Europe in WWI, I could smell death. He was as grey and fragile as piñon smoke.

Katy said, "My god, Max, we gave him our word we'd not take him to the hospital, but what are we going to do? "

"We've got to find something he'll eat."

She left instantly for the supermarket and returned with the makings for a huge pot of chicken soup. She sat by his bed day and night spoon feeding him. Sometimes he'd take only a sip an hour, but she gradually got him walking. She cut the vodka, hid the pills, and put up with a madness that was even unnatural for him. Yes, Katy saved his life and put him going once more.

Bring Me the Head of Alfredo Garcia began with a fine original story by Frank Kawolski. Someone else wrote the screenplay, which Sam, during and after his illness, turned into an almost impossible, unshootable script. I told him it would be a disaster. He said, "Fix it." I worked continuously for two and a half days on it. When I handed it to him, he gave it an instant trip to the wastebasket without reading a line. The same as he'd done with Gordon Dawson's original.

This was the only time he ever had complete control of a film during his life. It came too late. He'd gotten up off the floor and fought back once too often. The years of consuming the liquid and other forms of pleasure in such vast amounts had already done the damage. He blew this picture simply because his body had his head in such a shape he didn't know the difference.

Warren Oates could verify this if he was still alive. Kris Kristofferson could, if he wanted to. We talked about it during the final editing while we were trying to get Sam into a tuxedo to go to the American Film Institute where they were honoring James Cagney. On his way to pick up his star, Isela Vega, he was involved in a fist fight at the hotel and got his picture in the newspaper. Then during the ceremony, in the middle of Jack Lemmon's tribute, he yelled for him to shut up and sit down.

After that, he straightened up the best his body would allow, but he was blackballed again and had to take whatever was offered if he was to remain in activity at all.

He was on Diet Pepsi when he brought *Convoy* to Albuquerque to film. I didn't go around him much for fear he'd decide we should have a drink and do something to important people. We did have him and his beloved brother, the judge, Denver Peckinpah, Katy Haber, and Frank Kawolski—his dialogue and second-unit director, confidant, and all-around hand—over to our house for dinner and a lot of quiet, enjoyable conversation.

There was hope for the picture, but it didn't work out. Sam invited Pat and me, together and separately, on the set many times, but out of respect for the picture's budget, we seldom went because when we did, he'd quit work, leaving his stars, equipment, and hundreds of paid extras standing around waiting.

On one occasion he called and said he just had to see me. He was in trouble. I went. When I arrived at the fairgrounds he left his friend James Coburn shooting second unit, and we headed for the trailer. He put his index finger to his lips for me to be quiet. He turned up the radio real loud. Through the sound I finally made out that he was trying to tell me the trailer was bugged and that the powers were plotting to do him in. He wanted me to find someone to scan everything for him and get him some equipment to return the favor. I agreed to try to help. (By the way, I was with him years before, when he did find a "bug" in his studio office.) Ali MacGraw finally got tired of waiting for her scene and came over to the trailer and visited right along with us. Over an hour, and probably a hundred thousand dollars, passed before he'd let me leave. The way the film turned out it didn't make any difference. I might just as well have accepted the job he'd begged me to take and gotten at least half rich. It wouldn't have made a visible dent in the final budget.

Journalists keep mentioning his having worked on *Gunsmoke* and *The Rifleman*. Well for the record, he also did *Pericles on 32nd Street*, *Noon Wine*, *The Losers*, and a series starring that marvelous all-around actor, Brian Keith, called *The Westerners*. All TV classics. Film is film—no matter what the form.

It is no less than miraculous that Sam accomplished what he did after *Ride the High Country*. He told me a couple of times of the hurt and anger he felt when he first screened the film for studio authorities. One of them actually went to sleep and was snoring like a hog.

What saved Sam and the picture was the European response. Critics there called the film a masterpiece and backed it up with a huge attendance record. The film was an absolute smash in France and it beat Fellini's *8½* for the Grand Prix at the 1963 Belgian Film Festival.

I think Sam's final cut—the one so few Americans have seen—of *The Wild Bunch* is one of the two or three best American films of any kind ever made and certainly the best and most influential western of any time. *The Wild Bunch* and *Ride the High Country* are both bound to appear in any list of the best fifteen western films; so is the under-rated *Junior Bonner* from Jeb Rosebrook's fine script. Add the mellow, loving *Ballad of Cable Hogue* and you have four Peckinpah films among the top twenty westerns made in history.

In other categories, *Cross of Iron*, co-authored by ex-Taoseño Jim Hamilton, will someday be recognized as the first-rate film it is. Sam made it in Yugoslavia on a broken shoestring; he had to make three tanks look like the whole armored Russian army. *Straw Dogs* fits into no category. Sam swore to me several times that he made it to show the latent violence in the mildest human so that maybe a few of us could recognize and control this ancient emotion. Pauline Kael of the *New Yorker* called it a fascist masterpiece.

These films are the true heritage he left us. We'll probably never know if he was desperately trying to show us that violence hurts, damages, and exists in us all unless we expurgate and acknowledge it. Some will say he just naturally loved violence for its own sake.

Pat Garrett and Billy the Kid had long moments of brilliance, but doesn't hold up as a whole. *The Getaway* was a piece of wild action and pure fun. If Eastwood had made it the film would be applauded artistically. The others, down to his last feature film *The Osterman Weekend* fail, but still give us flashes of the genius that was there when the body was full of adventurous fun and could still handle the uncaring abuse. It is an interesting postscript to Sam's career that he directed John Lennon's son Julian in his first two video tapes, including the big hit "Valotte." The London producer of these told me this work with Sam had been the greatest adventure of his life.

Charles Champlin, film critic for the *L.A. Times*, wrote, "What Peckinpah did make has a power that the years are not likely to erode. It is just that there should have been one more that was a march to glory and not an ambush in a box canyon. But there seldom is, and there wasn't for Sam."

Sam Peckinpah died swiftly, as he lived. They cremated him and threw his ashes in the Pacific off the coast at Malibu, where he'd created so many of his films and so much of his life. He'd once written a thousand dollars into his will for his friends to celebrate his demise. Later, he quit drinking, so he withdrew this codicil. My old writer friend Jim Hamilton said, laughing, "Well, Max, he stiffed us again."

Then his sister, Fern Lea Peter, called to say they had decided to have a memorial service for him at the Directors' Guild Theater, Sunday morning, January 13, 1985. There would be no public announcement; only the family and a few friends would be told.

It was blowing a proper blizzard when Pat and I caught the plane out of Albuquerque. Director Burt Kennedy met us at the hotel to take us to the Directors' Guild headquarters. The family all came, and so did droves of friends. There were stars, other directors, stuntmen, producers like Norman Powell, crewmen like Bobby Viciglia, cowboys like Alan Keller—it would take forty pages to name and describe their varied occupations. There was more hand shaking, hugging, and kissing than you'd find at a brush-arbor revival meeting. New Mexico was represented by Pat and me, actress Rita Rogers, and her son, Robbie, as well as Taoseño Dennis Hopper.

The tribute was, fittingly, forty minutes late starting. Sam's brother-in-law, Walter Peter, gave the eulogy with great dignity. Three hundred people sat in a trance. The famed director, Don Siegel, told of hiring Sam for his first film job as a go-fer. They were trying to get permission to make a film in Folsom Prison. The warden was interviewing all staff personnel. He didn't even look up from his desk as he dismissed the director, the producer, and everyone on down to the young man last in line, a twenty-five-year-old fresh-faced Peckinpah. When he heard Sam's name he rared back and looked up.

"Did you ever hear of Peckinpah Mountain?" he asked. Sam said, "Yes, sir. I hunted there often when I was a kid."

The warden went on, "Did you ever know any of the long line of Peckinpahs who were all judges from up around Fresno?"

Sam answered, "Yes, sir, they're my family."

The warden got up, walked around his desk and put a hand on Sam's shoulder, and said, "Now, if there is anything you need on this film, anything at all, you just come to me personally," and he led Sam past all the gaping high authorities.

James Coburn talked touchingly and with humor about his friend Sam. So did Ali MacGraw, L. Q. Jones, Brian Keith, Mariette Hartley, Jason Robards, Robert Culp, and Lee Marvin. An aura of ineluctable tenderness filled the building. The spirit of this man who had been so deeply loved and so violently disliked, sometimes both at the same time, was present with a final revelation of his powerful personality. He seemed to be directing his last show on this earth, and it was going well. There was crying and laughing. The tragicomedy that is the truth of life and the ultimate of art was taking place.

Richard Gillis sang "Butterfly Morning," his haunting, original song from *The Ballad of Cable Hogue*. People wept.

Walter Peter finished reading the last of the eulogy, written by Sam's writer nephew, David Peckinpah, his brother Denver's son.

I'm not going to talk about the films left behind; but I like to think about the one he's making now. He got a start date a couple weeks ago. A hell of a cast: Steve McQueen, Robert Ryan, Bill Holden, Warren Oates, Slim Pickens, and Strother Martin. Bruce Geller collaborated on the screenplay and Ferry Fielding is doing the score.

No studio, no producers, no schedule, no budget. The first assistant is pounding on the trailer door, . . . "We're ready on the set, Sam," he yelled.

Kris Kristofferson did a song he'd lovingly and especially written for Sam. Paul Seydor screened brief samplings of a few of Sam's films: *The Wild Bunch, Junior Bonner,* and *Ride the High Country.* It was quite a production . . . a fitting tribute in high style and beauty. It was over.

One evening in 1984 I had dinner with Sam at the Mikado, a Japanese restaurant in North Hollywood. At first we talked about Sam's other trailer house in Baja California, Mexico. He wanted to take me and his actor-producer friend, Walter Kelly, down there the following April.

I agreed to go if he wasn't working. About half way through, he raised his glass of water and said, "Nobody's ever gonna believe that you and I are sitting here together stone sober, nothing but water in any of these glasses and not even a cigarette in our pockets."

"No, Sam," I agreed, "they won't believe it."

Carol O'Connor, a lady friend he went to see later that night, said he'd talked about our odd dinner at least twenty times over his last few months.

I spent several hours with him on Thanksgiving day, 1984, and he called me a few days before he made his final trip to his beloved Mexico. He really felt good. We were planning another run together, this time on *My Pardner.* He said, "Call me right after the first of the year and we'll get it on." I called—no answer.

There is so much that could be told—more than ten biographers could handle. But what I want to remember most is being camped out in the high Sierras at Benton Hot Springs, California, near the Nevada border. I'm there with Sam, his adored brother, Denny, brother-in-law Walter Peter (his friend for thirty years), and two or three other allies. I'm going to remember the dancing clean air and the far blue-misted mountains, the smell of curling bacon, the taste of chile beans with a little wood ash in them, and the healing feel of the hot mineral water on my weary body. That's where we all belonged.

Sam had the soul of a Mexican general wrapped up in a gringo hide. He was as mean and crazy as a gut-shot javelina, and as tender as a windless dawn.

The credits are rolling. The theater is empty and dark.

I wish we could play it again, Sam.

King John

A Memoir From the Heart

How do you write about a colleague who was a close friend, a publisher of some of your favorite works, a legendary supporter directly or indirectly for over thirty years of all writers of the contemporary West when the world's publishing industry almost completely ignored, snubbed and, most often, insulted our words? How, indeed? In this very special case maybe one would just start writing and let the spirit of the heart be the guide.

Up until I was thirty-five years old I thought it was in the constitution of the United States that you had to attend, and often participate in a 4th of July rodeo. By the time I was thirty eight and about forty arena and other wrecks later, I finally caught on that this law was unwritten and could therefore be broken without heavy penalty. At this moment all over America, folks are celebrating this holiday by having outdoor cookouts, beer busts, large family gatherings and picnics, patriotic speeches by the tens of thousands, mighty musical concerts and sky altering displays of fireworks and yes, a million or so will attend local rodeos. That's right. I'm penning this on the 4th of July, 1995. A small gesture to a great man.

Unlike most of the lasting friendships of my life I did not meet John by accident but by invitation. Rose Woodell, a popular citizen of Taos and the third wife of writer Frank Waters, phoned and said somewhat thusly, "Max, Frank and I are having a small party Saturday about three p.m. John and Lynn Milton are visiting here from South Dakota and they're going to be here. I think you and Pat should meet them. Just last year John started a literary quarterly—*The South Dakota Review*. Frank is really high on it."

I was never much for organized parties, but my wife Pat and I decided to go. It was one of the very few wise decisions of my life. It was the summer of '64.

The Waters's home is near Arroyo Seco, a tiny village north of Taos in the foothills of the sacred Taos mountain and joining the Taos Pueblo reservation land. What a glorious and fortuitous place to meet. I only remember Frank and Rose, John and Lynn, and Pat and myself being there even though there were about twenty other guests. I know now that was the way it was meant to be.

During this first meeting I told John about my contemporary novel *The Rounders* being turned down eleven times before a reluctant signing by MacMillan Co. Instead of sympathizing with me he said it was a miracle that a book of the New West had been accepted at all. I knew in that instant we had a mutual understanding of the massive struggles ahead to get the writing of the Contemporary West recognized. Of course, we all talked of many wise and foolish things that afternoon as people in the world over do when their blood is blessed by good wine, the mind has been stimulated by needed and heeded conversation, and one has a new friend of warmth and dedication.

As I saw the light of the mighty orb of all life casting its last watermelon rays on the mother mountain, John and I sauntered a piece down the lane seeking a proper place to view in silent wonder and respect this eminence that dominates Taos Valley and the souls of men and women who have opened to it no matter where they are on the rest of the globe. Without words I knew that John had bonded with the sacred mountain as Frank and I had already done. However, an everlasting working friendship between us had been welded as well.

I do believe that moment was critical in his love of Taos and the Southwest just as some other special moment, I shall never know about, forevermore gave him to his beloved South Dakota and his quarterly of much quality.

At this time, Frank Waters only had *The Man Who Killed The Deer* in print. John Milton, out of a genuine faith in Waters' work, began a constant mention of Frank's books that no doubt helped greatly in the resurrection of his worlds that continued until their deaths only a few weeks apart of this year 1995.

Reversing. Waters encouraged John to finish his most ambitious work *The Novel of the American West,* University of Nebraska Press. I will point out in later paragraphs how our meeting that day at Waters' home and our subsequent absorbing of the symphony of Taos Mountain led to his publishing some of my best original work and keeping my work alive although on a much smaller scale than Waters. There are countless others who reaped his sometimes overly precise, but in the end, generous benefit to their own words. Without question this 1964 meeting was fateful and fruitful.

I had been through a four-year period after the publication of *The Rounders*, 1960, *The Hi Lo Country*, 1961, and the *One-Eyed Sky* trilogy, 1963, with so many highs and lows that all middle ground had simply vanished. However, the high desert winds were becoming more favorable about the time we met John.

I had finished a new novel, *The Mountain of Gold*, and the money through subsidiary rights of *The Rounders* had paid off the $86,000 in debts accrued during a briefly rich—and altogether adventurous—mining career. *The Rounders* was scheduled for filming with Henry Fonda and Glenn Ford in 1965, and *The Mountain of Gold* for publication the same year. Things were sailing in the paths of eagles—at least, lowflying ones. I had done several more short stories and novellas—a couple were for *The South Dakota Review* that have since been reprinted several times. We had five stories under option in Hollywood and five screenplays were being written. We were not rich, but were doing far better than ever before.

From 1964 through 1968, John Milton and television station KUSD (a PBS affiliate) brought to the University of South Dakota at Vermilion several writers to do six one-hour interview shows on film. Writers selected were: Frederick Manfred (Minnesota—John's birth state), Frank Waters (New Mexico), Michael Straight (from the east who had written about the west), Max Evans (New Mexico), Vardis Fisher (Idaho), William Eastlake, Arlene Zekowski and Stanley Berne (New Mexico). Three more writers who had not been able to make the trip for various reasons were audio taped: Walter Van Tilburg Clark (Nevada), Harvey Fergusson (New Mexico and California), and Wallace Stegner (California). One, A. B. Guthrie (Montana), was evasive. Milton and KUSD future plans included Paul Horgan, Ed Abbey, Jack Shaefer, Forrester Black, Larry McMurtry, Milton Lott, Henry Allen and Oakley Hall. This was an enormously ambitious and important project for a small school. At that time I didn't fly in planes, so Pat and I caught trains—several trains—to Omaha, then took a bus to Vermillion. It wasn't the easiest way to get there, but it sure was fun. We returned the same way except John and Lynn drove us to Omaha.

We started filming the next day. Unbeknownst to me Frederick Manfred had arrived in the control room, and when the filming was over the gentle giant charged down the stairs and roared his approval of some part I do not recall, "Every movie producer in the world should be sent a copy of that," he said.

Pat and I visited with Fred for several hours, met many of the faculty members at several special gatherings and parties and had a really great time. The filming finished on a Friday. The next morning we were having breakfast with John, Lynn and their daughter Nanci at their home, and I started talking about a book I was finishing on Sam Peckinpah and the madness that occurred during the filming of *The Ballad of Cable Hogue* with Jason Robards, Stella Stevens and Slim Pickens.

John said, "Max, why don't we publish it here at Dakota Press?" And I said, "Well, Okay." So it was. That's how simple the deal was done. We didn't even have to shake hands. Pat typed it up, John did an introduction, and Lynn did a fine modernistic jacket to sort of complete a family affair of friends. (All you publishers take note and heed). The title is: *Sam Peckinpah—Master of Violence*, and the book is now a collector's item and has been quoted from widely by critics and others. It was also published in book form and in magazines in Japan, Britain, and Italy.

The series of filmed interviews were shown around the country on PBS stations including KNME in Albuquerque, but there was a terrible hitch about to throw a kink in John's work of love and importance. This particular type of film was rapidly deteriorating and funding failed to come in order to supplant with permanent film. They also had to curtail recording the other writers scheduled. A mighty low blow to John and history. John, in desperation, made a typical cowboy move. He made do with what he had. He saved the audio for posterity and published a popular book *Three West* involving conversations with Vardis Fisher, Max Evans and Michael Straight. He also talked Lady Dorothy Brett, famed artist and intimate friend of such notables as D. H. and Frieda Lawrence, Mable Dodge Luhan, Georgia O'Keeffe and Frank Waters, into the first publication of her autobiography. The issue also included another interview with me in a special Southwest edition of *The South Dakota Review*. It was the best seller published to that date no doubt because of Lady Brett.

John, with sacrificial effort, had turned a disaster into a historical success for all of us who care deeply about the West. A majestic deed.

We were having some of this sort of turbulence at the Evans' household. We had moved from Taos to Albuquerque. I had been asked to be on the film committee for the State of New Mexico headed up by Governor David Cargo. I became so obsessed with helping to create this clean industry for our state that I totally neglected my writing and other business. Our personal film deals dried up like a Sahara drought. It hadn't yet dawned in my numb head that we were the only ones spending our savings while everyone else in the entire state would benefit, and were benefitting. But it all worked, and the state has profited by well over a billion dollars of environmentally nondestructive filming. I had no regrets then, nor do I now.

I went back to work peddling options when and wherever I could, even doctoring screenplays—without credit—to survive. At this place in time, I, like Frank Waters, had gone mostly out of print. During this period of recovery, 1972, John published my novella *Xavier's Folly* in an issue titled *The New West*. It had an abstract cover by R. C. Gorman. I was able to option this story of a Mexican plumber from Taos who becomes obsessed with importing the greatest of all Russian ballerinas to the high desert for a performance. The first script didn't work nor did the second. (I didn't write either one). The producers renewed the option, and we had acceptance by Hallmark Hall of Fame, subject to getting one or the other of two stars. One was not available and the other wouldn't do it. Later we optioned it in London for a stageplay. The Brits spent lots of money on music, etc., but could never get it all together. No matter, the story has pulled us through some financial spots tighter than a badger's bite. That's tight. The debt of gratitude grows on.

John once warned me to be very careful in Hollywood or I might end up wounded like Faulkner and so many other writers before me. I told him not to fret about me, but instead worry about what I would do to them. At his double take I said, "These are just little token jobs to get me on to my real work."

Through the down years John and *The South Dakota Review* published five of my short novels: *The Third Grade Reunion*, *Candles in the Bottom of the Pool*, *The Orange County Cowboys*, and *Old Bum* and, of course, *Xavier's Folly*. Three of these are included in my own choice as my best seven in our newest book *Spinning Sun, Grinning Moon,* by Red Crane Books.

Until recent years, one of the things I was very naive about is awards—I didn't know that stories had to be officially entered to be eligible. It never occurred to me to enter anything, I guess I thought that someone accidentally saw a story in a dentist's office or bought a book and this somehow led to the awards. It was only about eleven years ago that I first found out the difference. So later I entered *The Orange County Cowboys* in the WLA annual Spur awards and it won. Then I entered *Old Bum* and it was a runner-up finalist. All through the Sunset Boulevard scrambling, John was feeding me oxygen by asking for stories and putting deadlines on them so I'd be sure to get them written.

I was staying at director Sam Peckinpah's mobile home at Malibu doing a little of that undercover script work for him when Pat called and forcefully reminded me that I had promised John a novella for the 10th anniversary issue. I wrote *Candles in the Bottom of the Pool* in three days while John held up the printing. This publication was one of my proudest moments. All the thirteen writers are listed on the front page book-ended by myself and Walter Van Tilburg Clark. With, among others, Ben Black Elk, Paul Horgan, and William Eastlake. Powerful forces in the middle listing. *Candles* has been reprinted in an anthology, *The American West in Fiction,* by New American Library, also by The University of New Mexico, The University of Nebraska Press, and now in the Red Crane Book edition. All told the short novel has been anthologized eight times. All the short stories and novels I've done for John Milton have been sought after and reprinted. It just seemed that when he would ask me for a piece or I would write something with him especially in mind, I just did a better-than-average job of writing. It was the faith and unbounded friendship we had in one another that inspired this. The understanding that comes from looking at a special sacred mountain with twin eyes and souls, and actually hearing and knowing its music is everlasting. In all our phone conversations and the scores of letters and the precious visits in Taos, Albuquerque, and Vermillion we shared with the Miltons, I could not tell John that I'd been researching, making notes, congealing thoughts for what would be the ultimate life's work for me: *Bluefeather Fellini.* But he knew just the same. You see, on his many forays into the Chicano villages and pueblos of New Mexico he had come to love, respect these people and their innate mysticism. And he, too, became a mystic out of reality. We also shared this special understanding without question and always with esteem. He published works by many of these people who have a feel for spirit such as Ben Black Elk, Vine Deloria, Rudolfo Anaya, Frank Waters, Vincent B. Price.

All our meetings in Taos were very special, but naturally the last two were more so. We drove up from Albuquerque and met them in that ancient village in the early winter of '92. The Miltons had scheduled visits with the great Navajo artist R. C. Gorman, their special friends, Frank Waters and Barbara, his wife and soul mate since 1970, and Dr. Henry Saurwein, head of the Wurlitzer Foundation. Pat and I visited briefly with a couple of our friends and then drove all over Taos Valley. To our intense pleasure and surprise we found many of the great old adobe homes and pastures from our youth still there still intact. I felt again "The Taos Presence" emanating both down from the pulsating sky and upward from the breathing earth. Pat felt it as well, and I knew that John and Lynn were sharing this with us wherever they were in the valley. I feel John is partaking of this special thing this moment.

After several wonderful visits, we had to part and depart. The bags were loaded in both our conveyances. From the sidewalk in front of the motel we looked beyond the plaza of Taos village, on past the pueblo and up to the white sparkling crown of the mountain. The sky was so pure and blue it healed. I looked all around several times unbelieving. I said, "John, do you remember a single time when we've been together that the Taos sky was absolutely cloudless?" We all four scoured the immensity. "No," he said softly in justified reverence. We hugged and left for our homes and our work of words.

Back in 1966, John had published a summer edition of *The South Dakota Review* simply titled "The West." It turned out to be an extremely important journal of the contemporary West as well as the old, especially to me.

The lead piece by Max Westbook was titled: "Conservative, Liberal and Western: Three Modes of American Realism." There was an essay on Berger's *Little Big Man* and Walter Clark and two by different authors on D. H. Lawrence in Taos. It also contained a review of a biography on Vardis Fisher by Richard Etulain who would go on to become a noted western historian, also three poems by Taoseño Larry Frank. There was a powerful full-page photograph of Frank Waters by Sam Sprague and a follow-up complete bibliography. However, the essay that concerned and impressed me was by the late C. L. (Doc) Sonnichsen—"The New Style Western." Here in one volume back in the mad-mad sixties were the two men from the academic world who would keep faith with me throughout their life times. John had published it and Doc had listed the first four of my novels along with the works of Larry McMurtry and Benjamin Capps as the leaders of the new high road. I had read a couple of historical pieces by Doc, but didn't know any more about McMurtry and Capps than a working cowboy would know about caviar—and I'm certain they had never even heard of me and probably haven't until today. Sonnichsen skillfully pointed out our three entirely different approaches and used segments of our works to emphasize this. In my soul I believed that this issue of John's journal and this essay by Doc would forever make *me* feel I was on the only track that would properly deliver my words. I didn't meet Dr. Sonnichsen until fifteen years later although we had already become pen pals and more.

So, forgetting this personal lift to me, these two men never put the old west down as long as it was well written, but also never quit during their exemplary and productive lives pursuing and opening the great rusted iron doors that had locked the new west writers out of the game. In that issue they had done it together. The debt to these two special writers and teachers by the men and women who love the West is incalculable.

John was always conjuring different and special editions. In the autumn of 1975 he really went full powder with "The Writer's Sense of Place." The symposium part of volume 13 contained eighteen writers such as Frank Waters, Erskine Caldwell and myself, amazingly including thirteen essays by others from around America including Wallace Stegner and Karl Kopp. Since I've never known what my pen will lead me to express and because I had done what I felt was a poetic rendering of the writer related to the land in another issue, I was surprised at the way I answered John's query thusly:

1. *Are you conscious of place in your life and work? Of having your place?*

I am very conscious of place. The place next to a wino in a stinkin' bar. A place where I'd hit the ground after having been bucked off an ornery ol' bronc, and I have always hoped there was a place someone could properly apply the human soul.

2. *Do you, as an artist, need a place to sustain you?*

Yes, I used to have to look at a desert or mountain occasionally. Now all I need is a place to put my ass and my typewriter.

3. *To what extent does your work depend upon, or reflect, your region ?*

My region is wherever I hang my hat the most or any place that I had a good breakfast and didn't spend the night before in jail.

4. *How important are roots to the artist?*

After having read and admired Somerset Maugham, that great underrated artist, who did nothing but travel the world, dining on the finest foods and drinking the best wines, leaves me rootless for an answer.

5. *What are the differences between rooted and rootless art?*

I don't know.

6. *Do you think there is a need to stress the regional again— rather than the nationalistic—in the arts?*

Yes, because all regions are microcosms of the world and the universe anyway.

7. *Do you find "regional" to be an offensive word?*

A ghetto is regional; Park Avenue is regional; the Left Bank is regional; the plains of South Dakota are regional. It's just who the hell do you bump into?

8. *"The mind creates the world," OR "the world creates the mind": how does this distinction fit your own theories?*

When I was a kid a fella charged me a quarter to look at a caged hyena. He majestically pointed out that this wondrous creature was the only one in the whole world. He said it has the brow of a bull, the smile of a bear, the ears and teeth of a vampire bat, the neck like a horse, the body of a razorback hog and the testicles of an orangutan. I believed the son of a bitch. You pays your quarter, you takes your choice.

Now the modesty of this great communicator, John Milton, was recognized by all who knew him. It fit his surface appearance of the professor of the imagination greying beard and hair, modest stature, etc. However, he had a handshake like a farrier and was made of honest intellectual alloyed steel inside. But here from one of his usual "Literary or Not" introductions to each issue we see the dominant modest side of John R. Milton. I quote from a portion of the winter issue 1991:

> And that raises the question of whether creative writing can be taught, or whether the teacher contributes his own understanding of the writing of fiction and poetry and other than that provides encouragement and discipline of the kind needed by young writers. That method seems to work, at least here at a small university of South Dakota located on an invisible line (well, almost invisible) between Midwest and West. Among the published writers emerging from the University of South Dakota have been some who attracted national attention: Pete Dexter, recent winner of a National Book Award for his novel *Paris Trout;* Dan O'Brien with a volume of short stories, a nonfiction book, and two novels, all during the last four years; Elly Welt with two novels; Michael Doane with several novels; Bill Earls, whose novel had its beginnings in his masters thesis; and Linda Hasselstrom, who has published both poetry and prose while running a ranch in western South Dakota. For about fifteen years Frederick Manfred furnished guidance while I served as the nasty critic. But I believe that Frederick would agree with me in saying the real success of "our" writers comes from their determination to be writers. Teaching, if it can be called that in this case, was secondary to that determination.

In October of 1994, we fulfilled our last earthly meeting with John in Taos. I was having a signing of *Bluefeather Fellini in the Sacred Realm* at Mr. and Mrs. Art Bachrach's Moby Dicken's Bookstore, ironically located in the Long John Dunn house on famous Bent Street named after Governor Bent who had been assassinated there in a pueblo uprising. I wrote my first nonfiction book about the wonderful old outlaw, and personal friend, John Dunn, published in 1959. It seemed altogether an appropriate setting. John joined me in visiting with Art Bachrach, Tal Luther, noted book-man, and David Hill who took a snapshot of John and me laughing like kids at a Laurel and Hardy movie, Pat and Lynn went shopping and we all met at the Kachina Lodge and had more fine conversation and food. This was good because the next day John had scheduled a long interview with me to include in a new book he was preparing on writers. We had a lot more laughs mostly at our foolish selves, but even so he was meticulously taking notes.

I must confess that I don't remember most of it because that was *his* job. But I do indelibly recall a few things we discussed. For one, how important mysticism was to the earlier inhabitants of this huge, multicolored and shaped southwest and the importance and responsibility of never selling the emotions, beliefs and traditions short. Almost seven magical hours had passed before the women returned just as we were winding down.

I also remember both of us agreeing it wouldn't have made much difference what kind of writer Frank Waters had been, he was a truly great philosopher. John believed to this moment, among several other older writers, that Waters, Harvey Fergusson, and Walter Van Tilburg Clark would last. But he was adding a few younger writers to his list and told me he was going to make a slight adjustment in his final opinions. Of course, we will never know what those were.

John had a far-ranging interest in everything west of the Mississippi. On their yearly trips to California to visit daughter Nanci at Berkeley, he and Lynn took many side trips to visit west coast writers, and he published several of them. In the winter issue of 1992 he printed a marvelously warm photo essay of his own about Winnemucca, Nevada. He had fallen in love with the mountain desert town and many of its characters. He was looking forward to stopping over there on their next trip to visit his beloved Nanci.

We wound up our last meeting on a high note for sure and we had some real chuckles about it. In our usual back and forth habit of him asking me to write a piece for a special edition, or my saying I was doing a story I felt was unique, and did he want a look at it, I agreed in 1969 to do one if he would publish a story of his own at the same time. I had read in manuscript and loved his story about a young Indian girl called "The Inheritance of Emmy One Horse." John said he didn't feel he should print his own stories in *The Review*. I kept on horse trading and convinced him he could do it under a pseudonym and we would have some secret fun. Damned if our foolishness didn't work. *Best American Short Stories* contacted him and wanted to publish it. They called again and said they needed more information about this writer. John didn't know whether to hang himself or go fishing in Alaska. He called me and I told him to admit he did it and get his name on it. If he was afraid of that, I generously volunteered my own name. That did it. We laughed. He took his due credit. The story got top reviews. It was translated into Chinese for Voice of America broadcasts and also translated into Dutch and reprinted in a London women's magazine. He told me at our last Taos go-round that this highlighted his career personally.

He had already published 15 books of prose, poetry and non-fiction to small acknowledgement, but didn't receive his media and awards due until the last years of his life. They included: The Governor's Award for Achievement in Arts, induction in the South Dakota Hall of Fame, and he read his touching poem *Legacy* at a memorial for Governor George Mickelson and seven other men who died with him in a plane crash. It was reprinted all over South Dakota.

Several years back an acquaintance sent me a copy of *New York Review* listing the best "little" magazines in America. They said, "Surprisingly it's *The South Dakota Review* from a small college in that state," and went on to say that this was because of the highly talented editor, professor of English, John R. Milton.

It was one of the proudest moments of my life to mail this on to John. Typically he never mentioned it to me—not even once.

Most of the world's beliefs and ancient traditions see the circle, in all its variations, as the true continuity of all life. Some of us then may have one circle, others a few, and then another person may have endless circles spinning into spirals. Out of this it seems have come two common phrases: "The family circle" and "our circle of friends."

As earlier stated, the meeting that day so long ago in living time at Frank Water's party formed one circle that is still whirling. John was a powerful part of bringing Frank's work back into print and prominence. And he kept me in some form of print during my slow times as well.

Back in 1949 when Frank was editor of the *Taos News* (*El Crepusculo*) he took the word of art reporter, Regina Cooke, that Woody Crumbo—the late great Pottawatamie pioneer artist—was being shunned because he was painting in nontraditional oils. Frank told Regina to give Woody a full page and he saved one hundred tear sheets for the artist. Woody mailed them out around the nation, the press became huge, and a great artist was reborn. Right at this time, Woody had become my artistic and spiritual mentor. Frank's action had set him free to teach and inspire me. The circle of eternity moves on.

Without the spirit of Woody Crumbo, I never would have been able to write *Bluefeather Fellini* and *Bluefeather Fellini in the Sacred Realm*. John's powerful report on these books to University Press of Colorado facilitated and helped their publication and success. So, this particular circle, Frank Waters, John Milton, Woody Crumbo, and myself led to many wondrous things for us all.

John and I shared a special world of words for over thirty years. He shared his world with thousands of others, and I do believe the ripples of his influence are still widening in never-ending circles throughout the West and beyond. Far beyond.

The highly respected book-man, Dwight Meyers, in the June 1995 issue of *Book Talk—New Mexico Book League* said, "We lost a giant on January 28. The unexpected death of John R. Milton (70) silenced the strongest supporter of western writers and western literature that this century has produced."

He was a loyal friend with great talent and compassion. At first I felt the massive vacancy he had left, but now I feel him near. And I feel good. He changed the landscape of western writing and the landscape of the western soul. We will be fortunate indeed if another of his quality and dedication treads forth during any of our lifetimes.

To the true "King of the Little Magazines" I give a humble bow with a tear in one eye and a grateful smile in the other.

Long John Dunn of Taos

Long John Dunn was screaming and raising hell when he was born in Victoria, Texas, in 1857.

He made racket for almost 100 years until he passed into the Great Mystery, an unassailable legend at Taos on May 22, 1953.

His beginnings on a dry-land, slow-starvation farm put toughness and determination in him instead of the "poor me" attitude. He snared rabbits and trapped quail to help keep his younger brother, his older sister and his mother fed while his father was off fighting in the Civil War. His mother sewed for any and all stores who would give her piece work. It was a rough go and deteriorated further when his father returned from the war wounded and disabled and, shortly thereafter, died. Young John dug the grave himself and built the wooden casket. With blistered hands and a hurting heart he made up his mind to elevate himself out of this poverty any way he could.

He was loaned out to an uncle Dunchee who was supposed to pay regular wages. Dunchee worked John every daylight hour and all the chores that could be done in the dark. Old John laughed at the telling.

After several empty paydays, John had had it. He saddled his horse. Spotting a rope on the ground, he picked it up and rode off. A mile or so later he discovered that a fine bay horse was tied to the other end. He sold Dunchee's horse and rode on west whistling pretty tunes. John soared to 6 feet while in his midteens and was quite an all 'round cowhand, becoming especially expert at roping. He would win money at many rodeos through the years. He also became proficient at breaking horses—at $5 a head—and specialized his way on farther west.

In the Big Bend Country he took a regular job on the Half-Brothers Ranch south of Fort Stockton, Texas. Their ranch reached all the way to the Rio Grande on the south, a river where

John would eventually make history far to the north. The Half-Brothers decided to trail a herd north to Abilene, Kansas. John was first to volunteer.

Before he was 20 years old, he made many trail drives. The first three were to Abilene, Caldwell and Dodge City, Kansas. In Dodge City the cattle were quarantined for a month, so he began observing the gamblers, learning their tricks and elatedly started winning. He kept a pack of cards in his pocket and practiced at every chance.

He and some other cowboys were over-the-limit celebrating and John bet them all their pocket money that he could rope a train. He did, all right, clean around the smokestack. It jerked John and his horse down, almost killing them. The men paid off their foolhardy bets figuring John would die and they could take their money back. They were wrong as many others would be in those go-gettin' years to come.

His last trail drive was to the N-Bar-N Ranch in Montana on the Canadian border. There were the expected floods, burning sun, resentful Indians to fight, snakes, biting insects and other small irritations to contend with, but his card playing was improving.

John, fearful of the horse stealing charges that surely awaited him, finally worked his way back home. But old Dunchee had never filed official charges. He wanted more personal revenge. This plan was cut short when one of Dunchee's short-changed hired hands shot and killed him. John said, "I wanted to buy that man a new hat, but I never could find him."

Now one of those life-altering events happened. John's beloved sister had been badly abused by her husband. One night she stumbled to the Dunn home bleeding from the nose and mouth. John immediately prepared to "blow the bastard's head off," but his mother talked him out of it.

A few days later John confronted him on the streets of the frontier town. Unlike most bullies, John's brother-in-law was truly tough. He knocked John down in the dirt. John got up. They fought savagely. John landed a final blow. His opponent went back and down, fatally smacking his head on a hitching rail. John was sent to the state penitentiary then at Rusk, Texas, and was shortly transferred to a leg-chain prison farm on the Sabine River. He smuggled a file. Nightly, he tediously filed on his chain.

A flood came. The prisoners were called out to work on the levee. All prisoners were granted permission to pick up their leg chains. John snapped the chain and ran. Two others tried to follow and were killed. His only chance was the river. He dived into the deadly torrent, grabbing a floating log. Choking, he was hurled on shore by the surging river. He stole a farmer's horse and made it with great sacrifice to Matamoros, Mexico, where he honed his gambling techniques. From forced experiences, he decided that transportation was the key to the world—it most certainly was to his part of the West.

After polishing his art of gambling, he headed north—this time riding a fine horse. He rodeoed, gambled and had fun taking his doctorate of dice on the road in Montana, Nevada, and other Western states. Then he made it back to a gold boom at Elizabethtown across the mountains from Taos. His gambling tables flourished, eating up the miners' and outlaws' money like a hog does sweet-milk slop.

The transportation obsession called him over the mountains to the adobe town of Taos, famed for fandangos, mountain men, Tiwa-speaking Pueblo Indians and later, world-renowned for its artists. He got into a plural gun fight, eradicating a bully of a marshall. Understandably, John could never suffer bullies of any kind. One of the shots that did the marshall in was from a shotgun—John's favorite weapon. He then, all by himself, took over the neighboring town of Red River and set up his gaming tables after shooting a gun from a resenter's hand with both barrels.

His business ventures were flourishing. Besides controlling Red River, he had two profitable gambling joints in Taos—one in the old Don Fernando on the Plaza, another south of town. He was ready to fulfill his second dream. He ran stagecoaches to and from Taos junction with passengers, and had the mail contract for the valley. He bought two competing toll bridges across the Rio Grande. A flood washed out the main one, but he rebuilt it higher and stronger. Soon he was taking in $250 a day for sheep, cattle, horses and people to cross.

He built a hotel at his bridge near the mouth of Hondo Canyon and kept the travelers there overnight. They welcomed the stop after the bumpy, hairy ride up the steep, curving, rocky river road. He profited while they rested. He imported his mother to manage the hotel, giving her every comfort and luxury.

Then he went to Denver and convinced the manager of the Denver & Rio Grande Railroad to build a line from Taos Junction to Servilleta. John took contracts building on the railroad and it finally reached Española. This was the boost Taos needed. He met the railway at Servilleta in his horse-drawn stage and hauled scores of famous personages into Taos—including world renowned artists. Later he would run a motorized stage—licensed in four states—to pick up most of the famed dilettante Mabel Dodge Luhan's noted guests who arrived at the Lamy rail station south of Santa Fe.

John married a beautiful, vital Hispanic woman named Adelaide. They raised four fine daughters and a son, John Dunn Jr., who died at age 11 of influenza.

John respected the artists. They loved him. He respected the dominant Spanish and Indian cultures. The feeling was returned. They traded as partners with one another.

Including his three surviving daughters, there are probably fewer than 10 people left in the world who know of the secret recreational site called "The Office" that was located on famed Ledoux Street just south of Taos Plaza. There in an opulently furnished home, he and Mabel Dodge teamed up. John furnished plush rooms for assignations between the opposite, and sometimes same, sex prominent friends of Mabel's. Frieda and D. H. Lawrence, Georgia O'Keeffe and Leopold Stokowski were among the frequent guests. The arrangement gave John a select list of often wealthy suckers for his many games of chance—which he operated personally. He laughed and joked through his broken nose and raked in their money. They felt privileged to lose to him.

All this, and so much more, was accomplished while he was a wanted man. Such things as: he and his dear friend, Mabel Dodge Luhan, were the driving forces to get a hospital built for Taos. When he was in his 80s, the governor of New Mexico delivered to Long John a full pardon from the governor of the State of Texas for his discrepancies therein. A grand moment.

This ladder-straight, 6-foot-four man of the real West, killer of many—mostly in self defense—gambler, builder, friend of the art colony, working cowboy, rodeo hand, horse thief, trail driver, mail contractor, railroad and stageline builder, card sharp, visionary and fine family man was unique beyond compare. One would be hardpressed to imagine such unceasingly written-about Western luminaries as Billy the Kid and Jesse James even sleeping in a corner of the totality of his huge shadow.

The new steel bridge across the Rio Grande at Hondo Canyon is still named after him. His old home on Bent Street houses the first-rate bookstore, Moby Dickens. His old dice table—complete with his special monogrammed poker chips—appropriately stands in the entry of the brand new Van Vechten-Lineberry Taos Art Museum, which houses a vast collection of the work of Taos art colony founders.

John Harris Dunn is buried in Taos' Kit Carson Cemetery next to his beloved mother, Susan Jane Dunn. They surely must visit and laugh at the impossible odds they beat all to hell and laugh even more at the ridiculous, mostly wimpy world driving past so near and yet so unreachably far away.

Dinner With Frank

Sometimes you just can't make a bolt fit into the hole, even though everything started out with apparent blessings upon us. I had been in Denver for a three-day Western Historical Society meeting of some kind—I can never get that part correct—with Marcia Keegan, the noted photographer of Indians, her husband and business partner in Clear Light Publishing, Harmon Houghton, and Howard Bryan, the western writer of oldtime outlaws.

The last session of "outlaw history" meetings had ended the night of July 17th, 1992, with almost everyone pleased at the results. The next morning the four of us met for an early breakfast at Hotel Brown, and set about laying plans to meet in Taos that evening with Frank and Barbara Waters for a scheduled dinner.

First, we must finish breakfast and pack, then on our way out of town, we would take Harmon to the airport for a flight to New York where he had meetings set up pertaining to publicity preparations on their new publication entitled *Exiled: In the Land of the Free.* Sounds simple enough.

Secondly, the remaining three of us would drive on to Colorado Springs where Marcia planned to photograph Howard and me holding a banner under the sign that reads: Frank Waters Park. The banner would say, "Happy 90th Birthday, Frank. " The park and granite rock with Frank's name, and his honor carved in it, sits directly across the street from the house he was born in almost ninety years ago. Marcia would photograph that, as well.

Third, we would drive on to Taos to meet Frank and Barbara for dinner at 7:00 P.M. Seems easy as sniffing snuff, doesn't it? Wrong.

We drove into Colorado Springs looking for the street that turned off the main business drag to Frank's Park. It was Sunday. Hot and muggy. We were excited because none of us has seen these historical monuments to Frank Waters' momentous life.

Then the Cadillac fell dead without warning, without conscience. Marcia coasted to the curb. We all climbed out and Howard raised the hood. The two of them were looking at things under the hood, and now and then each courageously touched these things. Things I didn't dare even look at, much less feel. In fact, I didn't even kick the tires, but politely retired to a shade tree near the sidewalk. I have always had a tendency to innocently break, beyond fixing, most mechanical contraptions I become overly familiar with.

I could tell by certain grumblings and humming sounds emanating from my two friends that they were having some difficulty resurrecting the deceased. I knew this for a fact when Marcia looked down the street, hands on hips, and said,

"I think we'll need help, and where can I find it on Sunday?"

I answered warily, but hopefully, "The phone book?"

She looked at me, then at Howard, and decided the two wrecks she observed were not in much better shape than the car. "Okay, I see a phone booth down there in front of that restaurant." Being far younger, and much smarter than the two old worn-out writers standing there as pitiful as it is possible to look, she started across the street to initiate our rescue. Before she could reach the other side, a panel truck with large lettering on the side spelling out these magic words: MOBILE REPAIR UNIT pulled right up behind our disabled vehicle and stopped. A tall young man in his early thirties got out, along with his two small children—both under ten years of age.

"Need any help?" He asked.

I said, "It's broke."

Of course, he could see that, being in the business he was, but I didn't want to risk his leaving thinking maybe we had just stopped for a picnic and left the hood up by mistake.

Marcia joined him. Howard joined him. I even gathered the courage to walk up within two or three yards of the massive bulk of iron as they all three stared into the silent motor. Then the mechanic drove his van in front—almost bumper to bumper—and jump-started the car back to temporary life. He looked at it and listened, for less than a minute.

Then with the conviction of a Supreme Court justice that mechanic said, "There's a chain inside there that's busted. We will have to disassemble the entire motor to replace it."

Now, this huge motor fills up all that space in front of the windshield except for about three inches of wires on its top so thick they made me think of a cave full of hibernating snakes. This young mechanic was an amazing thing. I had read in the comics, and seen in movies, variations of the man with X-ray eyes. Well, here he was in person. This man could see through those wires and a foot or so of hardened steel all the way to that broken chain. He was either a liar, a thief, or a miracle worker. By the kind, but firm, way he treated his children, I decided it was the latter. That's the second time in my life I've been right about anything to do with a broken automobile. I can't remember the other occasion. It was probably a half century ago.

Now, I told Marcia my good feelings about the young man. She made a financial deal with him. He got on his car radio and in efficient order had us a reservation at a nearby Holiday Inn and a personal friend of his came in a cab and helped transfer our baggage from the stricken vehicle to the purring cab. The mechanic had a wrecker on the way to pull the car to his home repair shop and we were rapidly escorted to and checked into the motel. Marcia called Barbara Waters and told her we would be a day late and hoped she could change the dinner reservations to next evening, the 19th, at the same time. She could. She did. However, we would have to make it to Taos the next day or forget the dinner with Frank. The reason being: the mayor of Taos was holding ceremonies on the 20th to present Frank with an award for the massive import of his life's work. After that they would be too busy preparing for his ninetieth birthday on the 25th.

Our time allotment was growing desperately thin because the mechanic would have to work all Sunday night and the next morning to fix the car. So, there you have it. A mixture of minor disasters and a couple of little miracles. Ain't that the way most of our lives roll up the trail?

The next morning we took our packed bags to the lobby, checked out and waited. And we waited some more. Marcia kept looking at her watch, and fretted about our dinner with Frank. I remained sanguine and in good spirits because I knew a man of magic was working on her automobile. Sure enough, just in time, a Ford pulled up with another of this man's friends and drove Marcia across town to her soon-to-be-rolling conveyance. Now Howard and I waited.

At last we were once again on the road to Taos. I thought about Frank as the mountains of Southern Colorado came at us again near Walsenburg.

The man is the work. The work is the man. Had someone told me this? Or had I read about it somewhere? I couldn't remember, but it was true about Frank, nonetheless. I thought of what a monumental writer, philosopher he is, and even so, I felt he still had not been served his proper due. The movie colony had optioned, and abused, his writings. Over and over and over. Several times, he had been hired to write scripts, and the very fact of his vast knowledge of Indian lore, his obviously deep and penetrating understanding and love for the western earth he knows so well, and his long-proven mastery with words, had almost unbelievably been lost on the producers. A shame. A sin. A loss to us all.

Then I remembered my first meeting with Frank right after I moved to Taos in 1949. He was editor of the local paper. I pictured this tall, striking man with his mane of hair combed back as if he had been running into the wind, striding around the plaza, aware, but also looking somewhere far away into canyons full of mystic mysteries. Frank always, and to this very moment, exudes purpose. The one thing all great humans have in common.

It rained heavily as Marcia expertly drove over the mountain pass, down to Ft. Garland. I was remembering Frank's dry sense of humor, his close friendships with the likes of Mable Dodge and Tony Luhan, Lady Dorothy Brett—the English artist who followed D. H. and Frieda Lawrence to America—and his warm relationship to those who toiled in the fields, making adobes, or shearing sheep. His range as a man was as vast as the Sangre de Cristos bulking up in proclamation to our left.

As we drew nearer to Questa, a few miles north of Taos, Marcia was keeping close tabs on the clock and the miles left. It was too much for me to try and figure. I left it up to her. So did Howard. It was obvious, though that the minutes and the miles would run out at near the same time. Close. Then I really messed up-again.

There, way off to the west, across the Rio Grande Gorge above the sagebrush desert was a massive cloud formation that I've seen only in the Taos area. There were great hairy ape arms of moisture dipping towards the earth; some vanishing in the dry, evaporating air before they touched, others wetting the thirsty desert sage a bit. Mighty spotlights that only the sun can project pierced through breaks in the clouds that seemed to be heralding the birth of a new world.

I couldn't help saying, in an awed voice, "Hey, you guys, look at that sky."

I'd forgotten the road. So did Marcia. She looked and almost instantly pulled the car off the road. Grabbing her camera she practically leapt out. She moved down the fence line click clicking trying to capture the majesty of the greatest show on earth—the summer storm clouds of Taos.

The sun started pulling the shafts of light back behind the clouds, and we had to think of Frank and Barbara now.

Finally, in Taos, we turned right on Bent Street to the Apple Tree Restaurant right across the street from the Old Long John Dunn house—which is now the Moby Dicken's Bookstore in front with many other little shops behind. We got out of the car at the exact moment Frank and Barbara drove up. The bolt was tight and secure in the threaded hole, it would seem. Well, almost.

In spite of a heavy crowd of tourists we were placed at a table in the patio, by a lovely young Hispanic waitress whose father was a good friend of Frank.

The meal had been ordered and we were enjoying a glass of wine and visiting when a loud, cracking noise from lightning burst upon us followed by a drenching downpour. We managed to follow the waitress and get inside to a table before a great deal of damage was done.

Things started working for the better. The conversation turned to reminiscences and I was especially pleased to find out, after all these decades, that Frank, the editor then of *El Crepusculo*, the Taos Newspaper, had assigned Regina Cooke—arts reporter for over forty years—to do a full page write-up on Pottawatomie Woody Crumbo—who a few months later on would become my artistic and spiritual mentor. Woody had been pioneering painting in oils, and a lot of people resented his breaking away from the watercolor tradition. So here was a young man who had hundreds of paintings in museums around the world, getting turned down for art shows around the country. When the article came out, Frank saved Woody a hundred tear sheets which he mailed out. His career started changing back for the better. I would imagine, Frank's favors, such as this, are to those he believed in, uncountable.

It was good to hear the comfort in Frank's voice when he spoke of his classic novel *The Man Who Killed The Deer*. "It is hard for me to believe, but the book is selling more copies now than it was when it was published about a half century ago."

The trip had worked. At last we had our unforgettable dinner with Frank.

As busy as she was preparing for Frank's ninetieth year, Barbara was gracious about our delays and anxious for Marcia to bring the photographs back for the party at their home next to Taos Mountain at Arroyo Seco north of town.

One must simply enjoy good fortune. One must never gloat. Fate will come and knock your teeth out, if you do.

We were almost to Santa Fe when Marcia discovered she had left her camera bag with her camera and all of Frank's negatives in the restaurant. As soon as we got to her home she tried calling Taos. The restaurant was closed. Howard drove me on to my home in Albuquerque that night. We had worried all the way about poor Marcia having to sweat until morning about her camera and the film.

Anyway, I'll never forget the sparkles in Frank's dark, animated eyes that see ancient things and events few will ever know. We're lucky to have his great gift of books to try and realize his visions for ourselves.

Oh yeah, Marcia finally reached the Apple Tree Restaurant by phone the next day. They found and saved the camera and precious film for her. They immediately sent it by truck so she was able to have the pictures ready in time for the "big" party. The power behind the great storm over the Taos desert had smiled on us after all. Again.

Riding The Outside Circle In Hollywood

It used to be—when I was a youngster and working at cowboy labor—that the men and horses chosen to make the *outside* circle at a cattle roundup were supposedly the best. Since they covered a lot more country, the horses and men had to have more cow-sense and great endurance.

Now, working Sunset Boulevard, The Beverly Hills Hotel's Polo Lounge, the story conferences at studio offices, and deal-making at either "A" or "B" list Hollywood parties, is just the opposite. It is the small number *of inside-circle* riders who get the deals, the money, and the fame.

When I was first invited to Hollywood by Fess Parker, who was the star of Walt Disney's *Davy Crockett*, I was with an "A" list. Most of the world was humming or singing the Crockett theme song and the children of many lands wore coonskin caps. Ole Fess was rich, famous, and his head was filled with instant brilliant brains.

He had optioned my novel *The Rounders* for a movie, but let the project get away from us. Five long years later, I got it together with director Burt Kennedy who had been Fess' first choice to direct, then dropped for someone else.

You see, I didn't know anything about these kind of circles even existing. I was so naive I thought talent and dedication was all you needed. Instead of five years, even a little bitty *inside-circle* rider could have done the deal in five minutes. There is one thing, though, that remains the same on the outside circle in Hollywood and/or on a cattle roundup—endurance.

In 1961, when director Sam Peckinpah, *The Wild Bunch*, *Straw Dogs*, etc., called my agent and said he'd like to meet the guy who wrote *The Hi Lo Country*—only one year after the Fess

Parker fiasco—I was in with an "A" list man again. Ah, there would be many unpredictable hitches, however.

How could a little ex-cowboy, now trying to be an artist/ writer, living on a few acres four miles west of Taos, New Mexico, whose county was ranked as one of the most impoverished in the nation, be expected to expect the unexpected? I ask you again, how?

As they say in both Hollywood and the Hi Lo Country, "Sam was hotter than a $4 pistol." His classic western, *Ride The High Country*, had been thrown away by "A" list people at MGM. The French had discovered it and made it famous. Then the motion picture and its shepherd were rediscovered in America. Both the film and Sam suddenly became featured all over the major newspapers and periodicals, and everyone wanted a piece of the magic. Learning this would seem to call for celebration and rejoicing.

Well, Sam and I did both with extreme dedication. We developed such expertise at fun that we could perform well whether together or with someone else. We were also very hard workers. Life seemed full. But of what, really?

Sam took on the exciting contract of directing a major western epic called *Major Dundee*. He had Charlton Heston and Richard Harris as the leads and many character actors who would later become his ensemble players, such as L.Q. Jones, R. G. Armstrong, Ben Johnson, Dub Taylor, Warren Oates, and the Mexican beauty, Begonia Palacios, whom he would marry at least twice.

Sam and the producers on *Dundee* disagreed on almost everything and he made the often fatal mistake of fighting relentlessly for what he believed would make a great film. To his credit, Heston stood up for Sam as far as he could. Sam never gave in, but the producers hacked 27 minutes out of *Major Dundee* and destroyed the removed film clips so it could never be put back together like *The Wild Bunch* and *Pat Garrett and Billy the Kid* finally were.

The dedication to his art in *Major Dundee* was the very thing that had drawn him to my novel in the first place. *The Hi Lo Country's* hero, Big Boy Matson (or anti-hero, as you like) was a post-World War II, small rancher who was forced, for survival sake, to be a working cowboy on the side for other ranchers. He believed in the old-fashioned virtues of excellence and skill in one's work, a deadly sacrificial devotion to one's qualified friends,

169

and a maintenance of the culture of the so-called "old ways." It all fit Sam's attitude perfectly.

As for me, I had to live through all the spine-grinding bucking horses, the drying droughts and the marrow-freezing winters, the poker games and the brown whiskey, the fist fights and laughter and the eternal winds of the Hi Lo Country.

Then my best friend, who would later inspire and become the lead of the novel, was shot five times with a 38-special and killed by his brother. Thank God I had already moved over to the other slopes of the Rocky Mountains before it happened for I would not have been around to write it.

Shortly after *The Hi Lo Country* was published, a couple of friends and I got into a stupid barroom brawl in Taos with 17 other people. The incident was picked up by the United Press and spread around the world. My editor at Macmillan Company read it at the Brown's Hotel in *The London Times* and sent out orders for only 15 review copies to be mailed out obviously not appreciating all the free publicity. He then wrote me a spiteful, lecturing letter saying he could see no future for me in the book publishing world because I was bound to get killed soon; therefore I was a bad investment.

My place on the "list" had already gone down on one coast and Sam Peckinpah would sink it on the other, but I wasn't concerned because I was totally unaware of the existence of such so-called lists. That was the amazing part. Sam Peckinpah went on struggling, fighting, like no one I've ever known, and nevertheless would make the greatest western ever made, *The Wild Bunch*.

This early 1900s film was also wrongly cut when Sam was not present, but the deleted film was kept and, with the help of a few dedicated people, restored to its classic condition by his biographer, David Weddle and principally, film maker Martin Scorsese. With each personal destruction by the *powers*, Sam would go broke and be unable to renew the option on my book, but he never gave up. Neither did I.

I sold brief survival options in between to many producers. Even so it had the Peckinpah taint on it. The famed Broadway and film director, George Axelrod, took it to a major studio, with the help of my agent, Robert Goldfarb, casting Lee Marvin and Steve McQueen as the stars. I know how hard it is to believe this now, but the studio said, "It is impossible to understand how you could even entertain the thought of making a film with a falling down drunk and a madman."

There was a long line of stars, producers, and directors of the time who wanted to make *Hi Lo*, such as Charlton Heston, Brian Keith, and Lee Marvin, and some big producers such as Marvin Schwartz, David Dortort, and Phil Feldman, all told, a list longer than the alphabet.

Sam and I tried so hard that I would sometimes give him a temporary option with nothing but a handshake. Sometimes he'd give me a little money. Sometimes I'd simply donate it or trade it to him for some item of little worth.

Now the Hi Lo Country actually does—on the map—physically consist of the northeast quadrant of New Mexico, a slice of far West Texas, a bit of the Oklahoma Panhandle and another slice of the southeast bottom of Colorado. It is *big* I tell you—both up and down. The Sangre de Cristos—part of the timbered Rockies—run through the western edge, and the great well-grassed rolling hills, malpai mesas and canyons cover most of the rest.

It is a harsh and often beautiful land that not only is high and low physically but it's the very same emotionally. The heat, the cold, the wind, the price of cattle or coal see to that. I know, I lived there, my rope of life tied hard and fast, for many years. And I lived the book about it for many more in Hollywood—mostly with Peckinpah believing the film was ready to be made.

The casting began over and over and over for a quarter of a century. Then one of Sam's eternal wars with some of the very people who now praise him so highly would break out and the *Lo* part of our title would engulf us again. We still had a hell of a lot of fun amidst the furors. Sam was still struggling to get it made, along with one of my short novels, *My Pardner*, when he died December 28, 1985.

While I spent the next decade after his demise writing on the work of my life, the *Bluefeather Fellini* duo, and many essays and novellas, several people, including actor James Gammon, had scripts written on the book without a single piece of legalized paper. They were betting on the "come and lost" because I would not sign another paper unless everything was right, and it never was.

Then L.Q. Jones called me on January 2, 1995, and asked me to send a *Hi Lo* book to the great director, Martin Scorsese [*Raging Bull, Taxi Driver, Good Fellas*]. They had just finished shooting *Casino*, and L.Q. asked Scorsese why he had never made a western. He answered simply, "I've wanted to, but just never found one that was right for me."

I tried to put it out of my mind and kept on working. Then on February 2, 1995, I got a letter from Scorsese saying that he, like Sam, loved the characters. It all started again.

My agent, Robert Goldfarb, dealt with *Working Title Pictures* of London, which was acquiring it for Scorsese. They had made *Four Weddings and a Funeral* for $6,000,000, and it had grossed more than $250,000,000 and made Hugh Grant a big star. At this same time publisher Berkley-Jove was publishing *The Hi Lo Country* and another novel of mine, *Bobby Jack Smith, You Dirty Coward*, under a new title *Broken Bones and Broken Hearts*. Action, again. Nothing had changed.

It took almost a year of agonizing title work. At last we signed. Then we heard by FAX that Stephen Frears, *Dangerous Liaisons*, *The Grifters* and other highly acclaimed films would direct, Scorsese's company would produce. And by some unfathomable magic, Walon Green, who had done the Oscar-nominated screenplay for Sam Peckinpah on *The Wild Bunch*, called and said he was busy writing the screenplay for *The Hi Lo Country*.

Hey, Sam, after 35 years or so blacklisted, you're back on the "A" list forever. We have all "A" list people working on *Hi Lo*, and I am cautiously elated. There have been too many broken circles to quite believe. But, Sam, if you hear me let's have one last river-roaring laugh. Okay, ole pard?

Many Deaths, Many Lives

The first words I ever read about my own writing said: "If you read this at all, start at the end and read backwards. When you reach the middle throw the book away."

This review (of *Southwest Wind)* was in the *Santa Fe New Mexican* newspaper sometime in 1958, but it had actually begun in Taos a few weeks earlier. We were starving artists just like one is supposed to be. The phone, lights, water and car payments were all overdue. You know the song I suppose. It was about midnight in the Sagebrush Inn bar. I had sold a wet, unframed oil painting for two one-hundred dollar bills to a gentleman from Texas three or four hours prior. He was the greatest man who ever lived. A true angel of mercy. A man approaching Godhood. We enjoyed each other's company—the repasts and repartee.

However, into each life a flea must fall. A young man had been drinking at the bar and for some reason chose my companion of perfect taste to pick on . . . over and over. We both had politely asked him to desist. Finally, he put his hands on the table, leaned over and called my most gracious host and dearest art-buying friend, "A stupid, Texas bastard."

This was obviously untrue. The man had the great intelligence to buy my painting, several drinks, and converse upon many difficult but enjoyable subjects.

I said something like . . . no, that's better left unsaid . . . I beat him outside so he wouldn't hit me behind the ear. We had a brief bare-knuckle shootout. I won. I thought.

A while later I ran into him in a restaurant in Santa Fe. He apologized profusely, tried to pay for my lunch and was ingratiating as a D.C. politician up for reelection. The next Sunday *he* published the aforementioned review of *Southwest Wind* in the *New Mexican*. All you beginners heed this advice: Never, never, never strike *anyone*. He might be a book reviewer.

173

Long John Dunn of Taos came next and received modest to good reviews. Everyone enjoyed it, except of course this same guy who now reviewed books for the *St. Louis Post Dispatch*. There will always be ONE. Count on it. Accept it, if you can.

Now came *The Rounders*. Mr. Henry Volkening of Russell and Volkening, a New York literary agency—the L-word really meant something then—loved it and we went together through eleven major publishers with the book. Every one of them said something like "A superior book" "An odd-ball western of high quality and originality" "Sorry, we do not know what to do with it."

In the meantime the phone, the lights, the car payments, the twins' food . . . forgive me please, of course, you've heard that song before.

Finally after several eternities and a few deaths and resurrections, the editor-in-chief of Macmillan Co., Al Hart, Jr., published it. Then the company sort of threw it away. It lived on as a book to be called a classic by many. After five years and five movie options, surviving off Sunset Boulevard, while mostly broke, I optioned it to MGM. Burt Kennedy directed it. MGM threw the film away. They double-billed it—on the bottom. The film, like the book, survived on its own to become a cult classic and has been played more on television through the years than any film I know. It is an MGM/Turner video and just last week was shown on TV again. As the creator of the original work (the book) I naturally didn't get paid for the countless reruns and all that. As I write these very words I can't believe I kept on writing books, short stories, articles and doctoring screenplays. But . . . as they say in Hollywood "Let's cut to the real race."

In 1950, one year after I sold my little ranch near Raton, New Mexico, moved to Taos and married Pat, I wrote several short stories between paintings. I sold a few but most were rejected. One I didn't submit. It was eight typed manuscript pages entitled "Sky of Gold." I knew somehow that I wanted to make more of this story, maybe a short novel, my favorite length of reading and writing. As I charged on through this cockeyed life doing many silly and sad, sometimes outrageously funny things, the story grew in my mind—vision and the pile of notes grew. This little bundle of energy passed the novella stage, finally moving beyond the short novel, the regular novel, and at last became in my vision "Ol' Blue" or *Bluefeather Fellini*, a massive work of a lifetime of rank experiences and careful observations. Countless times I longed desperately to talk about it. For the past 30 years, my wife, Pat, knew that I'd been making notes and agonizingly re-searching on something different from anything else she had ob-served. She also knew I couldn't break my code and speak of it. I couldn't write a beginning word no matter how I craved to do so. I simply wasn't horse enough yet. I'd rather die than not do it right. There was always the chance that I would be sent back in another life to do it. Then at last, when I was 62 years old, I'd written a very short novel tentatively titled *The Mare*. Now I knew it was the *time of writing*. The main problem was the fact that I had enough notes and information for ten thousand pages. That would be at least twenty big novels or forty short ones. No, I must somehow distill this down to at least a thousand pages. I should have been a bootlegger.

From the day I wrote the first line which is: "It was a time of youthful jubilation, and Bluefeather Fellini—the chosen one—knew that never, never, never, before had anyone been so blessed," until five-and-a-half years later when I weakly scrib-bled "The End" I can't remember, but I'm sure I crawled to a bed and slept a week or so.

During those eons I lost contact with all my books even though the trilogy *Rounders 3* was published. I lost contact with friends and foes and in-betweens, and with making a living. There were hundreds of little sufferings, such as slipping on a wet walk and falling over a low retaining wall smashing in sev-eral ribs. An elongated swelling about the size of my lower arm formed over these skin and bones. Then I started coughing so that I could feel and hear the joy of ribs and cartilage grinding out a symphony from hell. I went to Dr. Christopher Merchant.

He was amazed that a now 64-year-old man had the child's disease of whooping cough. There wasn't a lot one could do at this age, he said. You either died or it wore out in six months to a year. The coughing and consequent grinding never stopped. I went to bed for two months hoping somehow to live long enough to finish what I was now calling the "damn thing." I couldn't hold back, so I wrote in bed as hard as my old previously busted-up hand would allow. Yes, that's right, I had decided that the Great Spirit would want me to do this book in longhand. My fingers swelled so that I had to tape them up every morning like a prize-fighter before a championship bout. I truly began to believe, with all the pain of body and soul, that I was going for the champion-ship with Ol' Blue, but I also felt the winner would not be an-nounced for maybe fifty years. I haven't changed my mind yet.

Oh, there were other little obstacles, of course, such as making a living, but who would care a holy hoot.

I'd been on the book over 40 years and had it all down at last. Pat typed and edited it. I edited it. Pat and I edited it again at her computer which I pointed at with a typewriter eraser not daring to touch the thing and break my vow of writing in longhand, as well as the machine. It was at last cooked, done. Now the real problems would begin.

I mailed a copy to my editor, Greg Tobin at Bantam. Then I had two copies made to send to my New York agent. At the bottom of the box, between the two copies, I wrote on a yellow page in big letters telling him to prioritize this to the famous editor, Marc Jaffe at Houghton Mifflin. I mentioned all this including Jaffe's phone number and address in a cover letter. I had called Marc and made him aware of the imminent arrival of my life's work. He was excited. Professionalism all around, right? No siree. Sorry. Oh, how we foolish people of books dream. About three weeks later I got a letter from my agent saying how much he liked *Bluefeather*. I knew he hadn't really read it, but may have skimmed the first part of it at most. I'm very often a gullible fool, but no one can dupe me on that. I waited and I waited. No surprise here. What's forty years in the entire scope of things, anyway? Yeah. Out of politeness I hadn't called Jaffe. Out of desperation I finally did. He asked, "Whatever happened to *Bluefeather*? I thought your agent was sending it on to me."

I ground my teeth down to bleeding gums to keep from catching a plane to New York. For reasons of safety all around I phoned my agent instead. He said, "Oh, I thought you'd sent it on to Jaffe yourself."

As I said, he hadn't even lifted the top down to the last page of the manuscript or he would have found the yellow page of explicit directions. He said my letter must have gotten lost. He finally got it to Jaffe's office who had now left for an editing vacation in Oregon. A longer incalculable wait ensued. At last I got a letter from Greg Tobin, senior editor at Bantam saying *Bluefeather Fellini* was the best work of my life and that I knew it. Well. Of course I knew it. I was delighted, however, because Greg Tobin was the first major editor to stick his neck out for the book. Nevertheless, I could tell by the tone of the missive that a paperback book deal was all that was there.

Let the sun rise and set uncountable times, allow the hands of a time clock to fully encircle its entrapped orbit until they are worn so thin they are invisible and you'll know how long it was, or certainly seemed, before I heard from Jaffe. The call did come. His first words were encouraging and unforgettable.

"Max, you've written a Homeric epic." We talked on for 40 minutes. He was very excited and would have no trouble wrapping up the entire deal including editor Greg Tobin's Bantam offer to publish the paper version. Right nice, huh? Whoops. Here we go again. The executives turned Jaffe down. Their excuse was that it was too big a book. He was devastated. I adjusted.

Then Bantam reorganized. Greg Tobin had beaten them to it and taken a high executive position at Book of the Month Club. A cold day in hell and in Albuquerque. After all the firings and hirings of editors, cancellations of author's book contracts, etc., Tom Dupree was hired to replace Tobin at Bantam. He flat out said *Bluefeather* was one of the finest books he'd ever read anywhere, anytime. He fought for the book and kept the paperback rights alive. I deeply appreciated all of that. He was at Bantam a few weeks longer while my agent and I were sending the book out by merry-go-round mail. Then he was transferred to head up the sci-fi division of Bantam and Tom Beer tookover the project and has done a first rate job with the paperback version.

Early on I had sent manuscript copies of *Bluefeather* to five special people. Each was a combination of writer, editor and critic. All were very successful in their own work. There would be no jealously. They were: Charles Champlin, arts editor emeritus of the *Los Angeles Times*, author of *Back Where the Past Was*, and a bio, *George Lucas: The Creative Impulse;* Robert Conley, Cherokee Indian writer, former college teacher of English, award-winning author of such classics as *Mountain Windsong*, and *Nickajack;* Dale Walker, who was director of Texas Western Press, a world-class Jack London scholar and author of several books and countless reviews and articles; John Milton, editor for over thirty years of *The South Dakota Review*, and author of many books of fiction and poetry; and Luther Wilson, director of University Press of Colorado.

Luther had built the University of New Mexico (UNM) Press from nothing to a go-getter. He went on to Syracuse, New York, and did the same thing there. He had just started repeating his expertise at University Press of Colorado (UPC) when I mailed him *Bluefeather* to read. Sadly, UPC's by-laws stipulated that they publish only nonfiction.

All of the above individuals answered, calling *Bluefeather Fellini* an epic, and two or three of them said it was a masterpiece of American fiction—there was nothing else like it. Hooray!

Then Simon and Schuster turned it down with little comment. Hyperion said they didn't publish books like that. I assumed "like that" meant original.

Berkley and the parent company, Putnam, had already turned it down, but editor Gary Goldstein covered beautifully, writing what a great book it was. Bob Gleason at TOR didn't like *Bluefeather* at all.

As the months ground by, just like broken ribs and whooping cough, I called Luther Wilson about maybe going fishing. While we conversed I told him I'd never settle for just a paper publication on this book. Suddenly we had negotiations going with two publishers, but I decided I'd rather go with UPC, if possible. Although it took a lot of courage, Luther presented the project to a ten-person board. All but one agreed to change the by-laws and risk it. The one "hold-out" insisted that John Milton write a report before he'd give it a "yes."

I had written and published more stories with Milton's *South Dakota Review* than anyone else, but during that thirty-year friendship, Id never known him to stick his neck out for anyone but Walter Van Tilburg Clark, Steinbeck, Harry Ferguson, and Frank Waters. He was, and is, a warm human being, but an extremely conservative, cold-blooded critic. He wrote a wonderful, powerful, and positive report on *Bluefeather* ending it thusly, "It is a true southwestern epic. There is nothing quite like it in American fiction."

The long ordeal was over—sort of. University Press of Colorado published *Bluefeather Fellini* (Fall, 1993) with Pat's jacket art. Ninety percent of the reviews were raves, the rest excellent. Except . . . yes, except for that *one* squeak we've already spoken of that is always there.

I had a dream vision and it ordered me to cut the book into two parts. We did. As I write this, the first part is going into a third, modest printing and I've had a few modest movie offers that I can't afford to take. The second three-fifths of the duo will be published by UPC in September, 1994, cover art by Pat Evans. *Bluefeather Fellini in the Sacred Realm* is wilder, bigger and better than the first two-fifths. Quality Paperback Book of the Month

Club will publish both together, where they belong, in the spring of 1995.

It is now four o'clock in the afternoon of a wondrous New Mexico spring day. Since I've written, straight through, these very words you are reading, two of my fingers are beginning to swell. Yeah, that's right. I had such smooth sailing and easy selling by using a pen I'm going to go right on to the next book, the next story, the next script—doctoring with this ancient apparatus.

It has now been 44 years since I first typed those eight pages back there in an adobe house under a blue-green mesa west of Taos. As the cliche goes . . . "It seems like only yester . . . no . . . only a million years ago."

Maybe it was.

Song of the West

"Just one more time I want to . . ." in the West. One hears that saying throughout the stretch of memory here in our wondrously wild, sometimes spoiled and rusted Rocky Mountain Range from Canada to Mexico.

"I want to make the rodeo and Frontier Days just one time."

"I want to climb the sacred Taos Mountain and see the silently shouting sunset in floral infinity just one more time."

"I want to drive down from the Rio Grande River's headwaters in the mountains of majesty above Creede and fly fish for the golden brown near Wagon Wheel Gap at the 4 UR ranch just one more time."

"I want to follow the great river and make those easy side trips to such intriguing little one bar–two church towns such as Magdalena and Hillsboro, New Mexico, on the way to the El Paso, Texas, border crossing just one more time."

It's an attitude of the land we hear, and there are more different viewpoints of the West than there are snowflakes at Aspen or Vail, Breckenridge or Telluride. Maybe our West is simply too big to cover and absorb even once, much less twice, physically or mentally, but we keep on trying.

In my youth I sold a little ranch over in northeastern New Mexico then moved to the art colony of Taos expecting to become rich and famous as a painter in oils, but first I ran into Doughbelly Price. He was an ex-rodeo hand, a gambler and ex-bootlegger turned real estate broker. He bragged that he had sold enough bootleg whiskey to float the English navy and get all of New Mexico and half of Texas drunk.

His newspaper ads read: *For sale: Hot springs. Buy this, take a bath and be somebody. Don't go around smelling like a man all the time. For sale: The Red Arrow Cafe on the account of too much business. For sale: Guest ranch in Moreno Valley, a place to freeze and starve at the same time.*

He sold me several acres of sub-irrigated land west of Taos with a falling-down pine slab house with no plumbing. "You couldn't buy *that* view," he said pointing to the sacred Taos Mountain, "for a million dollars." I believed. I bought. Of course, in a strange way he told the truth. The view he had so expansively pointed out belonged forever to the Taos Pueblo Indians. Doughbelly could only have invented himself in the West. He fit perfectly.

A while later a working cowboy uncle of mine stopped by and stayed a month before going on south of Tucson to winter on a ranch where it was warm. He had just spent a year working on a cattle ranch in the south central mountains of Colorado and said he would rather spend a winter naked in the Klondike than to repeat it.

This area's beauty of forest and streams is widely photographed in spring, summer and fall, and "ooohed and ahhhed" over like a firstborn child by tourists and newcomers who don't have to chop ice from ponds and watering tanks and scatter feed every day in belly-deep snow to feed and water their livestock so all can survive until spring.

I won't name this calendar-postcard ranch because they may need to hire cowhands again. Before my Uncle Slim (aka, Tex, Ion) Evans drifted on south, I made the grand gesture of pointing to the scarlet light rays on Taos Mountain and the glories of the mystic sunset to the west.

He took a quick forced glance, saying, "Ever since I've been here all I've heard is how purty these scenic views are. Well, let me tell you if a feller can't rattle a little change in his pocket (he proceeded to do so vigorously) them sights don't amount to a snowball in a hot skillet."

In spite of the obvious truth from his way of seeing the West, he never left it. His remains are slowly becoming part of the red sandstone mesas, pine-covered forests and blue-green sagebrush deserts that ranchers and miners, artists and artisans, philosophers and housing developers, hunters and monks, mystics and scientists are calling home.

Nearly anyone interested in the West knows that Ned Buntline (back in the 1860s) invented the western myth of the straight-shooting, fastdraw, always honorable and heroic, best-selling western cowboy.

What a contradiction ol' Ned was! He gave temperance speeches wherever and whenever he could, even inserting some of this preaching into his dime novels.

The fact is, however, Ned was a falling-down, knee-crawling drunk, who had four wives and several mistresses at the same time, often writing in an alcoholic stupor his little 10-cent myths of the never-lose, never-say-die, white-hatted heroes that covered the globe and became the enchanting western myth that most people of the world knew and believed—and still do to a certain extent. Amazing.

Thousands of movies and television shows perpetuated this Arthurian legend, and visitors—national and foreign—come West to see cowboys and Indians. Many western historical writers, carrying on the contradictions of their land, have transposed two of the West's biggest *losers* into very famous individuals: Billy the Kid and Col. George Custer.

A careless Billy was shot dead at 21, and I'm sure Custer wished he had been when he rode smack into thousands of well-armed, legitimately angry Indian warriors. Yearly, monthly, historians come out with new works on these two men contradicting one another to the last arrow, bullet and printed word.

When I was a kid-cowboy working on Glorieta Mesa south of Santa Fe, I used to stare from horseback longingly westward to the blue-misted Jemez Mountains out over 40 miles of corrugated foothills, mesas and canyons I was sure held all the mysteries and answers of the ages.

One summer day in 1937 I rode down off the mesa with an old cowhand from the 1870s hunting stray cattle. Old Burt had cowboyed most of his adult life with a little time off mining at Leadville for a silver company and for coal at Trinidad. He had also been a deputy sheriff somewhere in Montana. He was tall, bony and did actually have a *hawkface* as the pulpeteers always said.

To our astonishment we rode up on an encampment of Harvard archeologists. There were tents, barrels and odd equipment all over. These people were tanned, well-fed, healthy and strong-looking in contrast to a 13-year-old bag of bones and a taller bag about 75 years old.

These people were nice and polite, but also curious. We were invited to dismount for coffee and conversation. They explained that their *dig* was for some kind of sauros. They explained about the white plaster of Paris enfolding and protecting the huge petrified bones of the beast. They questioned thusly:

Harvard: "Was the West really as wild as they say?"

Burt: "I s'pose it was. There was lots more wild game, wild horses and wild cattle. Crippled up a lot of good horses trying to gather 'em."

Harvard: "Did you ever do any Indian fighting?"

Burt: "I did a little tradin' with the Comanches, but if I thought they were on the 'fight' I mostly ran off and hid."

This was not turning out as expected. The boss archeologist got a bottle of whiskey out of a canvas bag generously handing it to Burt. It held four long swallows less when he gratefully handed it back.

Another Harvard: "Were there a lot of fights?"

Burt: "Quite a few. Most smart folks hid behind a rock or tree and shot their enemies between the shoulder blades. Course if you could catch 'em asleep on their belly . . . that was best. You could get 'em before they even woke up."

The talk rapidly turned back to ancient sauros.

Another thing that has become a symbol of the West for me is the coyote, in spite of some of my agriculture friends having to justifiably protect their livestock and livelihood from its depredations. The creature's individuality and survivability truly are representative of its human tenants' traits. Only the cockroach can equal them.

Due to the rapidly compounding interest on the number of the West's inhabitants the coyote has been forced into becoming a *town dog*. They inhabit and survive in such disparate environs as Beverly Hills and Boulder. I understand their favorite delicacies are pedigreed poodles and imported maltese cats.

Every single time, for the entirety of my life that I've heard a coyote howl and another answer farther on, then another all the way out of sound I've felt an unexplainable sadness for all the blood shed and smeared—some justified, some certainly not—to inhabit this West.

At the sounds of the little prairie wolf's lament I feel all the lust for beauty, all the lost and found loves, all the terrible blizzards and dust storms howling in unison, all the countless books and paintings of the West leap from the covers and frames into living reality.

And that reality sways and moves to the chants of thousands of shamans. It's a song of the land, the sky, the water, and all creatures that move upon and in it. It is a song of the soul—the West. The West in all its high and low, mythical and real bigness is a singular place, a place of the heart, of the spirit. A special place of being. Home.

I do not know when there will be more fishermen than fish, more concrete poured than there is land to hold it. I do not know when the air will finally become unbreathable by the great forests and they will turn to brown and moldy wormwood. Maybe never. Maybe in 2050. Maybe tomorrow. Who can stop it? Who can change the current pincered movement west? I don't know. The grand canyons of our minds must somehow work the magic.

I was born here, but part of my ancestors were drawn to it long, long ago and they came just as people come now looking for the same beauty, bounty and freedom, I suppose. I make a prayer for the remaining wondrous wide spaces of the land.

The spirit of the West makes a music of eternal hope. While it's still here I shall love, appreciate and try to feel it all, *just one more time.*

3
Short Stories

The Ultimate Giver

Louis Valdez rode up on his worn-out saddle and jug-headed horse. On my trips to town every other day or so I passed his little rundown adobe house, but this was the first time I'd observed him up close. I'd seen his hungry kids watching me drive by. Their clothes were torn and shredded but clean. Louis sat his mount with some pride, but still rode as a sheepherder—holding the reins like a shovel handle and sitting with all his weight on his rump instead of balancing with his legs.

Just the same a true pride showed in his bearing. It was this projection that made me hire him. I couldn't know then that some months later he would offer me a gift more precious to him than his own heartbeat. But this he did. He gave me his wife.

I put him to work around the place patching up the barns, re-setting corral posts and such. He worked hard. He was short, powerfully muscled, and worked without gloves—said they bothered him. He laughed at anything that was half funny and some things that weren't. He wore a narrow brim, dude hat that looked out of place in this country. I suppose that's all he had. He constantly took it off and shoved at his black kinky hair. The thin-soled, brogan shoes he wore were always coming apart, but he kept sewing the soles back on, using a leather punch and some measuring cord.

He wasn't worth a damn working cattle. He'd herded sheep too long. I didn't know, but I would have bet he was a hell of a good sheepherder. I kidded him about organizing a sheepherder's union. He took it seriously, though, said all his cousins wanted him to go to Wyoming and herd sheep because the pay was so good. I learned later that he just couldn't stand to leave his family. He'd rather they'd go a little hungry than be apart. That's what made his later offer to me so precious.

I was new in the country and in no mood to make any fresh friends. It wasn't so much that I didn't like people, but because of recent disappointments in my intimate associates, I wanted to be alone except for the bottle. It wasn't the bottle that first started the trouble, though. It was oil. That's right. Forty gravity oil from seven thousand eight hundred feet under the grass-covered earth.

I had been just as happy as a big over-grown kid could be. We had twenty thousand acres of pretty good grazing land, all covered with cattle and good quarter horses to look after. I didn't take care of it by myself, but helped my father and a couple more hands. It was a good life. Mom did the cooking, and we all ate in the dining room, talking cow talk, horse talk, man talk. It was fun—the brandings, the roundups, the horse training. I got pretty good with a rope and was picking up a little money at local rodeos. Dad didn't go for *working cowboys* rodeoing, but he finally gave in, saying, "It's the times. These goddamn pick-up trucks have made everything too easy, too fast."

I feel now that he was right, but all I could think about then was whether my horse was following the calf properly and if I was improving my tying speed.

My sister had moved into town. She'd married an old boy who was a foreman or something or other of a supermarket. It left me out there on the ranch feeling like I was the big boss sure enough. Hells fire, I was really having fun. On Saturday nights there was always a country dance somewhere in the neighborhood. I had plenty of women—country women.

Then it happened! A dollar an acre for the lease. The big steel rigs moved in and started drilling. They meant business; three shifts, twenty-four hours a day. At night the multi-lighted rig looked like a carnival sitting out there in the hills. We tried to act like it didn't matter. Finally, though, we couldn't control it. Instead of talking around the dinner table about ranch work, we spent most of our time wondering how deep the well was.

Then it hit! Man, there was oil everywhere! The Snyder, Texas, boom was on. Everything went kind of crazy. Those rigs were everywhere, shoving steel into the ground. For a long time the steel came back out all covered with black grease. The town started filling up and then running over. Trailer houses were everywhere, and shacks sprung up over night. It was in the newspapers and magazines all over the country. So many new people moved into the Snyder country that it took all day to find an old friend to visit with. It didn't do any good to try to talk cattle any more. All anybody could say was "oil, oil, oil!" and "let's get rich!" If they didn't have any land to drill on, they figured out something to sell to those that did.

It upset our way of life. We built ten more rooms onto the house, new barns, corrals, and a great big steel cattle guard with our brand and name on it that could be read a mile away. We bought a bunch of high-powered quarter horses, and new trailers and Cadillac cars to pull them around. That damned oil spoiled us all in one way or another.

Mom and Dad got to staying in town a lot. They joined a bunch of clubs, church organizations and such, and did a lot of uptown entertaining. It was taking most of their time. After a while, they just turned the ranch over to me, saying that I was a grown man and they had always intended to do it anyway. I knew better, though. They just wanted to get into town and make the rounds of all those clubs, charities, and social functions.

Well, I took over. It seemed kind of silly to worry about the cattle paying off in the fall, what with five thousand dollars a day pumping out of the ground. Every time one of those pumps would stick its steel snout into the earth, it was inflating our bank account.

I pulled the same kind of trick my folks had. I hired Herb Jones to take over the ranch. He was an old-time cowboy and could be depended on *not* to go plumb crazy. I started running around to rodeos, pulling two registered quarter horses behind a blue Cad convertible. This didn't do me any harm with the women. Then me and a bunch of boys that couldn't quite afford the kind of drinks I'd learned to like started living it up. We just had one wild-ass party after another, and pretty soon all I could think about was curing my hangover before three o'clock in the afternoon so I could start all over again and wind up in the hay with some gal.

The old days were gone all right—just shot plain to hell. Then I met this little tail-twistin' gal. She wouldn't give in to me or anybody else. This came as quite a shock to me. I didn't know there was a woman on earth who could resist my charms. Well, this worried me. The boys kept asking how I'd made out. I couldn't answer. It was getting under my hide a little more all the time. She would lead me on till I was panting like a sunburned lizard, then she'd push me away and say just as positive as you please that final word, "no."

Oh, she was a looker, all right; brown shiny hair and soft brown eyes, big and kind-looking. She was just soft and lovable all over except her heart. But I learned this later. It wasn't too much later though, at that.

I'd say we'd been married about six months when it happened. We'd been doing nothing but running around playing the big-time. I'll say one thing for those oil wells, they had a job on their hands keeping ahead of this wife of mine. She ran through fur coats, high-heeled shoes and fancy dresses the way a fighting cow goes through thin brush. She got me to make a joint checking account, and then we started going over to Dallas to these cockeyed art shows. Now get this! She actually paid two thousand dollars for a painting that scared my dog so bad he wouldn't even come in the front door. If it had been left up to us, the ranch would have rotted and blown away.

All of a sudden she started making these art shows by herself. Then I got the letter. She said she was sorry, but she had found her true love. Well, now, that was a sure enough dinger and just kept getting better. The next check I gave bounced higher than a windmill. She had taken the money to Mexico along with this artist feller. I hoped she was happy.

That's when I started hitting the bottle and hanging around town sleeping with whores, and playing cards the rest of the time. All this began to worry my folks. They wanted to uphold the family name before all those joiners, and I was getting a little bit of rust on it. They gave me several talks. I listened, then went right back to doing the same things over again. Pretty soon they figured if they were going to keep all their memberships in good standing, I'd better be disposed of. I soon was. They bought me this swell little ranch up in northern New Mexico.

Well, I had lots of money and lots of time. This outfit just about ran itself. Everything was in good shape, and the grass was a foot deep. The cattle were fat and just lay around the waterholes licking themselves and soaking up the sun. I had a heck of a time finding enough for Louis to do. I spent most of my time going into town after a bottle. People in the little wind-blown village of Hi Lo were curious, but they kind of left me alone after they found out I wanted it that way. Besides, they needed the business very much. It was a poor country except for a few fellers like me who were being paid to stay away from home. An easy way to make a living, huh?

Finally, I couldn't think up anything else for Louis to do, but I wanted to keep him on anyway. He was proud, though, and that pride was getting in his way. He'd give excuses like he had too much work at his own place. I knew he had only forty sheep, one goat, one cow, one horse and three hound dogs. He also had six kids and a hard-working wife to look after them.

On my trips to town I'd drive back and forth past his place. One day a little pot-bellied boy about three, with dark skin and kinky hair just like Louis', waved at me from the roadside. He looked so damned pitiful that I stopped a minute and tried to talk to him. He was so bashful that no matter what I asked him he just twisted around a post and grinned with his head ducked down.

Then all the kids came out of the house—from about two years old up to twelve. The oldest girls, already filling into little women, were eleven and twelve, but they were the same size and looked like twins. They all began to talk at once. Then Louis came, yelling up at me from his rickety old barn. They all begged me to come in. I didn't want to, but it seemed a shame to turn down their hospitality. That's when I met Louis' wife, the mother of the six kids.

I was struck by her looks. Louis had bragged on her so much I expected a sure enough beauty. This woman was bigger than two mules, her front teeth were missing, and when she laughed her front shook in rolls of fat. It was almost impossible to tell what was what. She smiled that empty mouthed smile and said warmly, "Come in the house."

The place was clean but smelled like a bunch of kids just before their baths. It soon vanished in the scent of the hot coffee Jeemy made. I don't know even now why they called her that, but Jeemy seemed to fit. The first thing I knew we'd had a cup of coffee, and I'd gone out to the car to get a bottle of whiskey, then Louis was playing the guitar. I had three kids on my lap staring hard from those bright black eyes. Every time I took a drink they watched me swallow as if my life depended on it. Maybe it did right then. I don't know.

Now Louis is not the best guitar player in the world, but he *is* the most persistent. He never stopped except to drink, laugh, or talk the two oldest girls into dancing for me.

Soon I went back to the car and got another bottle. Jeemy was drinking and laughing more and more. Everything Louis or I said just bent her over with mirth. I noticed how long, thick and untidy her hair was. In fact, the only thing that could have helped that hair was a pair of sharp scissors or a steel horse brush. Louis kept insisting I dance with her . . . I did. She danced up close where I could smell her femaleness. She didn't push herself on me but neither did she pull away. I got so dizzy from all the heat and the whiskey that I just sat down right in the middle of the floor. Then we all started singing and yelling. It was the first good time I'd had in months and one of the best I'd ever had. The whole family made me welcome and meant it.

I woke up the next morning on a little pallet by the fire. Jeemy was moving about heating up some coffee. As I looked up at her from the floor all I saw was the fleshy curves overlapping one another and I was struck by the realization that Louis must still see her as she'd been fifteen years ago. She felt me looking and said, "Good morning. How do you feel?"

I couldn't think of much to say, so I told her the old one about my eyes feeling like two burned holes in a saddle blanket. I know she'd heard it a thousand times but she laughed loud and honest just the same. I got up and washed.

Louis and the kids got up then. We all sat around smoking while the kids ate a big bait of corn meal mush. I noticed it was all they had. Then Jeemy ran the kids outside and sent the two oldest girls to the barn to milk and look after the stock. She gave Louis a big bowl of mush, and before I'd noticed she put a fried egg in front of me. I knew it was the only egg they had. I didn't want to embarrass them, so I ate it and said nothing. When I think back on it, that was a mighty big gift, that egg. Of course, it was nothing to what Louis was to give me later on.

I got to liking those kids so much that I just couldn't let them go hungry any longer. At the same time, I didn't know how to get around Louis' pride. Then I figured it out. I'd buy two or three quarts of whiskey and a big box of groceries in town. I'd drop by and say, "Louis, let's have a party. Get that guitar to goin', boy. I brought along a little stuff to snack on later."

It worked. There would always be enough left over to last for several days. The kids lost that hungry look and began filling out. Jeemy kept her hair combed long and shiny now and wore a little powder and lipstick. I worried about their clothes now. They were all in rags, and I knew the two oldest girls needed perking up. Then I thought of a way to do something about it. 1 bought several different bolts of dress material—some plain, some print, all kinds. I had the clerk wrap them up and pack them in a box. I drove up one day and yelled for Louis. He wasn't there, but Jeemy and the kids came running out to meet me.

I said, "Where's old Louis?"

Jeemy answered, "He took the wagon and team to the hills for a load of firewood. Come on in."

I went in and after she'd brought me a cup of coffee, I said, "Somethin's worryin' me, Jeemy." She looked at me out of those wide dark eyes without saying anything—just looked hurt-like. I went on, trying not to catch her eyes. "I found a box out on the highway a while ago. A big box. It had Chicago marked on it. I guess somebody from Chicago must have lost it."

I walked out with all the kids following and brought the box in, and we opened it up. Jeemy's eyes grew large and she couldn't keep her hands off the material. The two oldest girls were having a fit about one of the long pieces of blue material. I could just see their minds pulling new dresses over those young bodies. Jeemy motioned them back and let the lid fall on the box.

"What will you do with it?" she asked.

I said, "Well, Jeemy, the way I figure it, Chicago is a mighty big town. It would probably be impossible to find the owner of this box, even if we knew the name and address. There's just one honest thing to do." She looked at me sort of sad-like, and I went on. "It would be an outright sin to waste this. Jeemy, don't you think you could take it and make up some clothes for yourself and the kids?"

The girls shrieked and everybody was talking, planning and pulling the cloth out all at once. I got out of there and went home.

One night Louis was playing his old violin—he was really much better on it than on the guitar. The kids had all gone to bed, and Jeemy and I, at Louis' insistence, were dancing. I kept smelling her powerful woman scent. It bothered me. I knew Louis worried sometimes about my not having a woman, but this was going a little too far. We walked outside to get some fresh air. It was a cold clear night. I could tell something was eating on him. Every time I'd taken him to town with me he'd made an excuse to drop by and see one of his good-looking female cousins. I reckon he thought I was crazy, but I was a little soured on females—couldn't get over the shock I'd had back there at Snyder, Texas.

Anyway, that night while we were standing outside, Louis cleared his throat and said to me, "You're my friend. My best friend! I just want you to know something. You can have my wife any time you want her." I looked at him, unbelieving, and he went on, "I mean it!"

Well, I just figured it was the whiskey and the cold air. I didn't answer. We drank all night, and Jeemy and I danced faster and wilder to the tunes from Louis' old violin. She was sweating, and I could smell the scents of her body again and it made me weak and dizzy, but I wouldn't have hurt either of their feelings for anything.

The next night we invited George Ellis and his wife over for a drink. George was a big son-of-a-gun. So was his wife. He was about six-four and weighed around two-thirty. Allene must have been at least five-ten and was big everywhere.

We got to dancing and yelling, so around two in the morning things were really picking up. Allene kept grabbing me and rubbing against me. It upset the hell out of me. I was half drunk and having a good time otherwise and didn't want any trouble, but one thing I hadn't had in a long time was a woman. Allene whispered in my ear, "Pour George another drink."

After a while with all those drinks, George started getting mean. He grabbed a butcher knife off the table and rammed it straight up into the low *viga* ceiling. He left it there, saying he was the only one who could get it down without a stepladder. Then he started singing. He sounded like a bull in a deep bog. It was messing up our party. I knew that was what he wanted.

He began telling Louis how sorry he played and nobody could sing to that music, much less dance to it. He looked at me and his wife when he said that. I felt bad and wished Louis would finish the tune so I could get rid of her.

Louis didn't like anybody insulting his music, especially in his own home, and I didn't blame him. He and George got to arguing loud and mad. George called Louis a dirty name, grabbed him and threw him over the table. Then he jumped over the table and hit Louis in the jaw before he could get to his feet. Louis was strong for his size, but he wasn't half big enough. He went down and George stood over him, breathing hard and glaring at me.

Allene yelled, "George, sit down and behave yourself! What in the hell's the matter with you?"

She knew what was the matter all right, and so did I. He wasn't really mad at Louis. It was me and his wife he was angry at. I figured he shouldn't have hit Louis. All of a sudden I got mad. I said, "You big dumb son of a bitch. You know so much about knives. Why don't you pull that one out of the ceiling and see what you can do to me with it."

He stared real hard out of his red, pig eyes and said, "That's just what I'll do!"

Like I said, George was sort of dumb. When he stretched up to get the knife I hit him right in the wide-open belly. That fist ran all the way to his back bone, and he doubled over with a big "whoof." I drew back and hit him right smack in the face. Then I went a little crazy myself. I knew I had him going, but I knew I couldn't let up. I laid them in there good and hard, one right after the other. He went down on his hands and knees, and a stream of blood ran out on the floor. Then I hauled off and kicked him in the side of the jaw. He rolled over, and I let him have another boot on the other side of the jaw. His head snapped around and his eyes rolled upwards. It felt good.

Louis got up and I said, "Louis, help me load this big boar hog in his car. He won't break up any more parties tonight."

We dragged him out and got him propped up in the front seat. You couldn't tell what he looked like for all the blood. He was moaning and taking on, but he didn't want to fight. He wanted to get the hell out of there. His wife was sure worried about him, all right. She whispered to me to take her down to the sheep barn. The temperature outside was setting at just about six below zero. It didn't help my woman situation a bit.

I didn't come back to Louis' for a week. I hung around town most of the time thinking about that last party. I kept hitting the bottle, and I wasn't eating much. After we'd gone back into the house that night Louis had said, "Why'd you do that to George?" I didn't think he'd understand all the reasons if I told him. I wasn't sure that I understood all of them myself. All I could answer was, "Why, Louis, you're my friend. I don't like people bothering my friends." Louis had picked up his guitar and started playing it and crying at the same time. I didn't know what to make of it.

After four or five days of hard drinking, I got about half sober, bought a bunch of whiskey and stuff and headed for Louis' again. I'd missed them all. While Jeemy got the coffee ready and the kids were leaning all over me, listening to every word, I realized how much I felt at home. There was something—I don't know what it was, but it was the only place in the world I felt this way.

I sat there watching, absorbing this family. They had so little and the possibility of having anything more was mighty slim. But they seemed so happy. They showed me the dresses and shirts

Jeemy had made out of the "Chicago" cloth with great pride. Whenever Jeemy or Louis asked the kids to do something, it was done eagerly without question. There was a unity about the whole family, and a closeness that I, an outsider, was allowed to share.

Louis started playing some old Spanish love songs, and after a time we whipped out a couple of bottles. We went on into the night drinking, dancing, having a big time. The kids went to bed. Louis played on and on. Sad love songs. I didn't know the words he sang, but I *felt* the meaning. Jeemy danced up close and warm and sweaty. I felt her heated, damp cheek plastered against mine. Louis played with his eyes shut, and he drank awfully hard. He seemed low and unhappy for the first time since I'd known him. He insisted we go into the front room where he and Jeemy slept, so we wouldn't disturb the children and where we'd have more room to dance.

The kerosene lamps flickered and made it all seem unreal and kind of unearthly, if that's the right word. The whiskey kept getting in my head more and more, and Jeemy's inflamed, woman smell got mixed up in it. The low passionate strains of Louis' violin were throbbing at my temples, and the desire in me was strong and painful.

Louis was playing softly from the room we had just left. Jeemy turned the lamp down low and pressed her massive breasts and stomach up against me. She held me tight but gently to her. I almost fainted and I wanted to run away, but I couldn't. Then I knew what I had to do—not for myself but for Louis. The last thing in the world I desired was Louis' woman. First, because she was his wife, and secondly, she wasn't my type, whatever the hell I thought that meant. I know that in all my life I will never have the love I received so unwillingly that night. Nothing expert or practiced, but just a feeling of closeness. Jeemy gave the same love to me that she gave to Louis, even though I doubt if I appreciated it as sincerely. Each to his own, is sure as all hell a correct cliche. The sacrifice was over at last. Then I lay quiet against her breasts with a powerful desire to fall out of that bed and run till I fell. But I gritted my teeth, slowed my breathing and stayed put.

Something made me glance towards the door. It was cracked open about four inches. I could see the lamplight from the other room encircling Louis' kinky head in a sort of halo. Then the head moved away, and the door shut softly.

I got up early the next morning and walked out through the kitchen. Louis sat at the table, his head on his hands, asleep. I noticed that the half-full bottle had been emptied.

I got to wanting a woman after that, and I found me a dandy—the daughter of a small time rancher down on the dry Cimmaron. I quit a lot of my drinking except for plain fun, and don't hardly leave the ranch at all any more. My wife, June, stops by to see about Jeemy and the kids every time she goes to town. I told her what fine people Louis and Jeemy are. I bought a little sheep ranch over north for Louis to look after. He makes it pay. He's the best sheepherder I ever saw. I've wished somehow I could have done more for Louis. He'd given me all he had.

Blizzard

It was at least an hour before sundown when the coyote howled from the rolling hills north of the house. A little farther on another answered and another and another. The way it sounded to me, every coyote in the world was having a say about things. I knew what that meant—blue norther. Besides, the leg I'd cracked up in the Cheyenne rodeo back in my better days was stiffening up. That was a sure sign.

Well, I had it coming, I reckon. I'd been down here on the lower camp for three winters, up until now the quietest winters a man could ask for. There were times when I began doubting how much longer I could hold out.

I remember when I'd first asked old Joe Rivers for the job. He'd said, "Mr. Manners, I've been running this outfit for over twenty-five years."

I interrupted. "Dave. Just call me Dave."

"All right, Dave. As I was sayin'. Twenty-five years of hiring men to work the lowercamp has made me just a wee bit leery about the matter. Some make it through the winter and pull out in the spring, but most leave in the late fall when we need 'em the worst. Always throws us in a tight. Have to hire some no-good and give him double pay to sit down there and roast his shins while the cows shift for themselves. I suppose a man gets lonesome thirty miles from the nearest living soul. I'll hire you if you'll stick out the winter."

"You've got a hand," I said. And he did have.

They'd furnished me good horses and fair grub, and that grub was what I was thinking about when I saw Sandy Malone. Although he was a quarter of a mile away, I knew it was Sandy by the way he sat in the saddle. Besides, he nearly always rode the bald-faced sorrel he was on now. I rolled a smoke and waited there by the corral gate.

As he pulled up, he let out a war whoop that to my mind must have answered all the howling coyotes at once, and then some. "Howdy, Dave, you old worn-out hermit. How about some frijoles?"

"Just took the thought out of my mind, Sandy. Turn your horse loose and we'll see what we can do about the hollow place in your belly. How are things at headquarters?"

"Fine," answered Sandy. "The old man sent me down to check on you before snow flies."

"You're too late, Sandy. She'll hit in the next twenty-four hours."

"Aw come on, Dave. You know better than to predict the weather in this country."

"You'll see, Sandy, my boy. You'll see."

Sandy had put his horse in a barn stall and pitched him a little hay and corn. We headed for the house. The sun was doing its last do over in the southwest where it went to sleep this time of year. I put the beans on the pot-bellied heater as soon as I had a fire blazing. I fetched a chunk of venison from the only other room in the lower camp house that I used for storing things.

"I've got to go over north and get another deer right away," I mentioned, as I dropped slices of the dark meat in the skillet. I had a little two-hole iron wood stove that I did most of my cooking on. It had a reservoir on the side that kept hot water whenever I remembered to keep water in it. The venison was juicy, tender, the beans just right. We washed it down with hot black coffee, and settled back for a smoke.

That's when it hit.

It got a little hard to breathe all of a sudden, as if all the air had been knocked out of the house. A window rattled warningly. Then, wham! It was upon us. Sandy got up and went over to the window to look out.

"Looks like you've got company for a while, Mr. Weather-Prophet," he said. "The old man will be worried silly, but from the looks of things, I can't do much about it." Sandy was right as rain.

By morning, everything was white—the ground, the air, the whole world, it seemed. The wind was getting stronger and stronger. I went out to let the horses into a hay stack. I was covered with the white powdery stuff when I got back to the house.

"Perty rough," I told Sandy. "I reckon the cows will drift down to the brush country east of here."

"Yeah, they'll make it all right, if it doesn't last too long," Sandy said encouragingly.

Sandy was a good-natured boy and laughed a lot. The two of us usually made payday in town together. That wasn't often, three or four times a year.

We passed the day off talking and eating. There's something about northers that makes a man extra hungry. Sandy was saying, "Remember the time we got in that fracas over at Santa Fe? That hombre thought you were trying to horn in on his gal because you said 'Excuse me' when you brushed her elbow, and took a sock at you."

"I'll never forget it," I said. "He missed me a mile and knocked his Suzy as cold as a judge's voice."

We got on stuff like that and talked for hours. And ranching, too—just about everything in the game. It was warm inside, our bellies were full and there was plenty of black coffee. With the resulting comfort, many memories came back—some sad, some so funny we'd laugh like idiots. Finally, way in the night, we played out.

The trouble that was going on outside had taken voice now. We could hear it howling like an abandoned baby.

I pulled out a folding cot and made it up for Sandy. Then I got out my own bed roll. I was sitting on the edge of it, pulling off a boot, when I heard a mouse gnawing in a little cupboard off the kitchen. I went over to the shelves where I kept my few eating utensils. On top, I found a couple of mouse traps. I set 'em, using a bean for bait, and went off to sleep in a hurry.

I've been in the habit for years of getting up with the sun. There wasn't any sun this morning, just greyness. I lay in bed for a couple of extra hours.

The wind was playing a tune to my memories. Neither the tune nor the memories were pleasant. I remembered the blizzard of my childhood. My father, mother and myself were traveling across country in a covered wagon. The blizzard had struck with terrible force. Father had tried to pitch camp, hobble the horses and gather firewood. The horses had become lost in the storm. The snow had driven so fast and hard, Father couldn't see to hunt for firewood. The three of us had huddled almost freezing in the wagon. The second day, Father had tried to go for help. He had frozen to death less than a hundred steps from the wagon. Mother had covered me with her coat. The storm finally played out. Trappers found us almost frozen and starved to death.

Mother died hours later. I knew I wouldn't be here listening to the wailing wind if she hadn't given me her coat.

I dreaded to get up. The room was cold. I could hear Sandy snoring away. Well, it had to be done. I raised myself to a sitting position, when I saw a mouse over there in the cupboard doorway. It was a big mouse, bigger than I'd seen since camping down here. Lighter in color, too. I had set the traps up against each side of the doorway. The mouse was standing there looking at me, eyes crystal-black and cunning. He was quivering all over, twitching his nose now and then like a rabbit. I wondered why he wasn't in one of those traps. Maybe he doesn't like beans, I thought. This irritated me a little because I've eaten more beans in my time than I've breathed fresh air. When I reached for my pants, the little dickens scooted back out of sight somewhere into the cupboard. I got up and shivering plenty had trouble getting my boots on.

Sandy woke up, yawning. "It's too cold for a fire to burn, Dave. Better get back in the sack."

"It's not polite to sleep when you've got company," I replied. "Besides, I don't want you to lay there and starve. Ground is frozen too hard to dig a grave. You're not the only company we had last night," I added.

"What do you mean?" asked Sandy.

"There's been a mouse moved in with us."

"Well, he's not getting my bed, even if he thinks I'm not polite to company. He can sleep on the floor or crawl in the bed with you, Dave."

I finally got the fire started. Slowly at first, then faster. It was really melting wood by the time Sandy got up. I told him I was gonna try to make it out to the barn and corrals to check on the horses. So maybe he could mix up a few biscuits and slice off some venison. Sandy agreed.

I put on a heavy sheeplined coat and tied on a bandana around my face; then with another I tied my hat on. I put it over my hat and under my chin. I'd lost good hats in this kind of weather before. When I opened the door, the storm didn't wait for me to ask it in. The icy blast nearly knocked me down and I could barely pull the door shut behind me. I thought I'd never make it to the barn. The air was made of ice with a million flailing arms to drive its coldness through a man. Here and there I could tell I was on a spot where the ground was swept bare by the whirling wind. Then I'd hit a drift waist deep. Once I fell, numbed . . . and it suddenly seemed warm and almost safe down in the snow. That's when I knew it was bad. It must have happened to my father that way. The memory flashed through my mind. I shivered, the cold rushing back into my body.

I made it all right out to the horses. They were bunched up on the south side of the haystack, heads down and painted white with snow. I managed somehow to get them into the barn. I paused for a moment's rest. When I had gotten my breath back, I started for the house.

The return trip wasn't so bad. I guess maybe because I knew there was a fire and warmth at the end of it. Sandy had venison on the table and was just putting the biscuits into the oven.

"Have a cup of coffee, Dave, and thaw out your clinking old bones."

"Man!" was all I could say as I took off the frozen coat. The coffee worked wonders, and Sandy's bread wasn't bad, although I thought I could've made better. We enjoyed the meal and were talking about the possibilities of the cows making it through the storm when the mouse made a dash across the cupboard and into the "junk" room. The crack under the door looked too small for him to crawl through, but he made it.

"That baby's too smart for my traps, but I'll get him tonight," I told Sandy. I got up from the table right then and set a different kind of trap. I got a bucket and melted snow until it was about half full. I then laid a piece of firewood so that it sloped from the door right out over the middle of the bucket. I took thin splinters of wood and laid them at the end of the firewood. I tied this down with a worn piece of string. On one end of the splinter I stuck a piece of venison. That was sure to get the little dickens. He'd smell the venison, climb the firewood, then crawl out to get the meat. The string would break and he'd take a dive into the bucket. I set the new trap right in the center of the doorway to the cupboard where he'd been standing. I could see where he had gnawed a hole in the floor. I wondered what kind of nest he had down there.

The day passed quickly. The wind had settled down to a steady roar now. Once in a while it hesitated, then blasted forth as before. The old wooden frame house was shaking a bit now and then. We didn't talk as much as before. We'd sorta talked ourselves out the past night. I got to sitting there waiting and watching for that little mouse. He showed up a couple of times all right. I wondered when he had crossed over again from the "junk" room to the cupboard. He ran right under the piece of wood on the trap and peeked at me from the side of the bucket. The little devil was ignoring the trap. This riled me a little, especially when Sandy said, "You've got to be smarter than a mouse to catch one."

Darkness had now spread its dim blanket. I moved my chair over by the cupboard. I held a stove poker in my hand, determined to bash in the mouse's brains if he took another peek at me from the cupboard. I waited and waited, getting stiff and uncomfortable sitting there. Sandy had gone to bed. I was about to give up, when I saw those dark, gleaming, beady eyes fastened on me. This paralyzed me for a moment. Then I let fly with the poker. There was a loud ringing noise, and Sandy jumped up like he'd had a rattlesnake for a bed partner. The mouse was gone. I'd knocked over the bucket and spilled the water. The ricocheting poker had sprung one of the traps I'd first set. I felt like an idiot about it all. I suppose from the way Sandy stared at me, I looked like one, too.

Sandy crawled back in bed and didn't say a word. I went to bed too, but I was a little shaky and lay there looking at the ceiling and listening to the song of the wind. I don't know what made me do it, but I got up and took my old 30-30 off the hooks above the door and laid it by the bed roll within easy reach.

I was just dozing off, when I felt something run across my chest. I bolted upright in bed and grabbed the gun. At that instant, Sandy said, "What in hell is the matter, Dave? That mouse get in bed with you?"

I cut him short angrily, then felt sorry about it. I realized too late that I needed someone to talk to. I didn't sleep a wink the rest of the night. I kept thinking I could feel that mouse scratching my head or crawling down my back. Part of the time I lay there with sweat breaking out all over me. I was afraid to move, even to breathe.

I rose before daylight the next morning, taking all the nerve I could gather together to do so. When Sandy woke up, I was sitting over by the stove drinking coffee and smoking cigarettes about as fast as I could roll them.

I was thinking about what the boys at headquarters had told me less than a year ago. Another man like myself, except that he had a wife, had been trapped here at lower camp. Their food ran low; then there was none. They'd been so hungry, he had finally dashed out into the blizzard carrying his rifle, screaming repeatedly to his wife that he'd get food. The boys found him sometime later with his hands frozen to a barbwire fence. His gun was lost.

The memory depressed me. I didn't see why exactly, except that I did have to make it for a while on beans.

By the time Sandy got up, it was daylight, and I felt better for a while. I even began wondering at myself for going off the cliff. But when I saw Sandy looking over at the 30-30 by my bed roll, and then looking at me on the sly, I got into a rage inside my guts.

The mouse made several trips back and forth from the cupboard to the "junk" room. I sat down on the bed roll, picking up the rifle. I'd wait. My head began to pound. I thought I could hear the mouse laughing at me in a screeching voice that seemed to keep time with the wind outside. I don't know how long he'd been standing there in the middle of the floor when I saw him. I jerked the trigger of the 30-30, working the lever feverishly. The noise sounded like a thousand sticks of dynamite going off at once. I stopped after the hammer clicked empty several times. I'd had genuine buck fever over a mouse.

I was standing now in the middle of the room, with nothing to show for my outburst except some holes in the floor and a loss of breath. I looked foolishly around at Sandy. He was standing over there by the cot with a forty-five in his hand. I knew that a moment before it had been pointing right at my back. The gun belt was hung across a corner of the cot. It hadn't been there the last time I looked that way. I always left it hung on a big nail in the wall.

I hunted up some shells and reloaded the 30-30. Sandy was lying on his side on the cot making out like he was asleep; but I knew he was awake and was watching me through the slits of his eyelids. I thought the storm had got him—driven him out of his senses. I figured he was planning to kill me.

The day went slowly. By nightfall, I was shaking inside and out. I didn't eat another bite, just sat and stared at the cupboard door. I even forgot Sandy. When darkness did come, I was afraid to go to sleep. I kept thinking things were crawling on me. Once in a while I'd think something was slipping up behind. It didn't matter which way I sat. I was scared silly. I kept the fire going and it cast funny lights about the room where it shone through the vent in the front of the stove door. It had been hours and hours since I'd slept. Finally, against my will and from sheer exhaustion, I dozed off.

I dreamed that my arm was hanging off the bed roll and the mouse was eating my fingers. I struggled and strained with all my might: I couldn't move my arm. He ate my fingers, my hand, my arm. His belly was getting bigger and bigger. I kept looking for it to burst. The little devil had started talking to me now. He said I'd been mean and tried to trap him, tried to drown him, tried to shoot him. He said he was going to eat my arm off and then go get a hundred more mice and let them have the rest of me.

I woke up screaming at the top of my voice. The mouse was crouching there in the flickering light. I hurled the covers back and dived at him with all my crazy energy. The world turned into flashing lights—all of them red, some in circles and some in straight lines that went off into space out of sight. Then it was soft purple and hard black and that was all.

THE LIGHT WAS IN MY EYES. It would have been sunlight except that sunlight couldn't get through the windows for the frozen snow. I was covered up in bed. My head was heavy and when I raised myself, pains shot all through my body. I struggled to a sitting position. I felt my head. It was swollen on top and there was a little dried blood.

Sandy's cot was empty. There was a note lying on it. I could tell by the broad line that he'd written it with the lead of a bullet. Guess he couldn't find a pencil. It said that he was going to try to make it in, as the old man would sure be needing him. I'd bumped my head and he'd dragged me back to bed. There was something else, but he'd scratched it out. Well, anyway, I wasn't scared any more. Maybe I was too sore and too cold to be.

As quickly as I could, I got myself into the rest of my clothes and stepped out into the world of glaring white light. It was still and quiet. I saddled a horse and rode down east to check the cattle. They were all right, browsing about in the brush in search of food. I felt good, not having any losses. Soon the horse was exhausted from busting shoulder high drifts, and I headed back for the lower camp house to get another.

As I unsaddled, I realized how long it had been since I had eaten, and how hungry I was. I built a fire in the cook stove and put the last of the venison on. Now I set about stacking the few plates on the table, getting the crumbs together. I reached for the half-biscuit left over on the bread plate, intending to finish it, when it fell from my fingers and rolled to the wall just by the door to the cold room. Suddenly I knew that's where I wanted it to be. "That's your grub, little feller," I said half aloud.

I thought I might as well get some beans to soak for future meals. They were in a hundred pound sack in the "junk" room. I took a pan with me and stepped into the icy place. There in the middle of the barren floor was the little mouse. I could tell by the stiffness of him that he was dead. He looked a lot smaller than before, there by himself.

Even with the fire going and the venison sizzling, the house seemed unaccountably cold. Empty.

Don't Kill My Dog

I would have gone over and killed Marv Jensen right then, but I was too choked up. I just squatted there holding that old white, shaggy dog's head in my lap. He was dead. I knew. It was just that I didn't want to admit it. It's not hard to figure, seeing how much I loved that old half-breed hound dog. I hadn't cried since I was just a snotty-nosed button, but the tears were there now.

I kept saying, "Get up, Rag Dog. Get up and let's go run a coyote. Come on, boy. We'll jump in the pickup and hunt the whole durned country before dark." I should have known old Rag Dog wouldn't believe that, even if he could hear me.

I'd heard some shots while out milking. They came from over west at Marv Jensen's sheep outfit. It sure never dawned on me that it was my dogs stopping the lead.

I went right on and finished milking, let the calf suck, turned the cow out to pasture, gathered up my bucket of milk and headed for the house. Then I saw Rag Dog coming across the rolling hills between my little starvation outfit and Marv Jensen's. He was pure white and stood out against the golden gramma grass like a hole in a saddle blanket. I was sick. I didn't know why exactly. It was just a feeling I had. As old Rag Dog got closer, I could see he was limping.

I set the bucket of milk down and took off afoot towards him. We kept moving closer together. I could see the red smear behind his rib cage running down on his flanks. He dragged one hind leg. He came right on up to me and fell down on the broken leg, looked up and wagged his tail. Those old honest brown eyes of his stared out around all that shaggy hair and seemed to say to me, "I've had it, Boss. I've had it bad." The eyes dimmed, he swayed and fell over. I dropped down by him and held him a minute or two before he died. I held him for a spell after. He looked at me once and then kicked a little and wagged that big shaggy tail. It looked like he said, "This is old Rag Dog's last run." It was.

Well, I got up and I was mad—just plain killing mad. The other three dogs were missing, too. Killing coyotes was what I did for a living, and they made it possible. It was all I knew. All I ever wanted. Hell, Marv was one of the fellers that helped pay the ten dollars a head for every coyote scalp. That's why I figured Marv had spotted a coyote among his flock and was trying to save ten dollars as well as some of his sheep. I was sure enough wrong.

I walked on back to that little rickety bachelor's shack I called home. I took the thirty-thirty off the wall and filled it plumb full of bullets. Then I stuffed a box of them in my jacket pocket. There were twelve or fourteen rounds in that box, and I aimed to put every one of them through Marv Jensen's guts. That is one thing I meant. I may not be much else in this world, but I am a sure enough dead shot with a rifle—and that goes for rocks, too.

My thoughts went back to when I was a little kid over on the flat, east side of the state at Humble City near Hobbs. I had a dog called Depression. My granddad named him after what was going on in the world. I didn't savvy any of it. See, I spent all my time with ole Depression running down young jackrabbits and cottontails for food. The cottontails he couldn't catch, he'd chase down a hole, and I'd twist them out with a forked barbwire. Hard way to help feed the family, some would say, but to me it was fun. I didn't really know the difference.

Then that Sunday, my uncle Gilt, Aunt Rosie, and their four-year-old boy, Hodge, came to visit. We'd had a batch of blue quail for dinner that I had trapped. They sure went good with the hot bisquits, gravy, and sorghum molasses. Everybody was full and visiting out on the front porch. Ole Depression was lying in the shade, full of dinner scraps, trying to sleep. Hodge kept pulling at his ears and bothering him all over. I told him about five times to quit. Everybody ignored me. Then Hodge picked up my dog's tail and kicked him you know where. Ole Depression jumped up and roared, knocking the kid down. He didn't bite him or nothing, he was just saying, "Let me sleep."

Uncle Gilt jumped off the porch and kicked Ole Depression in the belly as hard as he could. I reached down as naturally as I'd scratch my butt, picked up a rock and threw it. Thud. It hit Uncle Gilt right between the eyes. He dropped. Everybody, but me and the dog, gathered around to see if he was dead. He wasn't, but it took him an hour to stand up and a year to quit wobbling. He never did get close to one of my dogs again.

Funny how things from the past pop back into your mind when you're mad about something else. I got in that old pickup truck that I did all my hunting in and set the motor spinning. I almost turned over on the first curve. That little wagon-rutted road was not made for speed. I slowed down. It was mighty hard to do, but I wanted things in good shape when I got hold of Marv Jensen. The breath was coming out of my lungs scorching hot. I gritted my teeth till I could feel the enamel chipping.

Old Rag Dog was seven years old. As dogs go that's not old, but for a coyote-running dog it's just about his last year. I had a five-year-old stag and two young greyhounds. I was using Old Rag Dog to train these young greys. Man, were they working out.

Why, it had only been a week ago that me and the dogs had one of the best days of our lives. Over north about ten miles in a bunch of rolling grass country was where we had hunted. Some homesteaders had moved in here years before. They had one hundred and sixty acres of plowed land apiece. But they starved out. The fields had blown for a while and piled up in drifts, then finally the weeds took over. Some years, when the rains were good, the sunflowers grew up three or four feet high. It was home to Mr. Coyote. It was a fine place for him to hunt field mice, rats and gophers.

I had this wooden crate built on the back of my pickup, and when we'd jump a coyote all I had to do was reach out the window and pull a rope that ran through a couple of pulleys. This raised a door in the back. Out the dogs would come.

Old Rag Dog knew enough to look in the direction I was driving. He never wasted any time. He just bailed out in a dead run, whirling and heading out in front. Pretty soon he would see the coyote and the race was on. Naturally, the other dogs followed Old Rag, doing whatever he did. They knew he was the lead dog and would keep them out of trouble.

Well, on that great day we were easing along in second gear watching the sunflowers. This old coyote was plenty smart. He stayed down till we were past, then raised up and trotted off in the opposite direction. I spotted him in the rear view mirror. Gradually, trying to keep him from noticing, I fed more gas to the engine. At the same time I started making a big circle. The coyote kept trotting right along. Then all of a sudden, before he knew it, we were headed right back at him. I slammed the pedal plumb to the floor, and that old pickup like to have jumped out from under us.

The coyote caught on then and there. He whirled and headed at full speed towards a canyon about a mile to the northwest. He was too late. We were gaining on him fast. The pickup was bouncing up and down and sideways and every other way as we ripped across the rough prairie. The dogs were bawling to beat hell and jumping at the sides of the crate, wanting out. A hundred—fifty—thirty yards. I slammed on the brakes and pulled the rope at the same time. The dogs hit the ground running. I slapped the pickup into low gear and then back up to second.

Everything was moving at about the same speed now—the coyote out front running for his life, the dogs right behind stretched out in long smooth, prairie-eating strides, their bellies seeming to drag right on the ground, and me pumping the gas and dodging bear grass clumps. I reckon I would have driven right straight off into a deep canyon if I thought I would be there for the kill.

Just when I was afraid the coyote was going to make it to the canyon, I saw his tail start switching from side to side—a sure sign he was putting out all he had. Then I saw Old Rag move out a little ahead of the other dogs and close the gap. He moved right up beside the coyote and reached over to gather himself a mouthful of neck. They rolled over in a big cloud of dust. The two greyhounds went on past, whirled back and took hold. The stag had already dived into the breast.

I drove right on up and bailed out of the pickup almost before it was stopped. That coyote was done. Old Rag had the main hold on his throat, and the stag was crushing into his ribs, shoving those broken bones right through his heart. One of the greys was chewing on what little bit of the neck he could find, while the other had a jaw full of stomach—trying to tear it open to get at the guts. What a team of dogs! Old Rag Dog had stayed with the throat, never letting the coyote get a chance to bite one of the young greys. They were getting their confidence fast. A few more hunts and they wouldn't pay any more attention to a coyote's fangs than they would the bite of a baby flea.

I got my breath back, pulled the dogs off, and we all stopped for a little rest. After a smoke or two, I scalped the coyote. Ten dollars it was worth. Good money . . . and a million dollars worth of action.

These things, and more, were jumping back and forth through my mind as I drove over to kill Marv Jensen. Every once in a while I'd reach over and feel the hard steel of the thirty-thirty. In just a few minutes that same steel would be plenty hot. Old Rag Dog dead! He had to go and kill Old Rag! And maybe the others, too.

Seems like the times I'd been in bad trouble in my life it was over somebody abusing my dog. That old dog, Depression, never bothered anything but what I wanted him to bother . . . well, he did chase rabbits on his own, and he'd nip at the milk-cows' heels when I was driving them home. He was just helping and I loved him.

There was a neighbor kid in Humble City, where I was a boy, who had been throwing rocks at Depression for a spell. So far he'd missed. I'd warned him twice. He didn't listen. Then he whacked Depression on the side of the head with a big rock, and just stood there on his front porch laughing. Old Depression headed home just like Old Rag Dog had today. He was slinging his head and one ear was bleeding. I examined him to be sure he'd live, and I took off through the mesquite making out like I was going in the opposite direction. I didn't. I circled around and came up on the other side of the kid's house. He was pulling a rusty toy wagon with a wheel missing.

My granddad had given me a ten-cent pocket knife. It wouldn't hardly sharpen up and the blade would bend when I whittled if I didn't hold it just right. I chased that rock-throwing little sucker up on his front porch and threw him down and got astraddle him. I took that ten-cent knife out of my pocket and opened it, spread his throwing hand out flat, and stabbed. The blade didn't have time to bend and it pinned his hand to the wooden porch like Christ on the cross. While he was kicking and screaming, I told him never to hurt my dog again.

I really got into trouble over that one—even sent me to West Texas to stay with my grandmother. I didn't care. I took my dog with me and we hunted and had a good time.

I was thinking of Old Rag Dog, now, and the day of our great hunt. Old Rag had pulled a jim-dandy. I'd loaded the dogs back into their crates, then drove over to look off a rocky rim. Talk about luck! Just as I slowed down and reached for the door handle, a coyote came jumping up out of the rocks and took off down the rim. All I had to do was pull the rope. Out they sailed right in after him. Up ahead a little bunch of white-faced cattle were grazing. That coyote ran right out through the middle of them.

This fooled the two greys and the stag. They got mixed up and lost sight of the coyote. Not Old Rag Dog. I think he gained right then and there. Anyway, by the time I'd circled around the cows, I could see Old Rag straining to latch on.

The coyote knew his time was near. He did just what any animal would have done. He jumped right off the steep edge onto the sharp malpai rocks. Most dogs would have quit right there, or stopped to look for an easier way down. Not Old Rag Dog. He just leaped way out, and when he came down he had the coyote.

I drove up and fell out. There was one hell of a fight going on down there. That coyote was up and then he was down. The white hair was flying where he was tearing it out of Old Rag Dog's hide. They rolled over and over together. Then Rag Dog got hold and held on. I yelled for the other hounds and here they came. They all piled off the rim and down to help Old Rag. It didn't take long then, but I swear I believe that white rascal would have finally killed that coyote by himself.

We caught six full-grown coyotes and one half-grown pup that day. Seventy dollars! In one day, mind you, with *my* dogs. Only I didn't have my dogs any more. I didn't have anything to talk to and worry over and love. After hunting over all that rough country, the dogs' feet had been sore. For a couple of days I kept the dogs penned up while I soaked their feet in alum water to take the soreness out and toughen them up again. By the fourth day (which was today) they were restless, wanting to get out and hunt some more.

I pulled up at the gate about two hundred yards from Marv's headquarters. I could have leaned the thirty-thirty over the gate post and waited till he showed up outside the house. I know I could have got him from there. I didn't though. I wanted to see him kick. I threw the gate back and got in the pickup and headed for the house. I just hoped he was home. I didn't want to wait.

I drove the last hundred yards up to the house kinda slow-like. I was looking hard for Marv outside. Then I saw him out working on the corrals. I drove right up. Marv turned his heavy frame around.

"Marv," I said, and then I couldn't do nothin' but cuss him. I wanted him to suffer just a little before I killed him."

He opened his mouth and said, "The dogs, they were . . . ."

That's when I shot him. He was turned sort of sideways like maybe he wanted to run. The first one went through his elbow and side. It knocked him back against the corral. He turned to me, one hand held out in front. I shot right through that hand and saw a finger drop off. Everything seemed to be moving slow to me. Then I shot him through the bridge of the nose. He fell on his face and rolled over. I emptied the rifle into his chest. Every time it hit he jerked a little. When the rifle started clicking empty, I got on out of the pickup. I'd shot him through the half-open door.

I went over and looked down on him. The blood was oozing out all over. Then I heard a scream and saw Maggie, his wife, come running. She ran up and fell down, yelling crazy things. And then she started saying over and over, "Why did you do it? Why? Why?"

I said, "Don't nobody kill my dogs. Nobody."

I got back in the pickup and drove off up the road. About a hundred yards from the house I saw the stag lying stretched out over a clump of bear grass. Then I saw the two greys lying flat and still. I stopped, got out and walked over to them. Nine or ten dead sheep were scattered out all torn to pieces. One of the grey hounds still had a patch of wool in his mouth. I couldn't believe my dogs would attack anybody's sheep. They never had. Why, they never had even bothered the chickens.

I walked over and sat down on a stump. I could see several hundred head of sheep grazing peacefully off a ways. I had to face myself then. There was nothing to say, nothing to do, just think and look at it the way it was. That morning I'd turned the dogs out for a run and gone to milk. That was the mistake. After being penned up, those dogs wanted to run and kill. That's what I'd trained them for.

Old Marv and his wife had spent twenty-five years building up that flock of sheep. Blizzards, droughts, low prices, coyotes, he'd fought them all. I reckon he felt about those sheep something like I did my dogs. Well, there were still lots of fat sheep out there. They wouldn't do him any good now. I could get me another bunch of dogs, but that wouldn't do me any good either.

The Far Cry

Strangely, Jim Tatum wasn't tired when at last be finished the hard job of hazing his small herd of cattle up the steep, winding trail to the top of Piney Mesa. His saddle horse was nigh worn out, but Tatum was buoyed up with the satisfaction of knowing that the strong grass here in the high country would put flesh on his stock and give them plenty to eat all summer long.

How lucky Frances and I are to control this fine forest grazing land, he thought, and if only we now get a good crop on our flats ranch . . . .

"What's that over there?" he said aloud. "Heavy storm clouds building up. I'd better head for home."

With this, Tatum turned his black gelding back down the crooked trail on the malpais-studded and brushy slope which led to open country far below the mesa's top. But as the man let Blackie pick his own way, his pleasant thoughts ran on: If mid-June rains came, the dormant, empty pastures below would grow and ripen. He'd cut several stacks of hay and there'd be grazing left for the long winter!

Down, down the trail horse and rider moved, around and over the rocks; through sweet scented cedars and pinons. This morning cottontails had scurried through the underbrush; blue jays had squawked and a magpie had shrilled his resentful cry. Now it was quiet. A still, ominous quiet.

Tatum looked across the intervening miles to his home. He could see the smoke coming from Frances' old, iron range. It lapped over the house and seemed to move slowly towards the earth. A good sign of rain. His wife would be as glad as he about the moisture. She had sweated out the long lean years right by his side.

He looked up and back at the clouds. They were twice as big now—twice as close. Man, they were heavy with water! This rain would fix the pastures for the whole summer. A few showers in

August, and his grass would be made. The bills would be made. He and his family would be made for one more year.

He would sure be glad when Billy got a little older so he could help with the ranch work. It wouldn't be long. At six, the boy was already riding, but he couldn't hold out for a cattle drive. Jackie was only three and would be with his mama quite a spell yet.

Tatum felt the sudden stir of air and saw the cedars sway and the sparse grass of the hillside move. He pulled at his hat from years of habit. Then he noticed the pastures far below him turn dark under the shadow of the clouds. They were swiftly spreading over all of the sky.

"We're goin' to get wetter'n a baptising, Blackie," Tatum told his gelding. "It's goin' to rain catfish and big fat bullfrogs in about three minutes . . . I sure hope Frances remembers to turn off the windmill!"

The coarse mane of the horse flapped in the wind. The clouds were shredded and torn now, breaking away in parts and then sweeping back as if by call. The wind pulled harder at Tatum's hat, and it seemed as if the clouds began to roar, louder and louder.

"It looks bad," Tatum said grimly. "Blackie, old boy, we better move out. This could turn into a twister." As he spurred the horse faster on towards the bottom of the mesa, he saw the funnel dip and return and then dip again. It was still above the earth, mixed with the white fangs of lightning.

"I sure hope Frances turns off the windmill and puts out the fire in the stove. A twister might burn the house down, even if it didn't blow it away."

A black tongue snaked from the sky and lapped at the earth. Even in the beginning rain, Tatum saw the puff of dust where it had torn the earth. The thunder and lightning overlapped one another until it was solid, continuous, sound and light.

"I hope Frances has taken the kids to the cellar."

The wind pulled the horse sideways and almost swept Tatum from his saddle. Blue-purple sheets of rain were streaking from the clouds as the storm moved out between Tatum and his ranch.

"Blackie, I sure hope Frances thinks to stash some meat in the cellar. I wonder if she'll think to save some extra clothes, and a couple of lamps and some kerosene. It looks to me like the cellar's going to be our new home, old horse."

Eight gut-bustin', muscle-stretchin', sweating, hoping, praying years it had taken to get the little JT outfit where it was now.

Only this past year they'd finished paying for the windmill. Both of them—he and Frances—pulling against the traces together like a good wagon team.

"I hope Frances and the kids ain't gone to sleep and let this storm slip up on them."

Tatum pushed out of his mind her soft brown hair and eyes, her tender voice, her patient, constant care of the younguns. The love they made together. He must think of other things.

"Man, that windmill sure saves lots of work." They had had it only three years now. Before that, they had hauled all the water for drinking, washing, and for the milk cow, from a spring four miles to the east. It seemed as if nearly all Tatum's time was spent hauling water. They had to use a wagon and team most of the time. The old ford truck just ran when it wanted to, and that was seldom.

But he'd improved the ranch these last three years. The fences were now tight with strong water-gaps and gates. The roof on the house was patched and didn't leak. He had built a good round-pole corral for breaking his horses.

What a day when the well driller had told him, "You've got a good well of water, Jim. She'll never go dry."

It had been an even greater day when workmen swung the shiny new wheel in place on the windmill, and set the pipe, screwed the succer-rods together and turned it over to the wind. The water came bubbling out in a sweet, clear stream. And the harder the wind blew, the more water the well furnished. But now that same life-giving wind, whirling and growling, could take it all away!

The funnel came down out of the seething blackness and stayed. It ripped at the earth, tore the grass from its roots and gathered up the soil, the twigs, the insects, the life of the land, and hurled it up, up. All Tatum had, all he would ever have, was down there on the flats. The whirling beast meant to suck his own from him as he rode, helpless.

He screamed instructions to his wife into the wind. He knew she couldn't hear him—but maybe if he felt hard enough, strong enough, she'd hear. She would feel.

"Blackie! Come on, Blackie." Tatum spurred the horse's heaving sides, and Blackie responded. Once he stumbled and fell to his knees. Tatum yanked back on the reins, and the horse rose, hurled himself down over the rocks and out onto the flats and into the storm.

215

The wind, the rain, the thunder and lightning, the horse and his rider, all were one. The sky and the earth welded themselves together and ripped off into the great spaces above. Tatum grabbed his hat from his head and stuffed it inside the Levi jacket. A good hat cost a lot of money. He could feel the horse under him, somehow harder to ride against the force of the wind than a bucking bronc. The wind pulled at his arms where he held the reins and gripped the saddle horn. Now and then he felt the horse wrenched sideways as if he were a dry weed.

The man's eyes were so full of dirt he just clamped the burning lids tight and held on. Hard objects driven by the wind struck him in the head and all over the body. A mighty vacuum sucked and pulled at the rider and his horse, sucking the very air from their lungs and nostrils.

"Oh, if she just remembered to turn off the windmill."

With chest heaving, Tatum strained the thought from himself. "Frances, honey! Git to the cellar! Git the kids in the cellar! Turn off the windmill, Frances. He felt he would burst apart from the force of his will.

Then for a timeless spell he felt nothing, saw nothing. The blackness was deeper than the darkest night had ever been. Maybe they were right on top of the storm and would come crashing through to the torn earth when it quit. Or would it ever quit?

"It's been blowing for a month now, Blackie. Frances, turn off the windmill . . . ."

Something was changing. He could hear his own voice. Louder, he yelled, "Frances, Billy, Jackie!" and all the time his voice became clearer. At last he could see the ruptured barren earth. The wind was dying. He watched Blackie's mane gradually settle.

Then he knew the storm was past. The earth was wet and muddy. He was drenched and cold. Water and sweat ran from his tangled hair in tiny arroyos through the grime down into his stinging eyes.

It cleared fast then. First he saw the barn. It was still standing! But where were the corrals? They were gone. He spurred the staggering horse forward. The house was still there. And Frances stood in front of the cellar with the door pushed back. He jumped down and stumbled the last few steps to her. He held her close, saying nothing.

"The kids?" he asked.

"They're still in the cellar. I told them it was a game. It's the most fun they've had in ages."

Tatum plunged down into the cellar.

"Daddy, look here," cried Jackie. "I've got a frog!"

"It's half mine," said Billy, his large brown eyes gleaming in the light of the kerosene lamp.

"Can we stay down here and play, daddy?" Billy asked.

"Yes, son, you can stay all the way to chore time if you want to."

Tatum looked at the rifle, the canned food, the meat, and the extra clothing Frances had brought to the cellar. He walked slowly, thoughtfully, up the stairs. Close. Very close. Only the corrals were gone. Had Frances heard his far cry?

When he saw the fan of the windmill pulled tight against the wheel, motionless, he knew.

The Wooden Cave

It was quite a shock to Marvin Neal when the man handed him the papers to sign and then presented him with a check for thirty thousand dollars for just a mineral lease on his ranch land. It was even a greater shock when the company this man represented drilled for oil and hit it. Five hundred barrels a day of forty gravity oil in a pay called the Devonion. The steel rigs sprouted all over his place and it was always the same, oil and more oil, money and more money. Trouble, too, accompanied the wealthy into the pure white house but it came slowly by degrees until it built to a strange and unfathomable climax.

When Marvin, his sister, Janet, and his brother, Dewey, inherited the ranch and the great two-story white house on the hill, the indebtedness amounted to more than its worth. Janet and Dewey left for the city, but Marvin stayed on.

Gradually, year by year, he built up the qualities of his Hereford cattle. Surely, almost imperceptibly, he paid the debts, fixed the fences, cut logs and built new corrals. It was a never ending job from sun-up till dark and after. He broke his own horses, milked his own cows, slopped his own hogs and kept his own company. It was a lonesome, grinding, man-breaking life.

Finally though, he married Arline, a good, go-getting woman like himself. She didn't ease his load any, but only helped him do twice as much. They were happy at work and lived for the day they could buy out the other heirs. At last they succeeded.

They saved a little more and added another coat of gleaming white paint to the old house. Marvin's father, a careful man in his carpentry, had built the house himself. Everything was square, solid, built with seasoned lumber and set on a big rock foundation. The house had put him under such a debt that he never recovered to his day of death. It stood on a hill in the middle of the rolling mixed grass pastures—a castle, without turrets or princes but nonetheless a castle.

At the first fright of new found, easy riches after the years of hardship, the Neals had a talk.

"I tell you what, Arline," said Marvin, "We'll get a new pick-up and buy several tons of cottonseed cake for the cattle in case of a hard winter. We'll get you a new sewing machine, a new dress and a new pair of shoes. We'll raise some kids and let it go at that. What do you say?"

"All right, darling, sounds right to me," she answered.

So that's the way it was, very little change except, of course, they didn't have to worry nearly so much about the shape of things to come—or so they thought.

Then one day, Marvin's brother, Dewey and his wife Harriet dropped by. It was their first visit in years. However, it was rather a prolonged visit—days, weeks, months.

Janet and her husband Tom, a small-time building contractor also chose to make their first trip back to the old home ranch. With them came their three noisy, nasty tongued, thoroughly spoiled children. They, too, stayed quite a spell.

Upon arrival, Tom the building contractor remarked on how well built the old house was and even walked around with a square in his hand testing every corner, every window and every door.

"Amazing," he said, "Every thing perfectly square. Janet, your father would have made quite a building contractor. Well," he reconsidered, "at least, he would have made a top-notch carpenter."

Marvin, the happy host, turned over the entire upstairs of six big rooms to them. There was just one thing wrong as far as he was concerned and that was what Arline said about their company.

"Look, Marvin," she said, "You know good and well they're here just to get money from you."

"Oh, no," he answered in a pained way, "Not a word has been said about that."

"Just wait," she said, "just wait."

Marvin waited and sure enough one day Janet asked if she could buy a new car from some of the money that came from the depths of the old home place. Marvin bought her and Tom a new car. Dewey came around right after that and wanted one even bigger and shinier. Marvin, trying to be fair, bought him one just like his sister's.

Janet talked quite often of the new equipment Tom needed in the construction business and added that she had always wanted a dress shop in the city. Dewey mentioned several times how he would appreciate the opportunities of playing the stock market since he had the courage and cunning to gamble.

Marvin wished, in his quiet, settled way, that Janet's three kids would mind a little better and be somewhat more careful around the old house. In one upstairs room they had painted with orange and green crayolas a picture of Marvin handing bales of money to what was probably meant to be their parents.

Dewey loved to lounge on the front porch and smoke Cuban cigars. Marvin was so used to doing the chores around the place that he never asked Dewey to get up and help.

Arline said, "He doesn't need asking Marvin. He can see you could use help."

Tom never did anything but read home building magazines and order folders from construction supply outfits. These he left laying all over the place.

Arline said, "He leaves them around for your benefit, Marvin. Oh, can't you see what they're trying to do?"

Janet always managed to go shopping with Arline when she went to Amarillo and would pick up luxury foods in the grocery store saying, "Don't you think this would be nice for something different?" When window shopping, Janet would spy a dress or pair of shoes. "Come let's go in and try them on, just for fun," she would say eagerly. It was always Janet who tried them on. Then, she would pose with a gleam in her eyes and ask the clerk what he thought. Naturally, the clerk thought nothing else in the world would suit Madame better.

"Shall I wrap it up?"

"Well?" Janet would say looking at Arline.

There was very little choice for the wife of Marvin Neal but to pay. If they had been her kin . . . well . . . .

Dewey, Janet and Tom started using the mails to order various and assorted goods. They were all quite certain they needed these items. "And, anyway," Dewey told his wife, Harriet, "he's got plenty of money to spare." The orders were always made out C.O.D. in care of Mr. Marvin Neal. Marvin would shell out the cash.

It wasn't long until the two upstairs apartments were filled to the brim with all sorts of electrical appliances, new ranges, ice-boxes, radios, gadgets, clothing of the finest cloth and toys galore for the undisciplined little children.

At first, they had all eaten together in the big downstairs dining room. Now, only the night meal was consumed together. Marvin began to have a little faith in his wife's opinion of his relations, but as yet, he had reached no decision as to what to do about it. At least, he had held back on the construction equipment and the stock market hints that were uttered so often.

The thing that really set him to thinking was the day school started in town. Janet hired a private tutor and kept her smooth-skinned, little juveniles at home. The poor teacher would have died of nervous prostration shortly if she, too, hadn't held hopes of somehow getting her hands on a great deal of Marvin's capital. However, capital or no, she could take the brats only a short time and one day she up and left.

At dinner each night the talk rambled on and on, but Marvin and Arline had been getting quieter and quieter. One night the darkness was splintered with flashes of lightning and the sky reverberated from the malevolent boom of thunder. The tall cotton-woods swayed against the white house and brushed back and forth, like agitated spirits.

Suddenly in a rare moment of silence, Tom the builder, gulped down a thick slice of prime beef and his experienced eyes bulged from his head. Without a word he leaped up and dashed to the tool-shed. In a moment he was back, slamming the door into the wind and rain. In his hands he held a square. He dashed to an archway from the dining room to the kitchen and placed the square on the floor so one angle of it ran up the archway. There was a gap of several inches.

"My God!" he shouted, "The house has blown apart." It was plain for everyone to see.

"It must be the wind," whispered Harriet.

"Yes, it's just the wind," laughed Dewey, "The wind. Well, well," he continued, clearing his throat, "the old house ain't what she used to be."

As one body they arose and went to their separate parts of the house.

Arline asked Marvin, "Do you understand what's going on?"

"No, I don't. Nothing, I suppose. The square was probably bent."

Upstairs Dewey was silent. Harriet crawled trembling in bed and pulled the covers tight over her bead. Janet and Tom sat at a marble-topped table they had ordered from the biggest store in the city and stared at each other. Unaccountably, the spoiled little children rolled and mumbled in their sleep all night.

At last the morning came calm and clear. The sun burned down on the wetness of the earth and an atmosphere of peace and contentment spread over the whole of the pastures. The birds sang more than ever. The white-faced calves bucked and played about in the grass just now turning to ripened gold. The night was pushed down into the minds of all and a good will of sorts came to the surface. Everyone laughed and joked—perhaps a bit too much. Marvin even considered giving Dewey and Tom their wishes. He decided he would tell them that night at supper.

As each took his place at the great oval of oak for the nightly repast, their glances went to the square where Tom had dropped it and where Arline had left it. Tom studied the house nervously while he ate but it was evident that it was again perfectly square. It was, he decided something best forgotten for he knew the wind hadn't been strong enough to sway the house that much for if it had it would most surely have blown it right off its foundation.

All present ate fast—much too fast. Marvin decided if he were going to make his announcement it would have to be now. He looked at the children and smiled, though he despised their whining ways even in his kind heart. He smiled at Janet and Dewey and turned to Tom. What he saw was a man as pale as the outside of the huge ranch home—a man breathless and rigid.

Slowly, almost creakingly, Tom eased from his seat and slipped to the square. It dropped from his hands. The onlookers jumped. Then, with shaking hands he put it against the archway.

"It's . . . It's . . . at least eight inches off square . . . the other way," he stammered. He turned and ran from corner to corner but all was square except this one arch.

They all trembled in silent, inexplicable fear. All except Marvin, he was just plain outright puzzled. Arline seemed nervous but not to extremes. No one attempted any explanations. They waited only for the dawn.

The next and last time the group gathered at the table for dinner Tom failed to join them. He came rushing in late, grabbed the square and dashed madly from one corner to the other shouting, "See, its off four inches to the north. This one's off six inches to the east."

The spoiled little children screamed and cried out loud. Janet gave them the only real spanking they had ever had. Marvin thought how regrettable it was she couldn't have done this the times before when they really needed it.

That night Dewey and Harriet quarreled bitterly. He slapped her in the month bringing blood frothing from the inside of her tooth-cut lips. Harriet raked long, manicured nails down one side of his cheek leaving red zebralike stripes.

The obnoxious children kicked each other under the covers and one little boy pinched his sister on her budding breast and called her the dirtiest name in the world.

No one ventured downstairs the next day. The sound of shouting and cursing could be heard in the upstairs rooms and once a scream. The house moved first one way and then the other. The big print of a wagon train over the fireplace in the living room hung crooked on the wall. The next minute it hung lopsided in the other direction. All the corners of the house were out of shape. Gradually they moved so the human eye could follow.

Tom sat spellbound and watched for hours while Janet ranted and screamed and cried. Then a wailing noise came from the house as each board, so carefully nailed long ago, bent and moved and moaned. Cracks came in the floor and the boards humped and writhed like burning snakes.

Harriet cried, "It's that Marvin, the dirty rotten cheapskate. He's doing it! He's doing it all! Listen," she said suddenly quiet, "Let's poison him."

"But how," shouted Dewey, "I wouldn't go down those stairs for anything."

In another room Tom yelled, "It's Marvin. He's the cause of it all. I'm going to cut his head off tonight. The dirty son-of-a-bitch," he screamed and grabbed a butcher knife from a drawer. He started down the stairs, but they buckled and bucked under him until he fell. With a craven fear he crawled back into his room. His hand left a trail of blood on the floor like a white line down a highway. He had dropped the knife and picked it up by the blade.

"Wrap it up," he said holding the red stained hand out to Janet.

"Wrap it yourself," she shouted, and threw her hands to her temples trembling violently.

All over the place chairs slid into walls, dishes clattered and fell, windows popped out and crashed tinkling into the wind or onto the floor. Harriet ran about barefooted over broken glass until her tracks were etched in red wherever she stepped.

More and more Marvin spent his time comforting Arline and during this period the child they had wanted was conceived even while the bed moved about the room to the contortions of the white house.

The sound grew—forlorn one moment, agonizing in its intensity the next. Louder, up the scale and down the scale, but always louder. It rose to a crescendo of a million, mad symphonies. Splinters flew out of the walls and stuck in flesh.

Suddenly, Marvin raised up as a bird dog in the marshes. The silence was profound, and for a moment, more frightening than the terrible sound. It was over. He took his arms from around Arline. They walked through the dining room, upstairs and into every room of the house. Nothing was amiss. No glass was shattered. No splinters lay on the floor. All the furniture was in place, but the house was empty except for the two of them.

Marvin walked outside just as the rising sun turned the sides of the house to white orange. The new cars were not there. In the pasture the cattle grazed, peacefully putting on weight. Marvin turned and ran towards the house shouting to his wife, "Arline, let's saddle the horses and ride across the pasture. It's such a beautiful day."

The Third Grade Reunion

1

The propeller-driven plane and the eagle passed each other in the sky. Both were hunting. The bird searched for food; the geologist pointed out possible new drilling sites to an oil company executive. Among the derricks scattered below, the waste oil pools would, now and then, coordinate with the sun and reflect up to them a gleaming image of shimmering ponds of water—but this was only an illusion. The land was dry as death, and the southeasterly New Mexican town off to their left was barely visible because the stripping wind had erased the vegetation and whipped the dust around and above it.

Right after the 1929 crash, the sky had turned cloudless in the vast, flat, lonesome land. As the sun and wind seared and killed the grass and weeds, the once-fat cattle grew weaker each day, and then finally there were only piles of bones. The government bought them for a few dollars a head, shot them and left them where they fell. Only the coyotes and rodents became fat, everything else withered, including the people.

Even so, Hobbs, New Mexico, fared better than most of the towns in the nation. In 1927 oil had been struck, filling the prairies with steel, leafless, man-made trees. The population jumped from zero to thirty thousand in one year. They came from everywhere and were every kind—the dreamers, the adventurers, the greedy, the hungry, the clever and the stupid. As always, just like the coyotes, there were those who came to pick the bones. They came in old cars, trucks, wagons and teams. Some hitched rides in on anything that moved, and some came walking in, sore-footed, but with souls full of hope.

Everything was greasy. The streets were oiled down twice a week to settle the dust from all the wheels and feet that moved and churned back and forth searching for destinies, for dreams, jobs and money, for something, anything. The noise of groaning motors hauling loads of steel pipe never stopped. The babble of people, the clinking of glasses, bottles, doors opening and shutting, curses and laughter were ceaseless as well.

There infiltrated amidst all of this the non-productive, the cheats, the peddlers of false illusions, the dry-land sharks. There would be more to clean up than the ruptured streets.

Then, with the great depression and the terrible drought, oil dropped to ten cents a barrel, and with that price the population of Hobbs fell to three thousand. There it solidified, holding precariously together amidst the many empty buildings. What really kept it from turning back to a sandhill was government intervention again. The oil was prorated and the law said no one could sell a barrel for less than a dollar. This began to help, but it didn't bring a single extra cloud into the parched sky.

In the winter of '32 and '33, Franklin Delano Roosevelt had been president for only a few months, and the industrial production of the nation was at the lowest level ever recorded. Thousands added to thousands of men stood in soup lines and peddled apples on streets corners to keep from starving. More than twenty states declared "bank holidays" to keep from opening their doors. The president made his famous speech declaring that "The only thing we have to fear is fear itself, "and promised "Action, and action now," but a man with an empty belly had a hard time hearing these stirring words. Before the year was up Roosevelt would instigate action that would end the falsity of prohibition.

Now the year is 1933, the month is March, and things are about to start happening again in Hobbs. Most ranchers who didn't have the black liquid sold out for a pittance, but a few dry-land farmers stayed and fought it out. One of these was R. G. Warren.

On this particular day, R. G. and two of his sons stood by a hand-dug water well working on a rattling Cadillac motor they had traded from a Texas mortician. Finally it sputtered and started. They stood back and stared at the empty pipe shoving out across the land like a cannon barrel. The motor choked and stopped. They went right back to work on it. This time it ran, and so did the water—a full ten inches of rounded liquid gushed out and fell upon their dying land. The earth gulped it up blindly, feeling the life return like a lost heartbeat.

They yelled and whacked each other on the back. They laughed wildly and cried shamelessly. They had stayed and won. Soon all would know of this happy discovery more precious than oil. The revelation would only increase the inward flow of those who thirsted for the plasma of the toilers.

A few miles down the dusty road from the new discovery, Hobbs was having a very special outdoor ceremony in honor of their distinguished sheriff, John Strong. A fat, sweaty, little mayor, with a permanent smile, intoned to the generous gathering of people all the excellent qualities of Sheriff John, and handed him a scroll declaring this appreciation from all the citizens. The mayor went on to relate that John had arrived in Hobbs shortly after the sheriff and his deputy had been gunned down in a gambling raid. John had tried to stop one of the many fist-fights going on that night and two men jumped him. He flattened them both in about three minutes and made a lasting impression on several more. The mayor, having been present to witness these actions, immediately appointed him temporary sheriff. The following election John won by a huge majority.

The mayor finished up with, ". . . and has reduced the crime rate at least thirty percent annually, and in his three years with us has become a warm, personal friend to us all."

A roar went up from the happy crowd as John stepped up to accept his honor. He hunched his heavy shoulders a little embarrassedly, cleared his throat and replied, "I thank the mayor for all his . . . his kind words, but more than anything I want to thank you people standing here in this dust for the confidence and help you gave me durin' those first rough months when Hobbs was bein' run over by those with no respect for the law. And with your continued help I see no reason whatsoever why we shouldn't be able to keep our town clean and safe and just as crime-free as it is right now . . . ."

Across the street, from the second story of the Plains Hotel, Rusty Larkin looked down at the ceremony. He was a dark wedge of a man and even though his complexion was pale and sun-fearing one still got the impression that the second layer of skin was as dark as a sandstorm.

His binoculars followed Sheriff Strong through the crowd as he shook hands with some of the farmers, ranchers, oil-field hands and merchants, inquiring about the welfare of their families, dogs, horses and jobs.

Larkin lowered the glasses and smiled across the room at a pretty young woman sitting at the dressing table and said, "Yeah, it's him all right." Then he looked back out the window and said, "Lord uh mighty, Charlene, it really is him."

She waited for the rest of his explanation with her green eyes wide with anticipation, and said, "Who? Who is it, Rusty?"

"Well, if this don't beat all. We came here because of the mayor and I just found out that the sheriff of this town is my old third grade classmate."

"Oh, is that all." She turned back to the mirror and did some more prettying. "What does that mean to us?"

"Just about everything. That's what it means to us." He moved quickly across the room and pulled a sheet of paper from a folding file. It was a WANTED poster and the picture on it looked an awful lot like Sheriff John Strong.

Sheriff Strong was now sitting alone at the corner table in the sunny dining room of Millie's Place—a combination hotel, boarding house and restaurant. He lived and ate there, and tough old Millie Watkins was his friend. He drank the hot black coffee and wrote something on a piece of paper. The scroll lay in front of him and he touched it proudly and reflected on the events of the morning. His thoughts were interrupted by rushing footsteps and fast talking.

Millie marched into the room leading Todd, a freckled-faced, wild-headed boy of nine, by the ear. She said, "John, this little renegade just knocked Amos Carter in the head with a rock."

John sat up straight saying, "Whoa, now, did I hear you say that Todd knocked ole Amos in the head with a rock?"

" Just that . . . and it took seven stitches to sew him up."

"Todd, what on earth did you do that for?"

Todd rubbed some snot from his nose, pushed it into his hair and stared at a spot on the wall past the sheriff, and answered defiantly, "He kicked ole Romper in the belly."

"Why'd he do that?"

"Well, that little brat of his is always pullin' Romper's tail, and I've told him a hundred times to stop it and he don't pay no attention to me atall."

"What happened? Did Romper bite the kid or something?"

"Naww, he wouldn't do a thing like that. He jist growled at 'em a little."

The sheriff finished his coffee giving himself a minute to think, then said, "Now, Todd, the night I won you in that poker game you promised me you'd be a good boy."

Millie pushed the grey strings of hair from her forehead and said, "Huuuummmrph, that'll be the day."

The sheriff went on, "You should never bust a man's head with a rock for kicking your dog, Todd, 'cause it costs money to sew him up, and money is scarce."

Todd squirmed and Millie grinned around her few teeth and flashed a triumphant 'I told you so' look at him.

"What you shoulda done," John lectured, "was hit him up side the head with a flat board. That way he'd uh got the message without any unnecessary expense." He reached over and gave the boy a light cuff on the ear. "Gettin' some sense in that head of yours is like poundin' steel with a feather. Now go wash the crud off your hands and face, and stay outa trouble." He watched Todd dash out of the room, and said, "You know Millie, the boy's had it pretty rough in his short life." And he thought about how Todd had come into his life. His folks had both died, leaving Todd to be cared for by a worthless, drunken uncle who successfully failed at everything he did, and then he simply left town leaving the boy alone. The local gamblers took him in and let him run their errands and do some chores for his keep. One of them claimed to own Todd until the sheriff took a liking to him and one night bet the man three dollars and a quarter on a poker hand for him. For a while he thought he just might have won the biggest loss of his life, but now he was used to having him around.

The sheriff stood up, grinning a little bit, and said, "Awww, don't let it worry you, Millie, he ain't a bad boy. In fact, you might call him a bargain. Remember, I won him on a bluff—all I had was two dueces.

John reached for the papers on the table, and added, "You know what I'm fixin' to do, Millie? I'm fixin' to throw myself a celebration. You might call it a third grade reunion."

Millie's puzzled expression seemed to call for more explanation, so he continued, "I really cain't tell you why I'm doin' this. I guess it's lookin' back to old things and ways . . . getting this town straightened out, and gettin' this award and all. Well, I reckon I just want some of my old friends to come celebrate with me. Maybe I just want to show off to 'em. Brag a little, maybe."

Millie listened but still didn't quite understand. "A third grade reunion?" she asked, puzzled. "What's that?"

"Well, none of my bunch ever finished the third grade 'cause Rusty Larkin burned down the school house just before the summer vacation. Anyway, it didn't make any difference to me. I wouldn't have made it out of the third grade in ten years. I couldn't subtract."

"Oh," Millie said, enlightened.

He didn't say any more aloud, but he thought, "It's like leaving your home town poor and coming back rich, except this is my home now, and I've invited them all here. What's the difference?"

He stepped out on the porch and down to the oily main street on his way to the telegraph office to wire his invitations. He was feeling good—even excited. Then he heard the paper boy yelling, "Extra! Extra! Water has been found! Water—not oil!" He bought a paper, stuck it under his arm, and proceeded to finish his mission.

On the way out of the telegraph office he opened the paper and read the headlines. As he read a little more he became concerned. He quickened his pace back to the boarding house.

"Millie, looky here, R. G. Warren found water on his place."

Millie was pleased and said, "Why John, that's right fine news."

"Well, it is and it isn't. The whole damn town will boom again and go completely crazy."

"Well, maybe not *so* crazy this time. Anyway, maybe it will give folks a chance to earn a few nickels again."

The sheriff seemed to not hear this. "And I've done sent my friends those invitations."

2

Acee Hittson took the telegram from an associate, saying, "Excuse me, gentlemen," with polite gentility.

The four men at the table waited with impatience for him to read the wire. They were losing at five card stud. Acee was the only winner. This was the usual case. The surrounding decor of Acee's apartment was soft and plush and verified his success. Even the walls were carpeted, and the chairs were soft and comfortable—made for dozing. The walls were hung with paintings of the West—golden-aired landscapes of elk grazing, moose drinking, beautiful Indian maidens staring off across the glorious land with clouds like castles, and the sun bursting through like the first view of heaven. One could almost hear sweet hypnotic music emanating past the picture frames. This was purposely set up to lure the victims' minds away from the harsh reality of the green felt table in the center of the room.

Acee folded the wire and slipped it inside his silk vest, thinking to himself, "It's hard to believe . . . John Strong a sheriff . . . well, it'd be fun to see him again . . . anyway the Fourth of July is some time off . . . plenty of time to get ready."

Pulling his lips from around teeth as white as an angel's thoughts, he picked up the cards, and said, "Let's see now, gentlemen, it's my deal isn't it?"

Bessie Lou Jones' lady companion delivered the wire to her on a silver platter. She certainly hadn't always had things this way. The decor of her Kansas City establishment was no less elegant than Acee's but it was different. There were full wall drapes of purple velvet. The statues and paintings were of men and women frolicking about in various forms of nudity and inclination. In the outer-room, her ladies lounged about casually, revealing on purpose portions of their anatomy for the careful consideration of Bessie Lou's high-toned clientele.

She read the wire and placed it on a marble table, picked up her cup of tea and smiled, "Yes, it would be fun. I could use a little country air again . . . . but John Strong a sheriff?"

Dalton Van Allen signed the green, gold embossed stock certificate as president of the company. Then he rared back lighting a cigar and read the wire again. He looked out the window of his slightly worn Tonopah, Nevada, offices. He, too, smiled, but he was wishing the reunion was tomorrow. He was currently slightly oversold on gold and silver mining stock. ". . . but John Strong a sheriff! That could be very interesting indeed! . . ."

Waddie Thorton was taste-testing the latest run from his copper stills hidden in the brushy hills several miles from Fort Worth, Texas, when his brother brought him the invitation. The birds sang and the whiskey perked as he read it. He didn't smile, he laughed. He'd already heard about the oil town of Hobbs, New Mexico. "Why . . . no telling what opportunities might jump right straight up in front of me . . . especially having an old friend as sheriff . . . yet, how could that be . . . just didn't seem right!"

3

Rusty Larkin sat in his Hobbs hotel room sipping whiskey, looking out the window at the people of the town. This was not an unusual activity for him. He'd made his living for a number of years looking in and out of people's windows. He'd once described himself as a soldier of fortune, but neglected to say his living was mostly comprised of other folks' fortunes.

One could call him an opportunist and be reasonably accurate. A few years after burning down the Smackover, Texas, school house, he drifted around New Orleans and Atlanta a while, bumming, stealing, and even working now and then, if that work led to valuable information. He really couldn't pin down just how his special abilities developed, but a full statement of his final philosophy could be summed up that it was not what you knew about yourself that counted anyway, but what you knew about other people.

He'd drifted out west to an Idaho silver boom at an early age. It didn't take him long to find out that the people who came into power in these sudden spurts of wealth usually had many things in their pasts that were more valuable unsaid. If the price was correct, in his estimation, they remained unsaid. If not, he simply turned them in to higher state or governmental authorities, earning their thanks and sometimes collecting a reward. This, of course, led to his access to many "wanted" flyers which in some cases gave him a double stranglehold on his victims.

Like everyone else, during the great drouth and depression scarring the land, he'd had some difficulty plying his true trade. There just weren't that many boom towns around. He'd arrived in Hobbs because he had an ole ace in the hole. He was the number one lover of Charlene Miller, niece of the mayor himself. Pretty hard to top that. Anyway it was worth the gamble because this town had survived better than most.

He could smell the dull scent of oil under their feet, as he watched the clusters of people gather on the street. The smell was everywhere. It was even in the cleanest of bed clothes. It was in the wood buildings, and even in the pores of their occupants.

There was the old movement of anticipation about them he recognized so well and the thought of riches that would come their way with the discovery of irrigation water. Then, too, there were rumors everywhere that a large new oil drilling program was about to be instigated. He had waited patiently, for two days, for Charlene to return from her uncle's and give the report.

When he heard her knock on the door, he smiled easily and opened it, taking her into his arms and giving her an affectionate kiss. Then he said, "Well?"

"I'm sorry, honey, I didn't learn much. He's as honest as the Lord."

"You gotta be puttin' me on. The ruling leader of an oil town and he's honest?"

"That's right. Well . . . I'm sorry but it had to happen some-time, I guess."

"Sheeeiiit," he said with disgust.

She looked at him with sympathy and then a certain coyness before she spoke again, "I did find out one little thing that might interest you though."

He poured himself another glass of whiskey and waited.

"On the Fourth of July, our esteemed sheriff is giving a third grade reunion, and the whole town's invited."

"A third grade reunion?" He started to laugh, then sobered and went to the file folder. He began to get excited as he thumbed through the flyers. Then he said, "Whoopee! I have, believe it or not, a wanted flyer on every damn one of them. Hell, honey, we're going to turn this into a bonanza."

"But it's a long time until the Fourth of July," she said, pouting.

"Only about four months. Anyway, where else we gonna go? Huh? What else we got to do? Tell me that."

"Well . . . ."

"Now, you get your perty little tail back over to your honest ole uncle's. There ain't no tellin' what kinda information you'll latch onto before this is over."

She said, "I'll go in a minute, but first . . .," and she pulled him to her and fell under him on the squeaking bed.

4

The boom town followers came all right, one, two and three drifters at a time. In a country and a time when dollars were as scarce as shadows in a desert sky, they came to Hobbs. Those who had profited from the earlier oil boom began to loosen up. Gradually, the word spread about the water. The farmers to the south that had held on, dug more water wells. Somehow they scrounged pipe from the oil companies, and old motors and tractors and teams of horses. They plowed the crusted earth and pumped life into their limited acres. Hope sprang anew. Again.

Now the sheriff allowed some clean little saloons and a few night ladies to operate as long as it didn't upset the rest of the populace. However, as the empty buildings slowly filled back up, the drinking, the gambling and the need by these participants of female company increased. More and more people arrived to fill the growing demand for diversion. With this movement came an increase in crooked dice and cards, ladies who rolled drunks without other services, and consequently fist-fights and an occasional knifing. Human nature expressed itself. All were touched. All the movement of wheels and people started turning the town dirty again. The sheriff's duties grew in direct proportion to the action. But much to his credit and large fists, the town remained in fairly good moral shape, considering.

Millie Watkins grew up on dry farms and had spent the last two decades with her late husband on one. It was only after he'd worked and starved himself to death that she moved on and established her present business. She was a pure survivor.

About twice a week she and Todd would drive around the countryside hunting rabbits. They could survive where cows had starved to death, by finding bits of food under the mesquite and cat claw. They weren't fat by any means. In fact, their meat was lean and stringy, but it was food and cooked up fairly edible in Millie's famous "beef" stew.

She drove the old truck and Todd did the shooting with a single-shot twenty-two. After a time he became a phenomenal marksman. He couldn't help it. Millie insisted every round be a head shot so that no meat would be destroyed. When a rabbit ran in a hole, she showed the young man how to take a length of barbwire with a fork in the end and get meat. He simply twisted it down into the hole until it became entangled in the creature's fur and pulled it out. Rabbits contributed more to the survival of the West than all the preachers and politicians combined.

Todd was learning survival from Millie, and so it went to each his own.

The mayor was happy to have his niece Charlene with him and gave her a small paying job in his office. He and the city council were beginning to feel expansive again and looking forward to a few more years in office when they could actually get remunerated properly. They were especially encouraged when a certain Leonard Puft arrived from "back east somewhere" and set up a new office. He made a definite impression by actually painting the ramshackle wooden building, and putting up a rather large sign proclaiming:

LEONARD PUFT, REALTOR, IRRIGATED FARMS, OIL LEASES, ETC.

Mr. Puft seemed to assure the progress of the town. He was a man of six feet three, with a handsome belly that announced it had always been fed on big steaks and good whiskey. He kept his large face shaved except for a thick blond mustache, and dressed in suits that had never been seen here. He circulated among the citizenry constantly stating his confidence in the great future of the area; and since he spent money lavishly everywhere, everyone believed him.

No one but the sheriff had noticed the only small things about him—his little blue eyes. He kept these covered by heavy pale eyelids. That's what first caused the sheriff to take a good, steady look, but he wasn't saying anything against him for the present.

No one paid any attention when Puft bought out a couple of irrigated farms by acquiring the papers from the local bank and simply taking them over when the payments were found to be long overdue. At the time it just seemed to be part of doing business as always everywhere in the entire world.

He became the local prophet when the news leaked out—by Puft himself—that a large new oil strike had been made southwest of town. He went all over congratulating everyone, shaking hands gregariously and patting people on the back. He talked of beauty and bounties to come.

Suddenly the streets were full of people and once again trucks were groaning under heavy loads of pipe and equipment.

Every bus that ran emptied out the dreamers and the workers from all points. The oil-field trucks, Model A Fords and other contemporary automobiles churned up the dirt streets until they had to be oiled down twice a week again. The movie house re-opened with a Tom Mix film—and with it the whole mood of the town changed. It was charged up as if all were plugged into some huge dynamo. The newspaper published daily instead of twice weekly, each edition announcing a new hope, a new discovery, a new vision. It seemed as if the town and its boom had been rein-carnated and were living the same life again. Exactly the same.

Only the ranchers and farmers without irrigation wells still looked at the sunburned sky, and wept at the parched earth. The wind still whipped, and moaned, and killed, piling great drifts of sand on and even over the fence rows.

Even so, the steel bits were shoved into the earth and came back coated with slick black liquid. The farmers with the irriga-tion wells exulted at the new green peeking up from the wet earth, promising food and survival. But the town itself sweated from the increasing spring heat, and it sweated oil from every palpitating pore. Soon, as always, it would sweat blood.

The bootleg whiskey inundated the town. As fast as the sheriff raided one place, two more came into existence. On top of the fist-fights there was a shooting almost every night, sometimes more. The loaded dice rolled and the marked cards were dealt, the women were auctioned, and on the weekends at a constantly moving site, roosters killed roosters, and dogs ripped at the throats of other dogs. The onlookers bet with abandon, cheering, drinking, and fighting among themselves not unlike the roosters and dogs.

With the rest of the country in the agony of the drought and depression, Hobbs became the promised land. It was also an is-land of revolving madness.

5

The sheriff sat before the mayor and the town council. He lis-tened carefully to his honor without much pleasure.

"Gentlemen, we've tried to control certain elements here with dignity and consideration for what's, uh, goin' on. It just ain't workin'. We've got a drastic situation here, and I say we're gonna have to meet kind with kind."

The rest of the council mumbled and nodded in agreement. Then they all looked at the sheriff. He slowly raised his six feet two upright, put his hat on, pulled it down and said flatly: "What you fellers are sayin'. . . is you want me to make an example outa someone?"

The mayor said, "You got it, John. We'll leave the place and the means in your capable hands."

The sheriff nodded and walked out, replying over his shoulder, "Well, President Roosevelt said what we need is 'action and action now.' I believe the man was right."

Across the street in Rusty Larkin's room a meeting of another sort was going on. Mr. Leonard Puft was speaking, "Now look here, Larkin, I came out here on your word."

Rusty Larkin spoke back defensively, "You're doin' all right, Leonard. You got ninety percent of the action tied up."

"Doing all right while there's a boom on is one thing. Any idiot can pull that off. But this town will settle down again one of these days. It's gonna be solid when it does."

"Well?"

"Don't you see, we have to get control before that happens, or it'll be over for us. I thought your lady friend was smart enough to find the answer. She's right in the middle of the town fathers."

Rusty poured himself a whiskey, offering Puft one. He refused. Rusty took a long drink before he said, "Looky here, Leonard, she got you the tip on the new oil strike that made you a hero round here. What's so bad about that? And you know we'll have the sheriff in our purse come the Fourth of July."

"Well, Larkin, I can see you're just never goin' to get the whole picture. That godamned pious mayor has got to go."

"Go?"

"You heard me right, my friend. I have some . . . let's call them associates' in Chicago that specialize in taking this type problem off my hands, but I'll call them in later. I'll take care of the mayor in another way." He paused, then added, "By the way, you make damned sure you stay out of sight. Understand?"

While these two were enlightening one another Sheriff Strong and his three deputies were together discussing the newly proposed strategy.

That night they moved quietly through the darkness to a Chinese laundry about three blocks off the main street. The only cleaning going on was that of the customers' pockets.

John and one deputy hit the back door, kicking it in and leaping inside. Two others accomplished the same thing at a side door. The women screamed, drinks were spilled, glasses broken, card tables overturned and a man behind a small bar came up firing a gun. A bullet hit one of the deputies in the stomach knocking him slumping against the wall. The sheriff let the man behind the bar have the load in the right barrel of his shotgun, and a good portion of his face disappeared as he crashed among the bottles of bootleg whiskey.

A man in an apron came through the door from a back room with a thirty-thirty and the sheriff shot most of his arm off with the charge from the left side of his gun. At that same instant one of his deputies splintered the heart of a man on a narrow stairway, and shot him again as he rolled down into the main room. The dead man's pistol dropped from his hand. He stared up blindly. There came a sudden silence upon the place.

It took a little while for the law to separate the patrons from the proprietors. These last filled the jail to overflowing that night, and a few inhabitants of lesser charges had to be moved to an old shed. This entailed extra guards and expense. The law had moved, but the cost had gone up.

When the sheriff had done all he could this one evening, he wearily returned to Millie's kitchen saying, "howdy" to the black man on duty, poured a big cup of hot coffee and sat staring at the floor. He didn't see Millie come in wearing an old bathrobe until she sat down across the table from him.

He said, "What're you doin' up this time of the night, Millie?"

Millie pushed at a string of grey hair that always seemed to have escaped from somewhere, and yawned, "Awww, I been gettin' too much sleep. Makes for a slow mind and dull wits. How'd it go?"

"Lost Kincaid. Got three."

"Well . . . them's good odds ain't they?"

"I reckon, but there's more of them than there is of us."

"Won't take you long to get even at that rate."

The sheriff took his hat off, threw it in a chair, rubbed at his forehead and asked, "What's Todd been up to today?"

"The usual. Put a baby skunk in the teacher's desk."

"Well, that little devil. I knew he'd been into something." He laughed, "I did that one myself once."

"It ain't funny, John. They would expel him if they could afford to upset you right now."

"I guess you're right. I gotta have another talk with that boy. He ain't usin' any sense atall. He shoulda put a nice, clean horned toad in there instead. He just ain't thinkin'.'"

Millie snorted and whopped her head between both hands in exasperation, "I swear you're gonna ruin that boy yet."

"Now, he's just a regular kid, that's all."

"Well, John, he needs more of your time."

"Yeah, and I need more of his, but it just seems like I got about all I can handle right now."

Millie looked at him with much understanding. "Things'll settle down 'fore long, John, just like they did before. They always do."

He took the last of his coffee and lit a smoke and sighed, "Maybe. If there was any other place to go I'd leave."

Millie said, "No, you wouldn't. Hey, you forget you're talkin' to ole Millie."

The sheriff looked at her and a tired grin came across his face. "Okay, Millie, let's turn it in. Tomorrow's gonna be another great day for Hobbs and its worn out crime fighters."

He wasn't off much. The town seemed quieted the first day as people gathered in the streets, the stores and the joints discussing the raid. Their attitude towards the occurrence was expressed according to which side they were on.

The lull lasted for five days, as far as violence was concerned, but there was an undercurrent as the voices grew a little louder each hour. It was not unlike a far off, but oncoming, storm.

Over at the mayor's house, Charlene worked in the kitchen with his honor's wife, Tilda. They'd invited the sheriff, Millie and Todd for dinner to celebrate the peace, no matter how temporary it might be. Charlene was somewhat hyper. She had grown to like her uncle and aunt more all the time. Yet, she thought that tonight she might find out something of value for Rusty. She was torn. Rusty had demanded a lot of her the two years they'd been together, but after each score he'd been overly generous. During those periods he'd also been a lot of fun and she would really believe he loved her. Still?

The table was set. The chicken was turning golden in the skillet, and biscuit dough was ready for the oven. Two custard pies were cooling. All they really had left to do was make the milk gravy and finish making the salad when the time was right.

Suddenly the old shepherd dog barked outside and Tilda said, "Wonder what he's barking at. He doesn't bark like that at the mayor." She walked out of the kitchen, through the dining room, to take a look. Since they lived on the edge of town, with open prairie on all sides, Charlene said, "It's probably just a coyote prowling, Aunt Tilda."

The dog was silent now, and the perpetual wind sang around the house with many voices. Charlene poured herself another cup of coffee and put the pot back on the wood cookstove. She should be feeling good, but some kind of indecision, amounting almost to turmoil, increasingly possessed her. In another part of her mind she heard the front door open. Then there was a muffled sound, a little like gurgling water heard from some distance. She took the cup of coffee with her as she casually walked through the rooms to see what was tapping at the back of her mind. Then she saw Tilda by the open door lying grotesquely on her stomach with her head twisted sideways and the red wetness trying to spurt out from under her neck.

She dropped the cup shattering on the floor, and stood stiff as a fence post, her eyes stretched open with a scream entangled in her throat muscles. Then a hand clamped around her face and she was dragged away and out the door.

A little while later the sheriff turned off the winding rutted road to the mayor's house, saying, "I cain't hardly wait to get at some of Tilda's hot biscuits."

Millie said, "That shows good judgment, John. I taught her to cook when we were kids."

Todd announced, "I sure hope they have somethin' 'sides rabbit."

John said, "Why, son, Tilda's cookin' up somethin' real special for you. Somethin' you're plumb familiar with."

Todd asked, with perked up interest showing all over, "What's that, John?"

"Barbecued skunk."

Todd ducked his head and said, "AWWW."

They drove up and got out, finding first the dog with his head bashed in and then the mayor under some dying lilac bushes. His throat was cut and there were two wet spreading places in his back.

Millie gasped, "Oh, my God in heaven."

Todd just stared and got sick at the stomach.

The sheriff leaped on the porch and through the front door. Then he yelled back, "Millie, you and Todd go to the car!" He made for the old crank-handled phone. The brief time of peace was over, and now a coyote *did* howl across the blighted land.

After the funeral Sheriff Strong escorted Millie and Todd back to the hotel, and called an emergency meeting of the town council. He went through the facts: the town was without a mayor; the main jail and the secondary jail were full; and what was even more important, he was having difficulty keeping deputies he could trust. He revealed how often the information of a secret raid had been passed on before they arrived on the scene. There weren't many left he could put his faith in. Then he made his point. He wanted Millie Watkins appointed temporary mayor. At this he was greeted with incredulous stares and pronouncements. They were shocked at the idea of a lady mayor. It was unheard of. What would the voters think, and on and on.

The sheriff listened patiently, then said, "The eventual history of this town is going to be recorded in the next few weeks. We have to have someone right now we can trust. Someone who is tough and honest. I defy you to say that Millie Watkins doesn't qualify." There were tentative rebuttals from the council and then John ended it with, "You take her, or I quit."

They took her.

The sheriff and Millie got organized. They recruited men they knew from the surrounding farms and ranches to join them. They systematically set up raids that were effective. They struck at daylight and at midnight. Their adversaries were thrown off balance, but even more important, the enemy began to feel fear.

The town gradually came back under control of the law. Now John could look forward again to the pleasure of the third grade reunion. Maybe, too, he could spend a little time with Todd.

Many things were moving towards his town, however, like spokes into the hub of a wagon, but the center of the wheel was as delicate as nitroglycerin.

6

Acee Hittson drove south from Denver parallel to a mighty portion of the snow-crusted Rocky Mountains. He handled the custom Cord sedan with immaculate and dexterous hands. It responded to his wishes just like the cards and dice of his profession. He liked fine things, but his only capability to enjoy the better life resided in his skill at gambling across the tables. In the back trunk he had a suitcase filled with expensive garments and toiletries. Packed next to them were the marked decks and the loaded cubes that paid for it all. He also had a case of champagne for the upcoming occasion. At first he wondered and slightly resented John having requested their presence ten days before the actual reunion. Now he could hardly wait to get there. His recent knowledge of a boom going on in Hobbs had titillated him. He might just pay for the trip in advance of the celebration. He might even stay . . . at least for a while.

Bessie Lou Jones was sitting in the best compartment on the train as it moved southwest out of Kansas City . . . another spoke in the wheel. She was dressed in high fashion, and as she polished her long nails she felt her whole body relax. It'd been a long time since she'd been in the country. She looked forward to the vacation, and she anticipated seeing John again. She remembered him with great fondness.

Dalton Van Allen guided his refurbished Stuz Bearcat around the curves of Nevada's desert, moving exultantly southeast towards the Arizona border. He was full of plans. This early trip was a break for Dalton. Certain gold mining stocks he'd recently issued in Tonapah would soon be questioned. He would not be there to answer. Instead he'd be in Hobbs, New Mexico, with an old school chum who just happened to be the law. He'd always wanted to take a little dip in oil. These thoughts so excited him that he took a curve too fast and the auto careened off the road very close to a steep bank. Dalton righted the car at the last second and got it back on the road. This was sort of like his whole life pattern.

Waddie Thorton drove a new Dodge truck west out of the hills near Fort Worth, Texas. Trucking wasn't his business, but what they hauled was, and that was whiskey. The homemade version. Just for the hell of it he had two brand new copper stills hidden in the back under what appeared to be a load of straw hay. What with a schoolmate as sheriff . . . well, who knew, it might be time to expand.

Two days later, three Packard sedans pulled out of Chicago with four men in each vehicle. There resided black, cold and latently ominous, a submachine gun in each of the cars along with lesser weapons—sawed-off shotguns, pistols and rifles. In a box there were hand grenades to outnumber the human occupants. They drove in a convoy perhaps a hundred yards apart. Few words were uttered. They all knew what they had to do. It was an old, old game. Only the weapons changed.

7

The Leonard Puft oil-field equipment, farm and ranch supply warehouse sat in the middle of an otherwise empty block. There were several smaller buildings behind it. The sand and tumbleweeds had drifted about a foot deep around the base of the building except on the east side. The wind seldom hit there directly. East winds usually brought moisture in this part of southeastern New Mexico. There had been none of that for a long time. All types of vehicles were driven to and from the building tending to business. The front portion was for the public. The center portion was walled off for use by Mr. Puft's varied, mostly armed, associates, but the back portion was strictly for his private affairs.

At this moment he was raging. "All right, all right, but its been three days now since you turned those flyers over to the newspaper! Why haven't they printed it? What about some action?"

Rusty Larkin circled the floor in front of Puft's desk and said irritably, "I don't know. Maybe it's because they're so old and the statutes. . . ."

Puft interrupted him. "I don't care how old they are. We're not looking for prison sentences. We just want them to kick John Strong out of that sheriff's office."

Larkin said, "Maybe the newspaper editor is waiting for all the rest of them to get here for the reunion. Guess we'll just have to wait. . . ."

"Wait, wait, wait is all I've heard from you."

In a room with only an inside door, Charlene was listening. She knew she was a prisoner here even though Rusty had tried to convince her it was only for her own protection. It was just until things cooled down. After all, he was practically a prisoner here himself. He had fixed up the room with all the modern conveniences he could manage. There was plenty of food, and magazines, a couple of fans, a radio, and the kitchen was adequate. Still, that didn't alter her growing feeling of imprisonment, nor her realization that they might never let her go. Her knowledge could destroy her, just like Socrates.

She was working on an escape. She had been prying two boards loose behind her dressing table by using the handle of an iron skillet for a tool. It was a slow and delicate task. Fortunately, the table was on rollers so it could be moved back and forth swiftly. She would listen at the door until she felt she was alone except for the guard—she knew they always left one there when they were out—then for a few nervous moments she would work. She always turned up the radio so that no one could hear the rusty nails squeaking out of the dry boards. Of course, this presented another problem—she couldn't hear anyone approach either. By finite degrees, though, the two eight-inch boards were loosening.

Now she heard Puft declare, "Well, I've waited long enough. I'm fed up with this amateur operation. My old associates from Chicago are on the way, and they should be here any day."

Charlene put her head against the door and shivered in the summer heat.

8

Millie's Place was vibrating with a warmth other than that of the late June sun. This was the day of the long awaited arrivals. Everyone was dressed in their best clothes and hustled around carrying out Millie's instructions for the finishing details. The aroma of cooling pies and roasting beef filled the kitchen, and the dining room tables were pretty with their cheerful cloths.

It had taken Todd all morning to gather a bouquet of wild flowers for Bessie Lou's room, and the sheriff had placed a bottle of the best bootleg he could find in the room of each male guest. Everything was ever so special. Just about the only normal thing happening was Todd asking every few minutes. "When are they gonna get here?"

Finally the time came to meet Bessie Lou's train. She stepped off into the sand and oil and wind like a moving, perfumed oasis. The sheriff swallowed, removed his hat and said, "Bessie Lou, you ain't changed a bit . . . except," and he made a curvy wave with his hands, "maybe a little here and there."

She laughed and ran into his outstretched arms exclaiming, "John, oh John, you neither, except you did finally grow up."

John said, "I gotta introduce you to all my friends. This is Millie, our new mayor."

Bessie Lou took her hands and said, "Mayor? A woman mayor, how marvelous. This must be some kind of town you got here, John."

". . . and this here's my boy Todd." At her look he laughed and added, "No . . . no, I ain't married. I won him in a poker game."

She hugged Todd around the head saying, "John hasn't changed a bit. He's always kidding."

Todd broke loose, saying proudly, "No, mam, he ain't kiddin'. He won me with two deuces. It was a bluff."

She didn't question any further but added, "It would take five aces to justify a handsome young man like you." She gave him such a dazzling smile that Todd twisted and buried his foot in the oily sand. He was now hopelessly, helplessly in love.

The porters finished unloading the pile of baggage. It was quickly transferred to the Ford sedan and they were soon all back at the boarding house.

Everyone else had arrived by nightfall. There was a lot of handshaking, reminiscing, and much kidding about appearances and occupations. The meal turned into a banquet and the champagne was popped and poured. It was a real celebration.

The sheriff stood up and raised his glass. "Here's to the only member of our . . . uh . . . illustrious class that's missin'. I had no earthly idea how to reach him, but we are all indebted to him. Without his little arson trick we wouldn't be here tonight. Here's to ol' Rusty Larkin, wherever he is." They drank to the toast.

Acee Hittson, the gambler, remarked, "I wonder what really did happen to Rusty?"

Bessie Lou said, "Probably turned into a professional arsonist."

Dalton Van Allen, the con man, commented, "More than likely he wound up in government service."

Waddie Thornton, bootlegger deluxe, added, "I got a feeling he turned out good. Probably a preacher or a captain in the Salvation Army."

Todd's eyes were opening and closing with sleepiness but he blurted out hopefully, "Maybe he'll hear about the big celebration and make it here by the Fourth of July."

John spent the next three days proudly showing his old friends the city of Hobbs's attributes. They were all enthusiastic at the number of oil wells being drilled and pumping. They were also amazed and elated at the growing greenness of the irrigated farms. They asked John many pointed questions about the growth and future of the area. Any other time he might have been aware that their interest was not altogether altruistic—if he hadn't had his eyes and mind so heavily concentrated on Bessie Lou. Her almost childish excitement and interest in the smallest things intrigued him. It didn't hurt any that she was also a very good-looking woman. John had never felt better in his life. It was the rarest of things—a dream that was truly happening. He spent as much time with her as possible, sharing all his plans for the city, but leaving unspoken the plans building in him about her. The rest of the class was busy casing out the town's possibilities for their own ultimate leanings.

9

At three o'clock in the morning of the first day of July, a Packard sedan roared down the middle of Main Street. Both back windows were open. It moved in near Millie's Place and an object was hurled through the front window. There was a loud explosion. Glass and boards were shredded in this room and pieces of steel ripped out into others, both upstairs and down.

One chunk tore into the intestines of the night man just as another struck him in the temple, saving him much agony. A newly arrived geologist and his wife, sleeping in room number two on the ground floor, were riddled about the legs. They would live. The sheriff was jarred from his bed. He acted from instinct because there was no way he could know what was really happening. He first stumbled through the dark to check on Todd and Millie, then the rest of his friends.

While he was doing this the Packard charged in the same manner to the newspaper office and then the combined sheriff's office and jail. Following the three explosions two more of the Packards hit the street about thirty yards apart. They, too, had the back windows down. From each a short black muzzle exuded. The breaking of glass could barely be heard above the staccato bark of the submachine guns.

The attack was over in less than two minutes. There was just a moment of silence and then the night was filled with lights turning on, screams of the wounded and dying, dogs barking, and the confused babble of voices mixed with the suddenly rising wind. Peace that had come with painful slowness had left with shocking rapidity.

Only the children and the dogs went back to sleep that night. The little medical clinic could not handle the chaos. A station was set up in the school house. Bessie Lou, having had much practical experience, joined the two doctors and five nurses in treating the victims. Everyone did whatever he could. The casualty count for the night was seven dead and nineteen wounded.

Millie and the sheriff moved about the town consoling, trying to overcome the panic about to erupt. They had a difficult time getting armed volunteers to patrol the streets, but it had to be done to give a semblance of confidence back to the populace. They called on the need to protect their families, friendship, patriotism, and then used the strongest weapon of all—fear. Slowly it worked. By an hour after sun-up the town resembled a military camp after a bombing from the air.

An exhausted John Strong walked into the battered newspaper office where the editor and his two typesetters were struggling to get back in print.

John said, "Well, Irv, what's the damage?"

Irv Cohen looked up and said with both resignation and determination, "Looks like we'll have to print by hand for a few days . . . but the paper will be out." He gave the sheriff a straight-on look. "You got anything to say for print, John?"

"Yeah. It's a terrible and completely baffling thing that's happened here tonight."

"That's all?"

"Yeah, except we're sure as heck gonna get to the bottom of this before we quit. I reckon that's all the words I got for now. What the people need is action, not talk."

Irv put down the wrench he was working with and said, "Come back here a minute, John."

The sheriff followed his respected friend into a back room. It was scarred by shrapnel but was mostly intact. Irv opened a drawer in the rolltop desk and held out a stack of papers to John. He looked through them carefully, then raised his head and stared a moment at the editor.

"How long you had these, Irv?"

"About a week, I guess."

"Where'd you get 'em?"

"I was out when they were left. The boys didn't see who brought them in either."

"Well, level with me, Irv. What're you gonna do about them?"

"I don't know. I don't know what's right for . . . for everybody."

John looked at him again without speaking, then he turned and walked out, calling back, "I know you'll do what's right inside you. I gotta get on with my job."

Irv stood staring at the empty doorway a while before putting the wanted flyers back into the drawer.

John angled down the street to Millie's crippled place. People were already sweeping, repairing, and putting in what window glass was available and boarding up when that was gone. The armed guards walked about nervously watching. The thing was, they didn't know what to watch for.

The sheriff called a meeting of his schoolmates, Millie, and his two best deputies. He apologized for the unexpected violence that was marring the town and the reunion. He went back fully over the history of the town and wound up saying he felt it was all tied in some way to Charlene's disappearance after the murder of the mayor and his wife. He explained that he could call in federal help, but he believed that first they should make a strong effort to solve it on their own. There could be no doubt now—the movement was organized, and when you have organization you have a leader. He was asking the schoolmates to get out and mix with the elements that suited them best. Bessie Lou would mingle with the ladies of the night; Acee would involve himself with gambling and its participants; Dalton would try to infiltrate the shyster group and Waddie would contact the bootleggers.

"Now it just happens that you are all expert in the very lines that keeps the money flowin', and it's this illegal money that's brought this plague on us. Someone has gotta slip sometime. A single word may do it or even a hint. We gotta get to the brains and the power behind all this." The sheriff paused just a second and then finished, "And we gotta do it right now!"

They all went out among them knowing it was mighty risky, but then their entire lives had been that. The sheriff continued his rounds asking questions of everyone he could corner. Not one person would admit to having witnessed the attack or having any knowledge at all about it. There was a numb fear infecting the people. Well, he thought, maybe in a couple of days they'll relax enough to come forward. It was a stifling situation.

On July second, Millie insisted they stretch the canvas banner across the street announcing the first annual Fourth of July rodeo and the third grade reunion. Many comments were uttered about this frivolity when the town appeared to be under siege.

Millie ignored these accusations and her only comment was, "We're goin' to have the celebration, if it hare-lips the governor."

The carnival was setting up out in a big vacant lot. For the first time they could remember, no local kids ran in and out asking questions and looking for ways to sneak into the tent shows. Millie had some trouble, in fact, keeping them from loading up and leaving town, but the carny boss finally agreed that if a little old lady was so confident, it must be all right. They stayed.

The cowboys drifted in for the rodeo, staying together out at the grounds, wondering what in the hell they were doing in a war camp anyway. It was unnatural to them. They should be in town drinking, telling lies, and looking for women.

Just the same, Mayor Millie kept her wounded establishment going and had just about the only business in town of its kind. No matter what an individual's opinion might be of her, she exuded solidity and hope.

Late that afternoon, by mutual agreement, the sheriff's people met again. They agreed to hear one at a time. Bessie Lou was first. "It's organized, like you said, John, and it's very tight. I tried every trick I know, and . . . and I'm not sure I came up with anything helpful. I did overhear the name Puft mentioned a couple of times, but there was nothing really concrete said."

Acee, Dalton, and Waddie verified almost the same thing.

The sheriff said, "You may have accomplished a lot more than you think. We've been watching Puft for several weeks . . . I . . . well, I got to admit we haven't come up with anything we could move on either."

Acee asked if he'd tried a run-down with other law enforcement agencies on Puft, and the sheriff confirmed, "Yeah, we've got wires out all over the country, but nothin' to grab on to so far."

Just then a timid knock tapped the door to the meeting room. John moved over to open it. The waitress from Millie's place told the sheriff that a lady, the mayor's missing niece was there to see him. John excused himself and disappeared.

The group sat trying to make small talk, waiting. In a short while John returned, bringing Charlene with him.

"Well, folks, you were on the right trail with Puft. It is him. They have been holdin' Miss Charlene prisoner." He looked at the still-quivering young woman, "Now, don't worry, honey, we'll take good care of you. It's all gonna be fine."

Millie got up to get Charlene some coffee and a shot of Waddie's best. She calmed a little with the attention, and told all she knew about Puft's organization. With her information they could plan their counterattack. Then came the shocker. She told them about Rusty Larkin. They were stunned. Rusty had shown up way early for the reunion. They were all here.

10

July the third was a quiet day in Hobbs. Most people stayed in their homes with guns at hand, taking an occasional peek out a window, expecting something to come—something terrible because it was unknown.

The guards stood about hardly moving, shifting their eyes around carefully. None made any sudden motions. It was almost as if they believed that their own stillness would negate a movement from the enemy.

The sheriff, his classmates, Millie and the only two deputies he had left he could trust were gathered in the dining room.

John explained, "We're gonna be short handed, but we can't risk somebody gettin' word to 'em. We'll hit 'em just like they did us . . . at night. Now, if they do suspect anything at all, they'll figger on us striking early in the morning just like they did. What we're gonna do is move about an hour after sundown. Maybe, just maybe, we can catch 'em off balance." The truth was, John had wracked his brain numb trying to figure a way to take them without undue violence, but there was no answer because there was no time.

The room was stacked with rifles, pistols and shotguns, but John knew this was no match for machine guns. He had two rolls of dynamite tied together. He'd short fuse them when they were ready.

John went over and over the plans, making everyone repeat them back to him. Finishing, he said, "I don't aim to lose any more people. We gotta time it hair-thin."

The sun started down. A few lights came on in the houses, but the quiet pervaded. The night creatures out in the prairies hunted and hid just like the people of the town. When the sun would rise the next morning some would sleep digesting those that hadn't survived the night. The wind came in gusts, and then, suprisingly, settled.

The carnival lights blinked on, and then as the sun no longer affected the visible sky, the music suddenly exploded across the town. The ferris wheel started turning, and people looked cautiously out the windows at the garish lights, and listened to the incongruous music.

John's people waited, waited, waited. Then he said, "Well, it's time."

Everyone, including Millie, reached for the weapons. She picked up a double barrel and started stuffing a box of shells in her apron pocket.

John said, "Wait a minute. What do you think you're doin', Millie?"

"It's already done. I'm ready."

"Now, you listen here to me. You ain't goin'. If somethin' happened to you they'd run me outa the country."

"How come? I'm the best bird shot around these parts."

"Millie, these ain't birds. They hit back. You gotta stay here with Todd . . . in case something does go wrong."

"Bessie Lou can watch after him. I'm goin', John."

He looked at her a moment, then said, "Well, there ain't any time left to argue."

Bessie Lou reached over and touched John on the arm, saying softly, "I know how she feels, John. Don't worry about Todd. I'll take care of him."

They all eased out into the back alley where they had two cars and Waddie's truck parked. One deputy took Acee and Dalton and slipped out a back road to circle around the outskirts of town so they could come in behind the warehouse. The rest waited a while, then the second deputy drove slowly around the other side of town to their rendezvous. He had Millie with him.

Finally Waddie got into the truck cab. John whispered to him, "Now, you remember, don't you? Go down the alley three blocks and then left straight to the warehouse."

Waddie said softly back, "Don't worry, John. I got it all."

John loaded his weapons in the back of the truck and crawled in with the bundles of dynamite. Slowly, slowly the truck eased down the alley to the designated street. If Waddie went any slower the truck would stall, but he made it work. Then just as carefully Waddie turned left and drove towards the warehouse. John lived a few eternities there in the back of the truck. They were committed. The wheels moved on towards an ultimate destiny. He prayed that his other people were undiscovered and in position.

Now, ironically, the carnival was in full view as well as the warehouse. Its people stood around under the lights and whirling machines waiting, but no one came. No one. A coyote howled off in the prairie, but was drowned out by the music of the customerless carnival.

Now he had to light the fuses. If they were too short, he and Waddie would be blown up. If they were too long, it might give Puft and his men time to escape. He ducked down behind the cab and put the match to one bundle and then the other. He tapped on the window signaling Waddie and stood up bracing himself against the sudden lurch of the truck as Waddie jammed it into another gear and they roared forward across the open lot straight at the building.

John was having a rough time staying upright, but he did. Just as Waddie circled the truck near the building, he hurled one bundle at the back corner. It fell right against the building. Waddie gunned the truck parallel, and John tossed the other bundle high into the air. It came down somewhere on the flat roof.

They were just past the front when the first explosion blew the whole corner from the building. One beat later the roof was splintered apart and pieces of the building shot out through the dry night air.

Waddie jammed on the brakes at the bar ditch and he and John bailed out with their weapons into the sand. There were yells now and a fire leaped up. Then the first shots came from the two rear positions. Two figures burst out of a back building. John dropped one. Waddie got the other. He flipped over skidding against the ground; a submachine gun clattered from his hands.

Three figures dashed from the back of the main building, firing wildly, confusedly, into the night. One burst caught the bed of the truck above John and Waddie, but shots from somewhere in the rear dropped them. Another fell out into the back with flames eating at his clothing and flesh, screaming, rolling madly upon the ground in desperation. Then the body was still. The burning clothing died down to smoke.

John yelled, "All right, rake the buildings low!"

They grabbed fresh guns and fired until they were empty. They could hear shots from the other side, and some from the out-buildings, but they were slacking off.

John had just reloaded his rifle when one of the Packards came from somewhere behind and bounced across the empty lot at an angle away from them. John and Waddie levered the shells with all the speed they had, blasting two tires flat, shooting into the motor, and then into the car. It wobbled a moment, straddled a large mesquite bush, and died. The door nearest them opened and someone fell out.

John and Waddie ran down the bar ditch ducking low and then came up in front of the car through the mesquite. The driver's door was open and John spotted a figure crawling out onto the ground. He moved to him, put his foot on the hand that held a pistol, and shoved his rifle up against his head. The head turned and looked up with horrified eyes, dying eyes.

John said, "Well, I'll be damned if it ain't ol' Rusty Larkin. Welcome to the third grade reunion."

There were no more shots now. The cracking of the fire sounded extra loud as it inhaled the dry wood of the warehouse. The light of the blaze dimmed that of the carnival, but the music still rolled out across the soot and blood speckled land.

11

By noon the next day, the Fourth of July, the schoolhouse morgue was lined with bullet perforated and charred bodies again. This time, however, there were no local mourners to be seen. The few lightly wounded had been jailed. The sheriff had wired the Feds to come check out the living and dead remains to see if they had any claim on them.

By mid-afternoon the shock and fear had begun to subside. Small groups of citizens headed out to the rodeo grounds to cheer for their favorite contestants. By night the whole country pulsated with life again. Just about everyone went to the carnival.

Acee had a crease across his head. Dalton carried his arm in a sling. The bullet had only chipped the bone. They'd both be all right soon.

John and his group moved about the carnival, taking congratulations and lots of hand-shaking and back-slapping.

Laughter rang out from the children again as they forgot everything except filling their bellies with soda pop and cotton candy, the wondrous whirling rides and the magic promised behind the flaps of the mysterious tents. Somehow there was money afloat for everybody that night. For just a little while, the rich and the poor were the same.

Todd was treated by the sheriff's whole group until he was plain dizzy and satiated. He manfully endured. After all, he might never be so spoiled again.

12

The next day John checked out everything at the morgue and jail. He headed back down the street to Millie's, suddenly starving for food and the company of his friends. He ran head on into Irv Cohen. He'd forgotten!

They looked at each other a moment just as they'd done the last time they met.

Finally John asked, "Gonna get out a special edition, Irv?"

"Yeah, but it'll take us until tomorrow. We still haven't got everything repaired."

"Well, that's good news. Care to have lunch with us?"

"No, thanks. I just came from Millie's."

"Oh."

"Yeah. The stew's better than ever today. Oh yeah, I goofed up this morning and threw those flyers out with the trash."

John couldn't hold the big grin back. "Thanks, Irv."

"Awww, nothing to it. Uh . . . you did shoot that man in Billings in self defense, didn't you?"

"Why, of course. You knew that all along. Well, I gotta get on down and see the folks. The Feds will be in tomorrow and I'll have all I can handle for a few days."

Irv said, as they walked apart, "You can handle just about anything now, John."

They all had a carefree lunch together talking about everything except what had occurred in Hobbs.

Then Acee said, "Well, I suppose I better pack."

The others decided they better do the same thing. Each one made some kind of comment about how they'd like to stay and maybe operate here a while, but since the law was now in full control of this town it might not be expedient.

They left the room to get ready for departure. Only Todd, Bessie Lou, and Millie remained at the table with John.

Hesitantly Bessie Lou stood up and said, "Well, I've got some time before the train comes, but it won't hurt to be ready and avoid getting in a rush later."

They all looked at her, willing themselves to say something appropriate, but only John stood up.

"Well now, Bessie Lou, it makes sense for the others to leave . . . but it seems silly as all hell for you to . . . ."

"But, John . . . ."

"Now, now. You fit in here real good. There's gonna be a lot of work for us all."

"But, John . . . ."

"And I'm gonna need help the most of all."

"But, John . . . ."

"I won Todd in a poker game. Might as well flip a coin to complete the family." He flipped the quarter almost to the ceiling, saying to her, "Heads I win. Tails you lose." It hit the floor, bounced, and rolled under the table.

Todd fell down instantly, crawling under and grabbing it. He scrambled back out and held it up, grinning broadly.

"See! We won again!"

They all laughed, and for a moment nobody heard the goddamned wind blowing.

Sky of Gold

It might take two or three days, but just the same it was upon him. It was the time to die. The legs beneath his thin, shaky body moved with a stiff certainty beyond their strength, for he had been here a long, long time. He must get away from the town. He could feel its pull, reaching out to him. He could hear it say, "Come, Old Pete, sit by my dusty streets in the shade of my trees. Loaf and dream in the sun on my porches and warm your worn old legs. Come and die slowly here, looking out at the far distant hills." He moved out in front of the burros, the voice of the town becoming weaker with each halting step. Up there somewhere in the hills was a secluded spot where he could die without interference from the town, from all the towns and cities, where no one could ask him to recount the tales that belonged to him alone— tales that only he could understand.

Old Pete had lived as he wanted. Surely now he could die as he wanted. Just a hidden spot of hard earth somewhere in the rough hills that had been his home where he could lay his head and depart. Where he could make a meal for the coyotes, those singers of the night who had been his partners in loneliness these fifty odd years, who like himself had scratched their breath and sustenance from the hills.

He felt no pain. His heart still pumped his blood, and though his legs were stiff and very old they kept him upright. Still it was his time, and he knew, and like a gut-shot wolf he hunted his true home. There it was out ahead—dry, washed, worn, cruel. It was his. That was the difference. He'd long ago earned his place here.

He stopped to rest after a while. The burros grazed about in the thin patches of grass as Old Pete looked back. He had made better time than he thought. It was about noon, and the paved road splitting the village of Hillsboro looked narrow and fragile. He could see the trucks. He could hear their endless drone that spoke of things he felt no part of. Maybe by nightfall he would be free of their sounds.

The packs on the burros were light. Soon he would free them of their burden and turn them loose. They, too, could roam free and unmolested. But he would need them for a while yet.

"Haaa!" he said. "Let's move out, Old Mary, Old Nancy." The burros raised their heads and followed, their sharp black hoofs pitching tiny balls of dust at each step.

Now they entered the arroyos and the small, rolling, cover-less hills. In and out they moved, up and down, around the sage and cactus. Slow, steady, sure.

It had been a good life—and he had found his gold. Four hundred dollars to the ton. He had dug and blasted it out in a month. The vein had narrowed, pinched, and then petered-out altogether. He had crushed the quartz a little at a time in a hard mortar. He panned out the gold and sacked it. Eight thousand dollars worth at twenty dollars an ounce. What a time he had! The town was his then—the drinks, the tender women, the feasting, the dice table—they had been his. Then it had ended. The town turned its cold side to him. He went away and though he returned many, many times, he never gave of himself to the town again.

The tiny, sunken, blue eyes pierced out beyond the sharp eroded cheekbones to the land ahead. The great red mesas edged nearer. On beyond, the high, breastlike mountains called.

What had started this search so long ago and kept him at it all those years? Was it the gold? Was it? he couldn't answer that. He had been young when he started. He was strong then, and he was strong for years after. Before his strike there had been moments of indecision. One summer, far, far past, he had dug and panned nine hundred dollars worth of gold. "We can start a feed store," the woman had said. "You can settle down. You can sleep in a feather bed every night. My body and my heart will be yours, and I will cook and sew and raise your kids, and we will grow old together happily." That was Mary. Every burro he had ever owned had been named either Mary or Nancy.

He must have been about thirty-five or six when he met Nancy. That was the time he had failed to raise a grubstake for months he now remembered. Nancy was a dancing girl. Every young man wanted a dancing girl—this one wanted him, though. "Now, look, Pete," she had said, "I've been everywhere and done everything, I know men, but I don't really know you. You want my love—well, here it is, Pete, take it, but don't throw it away.

257

Come with me. I'll show the tricks of the cards to you, and we can tour the world. Just you and me. You'll never have to worry about the grubstake again."

She had made it sound so good, so easy, so sure. But the great secret magnet of the mesas had pulled at his life fibers, and he had been drawn back to the rocky slopes of the hills. Again and yet again.

He was growing very tired. The sun lingered just above the hills. He hadn't looked back for a long time. He would not look back until the night was upon him. It came swiftly and all at once. He knew that the sky just before had been filled with gold, but he couldn't make himself look.

He built the fire from a few sticks of wood on the pack saddle. They were still some distance from the scrub timber of the mesas. He fried the bacon and took the hard, sourdough bread into himself with little taste. He could hear the whish of the night-owl's wings and the cry of the coyote. In his lonely wail, his old partner sang to Pete of the Marys and the Nancys and the warm firesides. Of the things only they could understand—the things Old Pete had missed, and the things he had found.

Now Pete looked back and listened. There it was still—the drone of the mighty trucks. He was not nearly far enough into the hills. It would take another day, maybe two. He could see the tiny flickering red and blue lights blinking from the village below like a small cluster of earthbound stars.

Old Pete slept little that night. It was the longest night of his life. He lay in his blanket and stared and felt the earth throb beneath him. This earth was his. It was his love. He craved to have it devour him. But he must live the night out and move on beyond those lights and noises below. The voice of the coyote kept him company, crying into the night from one valley, then the next. Raising his head atop the hills and voicing his concern for his compadres who sleep alone on the desert sands.

It was almost noon the next day before the stiffness left Old Pete's legs. It only proved how right he was. He could no longer roam these wastes searching for his treasure. The burros threw their long ears forward and shied sideways. The diamond-back lay coiled, black tongue flickering, quivering in tenseness. The rattles were a blur on its tail as it shook its warning.

"No need for that," Pete muttered. "I'll give you back your land very soon. I will walk far around you. You were here first. It is yours."

He climbed on up through the scattered timber above the desert floor, the burros following slowly in single file behind. His stooping shoulders ached, and it was now a great effort to put one foot in front of the other, but on upward he moved. He saw the deer and the bobcat tracks in the soft sand of the washes, and he saw the fresh droppings of the coyote matted with rabbit hair.

He turned and looked behind him, taking his ragged old hat from his head so the light breeze could blow through his greyed and tangled hair. He looked close. It was gone. The village was gone. He strained his ears. No sound but the distant calling of a magpie. He was beyond it, but they still moved on up—the three of them.

They topped the high long mesa and struggled up into the thicker timbers. Pete could feel the blood beating hard on his ears now. His breath rasped through his worn, broken teeth. The rat-tat of the woodpecker told him they had reached the timberline.

Then he found the game trail into the oak brush. It was very steep. The timber thickened. He saw in the trail the lion's round track as big as his hand. Yes, he was near his destination, for the lion, too, feared the same thing in his own heart and had moved to the outermost reaches. It was just a matter of finding the spot now—the right place to return to his earth.

Pete walked and looked for a long time. Then he found it. A flat place on solid rock. A mighty tree-fettered canyon lay below. He could look down the canyon and out into another desert to the west. He could see as far as his eyes could reach. He could hear as far as his ears allowed. Only the sounds of the desert and the forest above were audible.

He unpacked the burros. He neatly piled up his equipment, his blankets, his pick, his shovel, his gold pans. He yelled, waving his bony, trembling arms at the burrows. They looked puzzled for a moment, then seeming to understand they turned and moved down through the brush.

Beyond the purple-bottomed mist of the canyons Old Pete saw the sky redden to the west. Then it turned yellow red, gold red, and then pure gleaming molten gold. He lay back slowly and settled himself. The trembling stopped. The breath came slower and slower. Only the sound of the forest was here. The elusive whisper of the nightwind soothed his tired old body. The thin chest barely moved.

He looked into the dark blue of the upper sky. His fading sight saw the twin streaks of white vapor forming behind the soaring aircraft, and he heard the harsh, shattering blast of its jets.

Mary and Nancy grazed peacefully back down the hill towards the distant village. Moving downhill it wasn't so far away. They would soon be there.

Author's note: "Sky of Gold" was written in 1950 and is the nucleus of the massive and major works of my life: *Bluefeather Fellini* and *Bluefeather Fellini in the Sacred Realm. The South Dakota Review* published "Sky of Gold" in the spring of 1995 as part of a dissertation on my two major works.

A Man Who Never Missed

Gus Morgan was the best deer hunter in the Hi Lo Country. There was no question about it. The meat was the proof and Gus always brought home the venison. As to Gus Morgan's other qualities there was doubt. Some folks called him lazy, others worthless, but they all meant the same.

Gus lived out a ways from the small mountain village of Hi Lo on a little one-section, starvation outfit, as he was prone to call it. He kept there a few head of poor cows and one or two half-poor hogs. In other words Gus only had one thing to brag about and that was his deer hunting. He didn't even have a wife to brag about beating the dickens out of.

Now every year when deer season opened you could bet your bottom-dollar that Gus was out in the hills with his .30-.30. And if you had another dollar beside that one, you could bet and win that within three days Gus would have his deer. He usually hunted alone, but occasionally someone would join him while out on a hunt and they invariably had quite a story to tell. It seems that Gus always put the bullet right where he was looking and that was through the heart.

This season something had gone wrong. Gus had hunted nine days of the ten-day season without bringing in a deer. He deserved credit for trying though. He had walked what seemed like a thousand miles. He had tried all the old familiar game hangouts and trails. But no luck. Gus, big man that he was in size, couldn't take this sudden departure of luck.

Evenings, when he came back through Hi Lo, he stopped at Lollipop's bar. Always before he had Lollipop's to show off his kill and hold up his reputation as the best deer hunter in the country. Now, however, he stopped and hung his elbows over the bar and drank all the alcohol he could pour down his long, gawky frame. That was considerable.

The town barflies had begun to gather every night in Lolli-pop's to watch the proceedings. Only one of them said anything, that was Carl Adams. The others just watched figuring that was the wise thin to do because of Gus Morgan's size and his foul hu-mor over the present situation.

Carl Adams, a Hi Lo merchant, reasoned that Gus would be needing some credit before the winter was over, so he ventured a remark. "Don't let it get you down, Gus. There's lots of has-beens around."

Gus just humped up a little more, turned a mite redder in the face and kept on drinking.

Gus went home that ninth night feeling confident of success the following day, but upon awakening the next morning, what with a hangover and one thing and another, he didn't feel so lucky.

He drove the old 1939 pickup as far into the mountains as he could. Then he climbed out and took off afoot. About a mile and a half up the mountain slope was an oak brush covered canyon that he had dragged many a deer out of. He had hunted it the first day of the season and saw only two does. Knowing the way of the deer, though, Gus figured that surely there were some bucks back in there now.

He walked faster than usual, feeling the limited time slip away from him with each step he took. His breath frosted in the cold mountain air and his boots crunched into the crusted snow of Johnson Mesa. He caught a glimpse of something dashing through some small cedars. It was a coyote. Breathing hard Gus lowered his gun. He couldn't afford to shoot now and chance scaring a buck up and out of the canyon before he got there.

"By damn," he muttered to himself, "I've got to get one today. That's all there is to it." He had never been known to go through a deer season without a kill. This thought made him lean over and walk even faster. The dark edge of the canyon was near. Gus bent low and eased his way up behind a clump of cedars on the brink of the canyon. The last few yards he crawled on his belly, not minding the snow that rubbed up into his coat sleeves and into the top of his pants. There it was—the canyon. There had to be a deer—a buck deer—in it or the reputation of Gus Morgan as a hunter was gone. He would be gone as well for that's all he had.

He scanned the canyon with narrowed eyes, gradually get-ting his breath back. He knew he had to quit blowing so hard or he might miss. His eyes ran up and down the little breaks that dropped into the canyon. Not even a doe.

Then suddenly his eyes were pulled back to a brush covered hump in the middle of the canyon. Something was there. It was a buck. Gus' heart pounded at his big chest. He eased the gun into firing position. Over two hundred yards down hill, it was a hard shot. He knew he had to make the first one good. His cheek lay over against the .30-.30. His eyes lined down the barrel and set the front bar in the rear V.

Just at that instant a shot rang out. Gus was so taken aback by this that for a moment he thought he had fired. Then he saw the deer thrashing around in the snow and the red blood of its life pouring out on the whiteness.

Gus lay there paralyzed as a man walked down from the other rim and up to the deer. It looked like Carl Adams, the merchant.

"Old Carl, huh?" he muttered out loud. A sickness rose up in Gus Morgan. For a moment he thought he was going to pass out. The sickness was followed by rage. Gus clambered down the slope. As he neared the scene of the kill, Carl Adams glanced up.

"Well," he said, "What are you doing here?" Before Gus could answer, Carl added, "I must have just beat you to the trigger, Gus."

"Yeah, that's right." said Gus.

"Tell you what." Carl said, "'If you'll help me dress this baby and drag it out you can have a hindquarter."

So, offering the greatest deer hunter in the Hi Lo Country a hindquarter to help pull a deer out of a canyon. What did Carl think he was anyway—a has-been?

Gus raised his gun slowly and took careful aim. At the shot a round black hole appeared in Carl Adams' forehead. The back of his head and half of his brains scattered out onto the snow. The impact of the bullet knocked Adams back on his heels where he was squatted. Then he fell with a limber slump forward on his face.

Gus wasted no time. He pulled Adams over to a crevice in the side of the canyon and in a short time had him covered with dead branches. He wanted to cover him with rocks but they were frozen to the ground. He surveyed the burial and decided it would have to do.

As he walked back over to the deer he picked up Carl Adams' rifle—a .30-.40 Krag, and hurled it into the clump of cedars where the deer had stood. Then for the first time he actually looked at the deer. Lord! It was a doe!

Gus stood stiff and dropped his gun into the snow. Even through his fear, he realized that he couldn't have taken the game into Lollipop's. Why, he would have been stuck for poaching. He cursed Carl Adams to the bottom of his heart—the ignorant peddling fool thought that was a buck. He whirled and saw the dead branches that had fooled both Carl Adams and the greatest hunter in the Hi Lo Country. He saw Adams' .30-.40 Krag laying out in the snow where it had passed completely through the cedars.

At that very instant he heard someone yell over on the other side of the .30-.40 Krag. "Hey, you seen Carl Adams around here? We heard him shoot a while ago."

Gus stood and watched the three hunting companions of Carl Adams moving steadily towards him. In their path the .30-.40 Krag shone black against the snow.

Big Shad's Bridge

Les Martin dropped his wiry arm around the shoulder of the woman Doreen; with the other he pointed down from the timbered mountains across the desert to the black scar of the Rio Grande Gorge.

"There," he said, "just to the right of that green valley is Romo's Crossing. When we get there, we'll have it made. Once we're on the other side we'll just follow the Rio on down to Mexico."

She looked a while and then turned her triangular face and dark slanted eyes up to his. "Are you sure?" she asked. "Really sure, Les? You know, a lot of other men have had this same dream and failed."

"Now look, honey, I tell you everything's set. I've worked on this for over a year. I've even made allowances for things goin' wrong. You're my rabbit's foot," he said gathering her small, supple form to him. "Just four days, honey. I'll be back here with the coin in just four days. Then it'll be all new for both of us from now on. No *more* pawing from drunk miners and cowboys for you." His sharp blue eyes showed an almost final determination.

"Please, Les," she said, "don't talk about it."

"I'm sorry, honey. It's just that I want this to go right so much for both of us." As he looked down at her from a battered, heavy-lipped face she seemed to him only four feet tall and delicate as a humming bird. She was an ex-prostitute, but he trusted her. She was his woman now. You can't trust a man to wait out four days of anguish—and if so, he'd probably shoot you in the back for the trouble, but you can trust a woman in love, as long as there's no one around to talk her out of it. Or so Les figured. Yeah, Doreen would be there waiting for his return, ready to die, if necessary, for their escape. This he believed.

Now he hugged her goodbye, looked over her lean-to, double checking to be sure all was right for her, then mounted the grey gelding and, leading three others, rode away from her tiny figure without looking back.

The Big Man, man of power, of decision and possibly of destiny, surveyed his bridge. It was his bridge by rights of ownership and vision. It was also his because of guts. It hadn't been easy. The Rio is a treacherous and deceitful river at all times, but more so at the time of the bridge's beginning.

When Big Shad started work on it in early summer, the waters still raged from the mountain snows of Colorado and northern New Mexico. The hired hands had refused to swim the heavy rope across the muddy agitated water, but without the rope nothing could be moved—no rock piers could be laid, no timber could be placed. Of course, he could have waited a couple of months until the water subsided, but Big Shad was an impatient man.

Big Shad had said, "All right, you bunch of cowards, I'll take it across myself. When I was hiring, you all talked like mountain trout and now you're as scared of water as opium den whores!"

He tied the rope around his chest and jumped in. Several times the water took him under. The hired hands, his gunmen, and even one of his dance-hall girls, stood on shore pale and trembling, but none moved to help. But then Shad would surface and fight against the current with his powerful shoulders and arms, struggling for what was more than life to him. This bridge would give him absolute control of the comings and goings to Taos. Sheer rock bluffs encased the river for over twenty miles in both directions, and Romo's Crossing, where the bridge was to be built, was the only accessible passage down into the gorge.

In Taos he already owned the gaming tables, and it was his own whiskey, made in his own still, that he sold across the bars. The dance-hall girls were his, too, because they either worked for him or had to move further down the river.

He'd been a long time getting here; from an early orphan in Texas to trail drives across the alternately flooding or scorching plains to Dodge City and past; from a mucker in a gold mine to a swamper in another man's saloon where he swept up other people's fun as it spilled out on the floor. But Big Shad had learned, and now his long fingers felt the cards and dice like a lover's hands on a woman's breast, like the lips of a virgin's kiss.

That day he swam across the terrible river, river of death and life that had tempted many at its crossings only to drown them on the fish-lined bottom. And the river, like a vicious woman, sucked at him, tugging and whirling his mighty body about on the rope which, he insisted, would conquer her.

On he fought, choking, strangling, blind in the muddy water. Tossed, turned, twisted and yet inching toward the far shore.

And then he was there, climbing up the bank, struggling, stumbling, rising again. Turning to the waiting ones, he held the rope in the air with the arm of a victorious gladiator. His spirit crept into all, and the bridge rose and spanned the water so that now a man could walk above the flow and smile down at its smooth green depths.

He turned to the little dark man beside him.

"Will it be finished tomorrow, Fidel?"

"*Si, Señor* Shad, *mañana* for sure." And for some reason he put his hand on the pistol at his right side.

"That's good. Very good. In a day or two the sheep will start moving across. That will be the test. If we stop the herders the first time and make them pay, the rest will follow like the creatures they herd."

"They will stop, *Señor* Shad. Do not worry."

A small hotel was being completed just back from the bridge. Soon he would have it all. The whole country.

Big Shad had learned that a rail-head would be laid to Servietta, a few miles across the river. It would connect Santa Fe and Denver. It would be *his* stage line that picked up the passengers to haul them to *his* bridge, where they, like the sheepherders, would pay to cross. Then he would hold them overnight at *his* new hotel. The next morning Big Shad's stage would take them on into Taos to stay in *his* hotel there, where they would drink *his* whiskey, buy his food and lose at *his* gaming tables.

And the sheepmen? He would make it easy for them to cross into the winter pastures of Taos. It would only cost them twenty-five cents a head. For cattle, horses and people, the toll would be an even dollar.

He shifted the buckshot loaded shotgun in his arms and said, "Tomorrow then, Fidel, we'll be in business.

"*Si. Mañana.*"

Orlando Espinoza looked over the backs of the flock scattered out before him moving, undulating, like a lake of wool as it followed the black goat with a bell around its neck. He stood in the shade of his horse and watched the dogs herd the sheep. Over to the side he could see his helper, Ramon Gallegos, riding back and forth, slowly, keeping the sheep moving towards the center probably thinking of the seven kids who were the other half of the world to Ramon.

Both men carried rifles and they had five dogs working. No less would do, for the coyotes were always hungry. The sheep were fat. It had been a good summer with desert rains to fill the waterholes.

The boss would be glad to see them now. They had crossed the Rio Grande to summer pasture in the early spring when the water was low, before the melting snow deepened and churned the river making it impassable. And now, in late summer, they were returning when again the water would be lowered and quietened so the sheep could be safely pushed across.

Tomorrow afternoon they would reach Romo's Crossing. There they would rest for a day and let the sheep graze on the lush grass where the Rio Hondo Creek emptied into the river. Then on to the sub-irrigated pastures of Taos Valley where the sheep would winter. That, too, was work, but before this would come the pay and the ten days in town with the wine and the whores. And all the summer wages would be spent in that time and a million years of fun would be had to make up for the million years of time in the silent desert.

The night came at them slowly in the pure air. The light lingered, fighting for another moment here before being overwhelmed by darkness as all things eventually must. The coyotes were talking across the sagebrush, yapping and smelling into the stillness. The sheep listened, but so did the dogs, bristles standing, growling low, ready to fight for their masters and their masters' slaves, with equal ferocity.

The purple and orange of the sky did not directly influence Orlando and Ramon. They felt its beauty without looking, its peace without knowing what it was. They were simple men. Dedicated men. They had known little else but the sheep. All their lives had been spent in this manner, looking after another man's wealth. They were apprenticed under their fathers when they had to ride hoseback because their legs were still so young they couldn't walk a mile without resting. With hearts and minds so tender, it had taken only gentle hands to mold them into what they were now, and what they would always be.

Some summers it was a desperate race to make it to the crossing and its lifesaving water. For in the dry spells that cracked the land and men's faces alike, the waterholes were two and three days apart. Then, the race for the crossing was one of life and death. It took all their skill, to move the flock at the right speed and tempo to survive the trek.

Orlando had always managed. Only once had he lost thirty-six head on the march and he'd mourned for three years—even though his patron bragged on him and said that other flocks had come to the wet banks of Romo's Crossing depleted as much as one-third. This did nothing to ease Orlando's dismay. He settled only for the best job he could do. All the sheepmen figured on a ten percent yearly loss to varmints, drought, or disease. Orlando had cut his to five, and with the exception of that one black year had held true to his dedication.

Now the night came, and visited a few hours. The dogs slept little because the coyotes stayed close and moved about smelling the sweet flesh beneath the dirty wool.

But none of the sheep were touched that night and Orlando could head for the river the next morning knowing he had served his master faithfully, and the sheep would be delivered into his hands whole, healthy, and ready to winter well and lamb heavily the next spring.

All was right in Orlando's world.

Les Martin rode higher into the mountains towards G-Town. It was slow going uphill leading three horses. It had taken a long time to select these animals—all dark greys. His days at cow punching, for twenty a month, had given him the knowledge to pick good mountain horses. Stickers. He'd chosen the color to blend into the mountain shadows and vanish with the night. He'd left two others staked in the meadow near Doreen's lean-to and the fresh spring water. They were all in good shape, ridden and hardened for months now. Doreen had helped considerably with the horses and she'd given him his plans for the big robbery for more reasons than just money.

Just recently he'd pulled a job on an express station down south and got slick away with it. It was the first since his prison stretch. That payroll robbery at Hillsboro had been a mistake. He'd been insufficiently mounted and was soon overtaken and captured by a posse led by Marshal Fred Gorman. Gorman was a born hunter, a pursuer of men, a wolf on horseback. The Marshal had set up a mounted posse with tough trained horses and men to be on call at all times. They rode Les down after he'd exhausted his ammunition firing at too long range.

Well, none of the things that happened on the Hillsboro job would happen this time. And now that Gorman had moved on to G-Town to handle the boom there, Les would even get revenge. He thought of that and tasted its sweetness. Then he thought of Doreen and the long nights they'd spent loving in the wolf trapper's cabin and the days they'd shared working and planning this one move that would take them both forever away from the degrading poverty and life they'd known.

Doreen hadn't believed him when he told her what he aimed to do that night in a Santa Fe sporting house.

"I'm takin' you out of here, girl. I'm takin' you for my woman alone."

She laughed cynically, and said, "Every drunken cowboy that ever bedded with me has said the same thing. You're all alike."

"Maybe so, girl, but we're leavin' in the mornin'."

The next morning, while the rest of the house slept off the night before, he'd ridden up with an extra horse for her, walked in, tied a gag over her mouth and carried her out. He slapped her in the saddle and tied her feet in the stirrups. Then he tied the stirrups together under the horse's belly. Doreen was mounted there solid as a professional bronc-rider.

He untied the gag about seven miles out of town and she immediately called him seventeen kinds of bastard and swore she'd have him arrested for unlawful abduction.

Les just laughed, kissed her hard and said, "There ain't no law against kidnapping whores. In fact, I might just collect a bonus from the city of Santa Fe."

Several days later in the isolated cabin above Taos all differences were reconciled. Doreen decided he meant what he said and from that moment on she was his totally. And she gave him the answer to the question all men ask of prostitutes—"Why?"

Doreen and her mother had been deserted by a drunken father when she was seven. Her mother washed clothes in a shack on the edge of El Paso for a living. At the age of fifteen Doreen was hired out as a cleaning maid in a downtown hotel. The second day she went to work. A man from Missouri, a gambler, had shown her a way to make a week's wages in twenty minutes. She had followed his direction these past eight years until Les had shown her something else.

Living with her new "master" hadn't been easy for Doreen. At first she swore she'd run away the second Les turned his back.

"Go ahead," he bluffed. "In the first place you'd get lost in the mountains, and if you did make it back, just where would you go? You know that ol' madam in Santa Fe wouldn't put you back to work after leaving her shorthanded like you did."

"Oh, you bastard. You dirty *bastard*, I'll kill you!" She grabbed a butcher-knife and lunged at him.

He stepped aside and tripped her. She stumbled and buried the knife so deep in the wall she couldn't pull it out. Les grabbed her hands and yanked her to him.

"Now, I ought to knock your pretty little head off for that, but I've got a better idea." He sat on the edge of the plank bed and jerked her belly-down across his knees, pulled up her skirt, pulled down her bloomers and beat her bare behind to the tune of curses, screams and finally choking sobs. When he quit pounding her rear end, he made other use of it on the hard bed.

She did not return his passion.

"Couldn't you have at least *faked* a little pleasure?" he asked her afterwards feeling suddenly ashamed and foolish.

She looked at him a moment, her face very sober and wet with tears, and said, "No, that's all I've ever done." After that Les slept on the floor in a blanket and never made the slightest suggestion of physical love to her. He was comfortable with her, though, and told her about all his plans. He even let her know that he needed her help to complete them.

One morning as he came back from the corral after working his horses, he found her on her knees scrubbing the floor. That night she tried to cook dinner, but since she knew nothing of how to prepare venison jerky and dried fruit, Les had to show her.

When night came, he could hear her turning restlessly in bed. He wanted badly to go to her, but somehow knew he must wait.

His work day started about sunup and although the work was progressing, it was slow. He was saddling his second horse for the morning when he saw Doreen coming toward the corral.

She said simply, "Saddle one for me and we'll get them ready twice as fast."

Now all was going smoothly. The horses were toughening and would soon be ready. One morning they decided it would be good for the horses to ride them up to the first spring of water beyond their camp.

It was fall and very still in the secluded natural park. Only the barest breeze stirred the tops of the golden trees. They got down and led the horses up to drink. Then while Les tied them, Doreen took some jerky and dried fruit from a pouch on her saddle. They sat down on the grass and she spread the food out on her skirt. Les was watching her delicate movements intently. Suddenly she blushed under his gaze. She paused a moment then took all the food from her skirt and put it back into the pouch.

Les said, "Say, what'd you do that for?"

She didn't answer, but walked slowly over and knelt beside him. She slipped a hand up behind his head and eased his hat off. Then she kissed him sweetly.

"Because," she said softly into his mouth.

Their boudoir was the whole universe, their bed the entire rocky mountain range, their cover the vast blue sky that peered down through the golden aspens on their naked love.

There was only a short time left before Les made his ride, but it was a fine time. Doreen delighted in everything she did for him. She kept his clothes washed, the cabin spotless and encouraged his plans endlessly. And at night in bed, when the wind talked in unknown tongues through the trees, she gave herself to him willingly, wildly.

Les stopped now at a spring, took one of the several ropes tied to his saddle and staked the first grey. He measured the rope carefully so the grey could just reach the water. The grass was thick and plentiful around the clear mountain pool.

He rode on hard, and later, in another similar secluded spot, staked another horse—again carefully measuring to be sure it could reach water. He had long ago axed all other brush and timber away from the springs except the one stump left for a stake. He put a swivel on the end of the stakes so there could be no winding of the rope and no danger of shortening it so the horse couldn't water. All had been worked out carefully. Every detail was exact.

He rode on, tired, tense, but elated, toward the last spring above G-Town. The night was coming and it would soon be cold. He was riding high into the trembling aspens now, which meant the altitude was between nine and ten thousand feet.

He staked the horses and stopped to eat some dried jerky and apricots to keep up his strength.

Then he slept awhile in the saddle blanket. Soon the cold came through it and into him. As he lay shivering, looking up at the sky between the thick timber, he thought of the warm bed he and Doreen were both missing tonight. It didn't matter. The payroll at G-Town was big, now that the gold mining boom was at full peak. They'd have enough to retire on a dandy little ranch down in Mexico.

He knew a certain town, about three hundred miles below the border, and he knew its people, and he knew that there the money would make him a king and Doreen a queen. He also knew that a lot of men before him had felt this dream and had it dissipate in the bloody sand by a lawman's bullet. But then, they had failed to plan thoroughly as he was doing.

He craved with an almost jealous desire to shame Gorman in his own lair, to rob a great payroll crucial to the welfare of G-Town and cause Gorman shame, ridicule and possible expulsion from his job and the community. He'd spent a lot of time thinking about it behind those thirty foot walls, and in the cramped ratty little cell of the territorial prison. It gouged at his insides like broken glass. Gorman was Les's opposite. He was the action to the reaction. To *kill* Gorman wasn't enough.

He listened to the two greys grazing and felt a pride warm him against the high altitude cold. Anyone who gave chase would have a hell of a time running down three fresh horses, even though he would be heavily loaded with gold coin and a plentiful supply of ammunition for a rifle and pistol. Most of the ammunition was for the rifle. He knew now that the short gun was practically useless for the long range firing of a mountain meeting. This mistake had cost him three years of prison slavery. He wouldn't make it again. He would have several surprises waiting for Gorman before the upcoming session was done.

The daylight was hiding the stars now. He rose and built a small fire. He took a pointed green stick and shoved it through the jerky and warmed it over the flame. He ate all he could hold and took a drink from the spring. This would have to do till nightfall, more than likely.

He saddled one of the greys, checked the ammunition in the saddle bags, looked again at his guns and mounted.

It was downhill now all the way to G-Town. He knew every gully, every patch of timber between here and the mining community. He'd ridden it until he could do it in total darkness like a wolf.

273

A little past sunup he tied his horse on a promontory above the stirring village. The miners moved out toward the black portal of the tunnel on the far mountain, and down below in a long draw the sluice-boxes were turned on. The gravel and water moved over the riffle boards to separate and capture the tiny gold nuggets and colors.

Les liked the sight of the smoke pouring from the chimneys. It reminded him of the trapper's cabin and Doreen. He knew where Gorman lived with his wife and four kids. They were up, too, having breakfast no doubt.

In a little while he saw the kids out playing behind the house and then Gorman was at the door. He kissed his wife and walked around the corner to main street and the jail office. Les could see and feel the steady searching hunter's eyes of Gorman—black eyes that saw great distances with accuracy—eyes that could almost look right through him. And yet all was well.

Les saw the payroll office shades go up and two guards seat themselves in chairs on each side of the door. In a little while one guard got up and went inside. Every move was being made just as Les had observed so many times in the near past.

Then up the road from the south came the stage with dust rolling out behind it like a hungry dog digging for a rabbit. Two armed guards rode horseback in front and two behind. The gold coin was there all right and tonight there'd be a bunch of fighting-mad miners in G-Town. Mining was gut-busting, sweat-pouring, back-wrenching work, and they demanded to be paid when due. Gorman would get his *dues* paid tonight. Les almost laughed aloud at the thought.

He was impatient now. His breathing speeded up and his heart made a dull thud in his chest that he could both hear and feel.

Time. *Time.* Slow eternal time. The long, long waiting was nearly over. The years of subdued desires were about to flame into actuality. But somehow time had reversed itself. Nothing was ever going to be consummated. He gritted his teeth and ground them across one another and clenched his sweating hand on the rifle. He wanted to scream curses into the village.

Then at last the stage left and the guards with it. He made his move. He rode down the gully from one clump of bushes to another and around behind the payroll office. He was naked in the world. He felt a million eyes looking into his mind and felt air-heated bullets tearing at his heart and lungs, but nothing happened.

He tied the horse and suddenly he was calm. He stepped swiftly, quietly around the corner of the payroll office. The guard had one foot up on the chair and a rifle in the crook of his arm. Luck was with Les. The guard was just reaching in his vest pocket for tobacco when Les stepped to him and whipped the pistol barrel hard against the base of his skull. Then he crouched low as the guard and his rifle littered the street.

The other guard dashed through the door and, just as one foot touched the street, Les shot him between the eyes. He turned a complete flip and lay spread in the dirt, dead as a century-old dream.

Les came through the door still low—almost on his knees. The payroll clerk clumsily brought a pistol out of a drawer and Les shot him in the arm as he raised it. The clerk fell up against the open safe.

By god, Les thought, *this is too good!* He wouldn't even have to use the clerk as hostage to get out of town.

He jerked the two long canvas bags from his belt and emptied the two boxes of gold into the bags and swiftly tied them together. He threw the boxes back into the safe and slammed it shut. At the door he yelled back at the wounded clerk.

"Tell Gorman to go to hell in an ore bucket—for Les Martin."

He ran to the horse, swung the gold over the saddle, mounted and headed for the hills. He could hear running and yelling and a bell ringing wildly. A couple of shots snapped somewhere above him. He didn't look back, but rode straight for the mountains. When he came to his hiding place and turned for a second, he saw that, sure enough, the bell had gathered them just as it had in Hillsboro. There they were—the picked posse, the tough horses, and the lithe almost slender figure of Gorman leading them out of town on his favorite dun gelding.

Les turned now and rode across an opening so they would see him heading south. Then in the thickness of the timber he cut hard around to the west.

As he rode, he analyzed his chances. They were good he decided. He had a strong lead and he knew the country better than anyone. His horse was tough and trained to a fineness. The one thing against him was the weight of the gold and the extra ammunition. Still, he felt he had the best of it. And this he did have for a while. Now and then he'd look back and realize the posse was sticking hard to his trail, neither gaining nor losing. He noticed the sweat turning the neck of the grey almost black and heard the great gobs of air bellowing in and out of the horse's lungs and he could feel the rib cage heave against his legs under the stirrup straps. Next, he felt the legs of the horse wobble a fraction. A man who lived in the saddle felt these things.

Then the legs weakened a little more. But now he could spot the rock outcropping behind which a fresh horse grazed. At that instant—his horse stumbled and almost fell. Les jerked up variously on the reins. The animal struggled valiantly and kept its feet, but it was lamed.

Les spurred hard but there was no speed, no drive now. The shoulder muscles had been torn. With only an injured foot the horse could have been spurred to cover the short distance, but with the shoulder gone the boot steel was useless.

Cursing savagely, Les jerked the saddle cinch loose, took the gold bags and guns, then stumbled towards the rock outcropping. He heard a yell in the valley below and the crack of a rifle. They were still out of range.

He struggled desperately up the hill. The gold weighed much more now than it had when he dashed from the payroll office. He fell, and fell again. Now he heard a rifle shot whang from the earth, but he made it to the blessed rocks and without hesitation turned his rifle down the valley. The posse was still on horseback, coming fast. He shot a bay out from under one rider and then looked for Gorman's dun. He caught a glimpse of it between the timber and fired. He had no idea whether he'd hit Gorman or not.

Now the answering fire came, and he felt a chip of rock split his left eyebrow. Close. He wiped the blood from his eye and quickly moved to the other side of the outcropping. He emptied the gun, knocking down another horse. He reloaded and moved again. He spaced his shots every ten feet into the timber, methodically estimating that distance to be the approximate spread of the gunmen.

Then he loaded his rifle, left the gold and rushed to the grey with his saddle. The grey felt his fear and excitement and jumped around making it difficult to cinch the saddle. Les kicked it in the belly and yelled, "Whaaa!" The grey froze, trembling. He raced back to the rock and saw a movement to the north. He fired from guess and heard a yell. He'd drawn blood. It didn't take but a few seconds to load the gold and saddle bags. He spurred away to the west again. He felt the bullets all around now and heard, Gorman yell, "Take your time and take sight on him. Get him, boys!"

As Les rode into a clump of aspens, he yelled out an imitation of the man he'd just shot.

Gorman roared. "We got him, boys! We hit him! Over there!"

Les reined hard back to the north ripping through the thickest growth of oak brush he could find to hide his tracks for a moment. It worked. He heard the milling about behind and then it grew less.

He turned back west and down hill again to his next horse. The odds seemed to have turned slightly back in his favor, even though he'd figured on everything but a crippled horse. Gorman had luck with him too, so far. Well, luck wouldn't win this race, only planning and cunning.

He rode on hard, but more cautiously, watching for the hidden rocks that had crippled his last mount. He couldn't hear the posse now. He didn't look back until he was saddling his next horse. Then he saw them topping a rise some distance behind. They were slowing and seemed to have lost his trail.

He had them now—there was no doubt about it. He'd ride them into the ground. The four riders left would soon be astride exhausted, crippled horse flesh. He reached down and felt the gold coins solid and real as the graveled earth they came from.

He thought of Doreen and moved on through the wilderness as night overcame the sky, towards his next mount and his woman.

Big Shad rode back into Taos the day before the completion of the bridge. He spent the night checking his gaming tables and ran the roulette himself from about eight till midnight in the Fernandez Hotel. The table always showed more profit when he took it over. There were ways to affect the outcome of the wheel that he didn't even pass on to his help.

He was a sort of hero in Taos, for the citizens respected most money and the power of politics. He had both. The money came from his own skill and crooked wheels, his cheap bootleg whiskey and the women he had for hire. The money took care of the politicians. Big Shad was left alone where lesser men were hanged. It had always been so in all the world, but this was Big Shad's world, and he intended to improve it by several fold with the bridge.

Big Shad was running as he'd always done from that empty purse and belly he'd known so long as a youngster. His ma and pa had been killed by the Comanches on an isolated East Texas farm. He'd built the coffins to bury them in and dug their graves at the age of twelve. For a while, he scratched a living with bare hands against the earth and then hired out for board and a hay-rick to sleep on. Later he graduated to saloon swamper for a little more pay. He wanted to get so far away from all of this that nothing could ever break down the wall he'd built with gold and silver.

This was going to be a great day. He'd slept well and his favorite girl brought him breakfast in bed. He stretched his huge frame. He shaved and bathed slowly. Then he put on a new suit, brushed his handmade boots and tied a scarf around his neck. This was the day the *king* was crowned. He felt the part and certainly should look it.

He rode, with an entourage of three gunmen, through the adobe winding streets of ancient Taos. He nodded and tipped his hat to the lounging Indians and Mexicans along the way. He could afford to give his attention because now they would all pay in one way or another. The world was his this morning. His huge lungs enjoyed the pure mountain air and his heart was beating steadily and happily at the thought of the sturdy new bridge across the Rio Grande . . . Big Shad's Bridge.

It was ten o'clock in the morning and the fall sun was just beginning to warm the earth. The aspen leaves gleamed like the gold in the sack across Les Martin's saddle. He reined slow through the aspen trees and then on below their growth level. He rode through the pine and spruce down to the lean-to of his woman. Doreen was waiting, ready.

He stepped down to her and she fell against him, and said, "You're safe! You made it! Oh. Les, you made it!" And then the first tear of happiness he'd ever seen her shed fell from the corner of a dark slanted eye.

He looked around. The horses were ready. He turned his loose, and then said regretfully, "Hell, that horse was still in good shape. Should've led him along with us."

It was too late. The horse, sensing total freedom, trotted off through the brush.

"I kept the horses off grass all night like you said and I watered them at sunup this morning. They're in perfect condition," she said proudly.

"Let's go, woman," Les said smiling and touching the gold bags for her to notice.

But Doreen ran back into the shack and stood very still a moment. She was leaving it clean as creek rock, scrubbed shiny and the few cooking utensils put carefully away in the rickety cupboard. She wanted the cabin to be in perfect shape for the next unknown occupant. It had been home. Her home and Les's—the only one she'd ever had. The only one she'd ever created for a man. Her man alone. She heard Les yell again and knew she had to go. She closed the door softly and walked to her horse.

They mounted and rode into the foothills where the cedar and pinion mingled thinly with the sagebrush. Doreen turned once in the saddle but now the cabin was gone from view in the timber. She didn't look back again. And then they moved out into the desert towards the gorge and Romo's Crossing, with no knowledge that a bridge, sturdy and brand new, now spanned it.

From the other side of the great gash in the earth moved Orlando and Ramon, five dogs and over a thousand head of sheep. They moved slowly towards the unknown bridge like the cooling lava that had once flowed beneath their feet millions of years ago.

Much else was moving across the lonely expanse of Taos country that day. Three miles south of Orlando's flock, two coyotes were chasing a rabbit in relays. One would run it while the other rested. Then gradually the rabbit would be circled back to the rested coyote, which would take up the chase afresh. They didn't crowd the rabbit because they had sure knowledge of an eventual catch.

But the earth and the sky are both full of surprises. A hungry hawk circled and watched the pageant below. On a sudden decision it dropped for the earth striking the rabbit at the base of the skull with a clenched claw, knocking it rolling. The hawk coursed up about twenty feet braking with wide spread wings, reversed its direction and swooped on the stunned rabbit grabbing it in each side with sharp talons and sweeping it away as the surprised coyote stood watching with stunned eyes at what had been his for sure, now moving a hundred and fifty feet above the earth out of his reach forever.

At this moment Big Shad arrived at his bridge. Far back in the aspens rode Gorman. He still came on although it looked hopeless. When his horses had failed in speed he'd ridden slowly south to a summer cow camp. There he'd acquired, under force, three good, fresh cow ponies. The riders resented being left with four worn out horses and a lame posseman, but Gorman had no time to waste. After the preliminaries he'd simply drawn down on them with a cocked rifle, disarmed the cowboys and rode away on their mounts.

He knew he was far behind and had lost the trail, but he was trying to think like Les. Romo's Crossing was the answer. Les would feel safe once he'd crossed the gorge. He knew that until he had gone a far distance he would never be safe. Gorman would pursue as long as he could requisition horses and find the slightest trace of a trail.

Yes, all was movement.

The sheep moved down the winding trail to the river. When the last of them dropped behind the lava rimrock, Orlando and Ramon saw the bridge. It was as if the devil had opened up hell and turned all the sinners of seven centuries loose before the eyes of the two sheepherders. They stopped their horses and stared.

"Mother Mary and Jesus! What is that?" said Ramon.

"It is a bridge."

"A bridge?"

"If I have not lost my mind."

"If that is so, we are both without minds," said Ramon, "for I see this thing that looks like a bridge, also."

"Well, that is a wonderful thing," said Ramon. "Now we can cross the river with ease."

"Yes, but where did it come from?" said Orlando. "Did the saints make a vision? Is it real?"

They found it was real, all right, when the sheep crowded hesitantly onto it, following the black goat. The bleating creatures shied and almost fell over the railing. It took a long time for the men and dogs to get the lead sheep two-thirds of the way across the bridge.

There they stopped and pushed at one another and cringed in a mass away from the five men who stood blocking the exit—five men with guns drawn.

Orlando rode through the sheep slowly. The horse shoving along, fighting hard to keep his feet with sheep in front, back and underfoot too.

Orlando said, *"Cómo estás, amigos?* Why do you stop my sheep?"

"Oh, it's nothing," said Big Shad. "You can move on in a moment."

"Oh, that is good. Thank you, *Señor*. Who built this bridge?"

"I did," said Big Shad.

"I know you," said Orlando. "You are Big Shad of Taos."

"That's right, amigo, and this is my bridge."

"That is nice of you to do this thing," said Orlando.

"Well, I'm glad you feel that way. You see this bridge took all summer and lots of money to construct. I have to pay for it in some manner. This is what you call a toll bridge."

"Toll bridge?"

"You have to pay to cross. Now I'm not unreasonable. It'll only be twenty-five cents a head for the sheep and a dollar for you herders and the horses."

"Twenty-five . . . " Orlando's mind blanked out. It was much too much to figure.

"I don't have any money, *Señor*." he said suddenly, sitting straight up in the saddle. "These are not my sheep, *Señor*. They belong to Demetrio Martinez, my patron."

"That's all right, too," said Big Shad. "These sheep are worth about eight dollars a head."

Orlando felt his chest go cold and the sweat cracked through the dust on his face. If they turned back, it would take three, maybe four, days riding down to another crossing and another three days back to Taos. A whole week would be spent on the trail. The sheep would lose much weight and strength. He would be late on his scheduled delivery of the flock to his boss. The long summer months seemed wasted to Orlando now. He couldn't give in to Big Shad. He must move the sheep across somehow. It was his duty.

Orlando stared speechless as he saw the man and woman ride up behind the gunmen on the bridge. *Did Big Shad need this much help?*

Les sat his horse, unbelieving. *My God there's a bridge across the river!* He hadn't been here in a year and there had been no sign of such a thing then. There was just one decision to make. He and Doreen were going across. They had to. They'd planned too long and fought too hard. Across the river was freedom—not just from Gorman and the law but from want and servitude. And here was a bridge full of sheep blocking his way—and two sheepherders and five gunmen.

He knew that Gorman was coming somewhere back there. If they went down river to the next crossing there was great danger that Gorman would overtake them. He could find horses on the populated east side of the river, but if they crossed here, now, Gorman would be at a big disadvantage. They could lose him in the vastness to the west of the Rio. And there would be no horses for the posses in the uninhabited desert.

Les started to speak, but Orlando beat him to it.

"Out of the way," Orlando suddenly shouted. "The boss will expect his sheep at Taos tomorrow. The boss he good man. He want his sheep!"

The shot was loud even above the murmuring river. Fidel had drawn and shot Orlando through the heart. As the sheepherder fell from his horse he was still trying to raise his rifle.

An instant later, Fidel lurched back and tumbled into the river where he sank out of sight threshing and clawing at the water. Ramon levered another shell, and the gunman to the left of Big Shad was knocked backward and down looking up at Les with his mouth and eyes wide open. He saw nothing.

Big Shad fired the buckshot at Ramon and the horse went down on its hindquarters falling over on Ramon who was still trying to shoot. Big Shad let go the other barrel and Ramon, the father of seven, lay still under the kicking, dying horse.

Les knew now without any doubt that Big Shad would stop him. He would spot the gold—Big Shad had eyes that saw such things. He liked gold even more than Les did. There was only one move left to Les. He threw up his rifle and shot Big Shad in the small of the spine. He flopped down heavily and the sheep milled and bleated all around him. His back was broken and a moan of unintelligible words frothed forth from his mouth where he lay paralyzed on his bridge.

Les caught the other black-bearded gunman in the nose and he fell spurting blood on Big Shad's heaving belly. But Les never got another shell levered into the gun. The last standing man on the bridge shot him with a forty-five in the Adam's apple. Les fell backwards off his horse.

Doreen spurred forward, screaming wildly and ran her horse over the man. The impact knocked him from the bridge into the Rio. He managed to scramble to the rock pier and hold on against the tugging water. His smashed rib cage made this extremely difficult. Doreen jumped from her horse, grabbed a rock twice the size of a tin coffee cup from the bank and ran down the bridge falling, clawing over and around and through the sheep. At last she was above the gunman and as he looked up at her with stricken eyes, she aimed the rock and dropped it square on his forehead. There was a crunching sound and the man slid under the water.

The sheep were following the black goat across the bridge now, bleating and shying around the bloody figures.

Then they came in a great solid mass as Doreen escaped from the edge of the bridge. The sheep moved over Big Shad. There was only a muffled cry and then nothing as a thousand head tromped the last dream from his mind and his body lay bruised, broken and still.

Doreen sat a long time and looked at the white face of Les Martin. She didn't cry. She just stared and stared. Then she said softly, "The only one. The only one there ever was."

She got up and caught his horse. She took the gold bags and threw them across her own saddle, and rode toward Taos.

About an hour before sunup she saw the riders coming at her across the desert. Their mounts were obviously tired, but she didn't try to run.

It was Gorman.

It came to her through the shock that the posse knew nothing of her. There was no one at the bridge who could inform them now. She was free, and if she was careful, the gold would be hers. She had always craved the freedom it could bring her. She rode behind a clump of cedars and watched through the branches as Gorman and his posse veered towards the river.

She felt of the bags, sensing the solid hardness there. The feel of the gold turned her mind to the feel of Les. But he was gone. A thousand times this much gold wouldn't buy one Les. Somehow he'd been a gift to her.

Tiny in the vast desert, Doreen rode on towards Taos, and then she was nothing as the sun settled beyond the gorge.

The sheep scattered out down the verdant banks of Hondo Creek, grazing. The dogs tried to look after them, but they were confused now without masters of their own. Soon they scattered and trotted aimlessly about, lost. In a day or so they would wind up one by one in Taos hunting a new master—just as Doreen would.

The Call

The old man stood stiffly washing at the tin plates as the wild game digested inside him. His chores done, he sat on a sawed stump in front of a rickety, unpainted table, slowly smoking a pipe, staring at nothing, and only occasionally blinking his tiny sunken eyes. Then he took a tattered Bible in hand and read . . . Genesis: . . . TILL THOU RETURN UNTO THE GROUND; FOR OUT OF IT WAST THOU TAKEN; FOR DUST THOU *ART*, AND UNTO DUST SHALT THOU RETURN . . .

Then he heard the scream. He bolted from his chair, dropping the Bible. Standing with his head held taut, high and turned to the side, his eyes rolled white and wild in their sockets. His nostrils flared in and out like a beast scenting fresh blood. One mighty rusty hand clawed at the long grey-streaked hair.

The scream—it came at him again now, piercing his ear drums, slicing into his inner skull and vibrating there like pounding gongs and exploding cannons. The hound dog cowered against him, trembling. The hair bristled along his spine.

This was the sixth night now. It came at the same hour of darkness. It broke away just as suddenly. It did not die gradually but stopped with startling abruptness, as if a sword as long as a pine tree had been swung by a giant and severed the scream in one swift cutting instant.

He stood a spell, as yet tense and waiting, but it did not return. His drawn old muscles slackened, and the dog lowered his bristles. What was it? What could it be? His ears were trained, as the hound's at his feet, to the sounds, the smells, the signs of the wild. A long time before he had rejected his own kind. He was *one* of these creatures of the forest. He had joined the animals and he had lived from them.

For over twenty years no one had been allowed in his canyon. No one except the fur trader who came once a year to pick up the winter's catch and leave the year's supplies in exchange. Even he was stopped at the very mouth of the canyon and waved back down the moment the transaction was complete.

Yes, the hermit knew the bearlike track of the coon, the round, padded ones of the bobcat and the cougar. He knew intimately the arrowhead-shaped print of the coyote and the three-pronged track, like one fourth of a broken rimless wagon wheel, of the wild turkey. He knew these wild things so well he could outwit them and exist from their furs captured by his swift closing steel traps. He knew the pointed track of the doe and the wider spread ones of the buck, and he could trail them and down them with one shot in the heart. He knew their sounds, their night calls, their cries of death. He knew them better than they knew themselves.

But he didn't know this scream that came pealing down from the rim rocks at the first touch of darkness. What was it that clung to the rocks and yet vibrated forth with great gusts of sound that struck at him like a flaming arrow? It seemed to be an infinite part of the rocks releasing the sound itself to torture him, to drive him mad with its unknown stabbing horror.

Strain as he might, he could not place it in his canyon. It was new here. It was not one of *his* animals. Was it some strange unknown beast invading his sanctuary? Had it come to challenge his superiority, to destroy his mind with sound alone? He could not say how long the sound lasted each time. A minute? An hour? An eternity?

Each evening from sunset on he stood poised, his hound rubbing against his bent legs, waiting. No matter how he prepared himself, he was always caught unaware. It was on him, around him, in him, before he could brace his being for the shock.

He moved back to his log cabin. As he opened the door, the hound dashed past him and crawled under the bed, growling and whining. There was no sleep now, only a numb listening through the night. He lay with the rifle at hand waiting . . . waiting. Would it always come at the same time, or would it break loose in everlasting sound, blanketing his canyon and stilling the movements of his animals? Would the maker of the scream leap from the bluffs and devour them all in an orgy of blood and hair?

The night turned into day, and the sun came up above the rimrocks and shoved shafts of yellow light between the pinion and the pine. The dog stood at the door sniffing carefully, wanting outside. The day was better. They could see now. But there in the atoms of their bodies, the dog and the hermit, the two hunters, lingered the knowledge that night, too, would return.

They breakfasted hurriedly on dry jerky. The trap line had not been run in four days now. The trader would soon be here for the winter's catch. Taking the rifle and putting a leash on the hound the hermit headed up the canyon to follow out his trap line.

He saw no fresh sign along the trails—not of the deer nor the furred creatures. Not even the rabbit. No birds moved among the trees. The forest was still. Yet, he felt them there, waiting, listening, watching him. The first trap was undisturbed, as was the second, and the third. He circled widely around them. No animal had been near. All tracks were old and crusted. The hound hardly dropped his head to the ground at all. There was no scent there for trailing.

On a promontory in a little clearing he stopped and studied the rimrocks. What deep shadow hid the scream? In what crevice did it crouch with huge hollow eyes staring at him, waiting to leap. For a moment the idea of leaving the canyon struck him. No! The beasts of the outer world lurked just as dangerously. If the thing would attack now in the light of day, he would make his stand and fight to the death. But no movement came to his vision. No sound. The hawks that usually circled above the rocks were gone. Not one flew in search of food. The sky was barren.

The sun moved on over the heavens and reached for the bluffs above the scream. There was only one more trap on his line. Each had been empty. The hound stiffened against the leash and moved toward the set in a little clearing. Something was in it. It had been a double set. One trap had caught a cottontail rabbit. The rabbit was half eaten. The ribs showed white through the dried meat. In the other trap was a foot—a large foot of a bird. It was a vulture's claw. The tendons strung out hard and yellow where the bird had pecked and torn free. It had eaten the heart out of the rabbit before it had stepped into the other trap. Where was the vulture now? Up in the rocks, perhaps, nursing its crippled leg.

The hermit stared again. The sun was resting on top of the rocks now, and he felt the first cold touch of wind that day. It brushed at him with ghostly fingers, and the chill-bumps popped out like measles over his body. It would not be long now until the terrible sound would shoot forth and flail him into trembling fear.

Where was the coyote's sunset howl? Where was the haunting, raucous call of the magpie? Utter stillness, muffling, smothering, quiet prevailed.

Suddenly, he whispered to his dog to come. He could bear it no longer. This seventh night of terror had drained him of the power to wait. It must be faced. He must see this screaming thing and look into its eyes and slavering jaws. It called to him silently now, as if the rocks were magnetized for flesh. He moved on towards the bluff. The hound turned with his tail between his legs and ran down the canyon towards the cabin without looking back.

The hermit's heart beat at his body and pushed his blood hard, forcing it through his veins in a swift, artery-straining surge as he climbed. His lungs were pained to handle the air drawn back and forth in struggling gulps. But he moved and clambered through the rocks. The sun had set, and the last rays weakened in the sky. He must be there at the instant of the scream. It drove him, this decision, beyond his actual strength, and the rocks jabbing and tearing at him were forgotten. Now every act of his life became as nothing compared with the desire pulling him higher and higher.

The orange sun and its beamed rays were gone. Twilight lingered a moment. On he struggled. There was only a faint glow now. The mighty boulders swelled around him, and the crevices split them sharply on each side. And then it was dark, and a crevice deeper than any he had ever seen was before him.

He leaned over, staring into its depths, searching. This was it. He could not see, but he could feel it. He leaned farther and fell down into the blackness. His mouth flew open, and a sound of terror hurtled from his throat. He knew now what the scream was and where it had come from, but it was too late to do anything about it. It had always been so.

4

Introductions and Forewords

An Introduction to Sanctification
and Humble Greatness

Considering the intense dedication and love the authors have for Patrociño Barela and his art, this would seem to be as near an impossible book to write as one could imagine. It was a formidable task, and I can only feel awe and gratitude for the skillful efforts of David L. Witt and Edward Gonzales. After a day of laborious devotion on this book, the drains of their shower baths must have run red with blood—in spite of the old cliché.

In the very early 1950s I witnessed for the first time a transaction between a professional trader and a pure artist. Patrociño Barela both sold and traded one of his carvings to Harold Street at the Taos Inn reservation desk. Harold handed Patrociño two or three bills and a fifth of Tokay wine. Patrociño carefully put the bottle into the brown paper sack that had previously held the piece of cedar art and shoved the money carelessly into his pocket. I didn't know it then, but I had witnessed a bit of recurring history.

I had 20-10 eyesight in those days and easily could have seen the numbers on the bills, but notions of politeness kept me from taking a closer look at them, or for that matter, at Patrociño himself. However, the cedar object was something else again, Harold was, as I would learn, looking at it from all angles for my benefit.

"Is it okay to handle it?" I tentatively asked.

"Oh sure, the oil from your hands helps preserve the wood," and he handed it to me with a rather careless gesture. No matter how it seems or sounds, I remember that thrill. My entire body was charged with a warmth that I felt surely must be glowing. I placed the piece back on the desk and turned it round and round as Harold had done, marveling at the perfect balance and rhythms of the oddly tilted heads atop the piece, one male, one female, facing in opposite directions with one arm of each reaching back searchingly towards the other's body. Strangely, that piece was easier for me to interpret than many of the others that would follow over the years. It represented to me both sides of our natures. It was the eternal male and female yearning. It was Patrociño Barela's world as well, I would soon know. I wanted the piece very much, but I didn't comment further after Street priced it at thirty dollars—which was too expensive for me at that time, because I also was a struggling artist in this town.

A week or so later I had sold a still-wet, unframed painting for fifty bucks to a guest at the Taos Inn. As I was leaving the establishment, planning to go buy some groceries and oil paints, I met Patrociño and his brown paper bag heading for the door to the inn.

I said to him, "Mr. Street has gone to Ojo Caliente for the day."

He turned slowly and looked at me. I saw the universe in those dark eyes. I did not then, nor do I now, maintain that I could interpret this vastness. I just felt it with an irrevocable certainty. I, slightly embarrassed, asked if he had a carving for sale. Without a word he pulled from the sack a religious work with three crosses and a heart and a dignified head carved upright and handed it to me.

This time I felt a chill—then that same indescribable warmth seeped over my being. I admired its balance, the curious rhythms I'd never seen before except in a few, a very few, of Gustave Doré's drawings illustrating Dante's *Divine Comedy*.

I was standing there in the greatly historical, but mostly poor, town of Taos, in front of the sometimes infamous, but more often famous Taos Inn alone with a truly "original" artist, privileged to be holding one of those masterful pieces in my hand. Since America is still by far the greatest country in the world it always comes as a shock to me, to discover and rediscover, that originality is a sin here. I was far too naive to know that then, but I'm pretty certain now that Patrociño did. He knew far more than most people realized.

I reached in my pocket and took out my brand-new, entire bankroll, selected a twenty dollar bill, and handed it to him. "Would you please let me buy it? I need the rest for groceries and gasoline." That was "our" price from then on.

He looked right through my head and a thousand miles on beyond it and took the bill with that enigmatic expression in his eyes and face that always seemed to be there drunk, sober, sick, or exalted. It was a look of not quite resigned acceptance of a cruel world and also an acceptance and slight smile at its fool-ishness. All who knew him will remember.

I suddenly felt a kinship and shook his powerful, but delicate, hand and asked him to come in and have a drink to celebrate our transaction. He didn't hesitate, but said, softly, "Not here. There," and nodded down the street to the El Gaucho Saloon a block and a half away, it was also known with great fondness as the Wino Bar. There's one in every good town.

We drank our Tokay and toasted the saints, and he said, "May they also drink and be blessed to have as much fun as we are having."

I was to learn that as humble and deeply spiritual as he was and as precious as the Almighty and the saints were to him, he honestly expected them to have an earthly sense of humor about the whole damn thing as well. I had always believed this as truth so we had a good solid ground for a forever friendship.

I wish I could say that we spent a lot of time together. We didn't. The times we did were always by chance, and I think we both understood why this was so.

Several hours later I drove home. My wife, Pat, and I lived just below the mesa next door to an old *morada*. I proudly placed two large bags of groceries and a few oil paints on the kitchen ta-ble and rather tenuously showed the Barela to my young wife, expecting her to justifiably berate me for such an extravagance but she didn't. She immediately gasped "Oh, what a beautiful Barela," Since she had grown up there and lived on the same road that Patrociño Barela trod from the plaza to his Cañon home, she knew him much better than I at the time.

In those beginning days of my painting and writing career, I was rapidly becoming a trader myself in order to buy paints, and for everyday survival. So, I wasn't privileged to keep the pieces I purchased very long. This in no manner dimmed my passion for the man and his carvings. He certainly understood, I can tell you.

All through the years I have praised his work in my writing wherever it fit. In fact, Patrociño is in both my Bluefeather Fellini books with all the honor I could give him. I kept on hoping someone of power would read, wonder, and act. I, too, had failed him. Until now it was all to no avail.

Before continuing further, I must tell of Luz Martinez—he was just as neglected as a carver. I had met Luz, in northeastern New Mexico, at Des Moines. We had both returned from World War II within a month of one another, he took his old job back with the railroad but was unhappy with it now. To my great and pleasant surprise, I learned he was taking a correspondence course in cartooning. We had an instant rapport since we were the only people in that entire vast and lonely cattle and sheep country able to sit down and actually discuss art and artists. He was a man of perhaps five foot five but like Patrociño had an aura of knowing about him that made him seem bigger than he was. His hands were also delicate but very large and powerful as if they belonged on a heavyweight fighter. His face was already chiseled like wood, and unlike Patrociño fires would flash in his eyes constantly and then dim until they were almost blank, and then fire again unexpectedly as a long dormant volcano suddenly flares up. We became very close, lifelong friends.

After I left Des Moines he had no one to talk art with, so he followed to Taos and lived with Pat and me for over a year using a slightly remodeled one-room house as his home and studio. He helped us gradually build three rooms onto our house as we could afford to buy materials.

For the first few months he did cartooning with disappointing success. Then he started building sturdy, attractive furniture out of slabs and scrap wood that we could use in our sparsely furnished houses. Later he advanced to beautiful carved furniture. We still have those pieces.

There is no room here for the marvelously untold story of Luz Martinez, but this he did. He wrote to a girl named Aurora Marcus, who lived thirty miles from Des Moiness in Union County, and asked her to marry him. He took a bus and met her in Raton, where they were wed. He brought her back to Taos to start life as the wife of a carver of furniture in a little house right across the driveway from the noted writer-raconteur Spud Johnson. Then Luz became a carver of saints, a *santero* but of a different sort. They were elongated like El Greco's figures, and he polished and waxed them. We still have his first piece, bought at Eulalia Emetaz's Gallery—who also did her best to handle Patrociño's artwork.

Then Luz and Aurora moved to Cañon just one empty field from Patrociño. Soon he quit carving *santos* and did mythological figures. He is included in the pages of this book mainly because he became such a close friend of Patrociño's. They had much crazy fun together, but neither one was an influence on the other as far as their art was concerned. Drinking, well that was many horses of many different colors.

One night I had somehow wound up with both of them in the Cañon Bar—probably because I was the only one who had a car—and we were having fun. I would do a Cherokee stomp, a Greek or some other silly kind of dance in honor of the two great artists and they did appreciate it and return the favor. However, Luz kept leaning over slowly until he would fall over on his head. He seemed to be unaware of this as he would talk all the way to the floor and keep on doing so as soon as he became fully conscious again. Frankly, I was getting tired of picking him up and also wiping the blood from cuts on his head. This didn't seem to bother Patrociño at all. He would gently help every time. Patrociño said what would seem like such a simple statement except to those few who really knew him, "Poor Luz, his head is heavy with *luz* (light). He cannot always hold up such weight." The truth and profundity struck me sober.

Once Patrociño and Luz were drinking at El Gaucho. Luz had just bought a piece of firewood with interesting potential from a wood-hauler. The idea of some special fun came to Luz. When he told me about it, I was surprised that Patrociño went along with the plan. Luz went next door to Sahd's Grocery and got a brown paper bag, put the firewood into it, and the two of them took it up the street to Mr. Street. Naturally Patrociño carried it.

Mr. Street played the traders game with the disgusted look most everyone puts on for drunken artists, but of course he finally just had to look at the piece. They had made him wait until his expression cracked. Luz said, when Patrociño so very delicately, so very slowly, extracted the uncarved wood from the sack, Street showed a trader's reaction never before seen. His eyes widened, his nostrils flared, and his hands clenched and unclenched, no doubt craving to attach themselves to wood-carvers' necks. This man of ultimate cool actually stuttered, "What, what, what is this?" Patrociño answered in his perfectly controlled voice. "Wood, Mr. Street. Just wood. The figure waits inside."

Luz could not help shouting back as they left the place, "You make the saint come out, Mr. Street, please, for it has waited a long time."

Vengeance is mine sayeth the Lord, or something thereabouts; even though it had all been conceived and carried out in fun, the two workers of wonders with wood staggered home that night holding one another up more from laughing themselves weak than from wine. I wish I could have been there, but of course it wouldn't have been the same for them.

Then there was this indelible incident imprinted in my brain as if by a red-hot branding iron. I was sitting in this little alcove of a Taos art gallery drinking hot tea from an urn provided by the establishment. Patrociño walked in. If he saw me he gave no sign. He walked right up to the carved wooden table and pulled a work from the every-present wrinkled paper sack with trembling hands. It was obvious he more than needed a drink. I didn't hear all the words exchanged as the possible buyer examined the priceless cedar saint, but I did catch some words as his voice rose in lecturing tones admonishing this great man, this great artist, this great soul in insulting and derisive manner about his wine addiction. Except for his shaking hands, Patrociño just stared at him unmoving.

It was extremely difficult for me not to get up and whap the gallery owner in the mouth. This same man, before he quit drinking a couple of years earlier and became sanctimoniously self-righteous, had drunkenly danced stark naked on top of a table in front of a group of both men and women. By itself that would have been sordid enough, but to do this with a massive whey belly shaking like a tub of lard was not quite in taste even in a free-wheeling Taos.

After he had properly chastised Patrociño for drunkenness—and I suspect the last remains of his own conscience—he got a bottle of Old Mission wine from a cupboard and slapped a dollar and a half on the desktop, saying, "Take it or leave it you wastrel."

Patrociño kept on looking him straight in the eye, and then somehow he controlled the shaking of one hand that was, with the tough years, becoming more gnarly with the nails thicker and harder. Without moving anything but an arm and hand, he methodically scratched a grove in the top of the table as the man stared stunned. Barela said in a calm voice, "What mark do you leave in the world, Mr. So and So?"

The trader was speechless as he stared at the fingernail trail, Patrociño pocketed his dollar and a half, placed his wine in its worn paper container, and exited the place with the greatest of dignity.

Several months later when I was doing better at selling stories in my way way-up and way-down life, I saw a sight that ripped my heart and guts like a Roman sword. I had picked up our mail at the post office—no mail delivery in Taos in those days—and drove on west to Placitas Road and turned right to head home. It was early winter and very cold just a few days before a big freezing snow came. There, working in the frozen ditch, was an old man—old far past his actual years—pulling and breaking dead weeds then placing them in neat linear piles. To my dismay I recognized Patrociño.

Two policemen sat comfortably watching him from a car. They had the motor running, the heater running, and cigarette smoke pouring from a crack in the car window. I pulled over and walked to the official car. They knew me, so after we said hello, I said something like "What in hell are you doing to Patrociño? Don't you realize he is the best we have? How could you abuse such a great old man like this?"

As stupid as this sounds, I demanded they take him home right now and I would pay his fine. To the cops' credit they were polite and tried to explain that they were just giving him a few minutes exercise and fresh air. I strongly denied that breaking off heavy dried weeds in the bone-arching wind was helping his fragile health in any way. They then told me in sterner terms that Patrociño had been on a two-week binge and his family had requested that he be picked up for his own safety. I insisted then that at least they could take him back to the underground jail, and I'd come over and pay him out. To my surprise, they agreed, but also chuckled, saying, "It will be a waste of money. He'll be right back in."

As they yelled at him to come get into the car, Patrociño walked over and said to me—he called me Maxwell by now— "Aiii, Maxwell, the cold she come, the wind she blow, singin' somethin' we don't know." Everything was freezing, but those wondrous dark, half-laughing eyes of Patrociño cast little waves of warmth even in this icy wind.

The little unplanned poem, the tormenting wind, and my own winding down made me consider and cool off a moment. I decided to get someone closer to Patrociño to do the rescue, so I drove to get Luz. Poor Luz, I'd forgotten that he had totally quit drinking some time before. I told him the story, gave him some cash, and said to him, "Whatever is left of the money you and Pat use any way you choose." I don't know what they did or didn't do, but I did learn that Patrociño was back in the Taos dungeon—as we used to call it—two days later.

When Patrociño was told about Luz Martinez's work being blessed by the Pope, he said, "The Pope, he a smart man." In that short sentence he had instantly congratulated the Pope as well as Luz Martinez and with absolutely no jealousy. Nor was it any bigger news to him than a *primo's* wife birthing another healthy baby. Could Hemingway or Shakespeare have surpassed this instantaneous response of both brevity and broadness? I doubt it. His work was the same way.

As I reflect back, I still wonder at the lack of respect Patrociño Barela received in Taos from those artists who had the international names and reputations to help him—as is thoroughly pointed out in this book—especially since he was the first Taos artist to be collected by the Museum of Modern Art in New York City, and such powerful publications as the *New York Times*, *Time* and the *Washington Post* trumpeted for all the world of this "discovery of the year" and on and on. Of course there were some people such as Ted and Kit Egri, the Domingues, Judson Crews and Mildred Tolbert Crews, the poet Wendell Anderson, Ruth Fish, *Taos Art*'s editor Reginal Cooke, modern gallery owner Eulalia Emetaz, Mary Chavez, Dr. Henry Sauerwein, and a few others who recognized his genius. And no matter what, we must give credit to traders Clark Funk and Harold Street for their belief and foresight, regardless of how they were said to pay him. The proof: they held onto most of his works. Even so he was mostly referred to as the old drunken wood carver and dismissed as a simple-minded, primitive man.

I did then, and I do now, deny this and become infuriated at this insulting shortage of vision on the part of such people. Just the opposite was true to me and a few others. He was so gifted, blessed, or chosen that under different circumstances than impoverished birth, child abuse, and extremely hard living as a shepherd, miner, laborer on the hardest kinds of jobs, he would have been world-renowned as a prodigy. He would have been recognized as one of them—one of those people who beyond explanation at the age of three, four, or six suddenly plays Mozart on the piano or violin without having had a music lesson or heard the great composers. And what about the others who can compute mathematics of the highest order instantly right from their head while only a very few years out of diapers. And those who suddenly burst out with enormously complicated drawings of almost impossible perspective while still untrained children.

Patrociño Barela was one of those. I believe it with my soul. It was just there, this mighty talent, all the time. It simply didn't leap out until the moment when he held that certain piece so precisely related in this Witt/Gonzales book, with the faithful photographic cataloging by publisher/photographer O'Shaughnessy.

As to his drinking: he was not *always* drunk while doing so, but I do know for a fact that, amazingly, he carved just as touchingly whether in the wine or shaking sober. I do not believe his was tortured drinking. He had too damn much camaraderie with his friends, too much genuine fun, for this to make a case. I think the key, the truth, was in his plain and pure understanding of Luz Martinez's head becoming too heavy with creativity for his body to hold it up.

Patrociño's entire being was so overloaded with visions of true tragedy, beauty, and the spirituality of the family, the world, the whole universe that his drinking, under Patrociño's sparse living conditions, was the one vacation available from the vastness of his innate knowledge of all things.

After these many years we must humbly give thanks that the trio—the Anglo writer David Witt, the Chicano artist/writer Edward Gonzales, and the Celtic publisher/photographer Michael O'Shaughnessy, came together to at last give greatness it due. They formed a trinity, if you please, of talent and inspirational love to get the honest images of Barela down properly at last.

Their daunting task of finding and photographing hundreds of individual pieces is a compliment to Patrociño Barela that we must be immensely grateful for. Barela has always, by his nature, been difficult to write about, and his pieces present a special problem to photographers. Where do the shadows of words and pictures go? How are both these applications properly illuminated? The answers are in these words of Witt and Gonzales and the photos of O'Shaughnessy. They maintained through those long months, even years, showing us so exactly the heretofore countless hidden elements featuring the artist in his glory, instead of the photographer and writers. Together they have given us a full view of a great world-class artist in all its astounding numbers and range of human emotion and divine spirituality. The neglect is over. Finis.

The authors wrote so revealingly: "The depiction of saints and of persons on a spiritual journey remained central to his imagery throughout his career. The uplifting strength of faith and a deeply held spirituality characterized both his life and art. Late in his life Barela described his work as having a *'santo* feeling.'"

His work was as powerful as Picasso's during his modern period, as fluid and full of the essence of spirituality as Michelangelo's in the Sistine Chapel. Señor Patrociño Barela was a walking poem written in cedar wood. He was a living *santo*.

Some Sweet Day Revisited

This book is true to its terrain. It is just as true to the hearts and foibles of the people thereon. Throughout printing history there have been fad after fad on the length of books. However, most volumes that have finally been classified as literature are vast indeed. Such classic, elephantine works as *War and Peace*, *Moby Dick*, *Crime and Punishment*, and *The Red and the Black*, and many others, have used millions of tons of paper and billions of words to tell their stories. Some, perhaps, could have been written and or edited to one half or less their length and said the same thing. The time spent by publishers and readers could have been used to irrigate the Sahara or invent a machine that would defy both gravity and the speed of light flying to far, far, galaxies in adventurous reality.

However, a few shorter works have been recognized as complete in what they said, and are of the highest quality: such works include Steinbeck's *The Pearl* and *The Red Pony*, Chekhov's *The Cherry Orchard*, Colette's *Gigi*, Faulkner's *The Bear*, Gogol's *The Overcoat*, Cain's *Mildred Pierce*, Hemingway's *The Old Man and the Sea*. They have been around long enough to safely say they will live on a spell longer.

Bryan Woolley's *Some Sweet Day* is one of these classics. All it needs is the readers, and time, because it has the universality of earthiness, tragedy, wry humor, love—and its companion—death. You can smell the creeks and taste the potatoes. You can see the coming storms, both human and nature's, and fear them. Yet you know that the inhabitants of this book will endure. Any tiny item or event past the simplest form and struggle of survival is something to be cherished—even celebrated. In a time when in-house authors consistently call each other's books—even mediocre to bad ones, and often without even reading them—classics, it makes Woolley's book even more special.

Woolley doesn't waste any words—or the other thing you really own, your precious, limited time—but you will have experienced about all you can handle in this deeply felt family of the Central and West Texas landscape. You can touch the people, hear the dogs bark, and the earth breathe. No one has ever done it better or purer about this part of the earth. Maybe some sweet day Woolley himself will, but he will have to get up before the quail and go to bed after the last hoot of the owl to do it.

The Hi Lo Country

The Author Looks Back a Bit

I must confess that this book was damn near as hard for me to put down on paper as it was for its characters to live it—and there was a lot of fun, and problems, in both cases.

First of all, the book was inspired by my best cowboy friend getting himself killed by five .38 bullets. At the time, of course, I didn't know I was inspired. I was just shocked numb.

Shortly before this shooting took place, I had sold my modest-sized cowranch near Hi Lo and moved to Taos, New Mexico, to become rich and famous. What I did, with great rapidity, is become a pauper and slightly infamous. It took me several years of living and learning—and three other books before I started putting this particular story on paper. When I was about halfway through it I decided it was time to stop for a deep breath and celebrate a bit. I went to my favorite bar where the events of the evening led to a very short fistfight with a fine and brilliant artist who had a skull like a Neanderthal man. I swung. He ducked, and I instantly found out that the bones in my right hand were far less solid than the top of his head.

Now I had to decide what the best course of action from this point would be. If I took my shattered hand to the local hospital, they would apply a cast and it would be a long time before I could use it. So, I decided to go to my friend the Indian medicine man. I had witnessed some of his miracles and had deep faith in his healing powers.

After hearing some mumbling explanations on my part, he reluctantly agreed to try to fix the hand so I could soon go on writing. He applied a mixture that looked like ground-up fish guts (it may have been), and then straightened the two most damaged fingers using popsicle sticks for splints and expertly tied it all up. This left me two swollen, unbroken fingers and two swollen, broken fingers on my right hand which made me mostly a left-handed typist for a while.

I finally finished the book and mailed it to New York. My agent liked it and sent it to an editor. The editor liked it, and when it was published it just naturally called for another celebration—but I really should have just gone fishing instead. Well, unfortunately, another fracas started, this time over a friend's bar bill. When it ended there were seventeen people involved. Three went to the hospital. Three of us went to jail. The battered condition WE three were in must have created a puzzling situation as to whom was to be hauled where.

The jail was an underground dungeon at that time. They've rebuilt it since then, I'm told.

My failure to arrive home that night made my wife Pat pretty upset. She thought I was out running around getting into some kind of orneriness. When we finally got word to her that I was merely incarcerated for simple brawling, she became angry at the other side. She showed up at the jail noticeably agitated, with a clean shirt for me—mine had vanished during the flurry of activity—and a basket of fried chicken that we shared with the other inhabitants.

The trial was held that afternoon. The three of us were fined all the law would allow, plus damages for broken glasses, etc. I borrowed the money for the fine, which took me a year to repay. This, however, was a small penalty compared to what came down in New York regarding my new novel as a result of this.

Unbeknownst to any of us there was a UPI man in the courtroom. He sent out a wire describing the battle in terms that would have made Zane Grey jealous. I also didn't know that my editor was in London and had just sold the British rights to my book before its American publication. He was having a sedate breakfast in Brown's Hotel when he saw this little UPI item in the London *Times*. He was incensed by it for some reason and wrote me a long, nasty, lecturing letter. I returned the favor with one of righteous indignation, strongly feeling it was too late for a lecture and suggesting that what I needed was a little compassion. Our previous, fine relationship ended. Inside sources later revealed to me that this editor had sent down orders that only fifteen review copies of my book were to go out and no advertisement for it at all.

In my mind *The Hi Lo Country* appeared to be as dead as last year's plans.

It wasn't. A "hot" young director named Sam Peckinpah read *The Hi Lo Country*, called my agent, and said he wanted to meet the guy who wrote it. We met in an Oriental restaurant in Studio City, had a fine old time and he optioned the book for a movie. Sam had three pictures booked ahead, so the option on the book ran out.

By now several other people had miraculously gotten copies. Among the many actors who wanted to be part of the film were: Brian Keith, Lee Marvin, Charlton Heston, Robert Culp, Slim Pickens, Ali McGraw, and others. Some of the producers and/or directors, besides Peckinpah, who wanted or tried to get it made were: Saul David, Buzz Kulick, Tom Gries, Marvin Schwartz, David Dortort. I sold so many options and there were so many scripts written and so much money spent that I truly have lost track. I horse-traded it back and forth so many times to Peckinpah that we once had to hire two separate firms of lawyers to find out who owned it. The book was batted around like a rock 'n' roll groupie, or the shifting wind of Hi Lo. Now, after almost two decades, I finally own the film fights clean and clear as distilled water. My agent thinks we'll actually get it made into a movie now, but I'm just happy to have it back in book form again.

Most of my novels and short stories are set in the country around Hi Lo. The geographical Hi Lo Country covers the northeastern half of New Mexico, the far panhandle of Oklahoma, a lot of southeastern Colorado, and extends over into far northwest Texas. The indomitable spirit of that land should cover the world and beyond.

In my early writing career I was aware that all the millions of words—mostly myth—from around 1870 to 1900, had been overly covered. From then through the '20s the myth continued, but at least Will James told about the real West during his time. I became obsessed with the fact that the West of the '30s, '40s, and '50s would also slip by and become mythologized out of recognition as the previous two periods had. I have nothing against the myth any more than I do fairy tales. However, I feel it is crucial that history be recorded close to the time it happens or the mists of legend alter it beyond recognition.

Since I had been brought up—or more properly "kicked up"—by several remaining old-time cowboys, and had been made a cowhand under them, I chose myself to attempt to put this period in time on paper, and I chose to try it in fiction. It seems to be more personal and more fun that way. So from *My Pardner* (1963) which was set in the '30s, through the early '40s and '50s with *The Rounders* (1960; Gregg Press edition 1980), *The Great Wedding* (1963), *The Hi Lo Country* (1961), *The One-Eyed Sky* (1963), *The Shadow of Thunder* (1969), along with many short stories and novellas, I attempted to show what the American cowboy truly was during those three decades and still is to a lesser degree today.

In the '30s the cowboys were still under the influence of old-timers and their ways in spite of the barbed wire. There were only a few old, flatbed trucks in use and hauling was still mostly done by wagon and team. The massive and final transition to the pickup truck was just getting started in the early '40s when World War II caused a postponement of the inevitable. After that terrible conflict the nation got slowly back into peacetime production; the pickup became more and more dominant. By the end of the '50s just about every ranch in the West had at least one. The transition was completed by Detroit, Michigan. Now this is not to say that the horse isn't used and needed on isolated ranches today, but the total dependence on the horse, and an era, is gone forever. I lived it and I've tried to write that period as straight and true as my ability allows. How well the words are strung out, only the readers can judge, but the actuality of those times are sure as hell there.

These deep emotions created by great transitions had always attracted Sam Peckinpah. In *The Wild Bunch* the railroads, automobiles and armies are going to crowd the horse-powered "Bunch" into eventual oblivion. In *The Hi Lo Country* we see the postwar pickup truck and societal changes doing this to the mind of its hero (anti-hero?) Big Boy Matson. I know that the drive to reveal this next great change in the West also drove Sam Peckinpah—for over twenty years—to spend more time, love, agony and his own money on this book than any other. Over and over it would be scheduled for filming and then one of his wars would break out with the studio . . . you know the rest. It is hard for me to grasp, but now Warner Brothers is releasing the uncut version of *The Wild Bunch* in special showings in New York, Los Angeles and San Francisco. A month later they will have a complete retrospective (TV work and all) at Lincoln Center in New York and in London. Then the greatest Western ever made will be released worldwide.

By the time you read this we will know if the world will still go for the best. If so, I strongly sense that someone will come along and film *Hi Lo* in the great Peckinpah's memory. That would be artistic justice done. Let us all dream on anyway.

The younger cowboys I worked, sweated, fought and played with are aging now. They will soon disappear just as most of the old-timers have who influenced them. Just the same I will always remember a few things. On a real working ranch the rope and "cow savvy" were always more important than the gun. Another thing—in my young cowboying days, I cannot recall a single cowhand sitting in a bar feeling sorry for himself. He was there to drink, try to find a woman, dance, gamble, have fun, and for a spell, get in out of the wind. The fistfights were just something to add to the short time of relief. Few held grudges and most were buying one another drinks before they could wipe the blood from their faces.

In the Hi Lo Country the wind blows hot or freezing about three hundred days a year. Fighting just that alone would cause a man to have a tendency to turn loose when he had a chance, not to mention the bucking horses, the kicking calves, the poor wages, the fence building and windmill repairing, the hay hauling in blizzards, and the chopping of ice with an axe from a tank so the stock could water. Then there are the droughts that shrivel everything on the earth: the grass, the wild animals, the cattle, the horses, the insects, the birds, bank accounts, and of course, the men and women responsible for the survival of all.

The Hi Lo Country is not just made up of cowboys. There are merchants, mechanics, railroaders, miners, bartenders, poets, inventors, whores, semi-whores, and elegant, dedicated, long-suffering women, every kind that's anywhere else on the globe. I think here, though, the land and the elements are finally in control. It is a country of extremes. You adapt or die, in body or spirit. Because of this, the inhabitants laugh and play to extremes; they speak with descriptive comparisons in extremes; and as some old cowboy once said, "What the hell, you just live till you die anyway, and the rest of the time you spend shoveling manure so you can get the cows in the barn."

I don't know if God ever intended to give his blessings to the Hi Lo Country, but I lived it, loved it and wrote about it. With all the high winds, broken bones and hearts, I'd like to do it all over again. Since I can't, here it is on paper the best I could do at the time.

306

As hoped for in the introduction—*The Hi Lo Country* has now been filmed by producer Martin Scorsese (*Good Fellows, Raging Bull*) and director Stephen Frears (*Dangerous Liaisons, The Grifters*), based on a screenplay by Walon Green (*The Wild Bunch, The Hellstrom Chronicles*). It stars such actors as Woody Harrelson, Billy Crudup, Patricia Arquette, Penelope Cruz, Sam Elliot, Willie Nelson, and James Gammon.

Introduction to *Final Harvest*
and Other Convictions and Opinions

C. L. Sonnichsen's *Final Harvest* is my favorite kind of book—small, but potent, like a palm full of precious jewels. The joy of earned wisdom is what we have here. At least this is so for those fortunate and wise enough to absorb its varied and flashing rays of brilliance.

Young Leland Sonnichsen's journey took him, on a mostly-straight line, from the rich soil of the Iowa and Minnesota prairies, to working his way through the University of Minnesota, by doing multiple odd jobs from mowing lawns to waiting tables in a Jewish fraternity. He was already revealing strong dedication and purpose. It is the most precious of gifts—making all life worthwhile even when stumbling over splintered stumps.

Young Sonnichsen did that too, but with style, as he moved on through the often sanctified environs of Harvard University to earn his doctorate. There have been uncounted, careless jokes about going from Hell to Texas and then spending one's life struggling to get back home to the eternal fire. Doc Sonnichsen came from Harvard to Texas—quite possibly a more difficult journey than the aforementioned—and stayed. Oh, how lucky we—worldwide citizens obsessed with the West—are for this early move.

There is no reason for my dwelling on those days here. Dale Walker did that in a concise and enlightening study, *C. L. Sonnichsen: Grassroots Historian* (Texas Western Press, 1972) on those early years.

What must be done here, add prayerfully understood, is the main thrust of Sonnichsen's work during the 1980s and early 90s. We will start, for reasons of space and expediency, with his Swallow Press, 1988, book entitled *The Laughing West*. It is an entertaining and important compilation of humorous fiction from the past and present with his personal observations and explanations—which may have been as difficult as a three-week-old puppy trying to run a grown jackrabbit into a hole.

Since I was raised on cow ranches by old poots out of the 1870s and 1890s, I found that *The Laughing West* espouses the truth of all truths about the mythical, illusory West. It combined the desert dust and pine forests so realistically the reader not only can smell and taste them, but even more importantly could feel them. Yes, *feel*, the "allness" of the region. No matter how broken-boned and broken-hearted the lives of these old cowboys were; no matter how bent, scarred and debased their entire lives had been; they found it possible to laugh at its ridiculousness. That's right. They laughed at bucking off on their heads, getting a broken nose in a fist fight, or being thrown into jail from having "too fine a time" while drinking bad whiskey. They, like Doc Sonnichsen, lived and related these stories with good humor and high style. Style? That's right, too. They could not have survived any other way.

The kind of humor emanating from our "vanishing West," that Sonnichsen is laboring so hard for us to understand, is the ultimate form of writing anywhere, anytime—namely tragicomedy. It became an art of survival over and over and over in a rugged, ragged life in a land that could, and at times can, be as hard as the head of a sledgehammer and as softly deceiving as an Arizona chameleon.

We have lately observed a few writers who have become famous and wealthy because they had first written about cowboys. Later, some of these same writers tried desperately to deny the broken flesh they had been launched from, demeaning the cowboy as a mindless, unfeeling creature no longer worthy of their exalted glances.

In a time when some well-meaning, and partially correct, radical groups are putting out great and persistent labors to destroy the dream image, along with the solid reality of our written West, Doc Sonnichsen's truth of tragicomedy being the glue and holding center of it all, becomes more important each hour. Also, in a time when the revisionists' quotes rampage across the written pages of books—and especially news reports—partially justifiable in some cases, destructive and self-serving in others, Sonnichsen has almost single-handedly gifted us all with a simple, enjoyable, undeniable truth in his landmark work *The Laughing West* followed by his *Texas Humoresque* published by TCU Press in 1990 and on to his now finished BIG BOOK on Western humor, *Don't You Cry For Me*, subtitled "Humor about, and of, the West that was."

He wrote thusly in one of my favorite books of all time, *Pilgrim In The Sun* (Texas Western Press, 1988), "The point to emphasize is the laugh-producing portrayals of the cowboy and his life are more than good stories. They show what has happened to the concept of the cowboy over the years. They contribute to history."

It is greatly desirable—yea, an absolute necessity even—that future historians heed his words.

Now, let us understand that Sonnichsen's humorous West is not limited to real working cowboys. He knows that the homesteaders, the merchants, the bartenders, the ranch wives, and those males and females who outlawed for various reasons, had this survivability quotient or they shriveled up and perished just as surely as showers in the sand. That part of the West *must* remain and be recognized today or there will be little left for worthy western tomorrows.

I feel it an absolute that we record here a quote of Doc Sonnichsen's introduction in *The Laughing West*, page three, paragraph two. Quote. "Similar calls for a saving sense of humor have come down to us through the centuries. [Note that he said "saving."] More often than not the theorists were talking about comedy in the theater, but always the basic questions were, Why do we laugh? and What do we laugh at? Nobody has yet found a satisfactory answer to the first, but everybody has had a try at the second, beginning with Plato, Aristotle, and Socrates. No two of them ever agree completely, but all concur in viewing comedy as a tool used by civilized man to get at the truth about life, change it for the better, or rebel against its failures and lunacies. Every important thinker has had his say: Cicero, Ben Jonson, Schopenhauer, Freud, Bergson, Koestier, and H. L. Mencken, to name a few." Unquote.

If one follows the works, teachings and life of C. L. "Doc" Sonnichsen, one realizes he knew the same truths as the above mentioned, highly-esteemed thinkers. He simply applied it to his chosen area of the globe—The American West, which has no boundaries of fantasies or amalgamated truths. It is an honor beyond my humble words to have shared some of Doc's inspirational knowledge and understanding of the sumptuous sound of merriment that will permeate the West like saddle soap as long as it exists. I join all the others in wishing him multitudes of birthdays, healthy with comical chuckles, and a few dollars to spend on . . . let's see . . . well, maybe a few comic books.

Rounders 3

Author's Notes to the Reader

Also being the account of searching for the roots of the Rounders *trilogy*

If there's anything to genes and heritage then *Rounders 3* started in Lynn County, Texas, approximately twenty miles south- east of Lubbock, before I was born. My Evans grandparents had a modest-sized cattle ranch there along with six sons and one daughter. One son, W. B., would later become my father.

It was the winter of 1918, the last year of the First World War. The eldest son, Elbert, had just been killed in combat in France. Before the family could overcome that shock, a terrible blizzard ripped down from the north. A great, black, rolling cloud stretched across the flat plains from horizon to horizon, leaving the family barely enough time to pen the chickens and open gates to corrals and haystacks. The horses and mules made it to these enclosures and survived. The cattle, scattered over many sections of land, turned their tails to the screaming wind and freezing snow, trying to move away from it. When they hit the long drift fence, they stopped and died.

The family huddled helplessly inside the shivering frame house for two days. Then it was over, and they moved out into the drifts to see what had survived. Most of the cattle were buried, frozen. The few that made it through the fence alive were found later in such pitiful condition that they had to be shot.

My Uncle Lloyd, of Levelland, Texas, recalls that the snow was piled so high in a plum thicket that they could walk right over the top of it. As the huge drifts melted and were dug away, they salvaged what they could—mostly cowhides. They split the hide properly, then finished peeling it off with a team of mules. It was a terrible struggle to save so little. Lloyd (who was ten years old at the time) remembers digging out what he thought was a cow and finding to his surprise a neighbor's hog standing up- right, frozen solid, as if it had stopped to rest.

My Uncle Bernard, presently of Houston, Texas, was five years old and the baby of the family. He said, "If I live a thousand years, what I'll remember most vividly of that storm is a fence covered with cowhides as far as I could see."

My grandparents sold the land, the few surviving cattle, the cowhides, and moved their family to Ropes, Texas. They bought a section of land right out of town, put in a mercantile store, and started over.

My father met and married my mother, Hazel Swafford, whose family had recently moved to Ropes from the Indian Territory near Manitou, Oklahoma. A short time later the newlyweds, driving a wagon and team were instrumental in organizing Hockley County. My grandfather, J. R. Evans, was soon the first elected judge of the new county.

The Evans family pioneered many other things in West Texas and eastern New Mexico. My mother was the first postmistress at Ropes. My Uncle Elbert was the first soldier killed from Hockley County in World War I.

One Evans son, Robert (a.k.a. Slim, Tex, and Ion), would, many years later, contribute considerably to the *Rounders 3* stories. He was a cowboy all the way down to his liver. He broke and trained horses for anyone who would hire him—and some who wouldn't.

He rode west to punch cows and ride rough strings from Mexico to Canada. He was eighty-three and working cattle the old, Spanish Vaquero way—horseback with the help of cattle dogs—when he died in the High Sierras of California.

My father traded for a modest-sized piece of ranch land just north of Hobbs, New Mexico, and set about establishing a town there. He moved his widowed sister, Pearl Nettles, and her children there to take care of the cattle on the east end of the land—the rest was turned into a town he called Humble City (and was it ever). The drought and depression both came right after he promoted a school and post office. My mother was a first postmistress again.

I'll never know how my mother did it, poor as we were and busy as she was, but she acquired some books and taught me to read. By the time I started school I could read almost as well as the teacher. I will be eternally grateful for this most precious of gifts.

It was a great place and time for a boy to grow up in. I loved the vast, unplowed prairies. They were full of all sorts of small game which I harvested and brought home for our lean supper table. I had a horse named Cricket and several dogs. When I wasn't herding my Aunt Pearl's cattle, I was hunting with my dogs or visiting my grandparents back in West Texas.

Farmers were just beginning to plow up all the Ropes area. The temporary exception was the famous Spade Ranch west and north of town. I resented them ruining those natural prairies, then and now. Some of it might have been fine, but *all* of it? No!

I remember when the hot winds of the drought blew the furrows barren and almost level. I wasn't too dismayed. I told all the local kids who would listen, "Don't worry, this drought is the best thing that ever happened. They'll never be able to raise a cotton crop again, and it's all gonna turn back to grass."

Well, in spite of my optimistic enthusiasm, my folks lost it all at Humble City—but it's still on the map. They moved to Lubbock, Texas. I was coming on ten years of age.

My father went into business with his Uncle Pit Emery, an auctioneer. The day came when he asked me to saddle and ride Cricket to an auction location just out of Lubbock. He told me to really rein the horse out and show him off for the crowd. We sold Cricket that day. It hurt for a while, but I learned, and accepted, that sometimes it's necessary to sacrifice one thing in order to get another. This particular transaction would lead to a string of adventures that were to change my life and partially guide me towards *The Rounders*, the first story of this trilogy.

My father and his uncle took the proceeds from this sale and bought a string of half-starved horses way down south at Jal, New Mexico. Then he introduced me to a one-eyed, extremely bowlegged cowboy named Boggs, gave us three dollars and directions into and across West Texas all the way up north to Guymon, in the Panhandle of Oklahoma. He told us to get there on an exact date with the horses in *better* shape. That was almost a cinch because I half expected the buzzards to start tearing at their bone-stretched hides while they were still walking.

There was a problem, to wit: we only had one saddle and it was mine. On the fourth day Boggs talked me out of it by demonstrating how saddles had bowed and ruined his legs permanently. He didn't want to see me disfigured in this manner. I rode several hundred winding, twisting miles bareback with a hind end raw as fresh ground hamburger meat.

Boggs was truly a drifting, hobo cowboy. But in the following weeks I found out that he had survival instincts as strong as a coyote's.

We zigzagged across Texas, "borrowing," as he so carefully explained, patches of grass, weeds, remains of old feed stacks, grain from many bins. We twisted rabbits out of holes with forked barbed wire, rescued chickens from locked henhouses, and did some midnight seining of catfish from privately stocked ponds. The horses ate. We ate.

We survived flash floods, great thunder and sandstorms, and arrived at a stock farm three miles out of Guymon the morning before the 1 P.M. start of the sale—and the horses *were* in better shape than when we'd left. It was a roaring success and gave our families a new start in the recently battered West.

I wound up with a tough ass, soft brains, and an uncommon craving to go to the mountains. Boggs had told me so many entrancing tales of his adventures across the deserts and mountains of Colorado, Arizona, and New Mexico that nothing could keep me from "experiencing" some of my own. Another key step on the road to *The Rounders* had been taken.

About this time I, my parents, and Glenda, my baby sister, were moving to the ranch and oil town of Andrews, Texas. When everything was settled in, I talked my parents into letting me go to Lamy, New Mexico, a tiny village a few miles south of Santa Fe, in search of my Uncle Slim. He was supposed to be in that area. I promised to return to Andrews in the fall for school.

It was a long bus ride to Lamy, over dirt and dippy gravel highways, but I could see the mountains ahead. I got off Wednesday morning at the railway station where, not too many years before, Mabel Dodge Luhan had met D. H. Lawrence, his wife Frieda, and the artist Lady Dorothy Brett. So many internationally famous people—Georgia O'Keeffe, Witter Bynner, and scores of others—had entered the world of the West from this little spot, and chosen to stay. I didn't know or care about any of them at the time.

I walked over to the nearest business establishment, the Lamy Bar. The only customers were two local Hispanics and a gringo wino. The bartender was a thin, fragile, pale man. He saw my one bag and asked who I was looking for. I told him my uncle, Slim Evans.

He grinned and said, "Sure, he's working for Pete Coleman. They come in most Saturday afternoons."

I was relieved, scared, and excited all at once. He let me sleep on a cot in a back room, and took me to the Harvey House next to the train station for all our meals.

On Saturday, Uncle Slim and the cowboys came. The very next morning they were moving Coleman's herd of cattle to a new ranch at Haney Springs on Glorieta Mesa. I was given the "honor" of riding a half-broke bronc on the three-day drive up on the mesa.

After a few weeks at the Coleman place, Uncle Slim decided I should try out for a job on Ed Young's Rafter EY Ranch. He said, "There's never been any kids make it on his outfit. He's hard, but fair. If you could hang in there, Max, you'd learn a lot."

I really didn't have much choice; jobs with pay were scarce. No one could afford to hire all the hands they needed, so everyone loaned and borrowed cowboys like coffee and sugar.

Ed did hire me. I made a fair hand mainly because I was naturally pretty good with a rope, but it took several seasons. Ed introduced me to a couple of "borrowed" cowboys as the new horse wrangler. What that actually meant was, I was the one who got up at daylight, saddled Ole P. Nasty, a silly-looking bay nighthorse, and headed out to gather everybody's mount for the day.

When I found them, they whirled and took off in a dead run towards the corrals. Hell, this was going to be easy; these horses were trained like circus seals. Ole P. Nasty laid his ears back and stormed after the remuda. About a hundred yards from the corral, before the horses entered the open gate, P. Nasty ducked his head and violently changed gears. He started bucking.

I can still remember thinking that this horse's head must have fallen off because all I could see was a black, flying mane in front of and below me. His forelegs seemed to be dropping into holes deep enough to strike oil. I was bucked completely loose on the third jump, but I couldn't fall off. Ole P. Nasty was miraculously bucking back under me. He came to the corral, bucked along the fence, then whirled back. All parts of my anatomy, from my hip pockets on down, were taking a hell of a beating as I came down and met nine hundred pounds of horse coming up.

I remember Ed Young running beside me waving his hat to keep the horse from hitting the corral posts and yelling encouragement. "Ride the son of a bitch, Max. Stay with the bastard. Spur hell out of him, son."

My balls were mashed; the breath had been knocked out of me several jumps back. The world was spinning faster than eyes could follow. What seemed like hours later, I was finally standing there clinging to the corral fence, when one of the cowboys presented me with Ole P. Nasty's reins. I took them like I'd been handed a blazing cow turd.

I knew I was doomed when Ed said flatly, "The horses turned back. Go get 'em. We're running late."

Somehow, I remounted, gathered the horses again, then rode twenty miles that day through rocks and brush, helping move cattle from a winter pasture to a summer one. It wasn't so bad. I changed to a good, gentle horse named Ole Snip, who knew what we were both supposed to do.

It was just like Boggs had said it would be—multitudes of long rides and endless new adventures. There were wild horse chases and sometimes capture, many wrecks out in the rocks and brush, the roundups and brandings, the rare trips into town. The good and the bad in abundance were here on the mesa.

Ed Young kept me working. Each fall I commuted back to Andrews for the football season. Some of the late winters on Glorieta Mesa made the high, sandy winds of the Andrews country seem like Hawaii.

Sometimes we'd have three or four extra "borrowed" cowhands around and other times I was loaned out all over the country. I looked forward to being temporarily transferred to the San Cristobal outfit just south of Lamy. That eighty-thousand-acre ranch was covered with the first black Angus cattle I'd ever seen, Indian ruins, petroglyphs, great white and red bluffs, and a wonderful winding stream that gave the ranch its name and life.

Ed Young's wife was known as "Mother" Young. The term was used with enormous respect. I never knew why I started helping her after supper, but thanks to any and all great spirits for the privilege. I'd chop and gather wood for the next day and fill the hot water reservoir on the side of the huge wood-burning cookstove; fill all the water buckets for drinking, washing, and cooking; help clear the supper table; and then—the real treat—stand and dry dishes for her. We talked and talked—even about books, paintings, and sissy stuff like that.

Her contributions were everywhere. She made the rag rugs that covered the floors, built the lamp stands from tree cactus or wagon hubs, painted the pictures that hung on the walls, cooked, cleaned, doctored, washed, ironed, and in true essence held the whole damned outfit together, as thousands of others like her did, and still do.

317

I have slowly realized that those tough, old ranchers would have been helpless without the Mother Youngs of the world. I know, because my wife, Pat, is a lot like that. Without her keeping a strong loop around our little art-addicted family, we would have long ago been lost in thick brush.

It is sad that back in those days, working cowboys seldom had a chance to meet the kind of woman they would, or could, marry. There were those they held in awe and respect, like Mother Young, and there were the other kind.

There usually would be three or four local dances held a year, but working cowboys seldom had transportation or money to properly date a girl, even after they met her. The old legend of a simple cowboy marrying the boss's daughter was extremely rare. It was nobody's fault. That's just the way it was. It has changed enormously, as you'll see in the stories of *Rounders 3*. In the beginning stories I wrote the women as they were viewed by working cowboys, and I end by describing the long-overdue respect they hold now. Any other way would have been false.

The first winter I spent on the mesa, Mother Young put a box of books on a little homemade shelf. There were three Balzacs in the bunch. I started reading them and couldn't quit. I was mighty impressed that anybody could take these varied characters and make me know them, see them, feel their loves and hatred, their fears, and occasional gallantries. It was a magic, different world the little potbellied Frenchman gave me here in this enchanted land of New Mexico. I could see the colors and smell the perfume.

Balzac's largesse carried over to Andrews. Income from new oil made this school one of the richest in Texas. They built a fine library where I spent hours and hours engrossed in its treasures.

Years later, after the first volume of *The Rounders* had been published, they put a picture of me in the Andrews High School Hall of Fame. It'll never be known if this was because of my work as a writer, an artist, or because of running so fast with the football. I was offered two athletic scholarships, to small colleges, but declined and became a rounder instead.

My Uncle Slim was on the lower Pankey Ranch gathering wild cattle that had been missed during several roundups. Naturally, he asked Ed Young if he could borrow me to help him. Ed agreed.

I rode down to the line camp on Ole Snip. He was the other favorite horse of my life after Cricket. Horses and catch ropes are just about the most important things in the cowboy's world. He will talk about horses he's known even more than the women in his life.

We worked the brush and rocks checking for tracks in openings, trails, and water holes. Slowly we dragged or drove the gather into a holding pasture.

Slim was having some trouble with a four-year-old roan horse. Everybody put their soiled horses and rough string off on Slim because they knew he could handle them.

The roan bucked Slim off at a water hole. It took me a spell to run the horse down and bring him back. Slim mounted and spurred the roan out. The sucker acted as if nothing had happened. He reined around like a champion cutting horse.

Several days later, Slim was riding this same roan. He dismounted to open a gate. We passed through and Slim closed it. The roan jumped, trying to jerk free. Slim hung on to the reins until the roan kicked him in the belly and ran off.

I knew he wasn't dead because he gasped, "Go get that mean son of a bitch."

We were racing down the edge of a twenty-foot-deep gully. the fence line and the arroyo formed a V. As the space narrowed, I thought Ole Snip and I would be cut to pieces by barbed wire; instead, we all three went off into the arroyo. The roan had more wind knocked out of him, in the wreck, than Snip or I.

We all scrambled up in the clouds of dust: I climbed back on Snip and continued the chase. He charged out of the arroyo into a fence corner. I threw the loop. It went out so far that I couldn't believe the roan had stuck his head into the tiny circle left at the end—but he had.

I returned the outlaw to Slim. He led the roan into the corral, took his catch rope off the saddle, doubled, it, and tied him to the snubbing post. Silence. He stood over by the corral and rolled a smoke, staring at the half-sleeping critter. He lit the cigarette and stared. He puffed. He stared. More silence. Then his long legs propelled him across the corral in about three strides and he kicked the roan in the belly so hard it went "Whooommp." the horse humped up like he'd swallowed a cactus. Slim repeated the performance.

I made the mistake of opening my mouth and even worse I asked a question: "What did you do that for?"

Slim snarled through grinding teeth, trying to ignore the pain of his hoof-imprinted belly. "The son of a bitch just shouldn't have been a horse."

Take three guesses and see if you can come up with who was *honored* to ride "Ole Son of a Bitch' the rest of our time at the cow camp. You got it!

This continuing education damn near killed me, but here's where I got the name and a lot of the personality for the satanic horse in all *Rounders 3* stories. I always thought this particular horse's name really was Son of a Bitch, because that's all Slim ever called him; but now and forever on the hard, rocky ground and the soft paper of the stories I'd write, he would be known as Old Fooler.

The drought and the depression were slowly going away. Hitler's war was spreading in Europe and other parts of the world. I was seventeen and in my senior year at Andrews High School.

My maternal Aunt Fay was a lady with real class and flair in whatever she did. I called her my "marryin' aunt." She had three deceased husbands. She was currently married to an M.D. from Oklahoma City. In lieu of a bad debt, he had taken in a small ranch, fourteen miles east of Des Moines in northeastern New Mexico. They hadn't even seen the property, but she sold it to me on easy payments.

I borrowed money from Mr. F. H. Chilcote, at the Farmers and Stockmens Bank in Clayton, to buy some cattle. Then I married my high school sweetheart, Helene Caterlin. We had a baby named Sharon. Life was really "whuppin' up" for me. All these things happened faster than the movements of a short-order cook.

Even though I was a lousy bronc rider, I took on strings of raw broncs to break and did day labor for neighboring ranchers to make a living.

Hitler's war was gaining momentum, so I sold all the livestock, sent my new family off to the kinfolks in Texas, and joined the army.

Naturally, since I had a horse background, they put me in the walking infantry. There was, in concentrated time, basic training, shipment overseas, landing (DI), France, on Normandy Beach. Shortly after the Saint Lo breakthrough, I was blown into the basement of a bombed out building by an artillery shell at Vire, France, and survived for several more months of combat all the way into Germany—by way of the Battle of Brest—then, back to northeast New Mexico to start painting pictures.

While I let the ranch slowly go to hell, I had lots of excitement and education in living—dancing, fistfighting, playing poker, and sundry other fun items.

In this readjustment period, I decided to change careers. I sold the ranch and moved into town. I bought a few acres just outside of Des Moines—still in New Mexico—with two houses on it. My close friend, woodcarver Luz Martinez, moved into one of them. I continued with even more dedicated oil painting and hell-raising.

Then came the divorce. I sold everything and moved to Taos—a mystical, savage, and loving spread of land with lush mountains and high, dry desert; so beautiful that no writer or painter has ever completely captured it.

I planned to become rich and famous here as an artist as I've said before. (I was poor and infamous within a year.) As soon as I moved there I bought, and paid for, a house with twelve subirrigated acres near the mesa three miles west of Taos. There was plenty of room to keep the horses necessary to maintain my serious hobby of calf roping. This kind of security, for most artists of any kind, might be a luxury; to me it was a necessity.

I was in Taos about four months when I met my future wife—artist and artist's model Pat James. After our marriage, we continued painting and I started writing. We didn't have much materially, but we had a lot of other things more important.

My artistic and spiritual mentor and friend, Woody Crumbo, the great Potawatomi Indian artist, gave us advice on selling art as well as painting it. Our sales and prices both increased.

Then Woody Crumbo and I became partners in the mining business. We climbed mountains over several western states, prospecting. We opened up scores of old tunnels, some that had been caved in for nearly a hundred years. We promoted mills and mines all over. We got rich. Then in one hundred and twenty days the price of copper dropped from forty-eight cents to twenty-four cents. We were broke.

Pat and I had twin daughters, Charlotte and Sheryl (both have become accomplished artists), as well as debts of eighty-six thousand dollars below nothing. We were out of money, credit, paintings, and everything else but desire.

Even during the years of mining and other things, I continued to write. I had two published books: *Southwest Wind*, a collection of short stories, and *Long John Dunn of Taos*, a biography. Some of my magazine articles and short fiction sold. This was not enough—I needed to work on a novel. About what? War? No, I wanted to forget that. Hunting? Possibly, even though by now I couldn't stand to shoot anything but a tomato can. Nature? I knew so much about coyotes that I loved them more than most humans.

What else did I know something about? Cowboys! I'd write a novel based on all those old-timers who were born in the 1890s—the ones who had raised me (kicked me up would be more accurate) and the younger ones who had worked and raised hell with me.

The Rounders was on its way. No steady paychecks were ready for me to pick up weekly, but we did have some western lithographs I had printed earlier at Woody Crumbo's suggestion. These were lifesavers.

I'd work on *The Rounders* a few days and then, when groceries became scarce and overdue bills plentiful, I'd take off for Taos plaza, or to Santa Fe, and peddle the prints. We managed fairly well, and I finally finished the novel.

My agent, Henry Volkening in New York, was enthused by what he called "a new kind of western." He had the power to get it straight to the senior editors at the major publishers. Eleven of them in a row turned it down, saying it was a superior, but too-different, western.

Finally, on the twelfth run, Al Hart, Jr., the editor-in-chief of Macmillan, took it on with enthusiasm. His judgment proved to be right—the reviews were all tops. Some called it the funniest tragicomedy western of its time. It made several bestseller lists; it was published overseas and in braille for the blind. The U.S. Army libraries ordered a thousand hardback copies. It was made into a fine little movie starring Henry Fonda and Glenn Ford. Noted film critic Judith Crist rated it one of the top films of the year. It was also made into a TV series for ABC.

The novel has been written up over the years in many academic books and journals, and taught in a large number of high schools and colleges. It finally paid off all the soul-bending debt from the mining days.

In Hollywood, director Burt Kennedy discovered a prepublication copy of the manuscript. The movie possibilities grabbed him, so he took it to Fess Parker. Fess was world famous at the time, starring in the *Davy Crockett* TV series. The title song blasted out everywhere, and millions of youngsters played wilderness in coonskin caps.

Fess Parker called me in Taos. He wanted me to come out to California so we could talk about an option. Pat and I went.

I sat on vast grassy slopes, just below Fess's semi-castle at Hope Ranch in Santa Barbara, looking down on the enticing blue-green of the Pacific Ocean. He sat next to me speaking in a voice as sincere and believable as God's. He told me not to have a single worry. He would never let anything injurious happen to my book. I was delighted and comforted to hear this.

I'm sure Fess meant all this at the moment, but in truth I'd just heard my first line of Hollywood bull and had failed to recognize it. In the many months of many years I spent out there, dozens of producers, directors, and just plain "script-packers" would lay this sort of thing on me. No bother. It's all part of the great poker game of illusion.

Fess or the writer who had done most of the *Davy Crockett* scripts, Tom Blackburn, to do a screenplay on *The Rounders*. Then Fess pulled off a miracle and later let it all slip away. He actually got director William Wellman to come out of retirement to work on this project. Wellman, a great World War I hero, had joined the Lafayette Escadrille and flown combat missions for the French. When he came home, he directed for the great financier, Howard Hughes, *Wings* and other classic pictures such as *The High and the Mighty, Battleground,* and *The Ox-Bow Incident.* He was now retired with wealth and world fame assured. Everyone was offering him lucrative deals to come out of retirement to direct. He refused all offers until he read *The Rounders*.

Not only did he agree to direct it, he sat with Blackburn almost daily, working on the script. He also traveled around the country talking to working cowboys; even crawling down in the chutes with rodeo hands.

The finished work was the truest screenplay, in the sense of authenticity and the use of its humor (which is the only survival mechanism that salvages life for working cowboys), that I have ever read—or believe I ever will. I was ecstatic.

Then the casting and the eternal meetings with United Artists started. All details but one were agreed on. Wellman and someone else had a clash of egos and wills on the casting. Wellman walked. Even though it hurt, I didn't blame Wellman a particle. In fact, his monumental efforts on behalf *of The Rounders* has brought only the feeling that I've been mightily honored.

We sold five options on the novel in the next five years. Ironically, Burt Kennedy and MGM came back into the deal and got it made. It has become a minor classic, having been shown on TV scores of times in recent years.

The Great Wedding was inspired, in part, by Old Santa Fe—all its art, its social life, my friends who were there, and the interesting strangers from everywhere in the world who came to soak up its unique charms. I have loved and visited this ancient city for over half a century. It seems like many lifetimes. I made a lot of trips there peddling art, books, mines; whatever I had. However, I have also spent a great part of my life writing about the little-known dignity of the coyote, and now Santa Fe artists and craftsmen have made so many wood, iron, or ceramic cartoon-type models of this wonderful creature they have cheapened his honor. My mind forgives the insult to my heart and to those noble animals.

The early Hollywood years, associating and partying with such wild and wonderful actors as Brian Keith, Lee Marvin, Slim Pickens, Warren Oates, and Morgan Woodward, and directors Tom Gries and Sam Peckinpah and his entire family, helped keep me in keen spirits to write *The Great Wedding*. Even though the time period in the book is the late 1950s and the early '60s, the book seems surprisingly, and almost exactly, up to date now.

All of the above, and many more, tried to get a film made from this book. Again, we sold a lot of movie options. Scripts were written, producers hired, money and emotions spent. In fact, our old family friend, Sam Peckinpah, was trying to get it made when he died in 1985. He loved the plot—one cowboy trying to get the other married to a rich woman for honorable purposes. He loved the concept of throwing two real working cowboys into the Santa Fe social structure and watching the explosion.

While *The Great Wedding* was intentional, the third story, *The Orange County Cowboys*, was triggered into action by an incident experienced by two California friends, Ed Honeck, an advertising writer and sports columnist, and Al Johnson, an international manufacturer. They told me of a little incident they experienced while relaxing at Al's "play" ranch up north. They had accidentally found a neighboring rancher's lost calf where it had fallen into a big hole. Their amateur efforts at saving the creature struck me as funny. They both hoped I would be inspired to use this as a basis for a short story. I agreed. Then it took on a different shape thanks to writer Joe Lansdale, who said I should write it as a short novel.

Well now, novellas are my favorite form of both reading and writing. I decided to wind up the *Rounders* trilogy, bringing the continuing characters right up to date, including their dealings with the Japanese. So everyone was happy. It even won a 1988 Western Writers of America Spur Award.

As the novels have progressed with the changes of time, so have the women. They are more at the forefront in *Orange County Cowboys* than they were in the other two books, which reflects their progress in reality over the last couple of decades. This is especially true in the business world.

A working cowboy must be a veterinarian, a part-time mechanic, an engineer, a tracker, a teacher, and much more. It is a complex, dangerous, and demanding profession. By the time he learns all the things he has to know to be a top hand, he is usually too old and too crippled to do all of them.

When I was a young man the word "cowboy" was only used as a point of great honor. One of the favorite sayings from these top hands was, "I may not be a cowboy, but I can take one's place till he gets here."

Now the title is insulted every time a group of corporate executives or high government figures get caught plundering or warring; they are called—and call one another—"cowboys." Or "Presidential cowboys." Or "savings-and-loan and corporate-merger cowboys." Even motorcycle and patrol car cops, along with grocery store butchers, are often called "cowboys."

Well, the old, open-range days are long over except in mostly mythical entertainment forms, and I give thanks for their continuance in this way. The contemporary days of transition combining cowboying with both the horse and pickup truck are about complete. The most glorious reflection of America's history may shortly be gone. Past.

Recently I read the following in America's largest daily newspaper: "Cowboy crisis grips West. Cowboys aren't home on the range anymore. Ranchers are having trouble finding workers."

Yes, they are becoming scarce. What a pity there are not enough monetary benefits to entice young people to the profession. It's true that most cowboys spend their last years in stifling poverty. Sad.

Yet, the wonderful western myth of the cowboy is the one constancy of admiration the rest of the world holds for America. This is only fitting; the American cowboy developed from every imaginable nationality. That myth has been spread to other nations by films, writings, songs, clothing, and uncountable other manners. Massive fortunes have been made based on the sweat and blood of these hardworking men. Careers have been born, world fame and worship enjoyed by many, while those whose guts, perseverance, and solid sense of humor had created the source of such success were being paid a pittance for labor that few have the courage and skill to perform. Even today there are those few who are getting their names in the papers and lining their pockets with donated money to destroy, actually eradicate, the cowboy from the earth he knows better, more intimately than anyone else.

I wish the public could be made aware that there is a vast difference between the big greedy, destructive mostly part-time ranchers and the other generational ranchers who are dedicated to caring properly for their land and its creatures. The cowboys that work for both kinds do the best they can under mostly adverse conditions.

It has been a long, bone-breaking, hide-splitting, joyous journey through the *contemporary* West for me. I've written it down, as I lived it, felt it, and loved it, the best I could. There are boozers and bankers, hookers and heiresses, merchants, artists, and practicers of many other professions throughout this trilogy. I genuinely hope the reader enjoys the trips half as much as I have.

∿5∿
Magazine Articles

The Cowboy and the Professor

It was Wyoming. It was June. It had snowed three inches the night before, but the sun was an hour above the mountains now and the snow was gone. The ground was still slightly damp beneath Luther Wilson's laced boots as he walked along the west bank of Crystal Creek looking for the right hole to cast his fish hook.

Sunlight darted across the creek sparkling like dancing diamonds. Damp ghosts of steam rose from the willow bottom in front of him. Luther decided to circle the willows and do his first fishing above them. About halfway around he heard a huge snort, a mighty whomping, splashing, and crashing noise. A monster was charging straight at him. He leapt aside, tripping on a cut bank. The creature's head looked to be about nine feet from the ground. It cascaded above and by him and must have weighed more than a ton. He reached for the .44 Magnum on his hip and felt a little foolish. He knew a moose can't hear or see very good, but they do have a needle sharp sense of smell. For that reason Luther felt it would not return. He was certain he needed clean underwear.

With swiftly returning courage, he marched onward. He found the right spot and cast the number 12 Adams fly out on the blue-green ripples. On the third cast, he hooked a twelve-inch cutthroat and banked it. The fishing was good. In thirty minutes he had five ten- to fifteen-inchers in his creel. Then the toothless cowboy rode up. He and his horse wore only what they needed, chaps for the brush, hat for the sun, rope for the cows—utility personified. He dismounted. Luther guessed him to be about his age-late thirties—even though he looked about fifty.

Legend has it that cowboys don't speak unless spoken to. Some accountants and bulldozer mechanics are like that, too. This 'un wasn't. He introduced himself and right off wanted to know what Luther's line of work was. Luther didn't know how to tell him that he'd graduated from college when he was eighteen, that he'd been in the Peace Corps, was an editor at Cambridge, Harper and Row, the University of Oklahoma Press, and was now doing an outstanding job as the director of the University of New Mexico Press. He was also a dead shot with a pistol and a right handy outdoorsman any way you looked at it. He had been raised in the Kentucky hills on a creek halfway between his aunt's cathouse and a preaching uncle's church. Luther told the cowboy none of this, even though he speaks seven languages fluently. He simply said in plain English, "I work for a school in Albuquerque."

The cowboy accepted this in his own way, replying, "Had any luck, Professor?" obviously referring to the fishing. Luther proudly showed the creel of fish. "Weeeeel now, ain't that some-thin'? Professor, you oughta be teachin' fishin'."

Luther went on about his casting while they "visited."

The cowboy asked, "Say, what kinda pistol is that?" Luther said, "It's a .44 Magnum. I'm wearing it because the game warden told me this is where they turn loose all the mean bears they remove from Yellowstone."

"Yep, that's right. I had a lot of trouble with 'em myself. Tore up our line camp twice . . . that is, they tore up what they didn't eat up. Headquarters sent us a big guard dog. Tied him to a stump right in front of the door. Thuh boss said he was a mean sucker. Never did know for sure."

Luther said, "How's that?"

"Rode in late one evenin' and that dog was plum gone. Weeeeel, not altogether-there was a little bit of hair stuck to the end of the rope."

Luther decided in mid-cast he'd change animals. He said, "Saw a moose this morning."

"A moose? Say, I did something awhile back I been wantin' to do for years." Luther turned his head to him and waited expec-tantly. "By God, I roped one of 'em, " he said, beaming through his squinty eyes and chomping his toothless gums in pure pride. Suddenly concentrating, he asked, "Say, Professor, you didn't happen to notice if that sucker was still wearing my rope?"

Luther's negative answer brought a change of subject. "Say, did you spot our line camp down below here?"

Luther acknowledged that he had.

"Was there two pickups there? A blue 'un and a green run?"

"No. There was only a green one."

The cowboy tied his horse to a bush and shaking his head in a worried way, said, "That's what I was afraid of. You see, head-quarters sent me a nineteen-year-old kid name uh Jack awhile back and I'll betcha a buffalo nickel he's over in Jackson Hole, agittin' drunk. I'm gonna fire him if he comes back—or hunt him up and kill him if he don't."

Luther said, "It sounds to me as if young Jack's a loser either way he goes."

"You got that zactly right, Professor."

Luther caught several more fish and noticed it was about lunch time. He had sandwiches, an apple, a banana, and a bottle of wine for the mountain repast. He offered to share with the cowboy.

"Naw thanks anyway. Outa the habit. Too much bother to carry a lunch where I ride."

"Well, some wine, then?"

"Naw, don't fool with it."

Luther was enjoying the lunch. He poured a plastic cup of wine. The cowboy stared at it like it was a rattlesnake and started another story.

"I was foreman of a jim dandy outfit in Utah awhile back. Had a good wife and bought a little house in town. The wife worked for the phone company . . . made good money. We was payin' everythang out, even the washin' machine and TV. Then me and ole Roger from the Cross W went on a three dayer . . . one of them knee-crawlin', table grabbin', head bustin' drunks. You know the kind I mean, Professor?"

Luther nodded his head in affirmation. He'd seen people in that condition from Sardi's in New York to Baca's Restaurant in Albuquerque, New Mexico.

As Luther washed down a bite of turkey sandwich with a big swallow of chablis, the cowboy continued, "Well, ole Roger run outa money right after I did. So we drove over to my house to get some more from the wife. I told Roger to jist wait in the pickup. I'd only be a minute. I knew the wife was home cause her car was and there was smoke comin' out of the fireplace chimney. I knocked on the door till my knuckles was about to swell. Nobody came. I yelled. Nobody answered. I walked around the house try-ing to find a window to open. They was all locked tighter than a pucker string on a loan shark. The fact is, she was inside and I was out. So when I got to the pickup, Roger asked me if anythang was wrong. Weeel, I didn't want him to fret none so I told him, 'No, everthang is just fine and dandy. I got her locked in where she'll be safe and sound till I git back.'" The cowboy was quiet a minute, then added, "you know what I mean, Professor?"

Luther acknowledged that not only did he have understanding, but also a great deal of sympathy.

The cowboy seemed to sense this honest compassion, for he soon went on with his story. "Well, there was a half bottle of whiskey in the pickup seat we thought was too sorry to drink earlier that morning, but we decided its time had come. A glass of water was settin' on the dash, and as I drove by a steep drop I just gave that water a good pitch out the window and told Roger to fill it with that good whiskey. A few days after I was fired, divorced and had moved to Wyoming I figgered out that my teeth was in that glass of water."

Luther had decided that here was a man that could use some kindness. He caught three more fish and invited the cowboy down to the camp to meet his wife, Judy.

The cowboy took off his chaps and threw them across the saddle. He removed his spurs, buckled the leathers together and slung them over his shoulder. He walked along beside Luther, leading his horse. This, of course, was utmost politeness because there could be no way he enjoyed this form of transportation. He was quietly thoughtful.

Luther took up the conversation. "You'll like Judy. She's lots of fun, a great cook, and she's sensible, too. She doesn't let any outdoor survival syndrome cloud her common sense. For instance, this morning I took a bath in that creek," Luther pointed to the stream, "but Judy drove into Moose, Wyoming, for a nice warm shower. Now that's sensible . . . because let me testify that creek water at seven o'clock in the morning, after a three inch snow, will make your hair hurt and turn your blood to bone."

The cowboy gave Luther a long, lonesome look, then mumbled something about Jack being drunk and disgraceful in Jackson Hole. Obviously the runaway Jack was weighing heavily on his mind because he suddenly stopped and asked Luther if he'd teach him to shoot the .44.

He said, "I ain't never fired one like that before, so maybe you'll show me how."

Luther pulled the gun out to explain the basic facts about it. Then he pointed to a small rock under a bush about ninety feet distance, saying, "Not much chance, but we'll try for that."

Luther took the .44 in both hands, raised the sights above the rock and as he came down to it, pulled the trigger. Although he knew he was a damned good shot he never expected to hit the small rock at that distance. To his pleasant surprise, the rock vanished. Having learned to think fast in many editorial meetings, Luther instantly handed the gun to the cowboy and said, "Your turn."

The cowboy tightened both hands on the bridle reins, thinking just as fast, "I better not. My horse is gettin' boogered."

Luther could have seen the truth in that from a mile away.

Finally they were in camp. The cowboy, the professor and Judy hunkered around the late afternoon campfire. Crystal Creek, now purple-black, gurgled by whispering in unknown tongues. Way off west, the snow peaked Grand Tetons tore at the sky like a row of great shark's teeth. The falling sun blushed the mountain tips orange a moment before retiring. A coyote howled at eternity.

Luther was frying the fresh trout. Judy was getting a pan of sliced potatoes ready for the fire. The cowboy held a big mug of steaming coffee and stared at the bottle of Jim Beam residing on a low camp table. Judy poured a shot of bourbon into her glass of soda. Luther picked up the bottle, twirling the liquid, studying it like a chemist, then tilted it up for three good gulps, finishing with a satisfying "Aaaaaahh."

Judy and the cowboy hit it right off since they were both from Oklahoma. He was born near Enid and she grew up on a stock farm at Chickasha.

The cowboy explained that he really needed his wayward hired hand back, since they had to ride all the time to keep the cattle shoved back out of the flats into the mountains. The high country was for summer grazing, so when the snow came there would be grass left in the flats for winter forage. Young Jack was sure throwing everything in a bind and the cowboy was worried about his double work load.

They ate and drank. Luther, warmed by the food, the fire and the Jim Beam, told Kentucky hillbilly stories of his childhood, and Judy, a much sought after CPA, chipped in with bits of her country background.

Luther kept the firewood coming while Judy cleaned up the dishes. She turned to the cowboy and asked once more, "Are you sure you wouldn't like a drink?"

The cowboy smiled, shook his head and replied, "No, thank you Ma'am, but I am sorely tempted to let loose." He paused a moment before continuing. "This puts me in mind of my old Uncle Pete. He was one of the fightin'est, drinkin'est, woman chasin'est rounders in that part of the hill country, but what he was really known for was his cussin'. He could peel the bark off trees and make a preacher go deaf. One day he was crossin' this little river on the edge of town with a truckload of apples when the tailgate came loose. The whole bed of apples went floating down the river. Uncle Pete crawled out on the hood and stared at all that work and profit floating away like autumn leaves. The town folks never seen him quiet like this when he was mad. They commenced to gather around waiting for the explosion of cussin' that was sure to shame all others before it. They waited till they was in nervous shambles. Uncle Pete jist sat and sat. Then finally, he stood up on the hood of the truck, took his hat off, and said, 'Sorry, folks, I jist ain't up to the occasion.'" Having made his point, the cowboy's stare now alternated from the fire to the bottle.

Soon pickup gears could be heard grinding in the near distance. Finally the cowboy broke his silence as he reached over and picked up the bottle, saying, "Weeeeel . . . on second and third thought I might just. . . ."

The gears ground close now and then lights flared luminous fingers through the trees. The cowboy held the bottle stiffly half way to his mouth as if he'd been suddenly petrified in that position.

The lights moved up and stopped. A door slammed on the blue pickup and a young cowboy came forward at a strange gait. Here was a man who could walk, dance, and stumble all at the same time. It was young Jack and he looked like he'd been in dedicated training to commit suicide.

Jack moved right up to the fire with his hands out. He snorted and yelled at the cowboy, "Aha! There you go again!"

The cowboy lowered the bottle, giving Luther a sick "I told you so" look. Luther urgently removed the bottle from the cowboy's hand and passed it to an appreciative Jack who tilted it up in a toast, saying, "Thanks pardner. We better drink this up before he ruins his life . . . " Jack took a long drink and then gasped out, "again."

Luther smiled knowingly at the cowboy. "Might as well let the song play itself out."

The cowboy threw a pebble in the fire, tipped his hat back off his head and scratched underneath it, saying, "I see what you mean, Professor."

The night birds called. The dark mountains listened.

A Horse to Brag About

I reckon just about every human in the world that was raised on a cow ranch, worked as a cowboy, or just plain rode for pleasure knew and loved a horse like Old Snip. In the memory of us all there is one old pony that comes to mind more often than all the others. A horse to do a little braggin' about. That's the kind of horse Old Snip was.

The first time I saw the little stocking-legged, blazed-face, snip-nosed bay, a long-legged bronc stomper named Robert Ian was hanging the steel in his shoulders. It was in a big pole corral at Cow Springs, New Mexico, and the dust was fairly boiling from under Old Snip. He bucked hard, mighty hard, with long, ground-bustin', neck-poppin' jumps, straight ahead till he hit one side of the corral, then he turned and put out all he had till he hit the other side. He bucked straight just like he did everything else in his life. But that was the only time he ever bucked.

Gradually he slowed and then quit altogether. Robert Ian worked him in and out around the corral letting him get used to the weight on his back, the steel in his mouth, the rein on his neck, letting him know that these things wouldn't hurt him if he behaved himself. The little old pony caught on quick and by the fourth saddling, Robert Ian decided he'd turn him over to me. He said, "Here, boy, get your saddle on this here Old Snip. He's gentle as a loggin' horse."

I was just a gawky, freckled-face kid hanging around the outfit wranglin' horses, patching fences, anything Robert Ian happened to think of that he thought I wouldn't mess up. Mainly I hung around to get a few square meals, listen to the tall yarns cowboys have a habit of spinning and maybe to learn a little something.

"You think he's broke gentle?" I asked cautiously eyeing the bay.

"Why, boy," he said, "this here horse would do to go to preachin' on."

I saddled up, gathered the reins up tight in my left hand, grabbing the heavy black mane at the same time. I took hold of the saddle horn with my right and stuck my left knee in his shoulder, swung my right leg smoothly over his back, and Old Snip moved out with a nice running walk. Right away I breathed easy again. I've never known a horse to pick up a fast running walk that quick. He was a natural at it. A running walk will carry a cowboy a lot of miles in a day and bring him back without his tonsils shook loose. Sittin' up there on him I felt just as good as an old coat that a feller's worn a long time and hates to throw away. He was already beginning to rein. The least pressure and he turned smooth as new grass, just where you wanted him.

"Now, listen, boy," Robert Ian said when I came back, "I owe Ed Young twenty dollars and I promised him this here horse in payment." My heart turned mighty cold at these words for I thought he was giving the horse to me.

"You been wanting to go over on that San Cristobal outfit and hunt arrowheads, ain't you?"

I said, "Yeah."

"All right, here's your chance. You can leave about daylight in the momin' and you'll be at the Indian ruins right around ten. I'll make out a bill of sale from me to Ed," he added. "You can stay at the old line camp across from Long Draw tomorrow night and make it in to Ed's the next day."

"Yeah," I said, not liking the sound of that *bill of sale* business.

"Something else," Robert Ian said, "If you keep your mouth shut, listen hard and work like hell you might get a job later with the San Cristobal outfit. A regular payin' job."

That last sounded good because all I'd got in the way of pay around there was a dollar Robert Ion gave me when we went to Santa Fe one time. That seemed like a lot of money then but I was a year older now and wanted to put on the dog a little.

Me and Old Snip were out on a piñon-crowded trail heading lickety-split for the San Cristobal Ranch when the sun came up. Boy, it was a mighty fine morning. A bunch of deer jumped up out of some oak brush and went tearing up the hill. A coyote crossed our trail and the magpies started screaming. The blue-jays flew from tree to tree.

By nine o'clock we crossed the highway between Cline's Corners and Lamy, New Mexico, and were well into the ranch property itself. The highway is fenced now, but then she was wide open. The August sun was warming up fast. I figured it was going to get hotter than blue blazes before noon. Sure enough it did. I didn't care though. Here I was mounted on a little animal that I figured the good Lord had made especially for me and I saw those sky-high, white and red bluffs sticking up like a bunch of cathedrals.

I took the worn out catch rope Robert Ian had given me and tied Old Snip to a piñon tree with a knot that wouldn't slip and choke him later on if he got boogered at something. Then I started out across those ruins with my head down and my eyes peeled expecting any second to see a perfect arrowhead.

Some college feller told me years later that these ruins were five or six hundred years old. They were brand spanking new to me that day in August. You could still see the outlines of the sandstone houses built in a big square. Out in the middle was the round kiva—a sort of church for the Indians. Broken pottery with designs painted on them in real bright colors was scattered about everywhere. There were lots of broken arrowheads and pieces of flint all over.

Then I found what I'd been looking for, a great big perfect arrowhead made out of black glassy obsidian. Man! Chills ran all over me and I knew what a prospector must feel like when he pans a big gold nugget for the first time. I got to walking so fast trying to—find another one that I probably stepped over several unseen. Boy, I had a pocket just smack full of flint pieces, arrowheads, and bright colored pottery.

Then I saw another one, white and small, a bird point. Just as I bent to pick it up I noticed a shadow spread across the ground around me. It was a cloud. As I straightened up I looked into the sky. There were lots of clouds, black and heavy with water. They hadn't begun to get together yet so I figured I had plenty of time to hunt.

Between the cathedrals and the line camp where I aimed to spend the night was a lot of barren, badly eroded ground and one deep-cut arroyo called Long Draw. Flash floods in the mountains caused these to fill with water and sometimes made crossing impossible. I was so wrapped up in what I was doing, I didn't pay the clouds much attention.

Then she hit—an earbustin' clap of thunder! I raised up quick-like and looked over to where Snip was tied. He was so wide-eyed you could see the white showing. It's not natural for a cow pony to get excited over a little rain storm brewing. But when Old Snip looked over at me and blasted out with a long loud nicker, I figured it was time to leave. I still swear to this day that horse was smarter than me and was just giving warning it was high time to drag out of there before it was too late. Sure enough it almost was.

Over to the east in the higher mountains, the clouds were having a family reunion and the more lively members were spitting out forked fire and deep down, rumbling noises. I could see the blue white sheets of rain pour out into the canyons and foothills. The storm was moving on out towards the flats and us, fast-like.

I buckled on my spurs, missing the hole with the buckle tongue a couple of times because I was getting a little excited. I untied Old Snip and mounted up. I leaned over in the saddle and away we went. Snip seemed to understand that the whole idea was to get across all that barren ground before the rain reached us. If it did, we might have to sleep out on this side of the arroyo all night without any shelter. He was really moving now, up and down . . . straining hard with his hindquarters on the upgrade and keeping his forelegs out in front on the downgrade.

We didn't quite make it. About a quarter of a mile out in the eroded flats, the rain caught us. I pulled up and took a look. There wasn't much to see, the rain was so heavy. As we moved out again I could feel the cold wetness already soaked through to the skin and the water running from the brim of my hat like it was coming off a tin roof.

Old Snip was beginning to slip and slide in the slick, muddy clay. We kept going just the same. I was so wet now I didn't feel the coldness so much. We finally made it to Long Draw. I reined down a gradual slope out into the gravel covered bottom. Water was running in little muddy rivers everywhere. Then all of a sudden I could see nothing but water. A solid stream of reddish, muddy churning water! We were in real trouble! The heavy rain up in the mountains was just now reaching this part of Long Draw.

Before I had time to think, the water swirled up around my boot heels. Then it hit, a great big wall of mud, water, piñon sticks, pine needles, and everything else that grows in the mountains. I dropped the reins and grabbed the saddle horn with both hands. My arms felt like they had been stretched out as long as a wagon tongue. I couldn't see and it felt like a whole ocean of water had spilled right on top of us. I knew for sure this was it. I wanted to do some praying but I couldn't get my mind on it for worrying about holding on to that saddle horn.

I began to strangle, and a lot of red, light and black spaces seemed to jump out of my head. I got a big suck at a bunch of air. It was mighty wet air as far as that goes but there wasn't quite enough water in it to drown a feller. We went splashing under again, up and out, down and under, over and over. After this had gone on for what seemed like about two long years I happened to remember hearing one old cowboy say a horse could swim better if you hung onto his tail instead of the saddle horn. They are only about two yards apart, but getting from that horn to that tail wasn't any simple act.

I had to take the gamble. If I missed I was a gone dog and I knew it. I turned loose and grabbed! One hand caught tail hair! I was washed sideways and every other way. By this time I was sure there was as much water in me as there was out of me. Somehow I hung on and got hold with my other hand. Everything was muddy at this point, including my memory.

A long time later, at least it seemed a long time later, I noticed a horse's hind leg next to my face. I counted one, two, three, four horse's legs. Then I realized I was lying in the mud and Old Snip was standing there with his head down, his sides bellowing in and out, breathing hard. I didn't mind that old sticky mud. No, siree, not one bit. I rightly loved it. I got up and put my arm across that bay pony's neck. I didn't say anything. I didn't have to. I knew he understood.

We stayed all night over at the line camp. Even if we were hungry and a little cold I didn't mind and I hope Old Snip didn't.

The next day about noon I rode up to Ed Young's place and let out a yell. He walked out, or I should say a hat came out with him walking under it, because he wore the biggest hat I ever saw. It was a real, honest-to-goodness old-time cowboy hat.

I said, "Robert Ian sent you this here horse," and I handed him the bill of sale. The best eyes in the world couldn't have made out what that piece of paper said. That old Long Draw mud and water had seen to that. "Reckon you'll have to get him to make you out another one," I said, tickled plumb to death. I figured I still had a chance somehow to come up with the wherewithal to own Old Snip for my very own. I told Ed what had happened, then I said, "Say, Robert Ian said you might be needing a hand."

"I might," he said, looking at me with those gleaming blue eyes across that hawk-looking, humped-up nose. "What can you do, boy?" he asked pointblank.

"Hell," I said, "I can do anything."

Several weeks later I knew that this was not exactly the whole truth. I know now that I stayed on at Ed's in the beginning because I wanted to be with Old Snip, but later on I liked it all the way around. That evening I helped him feed the horses and milk the cows. After supper I got up and helped his wife with the dishes.

This set real good with Mother. All the cowboys in the country called her Mother Young because she was such a top-notch cook, doctor, and anything else a woman had to be to make a good wife and mother thirty miles from town right smack dab in the middle of all outdoors.

Ed had some good horses in his own right. He had broken broncs for the old Waggoner outfit in the early days and a lot of other big outfits, and he wouldn't have anything but good horses around him.

I got to ride and work with them all. There was Old Sut, a coal black twelve-year-old. You could ride him all day and he'd never even break a sweat. Then there was Flax, the golden-maned sorrel—a good range roping horse; Apache, the big hard-bucking paint; Raggedy Ann, the little brown mustang that Ed had roped and broke himself; and Frosty, a blaze-faced chestnut—Ed's favorite. When the cowboys spoke about Frosty they would always say, "That Frosty's quite a horse, yep, he's one hell of a horse."

But none of them compared with Old Snip. As time went on he just got better and better. You could ride him all day without wearing him out because of his fast easy gait. He reined like a regular cutting horse, quick, but smooth and easy. Boy, that stop he had! Those hind legs would slide way up under him with his forelegs shoved out in front and you didn't feel hardly any jar at all. He learned to work a rope. He kept his head looking down the rope all the time and the slack pulled out.

I learned to heel calves on him. Ed and I worked a lot just by ourselves. It sure makes a calf easier to throw and brand if you rope him by the heels. I was getting so I hardly missed a loop when riding Old Snip.

One day Ed said, "We're going down to Eldon Butler's and help him brand about fifty head. He's interested in buying Old Snip. We've got plenty of good horses around here and I need the money."

As we worked our way down out of the mountains towards Butler's I felt sort of sick. I cleared my throat and said, "Ed, how much you asking for Old Snip?"

"Aw, around a hundred I reckon the way he's turning out." He added, "Now, I really want you to show off what a heeling horse he is. That'll do more to sell him than anything else."

We cut the calves out from the mother cows and held them in a pole corral. The mothers bawled to beat sixty and stirred up a lot of dust. The branding irons were heating in an open fire. Eldon was getting the black leg vaccine ready and Ed was sharpening his knife getting ready to castrate the bull calves, except one they picked out for a breeding bull because of his good conformation and markings.

I was thinking, a hundred dollars, at the rate I was getting paid, I would be a hundred years old before I had it saved up. I really didn't feel any extra love in my heart right at that moment for Eldon Butler. He was a fine feller too.

Ed yelled, "We're ready, boy."

I rode out among the calves on Old Snip. He eased in till we had one in the right position, then I dropped a slow loop under one of the big bull calves. Most fellers make the mistake of throwing too fast a loop to be good heelers. You've got to kinda let it float down. Then just as the hind legs move against the loop you pull the slack and you've got him. The big calf began bucking and bellering but I turned Old Snip and dragged it to the fire. Eldon ran up and got hold of his tail and over he went.

Pretty soon you could smell the hair burning where they put the brand to him. Ed castrated, earmarked, and vaccinated him while Eldon held. I let them have the slack, and the finished product got up shaking his head wondering what in the world had happened to him.

I caught four in a row and felt kind of proud of myself until I noticed Eldon looking at Old Snip with mighty admiring eyes. I don't know what happened after that but it was the worst branding I ever attended. It took me about nine loops to catch every calf and even when I did, it looked like Old Snip and me couldn't keep from getting tangled up in the rope.

It was something or other all the time. I reckon that's the sorriest work we ever did together. I could see the disgusted look on Eldon's face. Ed was downright pale after all the braggin' he'd done about Old Snip. I guess we were all glad to get the job over with.

It was after dark when we unsaddled that night. I told Ed to go on in the house and wash for supper if he wanted to, I'd take care of the horses. I shucked out several ears of corn and forked some hay in the manger. I stood there in the dark awhile and smelled Old Snip. He smelled just like a horse, but not just any old horse.

There always seems to be just a little bit of fun mixed up with all the trouble we have, like the time I sat up on Old Snip and looked at a white faced cow as if she were some sort of varmint. The fall before, we had moved all Ed's cows down out of the mountains to the home pasture for the winter. We didn't move them all at one time, I can tell you that.

Ed had a grazing permit on national forest land and those cows were scattered out in small bunches over about 200,000 acres of mountains, hills, canyons, rocks and timber, but all the rest of his herd put together was easier to round up than this one old cow. She always took off into the thickest timber or down some rough canyon. She was nothing but trouble, so that's what we named her.

Now there she was out in the bog. There was plenty of grass on the outside but she had to go fall off in it, and now if I didn't drag her out pretty soon she'd sink out of sight. I took the leather loop from the saddle horn and unwound the three wraps from the catch rope. I tied one end of the rope to my saddle horn and built a loop in the other end.

I whirled it a couple or three times and let it go. I had to catch her horns if I was going to be able to let her loose by myself. The loop settled down just where I wanted it and I spurred Old Snip in the opposite direction. Nothing moved. Old Trouble was really bogged down. I began to do some solid cussin' and sweatin'.

After awhile the old fool inched up out of the bog a little bit. "Now, Snip!" I yelled, "Now!" Old Snip threw all his weight against that rope and out she came. She struck dry ground running and hit the end of the rope hard. Old Snip was braced. I felt the back of the saddle raise and pull the flank cinch tight against Old Snip's belly.

Now, in the first place I should never have tried this by myself. In the second place I should never have got off Old Snip without somebody around, but that's exactly what I did. Old Snip backed fast, moving right and left trying to keep the rope tight. I worked in from the side trying to get to Trouble's head slightly behind her horns. She was slobbering at the mouth, shaking her head, and straining with all she had against the rope. Her main idea was to run one of those sharp horns right square through me.

I finally got to her and gripped down with all my strength on her muzzle with one hand, twisting and holding a horn with the other. She slung me around, but I stayed with her and pretty soon when she made a run forward there was some slack in the rope. I jerked hard and the loop came off her horns. I made a run for Old Snip and Trouble made a run for me. I could feel the breeze across my hind end as she went by.

To this day I've never mounted as fast. Even then I was a mite slow. Trouble turned back and ran her horns under Old Snip's flank. He leaped up and away! I almost fell off. She made a couple more wild passes at us before she turned and trotted. I reckon that was her way of thanking us for saving her life.

Old Snip learned to work in timber. It got so I could tell when and what he smelled even when we couldn't see it. For instance, if it was a coyote or some other varmint out in the brush, he would throw one ear forward and then the other while looking toward the scent. If it happened to be cattle hiding in the brush, his neck would arch and he would pull over toward them. This saved lots of riding and looking in rough country. If it was a bunch of horses, he got a little extra excited and quickened his gait.

One day we got lost. I did, anyway. Suddenly I didn't know exactly where we were. The country looked different than I'd ever seen it. I noticed the fast-moving clouds above. Then everything was solid gray.

The wind came first in big gusts, then the snow. It hit wet, cold, and mean. It was a blowing snow. I turned back down out of the high country, but I didn't really know where we were headed. First, the ground covered over; then the tree limbs began to pick it up. Every once in a while a big shower of snow would fall on us out of the trees when the wind shook it loose. My hands were getting numb in my thin leather gloves, and my nose and ears were beginning to sting. The snow came on thicker and thicker.

I reined Old Snip this way, then that. It just didn't do any good. I had to admit I was completely lost. The blizzard never let up, in fact, it was just getting started. Before long I could just barely see Old Snip's thick black mane out in front of me. He was plowing along with his head low. The snow was drifting. Sometimes we'd go in up over my boot tops.

Finally I let Old Snip have his head. I just sat in the saddle and hoped he didn't fall off a sheer bluff. Soon I didn't feel anything. It wasn't so bad. Then I remembered hearing that was the time of greatest danger. So, I began to move my arms back and forth, back and forth, faster and faster, until I couldn't hold them up any longer. Then there was just a world of cold white, with Old Snip and me right in the middle of it.

I sat a long time wondering why Old Snip didn't keep moving. Maybe he'd frozen stiff standing up! Then there it was—a gate, by doggies. It was the horse pasture gate into Ed Young's Rafter E Y Outfit.

After I fed Old Snip about three times as much as he could eat and stood with my hind end so close to the fireplace it just about scorched, I ate the biggest batch of Mother Young's hot biscuits, sow belly, and pinto beans that a man ever wrapped himself around. That was twice Old Snip had saved my life. I don't know how he found his way down out of that world of frozen white, but he did.

I worked for the San Cristobal outfit off and on on a loan out for a few years and then somebody got the idea I should go off and get some book learnin'. I had to leave Old Snip behind.

Ed sold him after I left to some rich Texas ranchers. Of course Ed didn't know him as well as I did or he'd never have done it.

I never did get a bill of sale to Old Snip, but I felt he was mine just the same. He belonged to me then and he does now— wherever he is.

Showdown at Hollywood Park
August 6, 1947

The race was at Hollywood Park, and it was a classic. In its excitement, color, conniving, and later importance, it had to be one of the top-matched quarter horse races of all time. The head-on bet of one hundred thousand dollars by the owners was chicken sprinkling compared to the vast amounts gambled on the side by the country boys for their favorite brush-track quarter horse, Barbara B, and the city slickers for their imported thoroughbred, Fair Truckle.

It all began in Texas. Barbara B's trainer, Lyo Lee, was in Houston waiting to see if the Texas legislature would legalize pari-mutuel betting in the state. The racing crowd was eagerly anticipating success. Lyo was there to have his horses ready before anyone else, but the bill failed to pass, leaving Lyo with twenty-five good horses and not much to do but try to scare up a few match races. That's when the call came from Ray Bell that would start it all.

Ray was a commission buyer, mainly in Europe, for such stables as C. S. Howard, the wealthy San Francisco entrepreneur and owner of Fair Truckle; and Louis B. Mayer, the movie mogul head of MGM Studios. At that time, Mayer was the highest-paid corporate officer in America, drawing down over a million a year. He had many stars under contract—Clark Gable, Joan Crawford, Spencer Tracy and Katherine Hepburn, to name a few. Just four years later the iron-fisted Mr. Mayer would see his power begin to erode because of his love for horses and horse racing.

Lyo and Ray Bell were long-time friends, but even if they hadn't been, Mr. Lee would have given him a good listening, This man dealt with wheels . . . the kind that breathe the dust that money is made from.

Ray knew Lyo was looking for some races, so he passed on the comments C. S. Howard had made about his fancy horse, Fair Truckle, after winning a thoroughbred race and leading from wire to wire. "When you go all the way to Ireland to buy a horse you're going to race in the U.S.A., you expect him to be good, and I'd like to see some of those smart-ass quarter horse men try to take him." Fair Truckle was good. He was unbeaten. He'd shown the roots of his tail to all contestants.

After the phone conversation with Ray, Lyo got moving. He called Barbara B's owner, Roy Gill, and told him they had a good chance to get a big win here if they played it right.

Roy Gill's Arizona family had huge cattle feed lots and farms all over. They were *big*. Roy got into racing with Lyo as his trainer, buyer, and all around man, so he could have extra money—lots of it—to play with. He didn't want to draw money from the family empire just to gamble with. He knew this would be heavily resented. He lived the highest life his winnings could buy wherever he was. There were always lots of lovely ladies in his presence, and some of these were escorted by men with much political muscle and moola.

Roy Gill didn't especially care about the art or sport of racing. It was a money machine to him. He expected to win and Lyo Lee delivered for him over ninety-five percent of the time. Gill wouldn't bet less than ten thousand a race. So, with anything below that Lyo was on his own. Gill took care of all expenses and Lyo received ten percent of the winnings, including the side bets made by Gill. Since Lyo was one of the best trainers in the world (he finally wound up with over 5,000 lifetime wins) and Roy was one of the finest spenders, it was a marriage made in horse heaven. At one time their stable had five of the top ten quarter horses listed in the *Quarter Horse Journal*. Among them were Tonta Gal and the great horse Pelican. When they cemented their partnership, Roy Gill had only one instruction for Lyo, "Win."

Lyo had some advice for Gill as well, "Anytime we find a horse that can outrun you, buy him. This rapidly eliminates the competition."

In further phone conversations with Ray Bell, Lyo learned that C. S. Howard wanted to run Fair Truckle at anything they had, but would bet no less than fifty thousand dollars with ten thousand up front as forfeit money. That put a lot of pressure on Lyo. He wasn't about to recommend to Gill they match the race until he'd done a thorough job of checking.

He went first to the Racing Year Book. Fair Truckle had been running at good West Coast tracks: Santa Anita, Golden Gate, and Hollywood Park. These tracks were all clocked with electric timers and the year book gave the exact time at every turn and quarter pole. These tracks all had a running start of twenty to seventy feet from the gate before the timer started. At Hollywood Park that distance was forty-nine feet. Fair Truckle was running the first quarter in 21.3 and 21.4 and had never been behind up to the three quarter pole.

Barbara B had never been timed with a running start. So Lyo got ready and gave her a go with the forty-nine foot advance. Well guess what? Her time would make scavengers and gold watch makers look wildly around and rub their hands together. Twenty-one flat, it was, and on a lot worse race track than the Irish-bred Fair Truckle had been using. Interest picked up around the Roy Gill and Lyo Lee stables like a banker's loan. Lyo didn't want this information spread around, but he wasn't worried. He said, "I had my help tied up so I could control 'em . . . not exactly a dictator, but close."

Lyo called Ray Bell and told him, "We'll run Fair Truckle in Texas for a hundred thousand." Gill was putting up fifty of this and a few close friends were picking up the other half.

Howard turned this down. He said he would only race at Hollywood Park under their rules and with their officials. He said he didn't want to risk such a valuable horse on rough country tracks. After further consultation with Lyo, Gill agreed to go to California. Then another of the many more snags came up. California pari-mutuel racing was only for thoroughbreds, not quarter horses, so the Racing Commission refused to let them race during the meet or any other time. However, the go-between, Ray Bell, went to Louis B. Mayer and some of his rich, politically powerful cohorts, and an agreement was finally reached that the race could be run on Monday, August 6, 1947, the day after the big meet closed.

Gill, Lyo, jockey Tony Licata, Barbara B, and the rest of the crew arrived in California with everyone doing his own special job. Roy's was a little easier than the rest—he was there to gamble and have fun. He was a master at the latter and with Lyo Lee's help, first rate at the former.

Roy Gill had let his sixteen-year-old daughter come to the races with him. She wanted to be in on the thrill of mixing with the Hollywood celebrities and high rollers. She mixed a little too well to suit her father. One of the younger men of the thorough-bred group mesmerized her into falling in love with him. Gill tried, to no avail, to convince her that the young man only wanted inside information about the race. To prove it, Gill offered to bet the suitor five thousand dollars, headup. Surprisingly, he took the bet.

By now word was out all over the quarter horse world about the big race. Phones rang back and forth from the California stables to all points, concerning every little rumor and chip of gossip. The match-race crowd, the bookies, the habitual and the part-time gamblers were all astir anticipating the day of action with almost a carnal craving. Finally the old, old question about the difference between a quarter horse and a thoroughbred had a chance to be answered. The press was picking up on the vast interest and excitement this race was creating. This put even more charge in the betting batteries.

C. S. Howard resided in San Francisco, so Lyo Lee drew up the contract himself and flew up to deliver it personally. The substance of it was that they'd use the seven and nine gates set exactly on the quarter pole. The post position would be decided in the paddock after the horses were saddled. This way no one would have the time or opportunity to alter the track to his own advantage. On a few rare occasions at match races, when the gate number had been decided in advance, the ground had been dug up Soft and deep in front of it and then smoothed over to look untouched.

Howard admitted he was afraid that some of these match race guys would attempt to trick him, so Lyo tried, in front, to make everything as up-and-up as possible. He included everything— the money, the track timer, the officials—that had already been verbally agreed. In spite of all Lyo's care, Howard refused the contract. He insisted the gates be left where they were—forty-nine feet back of an even quarter mile.

This would change the outside bettor's opinion of the race, most agreeing that the longer it was, the better chance Fair Truckle had. Howard and his people figured that Barbara B would slow at the quarter marker whether she was ahead or behind, and be slowing every foot after.

Lyo argued that this gate situation hadn't been mentioned until now and he complained, truthfully, that they would be out a lot of money in time, travel, and wages if the race was called off now. It did no good. Howard was adamant. He was what the town fellers call a "worthy adversary." Howard was a tough and clever man. He was also rich and powerful, having bailed General Motors out of a hole after World War I. He got a large block of stock and a percentage of every GMC car sold in California.

Lyo flew back to see Gill in L.A. feeling like he'd swallowed a bee hive—honey, bees, and all. He convinced Roy that they could beat Fair Truckle anyway, because he already knew that Barbara B could go three eighths. Lyo had saved back this secret information to put with his other forty-nine-foot ace he had in the hole.

Lyo flew back to San Francisco, and told Howard, "Well, it was tough, but I've finally convinced my people to go along with your terms."

Howard okayed the contract and they each deposited ten thousand dollars with the Racing Commission in L.A. If one defaulted before post time, he lost the money and, of course, there would be no race. The rest of the money was to be put up on race day. Then after they left the paddock everybody was on his own provided there wasn't an official foul in the actual race. The latter was included in the contract. They would take urine and saliva tests after the race as well. There would be no pari-mutuel betting, but the gates were open free to everyone.

The electricity was bouncing through the air. This race was crucial to advancing the status of the quarter horse, and could be the vital element needed for the legislature to pass the bill accepting the quarter horse into the parimutuel race tracks. At this time, the only places they could run under the pari-mutuel system were Tucson and Albuquerque.

It was in Albuquerque, in fact, that Lyo discovered Barbara B. She was entered in a handicap. Tom Snow owned her and they happened to be in the stall next to Lyo. He noticed, when they were shoeing her, that her feet were extra tender. She came in fourth, even with her feet in that condition. Lyo knew that here was a hell of a horse. He bought her for Roy Gill, at the extremely high price for the day of six thousand dollars. Barbara B was out of the stud Bar Hunter II and a Wagonner Ranch mare with rumors abounding that the dam had once sold for thirty dollars. Lyo patiently got her feet in shape and they started winning races.

Cal Kennedy, a horse trainer friend of Lyo's, came to him about a week before the "big 'un" with some information he thought Lyo might enjoy cogitating upon. Lyo knew Cal to be a knowledgeable man who would take every legal advantage to win a race—as who didn't in this world of worried inches.

Kennedy trained a horse named Three Bars. He'd run him three times against Fair Truckle at five eighths. Each race Fair Truckle had taken him, but also each time Three Bars had been lapped onto him at the quarter mile pole. Now Kennedy was all for his old friend Lyo, but he wanted to make a bunch of money by gobbling up a cinch. He explained that the only way to do this was to run Barbara B and Three Bars. If she couldn't take him, then the Gill and Lee stables better forfeit their ten grand and head for Texas, turning back a few thousand bettors on their way out. A dilemma, indeed. Lyo was under a glorious type of pressure from all angles.

"How much will she have to outrun Three Bars to be a contender against Fair Truckle?" Lyo asked Kennedy.

"A couple of lengths," he replied.

To keep Barbara B company, Lyo had hauled Tonto Gal out in the trailer and stabled her right next to the mare at Hollywood Park. Lyo didn't really want to give away any of his position, but when he made up his mind to go with something, he put all he had into it. He decided to run Tonto Gal with Barbara B and Three Bars.

Very early that morning, a lot of racebarn folks saw the three horses heading for the quarter pole in front of the gate and being lined up for the run. People were yelling and looking for stopwatches to time the race. (just what Lyo didn't want to happen.) Over a hundred of them watched the event.

Lyo decided to run Tonto Gal in case Barbara B got a bad start; he could still make a fair judgment because most of the time the two mares were only a head or neck apart.

Barbara B outran Three Bars by three lengths and Tonto Gal was lapped right on her. So now Lyo had what appeared to be a slick gut cinch . . . but instead of having 20- or 30-to-one odds, they were now dropping to even. Most of the track habituates knew Three Bars and a few seconds before had thought of Barbara B as a dog cow pony who Fair Truckle could outrun like breaking sticks. That had all changed. The word flew out like a West Texas sand storm.

The noted sports writer, Ned Cronin, who did stories for Pathe News and many large daily papers, dropped by the barn and asked Lyo, "Has she ever been in a starting gate?" Lyo answered, "Think so—once or twice before we got her, but I'm not sure." "Do you use a stock saddle or a racing saddle on her?" "Oh, whatever's handy." Lyo knew that Cronin was only halfway putting him on, but he liked the reporter and played the game with him. Cronin asked, 'Did you ever rope any calves or steers on her?" Lyo grinned and said truthfully, "Naw, I haven't rodeoed in years."

Lyo was having too many visitors around the barn now. Friends and acquaintances—hundreds of them—were beginning to arrive from all over the Southwest. The wealthier of these would be staying at the Coliseum Hotel on Figueroa Street in downtown L.A., because that's where Roy Gill and his "partying" party were headquartered. So were Lyo and his wife, but the last two nights he would stay at the barn with his horse. There were too many things that could happen to an unattended animal when hundreds of thousands of dollars were already laid down, and several million were yet to come. Lyo's pressures increased hourly.

Then another, more deadly form of squeeze play, unexpectedly entered the game. Two finely dressed men came to the barn. One carried a large black leather folding bag. With extreme politeness they asked to speak with Lyo in private. He took them to the tack room.

The man placed the bag down, saying, "You see this? It contains five hundred thousand dollars. Now all we want is a guarantee. Just guarantee us which horse will win the race and this bag and its contents is yours."

Lyo felt like he'd been gored by a Spanish bull; and he heard the gates of heaven swing shut behind him at the same time. After a bit, he convinced the two money men that he'd need the night to think it over. They reluctantly agreed and left.

Now, there was only one way he could guarantee the outcome of the race and that, of course, was to have the jockey hold the mare back. In spite of the race tests with Three Bars, where they were as close to a cinch as they could get, many strange things could happen to cost a man the race. Lyo had been in the game too long and too intensely not to know this.

He would spend a rough night. With a half a million dollars, he could go to a tropical island and be a minor king. He could envision the dancing girls and feel the soft warm sea breezes. Various temptations oscillated before his eyes, and he was truly entranced. On the other hand, he wouldn't be free to roam the country matching races anymore. The excitement of having a horse come from behind in the stretch and pound on to win with good odds would no longer be his. Doubt settled in like a Malibu fog. Then, too, there were all the people he'd dealt with over the years who had faith in his talents . . . most of them here at

Hollywood Park now betting on his abilities as a trainer. The golden sparkling thoughts of the islands washed caressingly across him again. Indecision. Agony.

The next morning he told the bag men to forgive him, but he just couldn't go along. Surprisingly, they made only one more pitch, then left. Of course, Lyo would feel a chilled ghost over his shoulder until the race was run.

The flag was to fall at 2:25 that afternoon. By eleven o'clock that morning there were over five thousand people at the track to watch the only race for the day. The final number of the gathering was estimated by different writers to be between 7,000 and 25,000, Lyo Lee figured the unpaid attendance at about 20,000. It was a tentless circus. Heavy newspaper coverage had brought a lot of the spectators, but several thousand were there by word-of mouth. The quarter horse enthusiasts from every southwestern state showed up to back their favorite Barbara B. The West Coast thoroughbred people and the rich, clubby followers of the financial wizard, C. S. Howard (justifiably known as Mr. Seabiscuit), arrived in even greater force. They didn't have as far to come, however.

This was an unofficial meet . . . two horses and one race. The money would either flow from the pockets of the booted, broganed, wrinkled suit crowd to the Brooks Brothers and silk shirt set, or vice versa.

The Fair Truckle followers were almost smug in their betting-and why not? They'd never seen anything ahead of their hero in nine races from wire to wire. The quarter horse boosters were more enthusiastic. One was heard to say that the brown, four-year-old mare could beat that "Eurrrupeein' horse pullin' a plow." Another said, showing considerable confidence, that Barbara B could win by a length and stop twice to graze on the way.

The movement of mouths and tongues was matched by arms and hands reaching in and out of pockets counting money and layin' it down. There was a vast kaleidoscope of color, erratic and pulsating movement, and a chattering symphony of sound made up of laughter, bantering, bragging, and ridicule. It was almost as if two massive brains were in mortal money-crazed conflict: one controlling the Fair Truckle crowd and the other manipulating the Barbara B bunch. It would finally boil down, though, to the more concentrated grey matter of the city-sharpened Mr. Howard and the brush and bramble seasoned Mr. Lee. The fact that Howard had bought the great horse Seabiscuit when he appeared to be no good and with his trainer had turned him into one of the fastest of all stake racers also enhanced this race.

The jockeys and horses are always expected to give their best in every race, but according to a perpetual race track yarn that started that day, Tony Licata could collect all honors for the most dedicated jockey of all. He was having trouble making the 114-pound weight for the race, so it was bandied about that he went out and had all his teeth pulled to lessen the pounds. (He did ride the race without his dentures.) Here was a racehorse man from the hocks to the gums. He was getting $8,000 for the race, win or lose. He'd bet every penny of it.

The even money was changing hands by the barrel, and the only way to get odds was to bet on the length of the win. That's the way it was until the horses entered the paddock. It took two men to hold Fair Truckle while he was readied, while Barbara B, always the lady, took the money-changing madness around her with such calmness that she looked like a sleepy, dead-headed cow pony. Deception unlimited. Between the paddock and the starting gate the Barbara B clan got odds on hundreds of thousands of dollars at four or five to one. Lyo had held off betting until this moment. Again figuring ahead, he had a friend get down ten thousand for him at three to one.

Billions of tiny bolts of lightning were heating the blood of thousands of people with the oldest passion in the world—contest fever. Unless there was a dead heat, one horse would have to chase the other.

As agreed in the contract, they had to flip a coin for the choice of a post position . . . gates nine and seven. Lyo was anxious to win the toss. Fair Truckle, having always come out of the gate ahead and leading all the way, naturally charged to the rail—the shortest route around the track. So, if he had to cut across from the nine gate instead of the seven, he would have a little bit more ground to cover. Lyo Lee's mother had not raised an unthinking son. He had taken this into consideration. Neither had C. S. Howard's mama birthed a son without the thought process. Where Lyo was hoping to gain maybe a few feet with the gate choice, C. S. had already fudged in a forty-nine-yard head start. Lyo won the coin toss and picked the number seven gate.

Now the horses left the paddock and the thoroughbred crowd became more fired up because Fair Truckle was prancing and dancing, led by a pony horse whose rider was having a little trouble. Barbara B just strolled along with her head down and the reins slack like a worn-out ranch horse.

The track looked fast, but Lyo had tested it carefully and found it cushiony underneath. He told the groom that there'd be no timed records set today, but the money being bet would break all gambling records on a match race.

Because he'd won the seven gate, Lyo loaded the mare first. She stood there calmly. Fair Truckle, on the other hand, was really acting up. When they finally got him in, he hung a hock in the gate. So they had to let him out and walk him around to see if he was all right. Several thousand hearts froze! He didn't limp, so they decided to go ahead and run him. During this little ceremony, Barbara B seemed to be catnapping.

They were off! Barbara B was neither a fast starter nor a slow one. Fair Truckle came out of the gate a good neck in the lead. There was just one thing though as Lyo had said:

"Barbara B reached full speed at the third jump and would be running faster at that point than any horse I'd ever seen. She was also hitting a stride of twenty-four and a half feet by then . . . I'd measured it many times. And that's how she won most of her races."

Because of the extra forty-nine feet, the gates were set back in a straight-away chute from the main track. By the time they hit that point, Barbara B had leaped out in front by a little over a length.

The great jockey, Johnny Longden, felt he now had a problem. He sure did! Fair Truckle had never been hit with the whip. Since he was always out front, there had never been a reason for it. Now there was, Longden figured. When he tapped Fair Truckle, he ducked in behind Barbara B and went to the rail. That move increased Barbara B's lead by another length as Lyo had anticipated.

The country crowd went slap dab crazy. The stadium waltzed and the air was shredded into slivers by the roar. Fair Truckle really put out. He pulled up almost neck and neck and held there.

Now it was the thoroughbred's touts turn to shake the earth and create vacuums in the air. The horses were sailing along on even terms so that now everyone could go mad at once.

Then! Then Tony Licata smacked Barbara B right across her gear box with the whip. Ned Cronin wrote about it in the *Los Angeles Daily News* the next day.

"Somewhere in Barbara B's clouded past there is a jack rabbit among her forebears. There's got to be. How else could she cut loose with a jump that almost took her out of her hide? As that jack rabbit blood bubbled and boiled through her veins, she sprang with a few such prodigious leaps that they carried her under the wire an easy winner by two and a half lengths in the respectable time of 21 and 3/5ths seconds."

Payday at the mines! Wild and good times for the Barbara B's. Lyo Lee, Tony Licata, and the lady with four fast legs had delivered the baby full grown. Most of the winners had traveled hundreds of miles to bet and sweat their all on less than twenty-two seconds. They'd sliced up C. S. Howard's thoroughbred club elites like venison jerky. The Final Score: Country team—several million. City team—zero.

There was great rejoicing in and around the Coliseum Hotel that night. Other areas of Los Angeles rang out with resounding victory yells and toasts before the grass and plow folks headed back home.

Roy Gill patted his daughter's suitor on the back as he collected his five thousand, and said, "Why, you're a fine young feller. You come visit us in Arizona some year, you hear."

Aside from the money, the real significance of the event was that it woke the racing world up to the fact that among all its other multiple and supreme abilities, the quarter horse was also a race horse. The momentum this highly visible, publicized race gave to the entire quarter horse industry is incalculable.

Ned Cronin and a lot of other journalists broke this fact to the world the next day with satirical force. Too few people remember that this race was instrumental in the legislature legalizing quarter horse pari-mutuel racing in the state of California.

Barbara B went on winning races, but she lost one to Miss Princess in Del Rio, Texas, after stepping on a small round rock and falling to one knee with her nose touching the ground. She still got up and made the acknowledged King Ranch Best in the World Champion run for it. In 1950, after Miss Princess retired, Lyo ran the seven-year-old Barbara B against the four-year-old mare, Stella Moore, for the generally agreed championship of the world at Sunshine Park, in Oldsmar, Florida. Again the national press, including *Time* magazine, picked up on the story and made several million more people aware of the quarter horse. Barbara B won the 330-yard race by a length and a half in 17.1 seconds.

All this is and should be recognized as a permanent part of quarter horse history. It was a vital part of the action that eventually led to the richest races in the world at Ruidoso Downs, New Mexico, and to the King Ranch recently purchasing the two millionth registered quarter horse. Considering the involvement of the West Germans and other countries around the world, in breeding and using of this very special breed, the number of three million or more will someday be announced. Even so, it will shower tubs full of hail in hell before a more momentous and exciting race will come along than the great matched shoot-out at Hollywood Park in August of 1947.

Lyo Lee and Barbara B—they made H-I-S-T-O-R-Y.

The Wild Bunch

Hollywood. The name conjures up images of the sky sliced apart by great blades of crisscrossing lights signaling—no, heralding—glamorous world premieres, limo after limo arriving and disgorging the famous, the perfectly beautiful as they absorb the adulation of thousands of pushing, screaming, worshipful subjects with flashing still cameras and hungry camcorders.

The name brings to mind emerald pools by white castles in Beverly Hills, Bel Air and other posh suburbs. We automatically envision Rolls Royces, Mercedes and Jaguars purring, slick and shiny as silk panthers along the palm tree-lined roadways where the sun always shines and the lawns are always thick green, and the wallets are the same.

The name evokes mind-images of cameras rolling as magic is created. Yes, magic and money, tons of money, where anything less than $1.5 million per picture salary makes you a character actor on the B-list.

Daily we are overdosed by the media with millions of blinding white teeth, thousands of long, tanned female legs and bounteous bosoms, and men with biceps and pectorals so thick and heavy they can break a score of large men into pulp in 30 seconds and lift pistols as big as cannons, blowing up entire blocks of buildings, vehicles and people into flaming oblivion to the rhythm of orchestral music that makes the sound of thunder seem timid. Lights, camera, action!

It ain't always like this.

Now as I look back, trying to pick out three or four incidents to sort of highlight my 30-odd-year association with Hollywood, I'm a tad indecisive. Should I relate my first meetings with actor Fess Parker (*Davy Crockett*) and one of America's great directors, William Wellman *(The High and The Mighty* and *The Ox-Bow Incident)*, on trying to film my book *The Rounders?* Or would it be

357

interesting to tell how in 1961 I was kicked out of Beverly Hills' last cheap hotel because I couldn't pay my rent in advance and then stood on the curb with my suitcase waiting for actor Morgan Woodward to come rescue me? I don't think so, because that would be a book in itself. We had lots of mad fun and survived 90 days on $500 worth of crackers, peanut butter and bourbon until he got a job on a Western series and I optioned a short story and was able to buy a train ticket back to Taos to begin again.

What should I tell? There are hundreds of incidents that had a little gleam to them with such film folk as Brian Keith *(The Westerner, Family Affair, The Wind and the Lion)*, Jim Hutton, Henry Fonda, Pat Hingle and close observations of such opposites as Jason Robards and Slim Pickens. Numberless.

I could relate in grinding detail how we formed the governor's first film commission to lure movies to New Mexico and how, when it stalled, I foolishly volunteered—on my own money and time—to go to Hollywood and set up a breakfast meeting in the late '60s at the Beverly Hills Hotel between filmmakers and the New Mexico Commission. How 57 major producers, directors and heads of three studios showed up at that meeting. Gov. David Cargo, being a natural-born actor, gave a great performance speech and the rest of the commission was pay-dirt charming. Luck! It worked! New Mexico is over the billion dollar mark in total returns today.

Perhaps I could relate a few happenings with some who on many occasions had been blackballed—those on the outside of the system, which just naturally brings to mind director Sam Peckinpah, the most vivid, insane, brilliant, maddening, black sheep bastard of them all.

Sam was shooting a Western TV movie called *The Losers*, starring Lee Marvin, Keenan Wynn and Rosemary Clooney. He borrowed several scenes from my book *The Hi Lo Country*. But that was all right, he had optioned and paid me fairly good money for *The Hi Lo Country* so many times we both lost count. Marvin read my book and wanted Sam to introduce us at *The Losers* wrap party outside a soundstage at Republic. I was honored and delighted. So much so that I invited the world-renowned painter Hugh Cabot III (now of Tubac, Arizona) to accompany me. The introductions didn't happen that day. Lee was drunk and couldn't remember his lines. So instead, he would sing the Marine hymn loudly. All the skilled people, nervous technicians, nervous actors and a surprisingly patient Peckinpah cajoled and pleaded with Lee to finish the last shot. Sam worked beyond any call of duty and slave-drove everyone else. They were all gut-weary-tired, yet tingling with anticipation of relaxing with the bountiful repast Sam had so generously supplied on a long table filled with Oriental delicacies from The Polynesian restaurant. Another table was loaded down with booze and a huge keg of beer. That's how it was in those days.

I suffered for the others and said to Cabot, "I wonder why one of those big old stuntmen doesn't whack Lee behind the ear just enough to knock him sensible?" You see, I hadn't yet really caught on to the power of the star system. Just as all seemed doomed, Sam said, "Print it. It's a wrap."

There was this mighty collective sigh of relief among the 70 or 80 people. Then something happened that shocked me to the liver. Lee was moving toward the booze table like Moses parting the Red Sea. He was roaring out a semblance of something between a great tenor choking in midnote and a bulldozer scraping granite. He stopped, suddenly silent. Swaying, he looked at the table of delicious food and then at the other table. He made up his pickled mind, erratically reached for a bottle, then with his free hand tipped the table over.

There was a horrified choking back of anguish from the film-making folk. Hugh (yes, from the speak-only-to-God Cabots) straightened his tie and the collar of his Brooks Brothers suit and the two of us dashed over to try and save the evening by righting the table and retrieving the few unbroken bottles. Others joined in the rescue efforts.

Lee wove on with his private bottle across the vast studio lot singing unintelligible songs and shouting certain profanities with a slight blue tinge to the uncaring sky. Sam handed a reluctant man a bill and said, "Take care of Lee. He's brooding."

As nerves settled some and food and drink worked their eternal soothing magic, I heard one stuntman express quietly my very thought. "I thought about bull-dogging him and tying him up, but then good sense kicked in and I changed my mind,"

Hugh turned to me and said, "Ahh, now I know why they call it the entertainment business."

The wrap party wrapped.

Cabot went on to Mexico City to visit some bullfighter friends. I stayed working my survival tactics in and out the environs of Sunset Boulevard.

I officially met Lee in a joint on Sunset called La Taverna. It was habituated by actors, a few producers and other vagrants such as writers like myself. Lee had a corner barstool and a private flamenco guitar player. After I introduced myself he politely asked me to join him.

We visited about trout fishing in the New Mexico mountains versus Pacific deep-sea fishing. To his credit Lee gave some attention to the guitar player and was polite when asked for autographs. He was gracious about a couple of women sticking notes in his jacket pocket. One did it twice. He did not encourage this at all. The woman's companion accused Lee of being a phony, and a fake, movie tough guy. We ignored this, enjoying a laugh or so about our mutual friend Sam Peckinpah when the man put his hand on Lee's shoulder pulling him around to verbally drive home his many contentious points. With a speed to do rockets and hummingbird wings justice, Lee kneed him in the crotch, whacked him with an open hand up side the head, grabbed the guitar from the talented and innocent musician and proceeded to bend it around the man's neck like an object in a Salvador Dali painting. This all happened before you could say, "Ouch."

My admiration increased when Lee picked up the victim, ordered a drink for him and the entire house, consoled the guitar player with a handful of bills and said, "Come on, Max, let's go to my house where we can drink in peace."

I went. He drove the huge black Chrysler all the way down the miles of curving Sunset Boulevard to his home at Pacific Palisades just like the Unsers when qualifying for the Indy 500. I wanted to jump out and race into oblivion, but I was too scared to make the necessary effort.

Lee proceeded to wake up his wife Betty to show her what he had dragged home this time. Me, a worn-out ex-cowboy, prospector, painter half drunk and still stiff from fright. Amazingly, Betty got up and was gracious to me. I said "to me." Somehow, because of his long time in combat with the Marine Corps in the South Pacific during World War II, his consequent tailbone wound and a long painful recovery in army hospitals, Lee would harbor no close friends unless they were combat veterans. Frequently, he brought home poor creatures in the middle of the night to introduce to Betty. He was mistaken about Sam whose Marine Corps duty was behind the lines. However, he had enough wars with booze, pills and studio executives to qualify. Among Lee's closest friends were Keenan Wynn, Jack Warden and

Neville Brand, all ground combat soldiers. The latter being the fourth most decorated warrior in World War II.

None of this mattered now to his wife. She served me drinks, conversing politely about numerous subjects, but the exchanges between her and Lee were satirically savage.

About four in the morning, Lee went upstairs to bed. Betty showed me to my room, said goodnight and then proceeded to forcefully pound out some sort of music on a piano in the room right next to mine, and directly under Lee's, until she fell asleep at the instrument.

I got up to check out the silence about the same instant Lee came bouncing down the stairs freshly shaved, showered and dressed, and freshly yelled "Hey Max, get your clothes on. I got an eight o'clock call."

With sandpaper eyes and a rolling stomach I listened to Lee chat on about deep-sea fishing—yeah, again—all the way to my motel, then he drove on to the studio as if nothing had happened. Nothing at all.

Oh yeah, I almost forgot, *The Losers* was shown six times during prime time in its first year and would have been turned into a series if Lee had agreed to the money. He didn't.

Several months later Sam would go direct a film in Mexico called *Major Dundee*. It was to be his Western epic. Instead it was a disaster of epic proportions. The film of a cavalry unit's pursuit of the Apaches into Mexico and consequent disastrous effects on the participants was a very big canvas indeed. It went over budget and many wars broke out besides those in the script. At one point Sam met a producer in the Mexico City airport, grinningly shook his hand, and while giving the proper *abrazos*, violently stripped the clothes from the man and left him standing naked before the gaze of all. The film was butchered in the editing. At least this once Sam was correct when he said they had cut the heart out of his huge child. Part of Peckinpah's heart was removed with it as well, never to be replaced. Even so, he had learned a lot, as some of his other great Westerns would soon reveal. The stars of *Major Dundee* were Charlton Heston, Richard Harris, Jim Hutton, James Coburn and a cast of the greatest character actors ever put together. Sam would use many of these actors over and over in his films. They included: Warren Oates, Ben Johnson, R. G. Armstrong, L. Q. Jones, Slim Pickens, Dub Taylor and the Mexican actress Begonia Palacias whom he would marry three times. A dream cast. A dream breaker.

In its butchered form *Major Dundee* bombed critically and financially, destroying Sam's career and soul to such a degree he never would fully recover. He had offered me a part in the film. I turned it down because I was writing a book. (I would later accept one of his acting offers, a part in *The Ballad of Cable Hogue* and publish a book about its filming.)

He generously asked me, my wife, Pat, and our twin daughters Charlotte and Sheryl, to baby-sit his unoccupied house on Malibu Beach, while he filmed and I wrote. We accepted the invitation, and temporarily moved from Taos to Malibu.

We were apprised, almost daily, of all the hell Sam was having on location, and gossip of every kind of disaster. Unfortunately most of these stories were true. Nevertheless, when he returned home he seemed in good spirits. He insisted that we stay and keep him company.

He invited Pat and me, his girlfriend, Keenan Wynn and Lee Marvin to a special dinner in Beverly Hills at one of those elite restaurants on Wilshire Boulevard where Cadillacs and Chryslers are ashamed to be seen—unless, of course Lee was driving it. This evening he was.

We had been served bountiful drinks and hors d'oeuvres, and I'm almost certain the conversation was scintillating. Since Sam was the young genius director of *Ride the High Country* and Lee and Keenan were thought of as stars by the management and waiters, the service was swift and a bit too deferential. But who could complain? We were all young creators of varying kinds and the world belonged to us, we just knew—and if it didn't it would. One should never have such gloating thoughts because just as you do either nature or human circumstance will knock you on your butt.

As the waiters approached with the main course Lee arose dramatically stating that a skilled master had taught him how to remove a tablecloth from under all these breakable objects without anything being broken, spilled or even displaced. The waiters placed their loaded trays on stands just as Pat and I saw everyone at the table scoot their chairs back. We did likewise—when in Rome . . . or Beverly Hills . . . .

Lee moved his hands about as if mentally weighing the objects on the table. Then he confidently grasped an edge of the red tablecloth. (I will remember this color red through many dimensions. I swear even now, I can hear a drumroll loud as empty bouncing barrels.) Then with a mighty gesture the cloth was

removed from the long table with Lee whirling it about him
gracefully like a bullfighter's cape. That part of the performance
had come off quite well. So had all the glasses, dishes, silverware
and remaining hors d'oeuvres. Things splattered and broke and
jingled and jangled for a radius that included the tables of several
other diners. A good journalist would say that pandemonium ensued. It didn't.

Never have I seen such efficiency. Everyone who worked in
the place instantly and magically cleaned up the entire mess and
we were all allowed to start over brand new. Sam placated the
manager and displaced patrons with calming words. No members of the law arrived, no fistfights occurred. Amazingly, everyone seemed to be pleased and entertained by the private sideshow.
Lee's only apology was said with a slightly puzzled air, "I don't
understand it. I must have been looking south."

Sam, with that thin grin of his that always belied what was in
his mind, asked Lee if he had any new fishing stories. The actor
immediately told how fish can read our minds and that they only
bite when you yourself are right with the world. If you were, they
would charge your hook by the schools. It went on from subject
to subject and we finished dinner with uneventful pleasure.

It was closing time. Sam and his lady left. Keenan left. Pat
and I stood talking to Lee for awhile. All the dining and drinking
places were closing up and down Wilshire as we drove our Buick
out of the parking lot, with Lee following in his heavy black Chrysler, into the suddenly heavy traffic. Our car died. Right there.

Impatient drunks immediately started blowing horns on an
entire herd of automobiles. Lee the Marine sergeant took instant
command.

Leaping from his car he directed traffic out of the way and
enlisted help to push our dead car back into the parking lot. He
did this swiftly and without raising his voice in anger. He took off
in a small run and stopped a passing cab, yelling back for us to
take his car—which he had left in the middle of all that traffic
with the motor running—and he'd be out to get it in a day or two.
He said he knew a place that was open all night. I wanted to go
with him but Pat escorted me to the Chrysler and drove us on to
Malibu.

The next day Sam drove us in and surprisingly our car started
right up without any bother. I knew for sure right then that inani-
mate objects do think and feel. That little Buick had taken

advantage of a chance to observe the wonderfully crazy ex-Marine and upcoming movie star in action.

Three days later Lee showed up in a cab at Malibu to retrieve his car. The visit was an entertaining one. At one point he proceeded to act out a cockfight. He convincingly played two fighting roosters by himself. He hopped around Sam's kitchen floor with imaginary wings, feet and feathers flying. Shakespeare and Tennessee Williams both would have applauded. We all did.

Our two girls and two of Sam's (all about the same age) came in from a playroom to watch the show. When Lee finished the act, he introduced himself to our 5-year-old daughters, Charlotte and Sheryl. They were polite, then Charlotte said, "Oh yes, I know you. I've seen you on TV a jillion times." Then they all whirled around and retreated to their room where they could finish playing their own games.

There is one place in Hollywood—the Polo Lounge in the Beverly Hills Hotel—that will always stand out. Howard Hughes and other movie and foreign royalty kept permanent bungalows at the hotel for whatever kind of frolicking they favored. More production and star deals have been cut in the Polo Lounge than anywhere else in the world, even though there are hundreds of other lounges that are more opulent. Why? Maybe because it is quietly elegant, has fine food, experienced help, available plug-in phones at the tables and many other services. Or maybe it's simply a habit that one gets used to like an afternoon nap or early morning coffee.

I had gone there several times for meetings and had actually sold an option on a short story and a short novel *Mountain of Gold*. It was during the delicate negotiations of the latter that I became acquainted with four mob figures and a pimp for high-class hookers. There were always at least two of the shady characters sitting at the relatively small bar from about one o'clock until around six in the evening, drinking, talking and taking many calls across the mahogany.

The pimp, I'll call him Geen for convenience, was about 5-foot-8, solidly stocky, impeccably dressed and genuinely polite and charming. He had wavy black hair above blue eyes that seemed perpetually amused at some private joke. He never sat down even when he took his calls from the private phone behind the bar.

Geen disliked the producer I was dealing with, summing him up as a cheapskate who never bought a drink for anyone but himself. So, when I finally got an option check from this fellow, I became a sort of instant hero and was never allowed to pay for another drink in the Polo Lounge as long as they were there. Convenient, huh?

Even back in the mid-'60s, Geen was handling $1,000-dollar-a-night girls. I saw a few of them actually keep rendezvous in the lounge as Geen proudly pointed them out. All were elegant. Without Geen's kindly observations I would never have known they were hookers.

At this time poor old Sam P. had been just as effectively blackballed as any of Sen. McCarthy's Hollywood "dozen" and was now doing what I had once done to survive: rewriting scripts without credit. Besides the countless tragedies associated with *Major Dundee*, producer Marty Ransahoff fired him from directing *The Cincinnati Kid*. The reason given: filming nudes at night. Actually Sam had called in a crew and shot scenes cut from the script of Ann-Margret nude under a fur coat.

Peckinpah called me at my motel room from his Broadbeach house. In a weak (purposely) voice, he explained in sad detail about writing scripts for little money and no credit and being so alone with no time or energy left to get a woman. He was almost crying. He knew I knew Geen. He wanted Geen's best hooker.

Without thinking other than a friend in trouble, I drove to the Polo Lounge in a rented car, found Geen and explained Sam's desires. Geen looked at me, with those sincere blue eyes putting a hand on my shoulder and said, "For such a friend as Mr. Peckinpah I will deliver the class of the show, top of the line all the way."

Well, I called Sam the good news from a pay phone feeling warm as you often do after a favor for a friend. He asked coldly, "How much?"

"A thousand at least. Probably more. This is his best, Sam." There was silence. "Well," I went on, "you said that's what you wanted." More silence. "Sam, what in hell do I tell Geen?"

"I'll meet you at the Malibu Holiday House at four o'clock this afternoon. Try to have her arrive between 4:30 and 5. I need a few minutes to talk business with you, okay?"

I made the arrangements hoping he had a movie deal going for us, I got there, ordered a drink and looked out the long window behind the bar at the contoured garden and the Pacific Ocean sparkling like a million tiny suns. I was graced with a nice warm feeling, by the beauty of the ocean, the cold scotch and the fact that even if I was acting as a go-between pimp, I had delivered for a friend.

Sam sort of snuck in, his head pulled down into his shoulders like a thin upright turtle. I ordered him a drink and he started cussing the sleazy producer he was doing the sleazy deadline work for. After a few minutes he said, "Now do you understand why I need a nice date without any complications?" I concurred, saying, "There she is now."

She wove her way, slim, supple and graceful as a Siamese cat, through the curving paths of the garden. She moved confidently into the place walking straight up to me as I stood and said "You must be Max." I found out later that Geen had told her to look for a guy with a busted face wearing cowboy boots. Introductions were completed. Sam had said nothing about a pending movie deal so I tried to leave, but he insisted I stay and have two drinks.

This gray-eyed lady had skin as smooth as a book jacket portrait, lightly tanned and everything about her suggested a top model who had simply gotten bored with the job. But her mind was another card. With a soft, controlled and confident voice she told Sam how she had enjoyed his TV movie *Pericles on 32nd Street* and then asked me about my novels—which of course, she like several billion others had never read. Then it happened. She said she had been reading Joyce Cary's books and how much she admired his gift for the tragicomedy. This sent my dumb brain quivering for this was my new favorite author. I changed the subject as swiftly as I could for I had experienced Sam's total possessiveness before. He got up without saying anything, went to a pay phone and made a call, then on to the men's room. I didn't even look at the woman. It was one hell of a strain.

Sam returned. He was pale with some kind of rage. He reached over and took both our drinks. He slowly poured them out on the table. Then he took his own glass and hurled it out the open door into the garden where it broke into shining little suns just like the ocean. Then he stormed back, saying, "You dirty son of a bitch. A man can't even go to the bathroom without you stealing his girl." And he strode swiftly out of the place as everyone stared after him in total perplexity, including the bartender who thought he knew Sam well. I had a sudden desire to race after him and at least disjoint a shoulder or something. Later, I had many good chuckles at how ridiculous we all are.

The lady showed why she was a thousand-upper by placing a hand on my forearm, saying, "Please don't do it. Leave his madness be. I'm used to it and you'll only lose a friend."

My breathing shallowed. I offered to buy her another drink. She refused with style and I walked her out to her car and embarrassedly tried to give her $40—all I had on me for her trouble. She said with a sincere smile, "Please don't let it bother you. Geen said Mr. Peckinpah acts erratically sometimes—an affliction of geniuses perhaps."

"And idiots."

She laughed and drove away with a kind of wave. Real class shows up in the most unexpected places. Geen forgave the debt except he asked me to introduce his only child—an 18-year-old aspiring actress—to my friend director Burt Kennedy. Burt took the time to interview her. She didn't pass the test. The hooker would have made it.

After the fiasco with Sam, I didn't frequent the Polo Lounge until we returned to Hollywood with the New Mexico Film Commission a few years later. My Beverly Hills bar friends had been raided and impounded. The place just never seemed the same after that.

Oh yeah, Sam called me the next day after the incident at the Holiday House, came into town and took me to dinner at La Scala. We didn't even mention the hooker, and I never told him she had a doctorate in literature. That day he bought another option on *The Hi Lo Country*. And was still trying to get it made into a movie, years later, when he died. He did, after all, have something to talk to me about that weird day, in a bar, on a beach at Malibu.

Sam went on to direct *The Wild Bunch*, the greatest Western of them all. Lee Marvin cut his drinking in half and won an Oscar for *Cat Ballou*. I don't know what happened to the thousand-dollar-upper, but I like to think she probably retired from teaching literature at some great institution of learning. If I were a gambling man I'd bet she has successful students scattered all over the globe. Maybe even some who have lunch in the Polo Lounge and participate in the perpetually running, unfilmed, four-star sideshows of Hollywood. The Name.

Super Bull

There are all kinds of bulls in the world, that's for sure Angus, Brangus, Charolais, Jerseys, but Super Bull was a Hereford—and if Jimmy Bason, cowboy and rancher, had known about this particular one, he probably wouldn't have bought the S Bar S outfit. This bull would give him more trouble than a street full of terrorists and drive him as crazy as a bee-stung bear.

The Bason's land starts just west of the historical little mining and cattle village of Hillsboro, in southwestern New Mexico, and goes all the way to the top of the Black Range Mountains. When Jimmy bought the ranch in 1962, it was the S Bar S, but his brand was F Cross and he intended for every animal on his spread to carry that marking.

He started riding and looking for strays. He soon found a bunch of wild Hereford cows and calves enjoying the springtime grass in South Percha Canyon. A few of the cows and all the calves were unbranded. This had to be changed.

Jimmy went for help to three absolutely top-notch, mountain cowboys, Joe Wiegel, and Mac and Bill Nunn. They brought with them their best rock horses. These animals could run a cow up a tree and back down a badger hole. And would they ever need them, because South Percha Canyon ranges from seven-to-ten-thousand timbered feet in altitude and is as close to straight up and down as they come and still have a rock roll instead of drop.

In three days of hard riding and skilled tracking, they'd gathered 17 head. They all agreed that there was at least one waspy, old cow and her bull calf left. Jimmy knew that these good hands had work and responsibilities of their own, so he thanked them and said they could go on about their business. It wouldn't be any problem at all for him and his Gruila horse, Billy Bob, to finish up.

Well, that old S Bar S cow was a smart one. She turned back on her tracks over and over. She'd run up and down the nearly sheer slopes in a zig-zag manner and then cut back and hide like a mountain lion in thick, brushy patches. The bull calf followed right along, making the same moves as his mother.

Jimmy and Billy Bob wore down after about four days, and as embarrassing as it was, Jimmy called on Rob Cox, another hellacious cowboy from the Organ Mountains near Las Cruces, to come give him a hand.

Two running, plunging days went by. No cow, No calf. Tired cowboys. Tired horses. Rob had other ducks to race, so, Jimmy was once more left alone to face the rugged wilderness.

In this rough country he had to work by sign instead of sight. He looked for freshly overturned rocks and broken brush, but mainly he trailed by tracks and by the squirts and drops of green, mostly digested grass that falls behind a running critter. The way it splashes points out the direction she's going.

This vast land of steep slopes is covered densely with pines, spruces and all kinds of brush and rocks and is some of the roughest terrain in America. To emphasize how wild it is, the great Indian leaders, Geronimo and Chief Victoria, chose it as their last stronghold after thousands of soldiers had pursued them for years.

South Percha Canyon stretches along Highway 90 for six miles, and along this whole distance there were only four trails dropped down from the road. Jimmy finally got the old cow and calf headed up one of these trails. He could tell by the freshly steaming, green droppings that he was right on 'em. Then he saw them top out and vanish on the winding highway. He topped out himself, and the green sign told him which way they'd turned. He *had* to get her before she reached one of the other trails. Billy Bob charged right down the pavement while Jimmy shook out his loop. He knew he could only catch one of the two, so when he pulled in roping range, he decided to take the cow. He figured the calf would hang around hunting for its mother. He threw the loop. He caught. Billy Bob set up, sliding his hind legs under and screwing his tail in the pavement. If he hadn't been a top rock horse, there would have been a hell of a wreck. The cow was jerked down hard right on the yellow line knocking enough breath out of her to turn a windmill for 30 minutes.

Jimmy bailed off with his piggin string to sideline her—that is, tie two feet together on the same side so she could move around and easily get her breath, but couldn't get away. He had flipped the loop of the piggin string on one foot when she found some lost wind and really started kicking and bawling. A tour bus full of Japanese had stopped on the highway and about 50 excited, camera-toting Orientals were circling around jabbering, scuffling, pushing and trying to take pictures. Here it was—the wild and wooly West in action right before their shining, dark eyes.

The old cow didn't like one human being much less a whole highway full of folks making more noise than a tenth class reunion. Billy Bob was boogered by all the racket, but kept the rope tight anyway. Jimmy was being kicked, butted and generally abused by the crazed cow. The more Jimmy yelled at the Japanese, the closer they came with the cameras, smiling, pointing, snapping pictures like they were recording the Resurrection itself. At last Jimmy got the attention of the bus driver and screamed at him to get these photographic maniacs out of his way so he could finish his job. The driver finally waved and pushed the crowd back. Jimmy tied the cow. The bus moved out with many smiling faces mashed against the windows.

Jimmy rode down to the pickup and horse trailer, then drove back to take the cow home. The maverick calf with tiny nubbin horns was off the road somewhere out of sight, but probably nearby.

The next day Jimmy rode leisurely back to the spot where he caught the cow, expecting to find the bull calf bawling for his mama. It wasn't there. He slid his horse off down the trail, confident he'd easily find the calf. They'd cleaned the country of wild cattle so any fresh tracks were bound to be the little baby bull's. Well, he rode for several days and although he found the sign, he never saw the calf. The little critter was running the same country as his mama, backtracking and pulling the same tricks she had. Jimmy was getting the first tiny inkling of the marvelous events yet to come. Well, no bother. He had fences, windmills, and other cattle to look after. He'd let Billy Bob rest awhile, then come back and get the little feller. Har! Har!

When Jimmy returned to the scene, he found the calf tracks and other damp sign. He saw him with his own eyes. He ran him with his own horse. The little bull would run—no, he would fall—off the mountains at least three times as fast as the best cowboy and horse possibly could.

Jimmy said, "That calf just wouldn't go where any 'well thinking' animal should. If I jumped him at the bottom of a canyon, he would charge up through brush so thick it would have stalled an army tank and then he'd bounce across piles of rocks so agilely that if a mountain goat had seen it he would have fallen dead from pure jealousy."

Jimmy never got a loop. He did get very tired. After three hours of this kind of games, Billy Bob was sapped out, too. So, Jimmy decided that all his other chores had suddenly become extra urgent, and besides, if he pulled out for a couple of weeks maybe a rain would eradicate all the old tracks and he'd have a clean shot at him.

Rob Cox came back to help again. They both made runs at the calf, but neither got close enough to throw a loop. The anguish mounted. Jimmy was finding it harder and harder to go into town now. The kind and considerate populace showed its deep concern by asking him about the elusive bull every place he went. One morning, as he was walking out to saddle his horse, even Sue, his patient wife, yelled after him, "Are you gonna go *play* with Super Bull again today, Honey?" That's the day the maverick got his name. Jimmy humped up like he'd been shot in the butt with a sackful of rattlesnake fangs, and with a great show of willpower kept his teeth clamped together.

Super Bull was getting bigger and stronger every day. Jimmy and Billy Bob were getting weaker. Sometimes Jimmy would spot Super Bull through field-glasses way across a canyon just lying in a flat, grassy spot looking back at him. All the time Jimmy was riding down the canyon and up the mountain, the calf would be resting. He had every advantage.

A lot of people, including Jimmy, had seen Super Bull grazing along the highway where the ditches fostered lots of tender, green grass and weeds. He especially like to graze there at night. He wasn't afraid of cars or pickups—only horsebackers. So? FIRST GREAT GRAND PLAN: Sue would drive the pickup while Jimmy rode in the back. He tied his rope to the headache bar, then they practiced driving slowly back and forth past Super Bull. At first the young bull didn't even look up from his meal. Then he started watching them as they passed by. He still grazed though. Jimmy tapped against the back window and Sue pulled the pickup over closer to the ditch so Jimmy could make his throw. He did. At the first swish of the rope, Super Bull knew something was wrong. He'd heard that swishing tune before. He took off. The rope sailed out and barely caught the top of his head and one short horn enough to jerk him slightly sideways. Sue gunned the pickup after him, but Super found one of the four trails before Jimmy could get his rope ready for another throw.

Jimmy crawled back inside the cab with Sue and said, "If his horns had been an inch longer I'd uh had 'im."

Sue said, "Well I guess we'll just have to wait until you both grow up." It was teeth and jaw grinding time again.

That winter, when the sun beamed and the wind eased, Jimmy made several runs in the snow. If Billy Bob had been a world class skier, he and Jimmy might have had a chance, because Super Bull busted in and out of the drifts like a dolphin in sea water and lost them every time.

Jimmy got more than a normal amount of remarks and ridicule from all his cohorts, which made for an extra long winter.

One rancher asked him, "Hey, Jimmy, you gonna call in the Air Force? They ought to get him easy. I hear old Super can't fly over a quarter of a mile without having to land." Just because Jimmy had been in the Strategic Air Command didn't increase his appreciation for this remark.

Then an out-of-work miner volunteered to use his dynamite expertise to close all the trails. Jimmy didn't bother to ask the miner how he would get down into the canyons to chase Super Bull if all the trails were closed. All in all, it was just more than a long-shanked cowboy could listen to without getting a skullache. Yes, it did make the winter longer and the obsession stronger. Spring came again in all its bird-singing glory, but Jimmy paid no attention to their merry chirping, nor did he smell the wild flowers, or notice how the water sparkled from the melted snow.

Super Bull was a yearling now with nice little horns. Jimmy and Sue tried the pickup trick again, but couldn't get close to him. Well Jimmy would just borrow a neighbor's pickup and fool the dumb animal. He soon found out that Super had now added ALL pickups to his list of no no's.

Then came SECOND GREAT GRAND PLAN. The flash of Einsteinian genius was blinding. Simple. They'd go after him in a car. He'd never expect that. They'd just wait until he was grazing by a strip of highway so steep it would be impossible for him to jump off. Jimmy would leap from the hood of the car and bulldog him. When Sue made her next remark, Jimmy began to suspect that the loyalties of his faithful companion for 15 years might be wavering in favor of the bull. As he pulled his hat down over his ears to prepare to mount the hood of the car, she said, "Now you be careful, Honey, and don't cripple poor little Super Bull. That's getting to be an expensive, valuable animal." Jimmy doesn't remember whether he shortened his teeth or not.

Jimmy tied a rope to the undercarriage of the car, then laid it in a coil on the front seat beside Sue. Jimmy would bulldog the animal and try to sideline him with his piggin string. Sue was to jump out and hand him the secured catch rope for insurance. If Super didn't tear the bottom out of the car, Jimmy figured they should have him.

They watched and waited until Super was in perfect position. The sides of the road dropped almost straight off for a half a mile and it was at least that distance to the next trail exit.

Sue eased the car along past him, turned around and passed him going the other way. Super grazed on, ignoring the car. The plan was working to perfection. The young bull, who now weighed around 800 pounds, was about to be had.

Jimmy put the piggin string in his mouth to free up both hands. Closer. Closer. Super loomed up in the car lights like a circus pet. There! Jimmy leaped. Super leaped. Jimmy grabbed both little horns, but had landed so far back he couldn't get enough leverage to throw the bull. Super charged out ahead bellowing and scattering the thin green with Jimmy desperately trying to pull himself forward to brace his feet.

The bull, suddenly and without hesitation, bailed off the side of the impossible drop. Super was really snapping brush in his descent. Sue could hear the racket from the car. She waited. She waited some more with the car lights locked on the spot of sudden departure. Just as she was about to take a flashlight and have a look, two hands grasped the edge of the highway. Then the forearms and a head appeared. Then the rest of the battered body arrived on the road. Jimmy's shirt was ripped like it had been run through a CIA paper shredder. His handsome face was peeled all down one side and there were knots and scratches from the top of his six two frame to the bottom of it. He still had the piggin string in his mouth.

As he stumbled wearily to the car to get a dose of well-deserved sympathy from his admiring wife, she said, "I see you didn't use your piggin string, so I assume Super Bull is alive and free . . . unless, of course, you broke his poor little neck."

"#*&#@@#&* . . . &&#%@$#*&+@@," echoed across the land.

Just the same, Jimmy maintained his vigilante pursuit. He couldn't very well stop. His closest friends, his nearest neighbors, his pretty little wife and even his four year old daughter, Stacy, kept it constantly on his mind. Only Brent, his year-old son, seemed to care about his predicatment. He had night-mares—he'd catch the bull, but the rope would always break. Once he dreamed he caught and jerked him down tying him per-fectly, but that changed and he was tied to the bull and they were sailing through a blue Western sky falling swifter and swifter to jagged rocks a mile below. Oh, if he'd never heard of that critter! Oh, if only *no one* had!

Super Bull was a year and a half old now. He was unbranded, unmarked, and gaining in weight, condition and brains. Super belonged only to himself. Something—anything—had to be done. THIRD GREAT GRAND PLAN had to produce better results.

Jimmy said, "I figured I was on my third great plan, but Su-per was on his sixth and probably heading for the seventh. Since it was such a dry year, I decided I could salt Super down the hill with some nice green blocks of hay."

It worked. Jimmy would drop the hay a little farther down the hill each day. Super would eat it and wait for the next batch of bait. He was moving closer and closer to the smaller hills and an open cattle guard gate. Once through that, Jimmy would shut it and capture him at last.

It was June. Jimmy and his neighbors were branding. Jimmy was having to get up at four o'clock in the morning, work all day then deliver the hay to the bull. Super Bull didn't have a clock so he was sleeping and fattening up while Jimmy was being worn all over like a ditch digger's hands.

Jimmy forgot about the work though, because he now had the bull taking the bait four miles down the canyon and still gain-ing. Glory, glory, hallelujah, and fried chicken on Sunday! Just one more block of hay and Super should be through the gate. Then it clouded up and started raining, raining, raining. The grass came up green, tender and delicious all over. Super had no use whatsoever for a dry block of hay. To make matters unhap-pier, some of Jimmy's gentle cows found the open gate and wan-dered up the canyon into the wild bull country. It took him three days, riding across the boggy ground, to gather them. He de-cided, however, the mud would be an advantage. He could run the bull now as fast as he could ride and the tracks would be clear and sharp in the wet earth.

He was giving Billy Bob extra grain and doing lots of talking to him. Since Sue's unfaltering faith appeared to be wavering, he could only share his woes with his horse. Well, Jimmy and his four-legged confidante ran Super Bull with all they had for three days. Even Super was beginning to tire, so he took a trail going to the highway. Jimmy followed the muddy tracks, and with a last surge of energy they were closing on him. It was three quarters of a mile to the next trail. Super was almost there. They had to do it now! Jimmy threw his 30-foot rope when Super was 29 feet away. It just caught one horn and the end of his nose. Billy Bob set 'er down. Super flipped over the side of the canyon and landed in the middle of a ten foot oak tree hanging upright with his four legs way above ground. Jimmy stood there and looked him right in the eye. He couldn't reach him, but he could have spit on him.

"We got 'im, Billy Bob!"

All Jimmy had to do now was side-line Super with the piggin string. The dawning. How was he going to get out there to the bull? He was wearing heavy leggings and a brush-popping coat. He couldn't risk the time to take off these cumbersome garments, but he wasn't any ballerina either. He put the piggin string in his mouth, stood on the edge of the road and jumped. He'd forgotten one little thing—a tree that's already holding up about 900 pounds of bull, might not handle an additional 200 pounds of cowboy and costume. It didn't.

The bull bellered, twisted, kicked and the tree slowly began to bend down. Down. Super Bull's feet touched the ground and when he got traction, he really zoomed out of the tree and down the canyon. With the main weight gone, the relieved branches snapped up—boing! Jimmy clung to the top looking around to see if a squirrel, a piss-ant or somebody had seen the event. Billy Bob was the only witness and he would never tell. Super Bull tore through the downhill brush still unbranded. Jimmy climbed out of the tree marked all over.

Jimmy didn't want to be inhumane to the bull so he decided to give Super a few days rest. During this period of recuperation he met a professional hunter-trapper who used a tranquillizer gun on mountain lions. Jimmy wanted to know if it would work on cattle. The trapper said, "Why, I seen 'em knock elephants down on TV, aint you?"

THE GREATEST GRAND FOOLPROOF PLAN OF ALL

Jimmy tried to sneak out without Sue seeing him. It didn't work. Not only did she go along, but she brought Stacy and Brent to witness the event.

They picked up the trapper and he said they'd just need one dart if he found the muscle. Jimmy insisted on four in case he missed. Jimmy drove the car up highway 90 until they found Super following a neighbor's cow who was in heat. Super Bull was harking to his calling, and like many males before him was vulnerable.

Jimmy drove slowly to within 15 feet of him. The trapper fired. Super Bull just kicked at the dart and went on sniffing the air. The trapper said all they had to do was drive up ahead a couple of hundred yards and wait about 15 minutes, then Jimmy could just walk over to the snoozing bull and tie him up. Easy pickens. At last the moment of truth. D-Day. He was glad his proud family was there to witness and verify his success.

One hour later, after some discussion, they decided to shoot Super again with a stronger dose. They did. The 15 minutes turned into another hour. They doubled the next dose with the trapper protesting that it might kill him. Super kicked at the dart with his hind leg and went on sniffing after the cow. This process was repeated, increasing the dose each time until all four darts were in him. Super maintained his pursuit of the opposite sex. He hadn't been watching TV.

Jimmy turned the radio up loud on Louisiana Hayride trying to drown out the unnecessary comments from the spectators.

He thought the bull must surely be groggy by now. He would make one last valiant effort. He mounted the car hood again, piggin string dangling from both sides of his mouth, and Sue drove him within jumping distance. Yipppeee, he had the thousand pound bull by both horns! He held them for about a hundred yards through the dense downhill brush. The crowd waited on the highway. Jimmy crawled back on the road into the daylight to a shattering round of applause. His piggin string was gone, but no one asked if he'd tied the bull.

The confused trapper had obviously forgotten to figure the difference in weight between a mountain lion and a bull, however, he insisted on ten dollars a piece for his lost darts. Jimmy rode back the next morning and found his piggin string and all of the brightly colored darts where Super had rubbed them out against tree trunks.

Surely a man who had a college degree, was a heavy reader, loved fine films, and had successfully flown the deadly patterns right up against the Russian border in the great missile crisis as an honored member of SAC could think of a way to catch a young Hereford bull.

As the weeks went by, Jimmy did make many more grand plans but kept them all to himself. He didn't even divulge them to his horse. It was such a rank, snowy winter he couldn't have used them anyway.

Spring came. Jimmy was driving his pickup over low rolling hills to check some loading pens that had a water tank sticking out on both sides of the corral. The pens were out in the flats not far from headquarters. He topped the hill and suddenly slammed on the brakes, leaned over the steering wheel and stared so hard his eyebrows joined his hairline. There was Super Bull ambling slowly along, bellering low in his chest, heading straight for the open gate to the corral where a bunch of cows were watering.

Jimmy eased out of the pickup thinking that every move he made sounded like a battery of cannons exploding. He crawled on his belly and crept from bush to rock like one of Geronimo's warriors. Then there was no more ground cover—just 50 yards of wide open pasture to the corral gate.

He crouched behind the last bush getting ready to take off like an Olympic dash man. It suddenly hit him that he and Billy Bob had done a hell of a lot of dashing without any results. He simply stood up and walked slowly, casually across the open ground like he was taking a course in daydreaming. This calm exterior camouflaged a heart that was pumping all the blood his plumbing could handle, and lungs that were overloaded to the bursting point with that clean mountain air.

When at last he placed his hands on the swung back gate his palms were wet enough to fill a sponge. He closed the gate. Simple as that.

The three-year-old bull had already picked out his next mate and was courting her with enthusiasm. As multitudes of males before him, he'd been captured by sex. Why not? He had nothing left to prove in the Gila Forest.

The next person to accost Jimmy with a sarcastic inquiry about his bullish escapades got this answer. "Oh, you mean Super Bull? Nothin' to it . . . caught him afoot."

At first Jimmy wanted to shoot him and even worse, castrate him, but instead he branded him with the F Cross and called his special friend, Rob Cox, to come look him over. Rob liked the young bull's conformation. Jimmy was relieved. Even though he couldn't stand to have Super around, he wanted him safe and happy. It was agreed that Rob would take him back to the Organ Mountain Ranch. A lot of bulls don't like the strain of doing their duty in rough, high country. It was plain natural for Super Bull. He was turned loose at 7500-feet altitude to live out the rest of his days eating and breeding in paradise.

Even now when Jimmy Bason rides the South Percha Canyon, he instinctively looks for the wild bull's sign. He's never going to find any. They just made ONE Super Bull.

The World's Strangest Creature

The boy had pulled off a good day for an eight year old. It was just past mid-sun and he was already back in town loaded with success. Unbeknownst to him his whole world, very shortly, would widen. His little bay horse, Cricket, moved under him, eagerly anticipating home and the early removal of the saddle, plus a good feeding. The two brown-and-black shepherd dogs followed, smelling at the ground now and then, but knowing the hunt was over. Three cottontails were tied to the old four-dollar saddle. The dogs ran the rabbits into holes and the boy twisted them out with a forked barbed wire. It was the middle of the Great Depression and drought. The rabbits were for human consumption and the few so-called inedible parts fed the two dogs.

Then the boy spotted the funny-looking wagon. That was easy because most of the ground around Humble City, in far southeastern New Mexico, was so flat you could shoot a marble and all it would do was spin in circles looking in vain for a downhill slope. The frame houses of the tiny town were scattered about one to an entire block. Some even had several empty blocks between them. The odd, out-of-place wagon was on one of these.

The boy's father started up a town on what once was their cow ranch. He purposely set the houses far apart in a vain attempt to make the town look bigger, and as he said, "give it room to expand." His idea worked for awhile. There was a one-room school; a combination filling station, general store, and drug counter; and the Post Office was in the ex-ranchhouse because the boy's mother was the postmistress.

Between the Great Depression and the mid-thirties drought, Humble City's existence was a miracle of the highest order. All that kept it there, squatting scared, scattered, and lonely was the fact his dad had accidentally struck an irrigation well while hand digging a cellar. Hope. Folks believed there would come a day when the bounty from the watered land would bless them all. It did. A couple of decades after most of them were gone, the land was covered with irrigation and oil pumps, and finally the oilrich ranching town of Hobbs grew around Humble City, and left its actuality only on road maps.

They were hard times, but the sandy-haired boy didn't know the difference. Supplying wild meat for their empty bellies was all an adventure to him. Fun. The fun was over today and Cricket was heading for the corrals of home when his rider reined him toward the new wagon in town. The tired dogs, not realizing the new adventure they were about to miss, went on to the house.

The boy rode up hesitantly, but so full of curiosity that his ribs were spreading. He'd never seen a wagon rigged up like this one. There was a big wooden crate with doors that swung to reveal its hidden treasure. A crudely painted sign was haphazardly lettered across the sides, saying:

THE WORLD'S STRANGEST CREATURE
MIXTURE OF TEN ANIMULES IN ONE

A man built like a thin, winter tree was feeding the team of horses. He spotted the freckled-faced visitor and smiled big with a mouth that seemed to run all the way around and hide behind his turkey neck. Yes sir, he had a smile, and not only that, it was mostly full of teeth. There were only two vacant spots to mar the perfect gleam of charming promise. His small blue eyes were something to think about as well. They could hardly be seen when he was smiling, but when the stretch came out of the mouth, the eyes flew open wide as a sunflower, and as blue as a painted sky. The boy could just tell that these were eyes that had seen many rare things.

With a voice as smooth and slick as new shoes on ice, he said, "Well, haaaalo there. How are you, Button. My, that's a fine lookin' steed you're mounted on, and I see you're quite a huntsman, too. Rabbits are gettin' scarce during these days of culinary disaster. Our stomachs may despair now and then, but I have here in this wagon a creature that will make the gray matter twitch and twirl for days. It's obvious a young gentleman of your upbringing and outdoor talents could never pass over gazing upon one of the wonders of the world. Huh? Huh? Whatta ya say, Button?"

"Uh . . . uh . . ." The boy's mind was mush, then he managed to utter, "What . . . what is it?"

"What is it? Can't you read? It's an animule. You got a quarter? That's all it'll take to feast your starving eyes upon this marvel of the universe."

The boy knew exactly how much money was in his pocket. "Gosh no, I ain't got but four cents."

"Well, this ain't no four-cent look . . . not this . . . this is a twenty-five cent look and the price might just go up in the next ten seconds." Sadness must have registered on the boy's face, for great pity came over the man's as if he'd just heard of his best friend's death, the spread of the plague, and the permanent cancellation of The Second Coming all at one time. "Well, I'm not one to keep knowledge from the young . . . far from it. It's within the nature of my sympathetic soul to give, not deny. Just hand me the four cents and that rabbit hanging on the right side and we've got a deal."

The right-side rabbit was the plumpest of the three, but the huntsman handed it over along with the four coppers and crawled down from his steed. He wanted to feel if the earth shook when the great vision was finally revealed.

The man stepped to the wooden crate. Stretching his long neck longer and twisting his head at the youngster as if he were going to show him how to make gold bars out of chicken droppings, he jerked the flaps back and said, "Cheapest education you'll ever get, Button."

The wide-eyed observer was speechless. His horse pulled back on the reins and snorted. There was a critter ceaselessly pacing back and forth behind iron bars.

"Just look at this, Son. Can you believe your staring eyes? Hump like a buffalo. Ears like a fox. Hind legs like a dog. Front legs like a tiger."

The man reached into a separate compartment of the cage and pulled out a large bone. He swiftly shoved it between the bars, and the creature snapped it in half with one crack. The man slammed the flaps shut then, and said, "Makes an alligator's jaws look like a mouse trap."

The boy's throat was dry as sand but he managed to stutter, "Could I . . . coulda . . . I'd like . . . Could I see . . . ."

"Now, now Button. You mustn't get greedy. I've done given you a fifty-cent look. Tell you what . . . you spread the word all over and you can look FREE . . . free, I say, all day long."

The dazed boy crawled back on his little bay horse and made a ride Paul Revere would have done deep knee bends over. He raced from house to house informing the occupants of the greatest animule of all time.

"Everybody's coming." He enticed the inhabitants of the land. He did have one piece of luck—several ranchers and farmers, along with the townsmen, were cutting mesquite bushes and building a brush arbor for a big religious camp meeting on the edge of town. While their husbands labored for the Lord, the country wives visited with the town ladies.

"You ain't never seen nothin' like it. It's made outa coyotes and elephants and bobcats and . . . ." The boy was getting a little carried away, but who could blame him.

The crowd gathered. They arrived afoot, horseback, by wagon and team, and then there were three Model T Fords and a shiny Model A. Even the boy's mother closed the post office and walked over. He was sure sorry his dad was on a trade on the other side of Hobbs and would miss this phenomenon.

The man was masterfully keeping the gathered crowd mesmerized. Finally he figured that he had about all the people Humble City, New Mexico, could provide. While he was collecting the looking money, the boy couldn't help saying proudly to a couple more of his age group, "I done seen it."

The man pocketed all the money he was going to get. He stood poised a pulsating second, then swung the doors open as if he were unveiling a Michaelangelo. There was a low gasp from the crowd. The man never gave them a chance to recover.

"See there! He's got teeth like a grizzly bear . . . and have you noticed those spots? Why, those are the spots of a leopard. And that head . . . why, that head belongs to a wolverine."

A woman said, "Whew, it sure does stink."

"There you are. Now, that's real observant of you, ma'am. This animule is even part skunk."

One old man interrupted, saying, "I seen a picture once and that there's a hyeeeni."

The man, sensing a slight murmur of rebellion in the crowd, recovered swiftly. "You got 'er there, Old Pardner. Hyena is an ancient Persian word meaning 'animal of many parts.'" Then he motioned to the front of the animal, saying, "He's high there," then he pointed at the animal's rear. "And eeny beeny there—like a buffalo." Then he threw another bone into the cage, and while